The American Drug Culture

The American Drug Culture

Thomas S. Weinberg
SUNY Buffalo State

Gerhard Falk
SUNY Buffalo State

Ursula Adler Falk

Los Angeles | London | New Delhi
Singapore | Washington DC | Melbourne

FOR INFORMATION:

SAGE Publications, Inc.
2455 Teller Road
Thousand Oaks, California 91320
E-mail: order@sagepub.com

SAGE Publications Ltd.
1 Oliver's Yard
55 City Road
London, EC1Y 1SP
United Kingdom

SAGE Publications India Pvt. Ltd.
B 1/I 1 Mohan Cooperative Industrial Area
Mathura Road, New Delhi 110 044
India

SAGE Publications Asia-Pacific Pte. Ltd.
3 Church Street
#10-04 Samsung Hub
Singapore 049483

Printed in the United States of America

Library of Congress Cataloging-in-Publication Data

Names: Weinberg, Thomas S., author. | Falk, Gerhard, 1924– author. | Falk, Ursula A., author.

Title: The American drug culture / Thomas S. Weinberg, State University of New York Buffalo, Gerhard Falk, State University of New York Buffalo, Ursula Falk.

Description: Thousand Oaks, California : SAGE, [2018] | Includes bibliographical references and index.

Identifiers: LCCN 2017031396 | ISBN 9781506304663 (pbk. : alk. paper)

Subjects: LCSH: Drug abuse—United States. | Substance abuse—United States. | Tobacco use—United States. | Drinking of alcoholic beverages—United States.

Classification: LCC HV5825 .W38335 2018 | DDC 306/.1—dc23

LC record available at https://lccn.loc.gov/2017031396

Acquisitions Editor: Jeff Lasser
Editorial Assistant: Adeline Wilson
Production Editor: Jane Haenel
Copy Editor: Mark Bast
Typesetter: Hurix Digital
Proofreader: Barbara Coster
Indexer: Nancy Fulton
Cover Designer: Candice Harman
Marketing Manager: Kara Kindstrom

18 19 20 21 22 10 9 8 7 6 5 4 3 2 1

Brief Contents

Detailed Contents

Preface

The original reason for writing this book is mysterious, even to us, the authors. In the spring of 2013, Tom Weinberg found a contract for a book on alcohol in his mailbox. It had been signed by him, Gerhard (Gerry) Falk, and the publishers of a university press. What was puzzling was that it was dated 1983! Tom immediately took it to Gerry and asked him about it. It seems that Gerry had been going through some old papers in his office and came across the contract. Neither of us remembered sending in a proposal for such a book 30 years earlier or getting a contract for it. "Why didn't we follow through on it?" we asked each other. Neither of us could supply an answer. Nevertheless, we thought that a book on alcohol would be an interesting idea, so we sat down, outlined the chapters, and wrote it.

We quickly found out that this was no longer a topic of interest to the university presses, to which we sent a proposal and sample chapters, nor were small independent publishers interested in the project. We then decided that this was the kind of book more appropriate for a large textbook publisher. Tom contacted Jeff Lasser, his sociology editor at SAGE, for whom he and a colleague, Staci Newmahr, had earlier edited an anthology. Jeff was interested, but he suggested that we include other drugs to broaden its appeal. We did so, and the result is the book you are now reading.

As we thought about what the book should look like, Gerry suggested that we ask his wife, Dr. Ursula Adler Falk, to collaborate with us on the project. She is a psychotherapist who has worked with alcoholics and drug addicts—some of whom are both—for many years. He thought that the addition of case studies would be an important supplement to our text, broadening its appeal beyond sociology courses and enhancing its usefulness to students and faculty. Tom concurred. We have integrated some of the case histories into a couple of chapters, including Chapter 11, "Becoming a Drug User: Careers, Personalities, and Interaction—Two Perspectives," cowritten with Dr. Ursula Adler Falk, which presents both the psychotherapeutic and sociological perspectives. In addition, the case histories are presented in two appendices. Appendix A contains the histories of Dr. Falk's patients with alcohol use disorders, and Appendix B presents the case histories of those with substance use disorders. Case studies may be used in any number of ways, limited only by one's imagination. For example, students can use them as archival data for secondary analysis or to generate hypotheses about drug and alcohol abuse. For more advanced students, especially those interested in ethnomethodology and textual analysis,* they can be examined as texts, to understand how psychoanalysts conceptualize the situation and prognosis of their students.

---

* See Rod Watson's 2009 definitive work, *Analysing Practical and Professional Texts: A Naturalistic Approach* (Burlington, VT: Ashgate), for examples of how this might be done.

Our objective for this book is not only to help students understand alcohol and other drug use and abuse but, more important, to show them how sociological perspectives can be used in that process. To that end, Chapter 1 presents some sociological theories as they are applicable to the study of drug and alcohol use. Chapter 2, "Alcohol, Tobacco, and Other Drugs," and Chapter 8, "Alcoholism," explicitly label the sociological perspectives being used, whereas in other chapters, those perspectives are implicit.

Acknowledgments

A number of people helped in the development of this book. First and foremost is our sociology editor, Jeff Lasser, whose belief in our project and support and encouragement kept us motivated and focused. We are also grateful for the support of Adeline Wilson, editorial assistant in sociology, for her attention to detail. Jane Haenel, our production editor, made helpful suggestions and kept us on track. Mark Bast, our copy editor, was meticulous and indefatigable in his commitment to our project.

Clifford Falk deserves our thanks for dealing with the vagaries of the computer. Several people read drafts of chapters and provided critical information and help in clarifying our ideas. Dr. Bonnie A. Beane read the alcoholism chapter and supplied some important ideas. Dr. Rod Watson read several of the chapters and gave us insightful feedback, directing us to sources with which we had not previously been familiar. Rod's friendship, enthusiasm for our project, and support are deeply appreciated. Dr. William Wieczorek, Director and Professor of the Institute for Community Health Promotion, Center for Health and Social Research of the Center for Development of Human Services, provided invaluable insight into the evolution of *DSM* terms, providing us with information that we had not previously known. Thanks are also given to Detectives Scott Sprague and Robert Goetz (ret.) of the Town of Tonawanda, New York, police department for providing material and information on the D.A.R.E. program. Discussions with the Hon. Paul S. Piotrowski, Town Justice for Cheektowaga, New York, about drug court gave us important information. We also would like to acknowledge the helpful ideas of Benjamin Woodrow about the mindset of substance users.

A number of our students read a draft of the first chapter and helped us make it more interesting and accessible to students. They are Shaniya Anthony, Austin Barker, Francesca Bond, Jhanice Buckley, Summer Byrd, Giannina Callejas, Christina Ferella, Sashae Fuller, Jeremiah Gonzalez, Desiree Gordon, Mark Granto, Ariel McClain, Shelby Metzger, Amina Mohamed, Meegan Petrucci, Hanif Raqib, Jillian Stenzel, Akeata Terry, and Shahadah Williams.

We also wish to thank the reviewers for their comments and suggestions, many of which we incorporated into the manuscript. Their ideas helped to substantially strengthen the book.

Kathleen M. Contrino, Canisius College

Kevin E. Early, University of Michigan–Dearborn

Scott R. Maggard, Old Dominion University

Jane L. Nichols, Southern Illinois University

Gerald S. Reid, University of Cincinnati

Scott Walfield, East Carolina University

Of course, the authors are entirely responsible for any errors in this project.

About the Authors

Dr. Thomas S. Weinberg is professor of sociology at SUNY Buffalo State, where he has taught since 1969. He received his bachelor's and master's degrees in sociology from Rutgers University and a doctorate in sociology, with a specialty in social control and deviant behavior, from the University of Connecticut. He was a postdoctoral scholar on a National Institute on Alcohol Abuse and Alcoholism grant at the University of California, San Diego, from 1979 to 1981. The recipient of the State University of New York Chancellor's Awards for Excellence in Teaching and for Scholarship and Creative Activity, Dr. Weinberg teaches courses in the sociology of addiction, social psychology, contemporary sociological theory, the sociology of sexual behavior, the sociology of deviant behavior, group dynamics, and introduction to sociology.

Dr. Weinberg is the author of *Gay Men, Gay Selves: The Social Construction of Homosexual Identities* (New York: Irvington, 1983) and *Gay Men, Drinking, and Alcoholism* (Carbondale: University of Southern Illinois Press, 1994), editor of *S&M: Studies in Dominance and Submission* (Amherst, NY: Prometheus Books, 1995; also published as *BDSM: Estudios sobre la dominacion y la sumision* [Barcelona: Edicions Bellaterra, 2008]), and coeditor (with G. W. Levi Kamel) of *S and M: Studies in Sadomasochism* (Buffalo, NY: Prometheus Books, 1983) and (with Staci Newmahr) of *Selves, Symbols, and Sexualities: An Interactionist Anthology* (Los Angeles: SAGE, 2015). He has contributed to several referred journals, including the *Journal of Drug Issues*, *Deviant Behavior*, the *Journal of Sex Research*, the *Journal of Homosexuality*, the *Bulletin of the American Academy of Psychiatry and the Law*, *Social Analysis*, *Psychology & Human Sexuality*, and encyclopedias and edited volumes in the areas of addiction, sexuality, and deviant behavior. He is associate editor of *Ethnographic Studies* and *Sexuality & Culture*.

Dr. Gerhard Falk is professor emeritus of sociology at SUNY Buffalo State, where he taught from 1957 to 2016. He received his bachelor's and master's degrees from Western Reserve (now Case Western Reserve) University and doctorate from the University at Buffalo. Prior to coming to SUNY Buffalo State, Dr. Falk taught at South Dakota State. He was a fellow at the University of Pennsylvania, served as a youth probation officer, and worked as a statistician in private industry. He is the recipient of the SUNY Chancellor's Award for Excellence in Teaching, the SUNY Buffalo State President's Award for Scholarship and Creativity, and the SUNY Research Foundation Award for Scholarship.

Dr. Falk is the author of 26 books and contributed many articles to professional journals such as the *British Journal of Addiction*, the *Australian Journal of Social Issues*, *Journal of Criminal Law*, *Criminology and Police Science*, *Criminologica*, *Criminal Law Quarterly*, *Deviant Behavior*, *American Bar Association Journal*, *International Journal of Social Psychiatry*, *Mental Hygiene*, the *International Behavioral Scientist*, the *International Review of History and Political Science*, *Journal of Educational Sociology*, and *Mankind Quarterly*. He also contributed chapters to a number of edited books. His wide-ranging research interests include criminology and deviant behavior (*Murder: An Analysis of Its Forms, Conditions, and Causes*, 1990; *Stigma: How We Treat Outsiders*, 2001; *Fraud: Deceit Among Scientists, Writers, Academics, and Philanthropists*, 2007; *The American Criminal Justice System*, 2010; *Assassination, Anarchy and Terrorism: A Sociological Analysis*, 2012), the sociology of religion—especially Judaism—(*The Jew in Christian Theology*, 1992; *American Judaism in Transition*, 1995; *The Restoration of Israel*, 2006), the sociology of social change (*A Study of Social Change in Six American Institutions*, 1993; *Sex, Gender, and Social Change*, 1998; *Man's Ascent to Reason: The Secularization of Western Civilization*, 2003; *Women and Social Change in America*, 2009; *Twelve Inventions Which Changed America: The Influence of Technology on American Culture*, 2013), and American culture (*The Life of the Academic Professional*, 1990; *Hippocrates Assailed: The American Health Delivery System*, 1999; *Football and American Identity*, 2005).

Dr. Ursula Adler Falk is a psychotherapist in private practice, with many years' experience specializing in working with substance abusers. She received her bachelor's degree from Ohio University, MSW from Bryn Mawr, and doctorate from the University at Buffalo. In addition to her work with alcoholics and patients with substance use disorders, Dr. Falk has a specialty in aging and nursing homes. She serves as a consultant to nursing homes and as a member of the New York State Nursing Board. She is the author of *Interviews With Patients in Psychotherapy* and (as Ursula Adler) *A Critical Study of the American Nursing Home: The Final Solution*. She also coauthored with Gerhard Falk six books: *The Nursing Home Dilemma* (1976), *Aging in America and Other Cultures* (1987), *Ageism, the Aged, and Aging in America* (1997), *Grandparents: A New Look at the Supporting Generation* (2002), *Youth Culture and the Generation Gap* (2005), and *Deviant Nurses and Improper Nursing Care* (2006).

CHAPTER 1

Introduction
Sociological and Other Explanations for Drug and Alcohol Use and Abuse[1]

The Growing Nationwide Opioid Epidemic

BUFFALO, New York—David Edick had always been close to his son, Benjamin. When he was a little boy, Benjamin enjoyed challenging his dad to Super Mario— and beating him at the video game.

Now, with Benjamin a grown man at 30, the father of a child of his own, the relationship revolved around cooking, working out together, and catching New York Mets and Denver Broncos games from the comfort of matching black leather recliners in David's house in Buffalo, New York.

In the spring of 2015, Benjamin moved in with his dad, having struggled with drugs for about a year. He had gotten clean, though, and had found work repairing gutters. Every morning, he'd meet with other members of a local support group—meetings that gave him hope, he told David.

When Benjamin didn't come home on the afternoon of July 23, David at first wasn't that concerned. He figured his son was working late. But by 10 p.m., David began to worry. He searched Benjamin's room but found no drugs. When his son didn't turn up by the next morning, he reported him missing.

Later that day, officers came to his door. "I thought, Oh, he's in trouble—he's in jail," David recalled.

Police told him his son was dead. He had been found in his car, head resting against the headrest as if asleep, the victim of a "heroin epidemic" sweeping not just upstate New York but the entire nation. (Daileda 2016)

Benjamin Edick was one of many victims of what has been termed a growing heroin epidemic in the United States (Horowitz 2017; Ingraham 2017; Owens 2017). Erie County, New York, the county that contains Buffalo and its suburbs, has been experiencing what officials are calling a "wave" of opioid-related deaths. In 2016, there were 357 confirmed or suspected opioid-related deaths, compared to 256 deaths in 2015 and 128 in 2014. In a period of just 11 days in late January and early February of 2016, there were 23 overdose deaths from a high-powered batch of heroin (O'Brien 2016). It is suspected that some of these deaths were caused

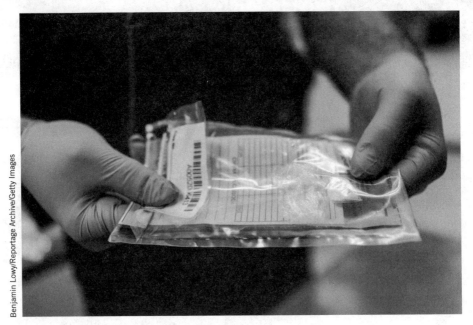

Photo 1.1: A lethal combination of heroin cut with fentanyl.

by heroin containing fentanyl, a synthetic painkiller 30 to 50 times more potent than heroin (H. Davis 2016; O'Brien 2016). The situation is so dire that the county executive expressed his fear that the opioid- and prescription-related overdose deaths will wipe out the county's population gains (Tan 2016).

The situation in western New York is reflective of a larger opioid epidemic sweeping the country ("Drug Overdose Deaths" 2015). Heroin is now the leading cause of overdose deaths in the United States (Glatter 2016). In fact, according to data from the Centers for Disease Control and Prevention (CDC), there were more deaths from heroin overdoses in 2015 than there were from gun homicides (Schumaker 2016). The CDC reports that heroin-related overdose deaths have more than quadrupled since 2010 and that there was a 20.6% increase in such deaths from 2014 to 2015 (CDC 2017a). The CDC notes that "the main driver of drug overdose deaths" is both prescription and illicit opioids, which were implicated in 33,091 deaths in 2015. Significant increases in drug overdose deaths during this period predominantly occurred in the Northeast and South. (CDC 2016c). The National Institute on Drug Abuse (NIDA) reports a 2.2-fold increase of deaths from all drugs from 2002 to 2015, with a steeper incline in deaths for males. Deaths from opioids during that same period increased 2.8-fold, again with male deaths showing a steeper incline than deaths of females. For heroin-related deaths, there was a 6.2-fold increase in total deaths, with an even larger and steeper rise in deaths for males than females (NIDA 2017). Deaths from fentanyl overdoses more than doubled from 1,905 people in 2013 to 4,200 in 2014 (Rettner 2016).

Why has there been such a dramatic increase in opioid-related deaths, presumably reflecting an increase in their use? The most common explanation is that this is due to the overprescribing of prescription pain killers such as Vicodin, Percocet, and Oxycontin, which became popular in the 1990s (Caba 2015; Eskew Law 2016; Ingraham 2017; Lopez 2016; Owens 2017; *The Week* Staff 2016). When people can no longer obtain these drugs by prescription, they first may turn to the black market to obtain them but eventually discover heroin, which, at $5 a bag, is one eighth the cost of pills and easier to obtain (Caba 2015; *The Week* Staff 2016). The strongest risk factor associated with heroin use is addiction[2] to prescription opioid painkillers (Caba 2015). "Over 50% of recent heroin addicts report that they began their opioid use through the abuse of prescription opioid medications" (Eskew Law 2016). Lopez (2016) notes that "a 2014 study in *JAMA Psychiatry* found many painkiller users were moving on to heroin, and a 2015 analysis by the Centers for Disease Control and Prevention found that people who are addicted to prescription painkillers are 40 times more likely to be addicted to heroin."

Although this explanation may help us to understand why some users of prescription painkillers acquire a heroin habit, it does not account for those users who do not go on to use heroin. It is only half an explanation. How do they differ from those who become addicted to heroin? In order to fully understand drug use, including alcohol and other nonopioids (e.g., marijuana, LSD, psilocybin, methamphetamines, mescaline, peyote), we need to look for other types of explanations. The difference between those who go on to use heroin and those who do not might be explained, for example, in terms of their personalities, past experiences, interpersonal relationships, opportunity to acquire drugs, and so forth. Formal theories from sociology, social psychology, psychology, and criminology help us to understand drug and alcohol use more completely. In the following section, we look at a number of sociological/social psychological and criminological explanations and illustrate how they have been used to examine substance use. Throughout the book we refer to some of these theories to help us understand drug and alcohol use and the drug culture. Our treatment here is by no means comprehensive or exhaustive. Its purpose is simply to give the reader a feeling for the variety of ways in which drugs and drug users have been viewed and can be understood. In Chapter 8, we present other nonsociological explanations for substance use, particularly focused on alcohol. These theories include psychological, genetic, physiological, and medical perspectives, as well as the Alcoholics Anonymous concept of alcoholism as a disease. In Chapter 11, Dr. Ursula Adler Falk, a psychotherapist, discusses the use of drugs from a psychoanalytical framework, supplemented with compatible sociological literature and theoretical perspectives. In this chapter, Dr. Falk provides real-life case histories to enable the reader to appreciate how theoretical structures enable us to understand how addicts view themselves, others, and their worlds. Additional cases can be found in the appendices.

The last section of this chapter looks at the many ways in which sociologists study drug and alcohol use. We provide examples of research using different methodologies and theoretical frameworks. Again, this section is not intended to be definitive, for this is neither a theory nor a methods book, but to give the reader insight into the complexities of the drug culture and how researchers attempt to understand it.

Sociological Explanations

This book uses sociological perspectives to examine the use of alcohol and other drugs in American culture. Sociological theorizing about drug and alcohol use has a long history. More than 75 years ago, sociologist Alfred R. Lindesmith (1938) proposed an explanation for addiction that emphasized a symbolic interactionist approach. In brief, Lindesmith applied George Herbert Mead's emphasis on the important role of significant symbols in an individual's construction of the self to an explanation of the process of becoming an addict. At the time, his theories were controversial, for the dominant position was a psychiatric one, which held that drugs were used by individuals to compensate for their feelings of inferiority. A few years later, E. M. Jellinek (1943) noted that though there was a large body of "sociological" research on alcoholism, there were few attempts to understand this behavior sociologically. He therefore called for the development and application of sociological frameworks in the field. He was an applied physiologist by training and not a sociologist, but Jellinek (1962) nevertheless developed a sociological theory of the progression of alcoholism.

In general, sociological theories may be roughly sorted into macrosociological and microsociological frameworks. Macrosociological perspectives focus on large-scale systems, societies, and social institutions and on their interrelationships and effect on social actors. Examples of macrosociological theories include structural functionalism and Marxian and conflict theories. Microsociological theories examine everyday life, including interaction between and among individuals and objects; how people construct, interpret, and manage meaning; and how they act in terms of these meanings. Examples of microsociological theories include exchange theories, behavioral sociology, symbolic interaction, labeling theory, reference group theory, ethnomethodology, and phenomenological sociology.

Some microsociological approaches, such as symbolic interactionism, labeling theory, phenomenology, and ethnomethodology, take what is called a social constructionist approach to understanding deviance, including substance use (as well as other social behaviors). This perspective, which was conceptualized in the 1950s and early 1960s by writers such as Harold Garfinkel (1956), Howard S. Becker (1951, 1953, 1963), Erving Goffman (1961, 1963), John Kitsuse (1962), Edwin M. Lemert (1967), and others, sees deviance as a subjective matter defined by some social audience (Becker 1963). From this point of view, deviance is a relative concept that varies over time and space. Because various groups and societies see the same behaviors differently, if they are not labeled or categorized in some way, they have no social reality, because they do not engender a response

(Thio 2010). For example, in some societies *homosexuality* does not exist as a social category, even though people engage in sexual behavior with members of their own sex (Amory 1997). Similarly, even though people were physiologically addicted, the labels *junkie* and *drug abuser* as descriptive categories did not exist in the early 20th century, before the passing of the Harrison Narcotics Act in 1914.[3] Prior to that legislation, the majority of opiate users were women, often of the upper classes, who were given those preparations by physicians to relieve the discomfort of "women's problems" (Kandall 1997). They were neither stereotyped nor responded to negatively as *junkies* or *drug abusers*.

Social constructionists are especially concerned with the creation and application of labels. For example, the pejorative label *dope fiend*, which first appeared between 1890 and 1895, was used to refer to someone who was addicted to opiates. In an article written in 1940, Alfred R. Lindesmith countered the prevalent image of the dope fiend as "the 'dope-crazed' killer or 'the dope fiend rapist'" (p. 199). Within the heroin subculture, however, the term has a different connotation. *Righteous dope fiend* is an accolade, rather than a deviant label (Bourgois and Schonberg 2009). Social constructionists understand that labels have power, for they set the parameters for how people are perceived and how they are responded to by others. Changing a label, or creating a new one, affects perception. The changes made in terminology by the American Psychiatric Association (APA) in the fifth edition of their *Diagnostic and Statistical Manual of Mental Disorders* (*DSM-5*) were partially the result of acknowledging this power. Psychiatrists and physicians are, from a social constructionist perspective, social control agents with the authority to make labels stick, with potentially negative consequences for those to whom they apply those labels. According to the Substance Abuse and Mental Health Services Administration's (SAMHSA n.d.) National Registry of Evidence-Based Programs and Practices (NREPP), "Addiction is no longer included in the fifth edition of the *DSM*, despite its common usage internationally, because of its 'uncertain definition' and possible negative connotation." The terms *substance abuse* and *substance dependence* were also eliminated, because the APA found those terms to be problematic. Traditionally, *abuse* was used to refer to an earlier stage in the process of becoming a drug or alcohol user than the development of dependence; however, in some instances abuse was severe. Also, *dependence* and *addiction* were often confused in clinical diagnoses. Although SAMHSA (n.d.) has adopted the APA's new terminology, other government agencies, including the National Institute on Drug Abuse (NIDA), and other organizations still use the labels *substance abuse*, *substance dependence*, and *addiction*. They are also used in the present text.

Social constructionists emphasize that in order to understand behavior, we need to be able to take a subjective approach, attempting to see the situation through the eyes of the individuals or groups we are studying. This is what Cooley (1909) called "sympathetic introspection." Throughout this book, we include examples of this approach.

There are two things to keep in mind when considering sociological theories. The first of these is that there are variations within each perspective. For example, there are different types of Marxian and conflict theories, such as critical Marxism, structural Marxism, and feminist Marxian approaches. There are several ways in which symbolic interactionists view the world, from the perspective of Herbert Blumer to the quantitative interactionism of Manfred Kuhn to the dramaturgical position of Erving Goffman.[4] The second idea is that there is often blurring and blending between and among various theoretical positions and levels. For example, Robert K. Merton's (1957) famous anomie theory is a conflict theory within a structural functional framework, which bridges macro and micro levels. Other theories, such as exchange and symbolic interaction, are easily combined. The following discussion examines some sociological theories as they are applicable to the study of drug and alcohol use.[5]

Structural Functional Explanations

Structural functionalism sees social systems (e.g., whole societies) and their various subsystems (e.g., social institutions such as political, economic, stratification, family, religious, and legal structures) as maintaining equilibrium such that changes in one system or subsystem affect the others. This perspective focuses on consensus and mutual support of societal components. An excellent example of the use of this perspective is Selden D. Bacon's discussion, "Alcohol and Complex Society" (Bacon 1962). In this chapter, he examined both the functions and dysfunctions of alcohol for the individual and complex society. He concluded that "the complexity of society is a significant factor in the relations of alcohol and man. It obviously enhances the uses of alcohol for man. It obviously increases the dangers of alcohol for man. Social complexity has added new forces and motivations for the production and distribution of alcohol. It has diminished the power of agencies of control which could once be efficiently used" (Bacon 1962:93).

Albert K. Cohen (1966) identified several functions of deviance in support of organization from a structural functionalist perspective: cutting through red tape, as a "safety valve," clarifying the rules, uniting the group both against and on behalf of the deviant, as a contrasting effect (i.e., accenting conformity), and as a warning signal. Two of these functions recognized by Cohen are especially applicable to this discussion. They reflect the ambivalence with which Americans view drug use (including alcohol) and drug users. Drug users are seen both as criminals (i.e., *dope fiends*—ironically a term of approbation in the heroin subculture, see Bourgois and Schonberg 2009)—an example of uniting the group against the deviant—and as victims, or at least as individuals worthy of sympathy and rehabilitation—an example of uniting the group on behalf of the deviant. The punitive response in the United States is strong; for example, in 2015, there were 1,488,707 arrests made nationwide for "drug abuse violations," or 13.8% of all arrests (10,797,088) that year. If we add to this total arrests made for "driving under the influence" (1,089,171), "drunkenness" (405,880, which used to be listed as "public intoxication"), and "disorderly conduct" (386,078, at one time reported as "drunk and disorderly"), the arrest rate for substance use violations rises to 31% of all arrests

(FBI 2015, Table 29, "Estimated Number of Arrests," https://ucr.fbi.gov/crime-in-the-u.s/2015/crime-in-the-u.s.-2015/tables/table-29). Nevertheless, drug users are also seen as needing help. Whereas President Richard M. Nixon, the architect of the "war on drugs," discussed in Chapter 2, urged strong measures against drug importers and distributors, he was more compassionate when it came to individual narcotic addicts. In a June 1971 special message to the Congress on drug abuse prevention and control, he stated, "Enforcement must be coupled with a rational approach to the reclamation of the drug user himself. . . . We must rehabilitate the drug user if we are to eliminate drug abuse and all the antisocial activities that flow from drug abuse" (Nixon 1971a). He further noted that

> the threat of narcotics among our people is one which properly frightens many Americans. It comes quietly into homes and destroys children. It moves into neighborhoods and breaks the fiber of community which makes neighbors. It is a problem which demands compassion, and not simply condemnation, for those who become the victims of narcotics and dangerous drugs. We must try to better understand the confusion and disillusion and despair that bring people, particularly young people, to the use of narcotics and dangerous drugs. (Nixon 1971a)

More recently, New York State governor Andrew M. Cuomo used the media as part of a campaign called Combat Heroin, which included 10 videos

AP Photo/Seth Wenig

Photo 1.2: New York governor Andrew Cuomo at a Heroin Task Force meeting.

featuring recovering addicts, to be shown in movie theaters. Echoing President Nixon's decades earlier call to unite on behalf of the drug user, Governor Cuomo said, "By using the stories of real New Yorkers who have struggled with heroin and other drugs, this campaign reminds us that addiction can happen to any family, and that we can all play a role in someone's recovery" (Michel 2014). To this list we can add that deviance often serves as a locus of social change. The changing status of marijuana, discussed in Chapter 2, is an example of this function.

Conflict Theory

Conflict theory sees elements of society in constant opposition, with the dominant forces attempting to maintain the status quo, while the subordinate segments of society try to assert themselves and change the prevailing social order. Conflict theorists, for example, maintain that the powerful in society make the rules that keep the less powerful in subservience. One example of the conflict position is the assertion that the laws regarding powdered cocaine and crack cocaine are differentially enforced. Crack cocaine users, typically poor members of minority groups, are dealt with harshly, whereas the affluent majority group users of powdered cocaine are given relatively light sentences (Inciardi, Surratt, and Kurtz 2011).

Robert K. Merton's (1957) anomie theory, often referred to as a theory of the middle range, examines the effect of larger structures on individuals' behavioral choices. Merton felt that much deviance in modern urban industrial societies was caused by a disjuncture between the norms and values of the cultural system, which define the socially appropriate goals and approved means for achieving them and their accessibility within a society's (i.e., a social system's) social institutions. Merton describes a number of ways in which individuals, whose opportunity to obtain legitimate means is hindered, attempt to cope with this disjuncture of goals and means. The most relevant to our discussion is innovation, in which deviant means are chosen to achieve success goals. As Daniel Bell (1953:133) puts it, "For crime, in the language of sociologists, has a 'functional' role in the society, and the urban rackets—the illicit activity organized for continuing profit rather than individual illegal acts—is one of the queer ladders of social mobility in American life." Using this framework, drug dealers, for example, can be understood as businessmen and entrepreneurs (Bourgois 1998a, 2003; Hoffer 2006).

In his classic *The Power Elite*, C. Wright Mills (1959), one of the most important conflict theorists of the 20th century, identified three major social institutions within which power is concentrated. "Within American society," he wrote, "major national power now resides in the economic, the political, and the military domains. Other institutions seem off to the side of modern history, and, on occasion, duly subordinated to these" (Mills 1959:6). These realms are intertwined, according to Mills, mutually supporting and influencing one another. He wrote,

"There is an ever-increasing interlocking of economic, military, and political structures. If there is government intervention in the corporate economy, so is there corporate intervention in the governmental process" (1959:8). In Chapter 2, we examine the relationship between large-scale corporations and the political structure. We note the vast amount of money spent by the alcohol and tobacco lobbies and individual corporations on political contributions to both major parties and the millions of dollars the government reaps in taxes from these products. Although they are our most dangerous drugs by several measures, tobacco and alcohol are nevertheless excluded from the federal government's drug schedules, which categorize drugs in terms of their currently accepted medical use and their potential for abuse.

Exchange Theory

Exchange theory is found on both macro and micro levels. It is applied to understanding relationships between large social systems such as social institutions as well as to interpersonal interactions. Exchange theorists see human behavior as being motivated by personal gain. For these sociologists, profit equals rewards minus costs. Relationships that provide a net gain, according to exchange theorists, will be kept, whereas those that incur a loss will be rejected. The theory applies both to financial and personal relationships. Hoffer's (2006) ethnography of heroin dealers provides examples of both kinds of relationships. He noted, for example, the often long-term symbiotic relationship between customers and local junkies. The junkies served as intermediaries between customers from outside the area and immigrant drug dealers, who were not addicts. By so doing the local addicts made sure that the often naive customers were not taken advantage of, and in turn, the local addicts were given some of the customer's heroin as a kind of broker's fee. A primary factor that supported the interdependence among the local addicts, customers, and immigrant dealers was, according to Hoffer, the social identity of the addict, who was seen by customers as both knowledgeable and trustworthy.

Kurt and Danny, the local dealers studied by Hoffer, were enmeshed in a network of relationships with distributors, who both bought and sold heroin, and customers. Many of these relationships were long term and characterized by the extending of credit to customers. This was one of the ways in which Kurt and Danny tried to keep their customers happy. Hoffer noted that the single most important threat to their business was the loss of customers. "Heroin dealing," Hoffer (2006:6) wrote, "like any distribution activity, involves a process of exchange. Heroin dealers coordinate the flow of resources. Customers receive heroin and dealers receive cash, goods, or services in return." Hoffer observed a code of conduct among heroin users such that if one user helps another, both expect this help to be repaid at some future date. "This norm of reciprocity among heroin users, particularly homeless users, proved to be the foundation of Kurt's career as a heroin dealer" (p. 14).

Symbolic Interaction

Symbolic interaction theory (and its derivatives such as labeling theory and reference group theory) is a micro theory, concerned with the day-to-day interactions of people.

Symbolic interaction theory conceives of people as acting toward others and objects in terms of the meanings these things hold for them. These meanings are learned through interaction with others. Humans have the capacity to treat themselves as objects. That is, they can figuratively step outside themselves and view and judge themselves the same way they view and judge others. This idea is captured by Howard S. Becker's (1953) notion of career and Erving Goffman's (1959) concept of the moral career, the changes that one passes through in judging oneself and others. Becker (1953:235), for example, in his seminal study "Becoming a Marijuana User" writes that "the presence of a given kind of behavior is the result of a sequence of social experiences during which the person acquires a conception of the meaning of the behavior, and perceptions and judgments of objects and situations, all of which make the activity possible and desirable." Marsh B. Ray's (1961) explanation for abstinence and relapse cycles among heroin addicts, discussed in Chapter 8 as it relates to alcoholism, is another example of the use of symbolic interactionist perspectives to understand the processes and progression of drug use, as is the work of Bullington, Munns, and Geis (1969), who studied how ex-addict paraprofessional street workers dealt with the difficulty of identity transitions.

Labeling Theory

Labeling theory is a derivative of symbolic interaction theory. This framework examines the processes by which people get recognized and labeled as deviant and how this may cause changes in their public identity. It also attends to the consequences for the individual of being publicly labeled (Goffman 1963). Becker (1963), one of the early labeling theorists, tells us that to understand deviance it is necessary to look at the labeling process. This approach requires studying the social audience, those who define, recognize, and respond to deviant behavior, and their relation to the "deviant." "The central fact about deviance," Becker (1963:8) writes, is that "it is created by society. . . . *Social groups create deviance by making the rules whose infraction constitutes deviance* and by applying those rules to particular people and labeling them as outsiders" (italics in original).

A classic example of the application of labeling theory is the work of Trice and Roman (1970). The authors were interested in how some alcoholics can be delabeled and then relabeled as something less "deviant." In their explanation, they identify some relevant factors. There is, importantly, the repentant role, which facilitates the acceptance of the now abstinent individual back into the fold. Access to this role is made possible by the widespread belief, promoted by Alcoholics Anonymous, that alcoholism is a disease. Additionally, people believe they know what causes alcoholism: alcohol. So long as an individual does not have alcohol on his or her breath and does not manifest any of the outward signs of drinking, others feel comfortable in assigning him or her a new label of *recovering alcoholic*. The authors contrast this situation to that of the mentally ill, who cannot get delabeled and relabeled because people do not understand what causes their behavior, which is hence seen as unpredictable.

Reference Group Theory

Reference group theory examines the effects of others on an individual's perceptions and behavior. Weinberg (1994), for example, found that the drinking behavior of a sample of gay men closely resembled that of their friends. Those men who "came out" into the bar scene at an early age and whose social life revolved around bars and other alcohol-related settings tended to drink heavily like their companions. Men who considered themselves to be moderate social drinkers surrounded themselves with like-minded peers. Those men who came out into gay community centers and whose friendships and social lives were centered in these institutions tended, like their friends, to be abstainers or light drinkers.

Phenomenological Sociology

Phenomenological sociology, also a micro theory, is a variant of symbolic interaction, focusing on the subjective experiences of the individual. The central idea of phenomenological sociology is that we can only understand why an individual does what he does if we understand how he views his world. It is often unclear whether a writer's perspective is symbolic interaction or phenomenological sociology for there are many similarities and blendings between the two related frameworks. A good example of the phenomenological sociological approach is the work of Rettig, Torres, and Garrett (1977). The main portion of the volume is the autobiographical account of Manny Torres, allowing the reader to see the world and his addiction through his eyes.

Ethnomethodology

Ethnomethodologists argue against classical sociological concepts such as macro or micro. Rather than a "micro" sociology, ethnomethodology is characterized as a praxeological sociology (i.e., one that focalizes on persons' culturally based social actions and interactions in context, Rod Watson, personal communication, April 2011). Unlike symbolic interactionists, who focus on the individual's application of meaning to his and others' feelings and behavior, ethnomethodologists are concerned with the *conjoint production* of situated meanings. People do this by using commonsense methods of categorization. For instance, one may identify another as a drug user (an underlying pattern) by recognizing the defining characteristics (indexical particulars) of drug users as one understands them. There is a reciprocal relationship between the underlying pattern and the indexical particulars in that one may reconstruct and impute indexical particulars to an individual once the underlying pattern is known. An excellent example of the ethnomethodological approach is Bittner's (1967) study of how police conceptualize their dealing with skid row inhabitants.

Ethnomethodologists have studied drunkenness and alcoholism. MacAndrew and Edgerton (1969), for example, looked at ordinary persons' culturally based knowledge of being drunk, "what-everybody-knows-about-being-drunk." Drunkenness is thus seen as a matter of cultural context. That is, in every group there are expectations and practices linked to a given context. So, for example, in the United Kingdom and the United States, the rules for drunken comportment for young people are that it is hedonistic, disorderly, and noisy. MacAndrew and Edgerton showed that the rules and expectations for drunken comportment in other cultural groupings differ from the hedonism model. This sociological perspective differs from other models such as the biochemical models of drunkenness or alcoholism.

MacAndrew and Garfinkel (1962) examined the commonsense cultural use of the term *alcoholism* as an account for making sense of persons' activity of repeatedly getting drunk, an account that does not exist in all cultures. They studied 62 Caucasian men who consecutively appeared at an alcoholism outpatient clinic for help with their drinking problems. Each subject, while completely sober, "was asked to describe in turn his image of himself as he is when sober (sober self), his image of himself as he is when intoxicated (drunk self), and the sort of person he wishes he were (ideal self)" (p. 254). The data were then subjected to sophisticated statistical analyses. MacAndrew and Garfinkel found that the men's sober and intoxicated self-images were "markedly different from one another" (p. 255). The men portrayed their drunken selves as worthless, undependable, contemptible, pathetic, bitter, resentful, and the like, descriptions that did not characterize their sober selves. "Taken together," MacAndrew and Garfinkel wrote, "these items constitute a compellingly consistent characterization of the changes that these subjects attributed to intoxication. There was a rise in feelings of disillusionment, bitterness and resentment, and a corollary demise of the 'togetherness' stance" (p. 259). "Why then," the authors ask, "do these people drink?" (p. 259). After considering alternative explanations such as the "Faustian" approach (i.e., the individual focuses on the short-term "benefits" to heavy drinking rather than examining its long-term costs) and the toxic-agent approach (the individual's drunken comportment is the direct result of the alcohol consumed) and finding them inadequate, MacAndrew and Garfinkel focused on a social systems explanation, attending to "the meanings accorded the resultant state of intoxication by the members of the system" (pp. 263–264). "Briefly," they wrote, "we propose that from this perspective 'being drunk' may be construed as a state of being-in-the-world to which society grants a provisional relaxation of the individual's institutionalized obligations, and particularly of the demand of accountability which is ordinarily required as a condition of accredited membership in the collectivity and sanctioned competence" (p. 264). Thus, "From this perspective, alcohol ingestion constitutes the socially understood and sanctioned *grounds* for the claim to 'being-in-the-world-drunk,' whereas in the toxic-agent approach the ingestion of alcohol is the *cause* of a physiological incapacitation. The claim to 'being-in-the-world-drunk' carries with it the prerogative that 'being after all drunk' one is free to 'act out' with relative impunity" (p. 264).

Criminological Explanations

Most criminological theories have been proposed by sociologists specializing in the study of deviance, and they are therefore based on sociological frameworks. Becker's (1963) discussion of the process of becoming deviant, and especially the stages he identifies in becoming a marijuana user, are examples of a classical socio-logical/deviance theory, using a symbolic interactionist perspective that is applicable to the study of drug use.

Sociologists/criminologists have proposed theories of the development of deviant subcultures and the functions they perform for their members. Whereas some of these are general formulations, easily adaptable to understanding the drug world, other writers focus specifically on drug subcultures.

Albert K. Cohen's Delinquent Boys Thesis

In Chapter 2 of his classic book *Delinquent Boys: The Culture of the Gang*, Albert K. Cohen (1955) developed a general theory of subcultures. He began by noting the importance of "the role of the social structure and the immediate social milieu in determining *the creation and selection of solutions*" to normal human problems of adjustment (p. 55; italics in original). Using the concept of reference group, Cohen noted the pressure to conform generated by these groups. If we cannot reconcile our needs with that of the group, he writes, "We are not so likely to strike out on our own as we are to shop around for a group with a different subculture, with a frame of reference we find more congenial. One fascinating aspect of the social process is the continual realignment of groups, the migration of individuals from one group to another in the unconscious quest for a social milieu favorable to the resolution of their problems of adjustment" (p. 58). Most critical in the formation of subcultures is, according to Cohen, "the existence, *in effective interaction with one another, of a number of actors with similar problems of adjustment*" (p. 59; italics in original). That is, individuals who share the same needs, problems, or perspectives have to find each other and be able to communicate about their common issues with one another. They do this, says Cohen, by carefully feeling each other out, using ambiguous exploratory gestures that can be quickly withdrawn if the hoped for congenial responses are not forthcoming. If a favorable response is received, another less ambiguous gesture may be proffered, until the individuals involved begin to freely interact. Examples of how this interaction progresses in sexual scenes are provided in the section on pickups in Chapter 7, "Alcohol and Sexual Behavior." The same process often unwinds in drug negotiations in which the participants are strangers.

As subcultures develop, a set of "group standards" or frames of reference emerge, which evolve to meet the needs of their members. One of the problems subcultures serve to solve, according to Cohen, is that of status. Subcultures, like the various drug subcultures, provide an alternative status system, based on established shared criteria. One example of this comes from the ethnographic work of Harold Finestone (1957), who studied young black men who were heroin addicts. These men had established their own criteria for prestige, based on their knowledge of fashion, music, and the "hustle" they devised for "making some bread" (Finestone 1957:4–5).[6] Among the jazz musicians studied by Becker (1951), subcultural prestige was based both on criteria of musical competence and whether the musician was seen as selling his integrity by going "commercial."

Another function served by subcultures, according to Cohen, is social validation. "It is only in interaction with those who share his values," Cohen writes, "that the actor finds social validation for his beliefs and social rewards for his way of life, and the continued existence of the group and friendly intercourse with its members become values for the actor" (A. Cohen 1955:67). Along with the greater reliance on the subcultural group for status and validation, a sense of being part of an in-group develops, with often hostile and contemptuous attitudes toward members of the larger society. Becker (1951) notes how jazz musicians perceive their audiences as "squares" and attempt to separate themselves, sometimes by using physical barriers, from them. "Musicians," he writes, "are hostile to their audiences, being afraid that they must sacrifice their artistic standards to the squares" (p. 141). They do this through what Becker terms "isolation" and "self-segregation." Finestone's (1957) "cats" had a similar attitude toward "squares," using drugs to emphasize their social distance from them. As Finestone notes, "It can be seen now why heroin use should make such a powerful appeal to the cat. It was the ultimate 'kick.' No substance was more profoundly tabooed by conventional middle-class society. Regular heroin use provides a sense of maximal social differentiation from the 'square.' The cat was at last engaged, he felt, in an activity completely beyond the comprehension of the 'square'" (p. 6).

In addition to the development, transmission, and reinforcement of attitudes and beliefs, subcultures also provide their members with access to whatever it is that they need. As Cohen observed, "Furthermore, to the extent that the new subculture invites the hostility of outsiders—one of the costs of subcultural solutions—the members of the subcultural group are motivated to look to one another for those goods and services, those relationships of cooperation and exchange which they once enjoyed with the world outside the group and which now have been withdrawn" (1955:68).

Cloward and Ohlin's Delinquency and Opportunity

Some criminological/sociological theorists have focused specifically on drug subcultures and their content. Richard Cloward and Lloyd Ohlin (1960) developed a model of delinquent subcultures—criminal, conflict, and retreatist—characterized by differential access to deviant opportunities and distinct patterns of behavior. One of the three subcultures, the retreatist pattern, "involve[s] the use of drugs . . . that are supported by a subculture" (Cloward and Ohlin 1960:25). "Subcultural drug-users in lower-class areas," they write, "perceive themselves as culturally and socially detached from the life-style and everyday preoccupations of members of the conventional world" (p. 25). In their description of the drug subculture, Cloward and Ohlin rely heavily on the work of Finestone (1957), which we have previously discussed. Echoing Cohen's (1955) observation of the importance of the social validation provided for the individual by the subculture, they write,

> His reference group is the "society of cats," an "elite" group in which he becomes isolated from conventional society. Within this group, a new order of goals and criteria of achievement are created. The cat does not seek to impose this system of values on the world of the squares. Instead, he strives for status and deference within the society of cats by cultivating the kick and the hustle. Thus the retreatist subculture provides avenues to success-goals, to the social admiration and the sense of well-being or oneness with the world which the members feel are otherwise beyond their reach. (p. 27)

In his autobiography, which includes a sociological analysis provided by his coauthors, Manny Torres (Rettig et al. 1977) describes his participation in all of the subcultures identified in the Cloward and Ohlin model. As an early teenager, Manny was immersed in a violent street gang culture (Cloward and Ohlin's conflict subculture). By the time he was 15, he was working for a "big bookmaker" (p. 31) who was part of a criminal organization (the criminal subculture). Manny had been running errands and doing odd jobs for Leo, the bookie, who decided to offer him a job with his organization, providing access to new illegitimate opportunities. Manny writes,

> Everything was divided up in the New York rackets in those days. And Leo had all the action around the neighborhood having to do with playing the numbers or the pools. As I was growing up in the neighborhood I used to run errands for Leo. . . . I was always around and ready to do him favors. As I got older I started doing him bigger favors, like running book occasionally when someone was jammed up. . . . So it was natural for him to offer me a job in his organization. (p. 31)

Manny's involvement in the heroin (retreatist) subculture began when his uncle introduced him to heroin. At first he simply snorted the powder, later graduating to injecting it subcutaneously ("skin popping" in the addict argot), and finally injecting heroin into his veins ("mainlining"). As Manny became more and more involved with heroin, his habit began to affect his work for Leo. Eventually, Leo had to let him go, and Manny's love affair with heroin, which he calls "the white lady," became all consuming. "By now I had a constant urge in my throat for junk," he writes. "I could taste it, touch it with every angry nerve ending in my body. Nothing else mattered a damn" (p. 38). As he became increasingly immersed in the heroin subculture, Manny began to develop a self-image as a "dope fiend," supporting his habit by engaging in secondary deviance, including drug dealing, shoplifting, working for a check forging ring, and armed robberies. Unlike Finestone's (1957) cats, who served as the model for the Cloward and Ohlin ideal type of the retreatist subculture, Manny's relationship with other addicts was not characterized by a need for group approval or prestige. Rather, the picture he paints of the heroin subculture is one of mutual use and competition:

> You have no values. There's no such thing as values for a dope fiend, none at all. The only livin' thing that counts is the fix. That's all that counts, nothin' else means a shit. . . . If it came to the point where I had a gun in my hand and you had the dope and you didn't give it to me, I'd take it off of you. And I'd of used the gun if I had to. I would kill you! Certainly! If you had the dope and that's the only way I could get it." (Rettig et al. 1977:13–14)

Irving Spergel's Racketville, Slumtown, and Haulburg

Irving Spergel (1964) examined Cloward and Ohlin's typology through an ethnography of three "lower-class" urban neighborhoods. Rather than being a discrete subculture, he found that heroin use was a subpattern in all three of the neighborhoods (i.e., the conflict subculture, the criminal racket subculture, and the criminal theft subculture) he studied. "The drug-addict pattern is considered to be one type of response by older adolescents and young adults, most of whom were former delinquents, to certain age-role and class pressures, rather than a distinctive subculture," Spergel notes. "No longer acceptable to, or desiring acceptance from, the delinquent neighborhood groups of which they may have been members, these young men now find in drug-use a way to ease their transition to adult status, conventional or criminal" (p. xvii).

Unlike Finestone's (1957) "cats," Spergel found that using heroin was not a source of in-group esteem: "In his present status as addict he obtained little positive recognition. His use of drugs made him undesirable in his self-evaluation, in the opinion of other drug addicts, or in attitude of the community" (p. 56). According to Spergel, for the young men he studied, heroin use "in part afforded individuals a collective support for escape from failure. It permitted and encouraged the support of the group in the use of drugs, giving rise to fantasies of success and personal well-being" (p. 62).

Sykes and Matza's Techniques of Neutralization

Gresham Sykes and David Matza (1957) were interested in how delinquents were able to engage in deviant behavior while temporarily eliminating or reducing shame and/or guilt. The writers hypothesized that they used justifications, which Sykes and Matza called "techniques of neutralization." These techniques of neutralization are learned in interaction with others and continually reinforced by the group. They write, "There is also reason to believe that they precede deviant behavior and make deviant behavior possible. . . . Disapproval flowing from internalized norms and conforming others in the social environment is neutralized, turned back, or deflected in advance. Social controls that serve to check or inhibit deviant motivational patterns are rendered inoperative, and the individual is freed to engage in delinquency without serious damage to his self-image" (pp. 666–667). Four of the five techniques of neutralization identified by Sykes and Matza are relevant for our understanding of drug users. They are the denial of responsibility, the denial of the victim, the denial of injury, and the condemnation of the condemners. Drug users often see themselves as victims, trapped by their addiction and forced to feed it in any way they can. For example, Manny Torres writes, "The white lady sucks, man. You think that you're sucking her up into the glass and mainlining her radiant ass. But the white junk lady sucks you in, man, until you belong" (Rettig et al. 1977:38). Seeing himself now as a victim of "the white lady," Manny can justify his secondary deviance as he desperately attempts to get money for a fix; he feels that he is no longer responsible for his behavior: "Like I would steal off anybody—anybody at all, my own mother gladly included if it meant the difference between a fix and no fix. I would do anything for money to fix. I would con, I would beg, I would cry; I would break bad and threaten. I would do anything at all to get enough money to fix" (p. 14).

Manny's autobiography also contains examples of the denial of the victim. In this type of justification, even if the individual concedes that his behavior causes an injury, "the moral indignation of self and others may be neutralized by an insistence that the injury is not wrong in light of the circumstances. The injury, it may be claimed, is not really an injury; rather it is a form of rightful retaliation or punishment. By a subtle alchemy the delinquent moves himself into the position of an avenger and the victim is transformed into a wrongdoer" (Sykes and Matza (1957:668). When Manny decided to rob his drug connections, he justified his actions by believing that they had taken advantage of him in the past. "For a moment I'm a little sorry, but only for a moment. 'Cause I've been buying three-dollar bags off him for a long time, about fifty or a hundred at a time. And he's never given me any special deal 'cause he knows I'm wired behind stuff and have to have it. . . . Besides the dope. I can knock off the connections that made me sweat" (Rettig et al. 1977:54–55). As Manny continued to rob both drug connections and bookies, he began to see himself, as Sykes and Matza note, as an avenger of sorts: "All that time we were hitting bookies I figure we're doing society a big favor. We're taking from rich criminals to support poor criminals. Like, we're the Robin Hoods of the underworld!" (p. 61).

In denial of injury, the individual believes that no harm was really done. Whatever "criminal" or "deviant" act occurred did not injure anyone. Many marijuana smokers, for example, believe that smoking that plant is a victimless crime and that its effects are not harmful. This position is reinforced by the legalization of medical marijuana in 28 states and the District of Columbia as of this writing and its legalization for recreational use in Alaska, California, Colorado, Maine, Massachusetts, Nevada, Oregon, Washington State, and Washington, D.C.[7] Some other states have decriminalized the possession of marijuana and treat it as a civil infraction or treat possession as a misdemeanor. Lenny Bruce (1963), who died of an overdose of morphine at the age of 40 in 1966, used this technique of neutralization in his book, *How to Talk Dirty and Influence People*:

> Alcohol is a caustic that destroys tissues which cannot be rebuilt. It is toxic, and damages one of the most important organs in the body—one that cannot repair itself or be repaired—the liver. Whereas, for example, no form of cannabis sativa (the hemp plant from which marijuana is made) destroys any body tissue or harms the organs in any manner. This is a fact that can be verified by any chemistry professor of any university in the United States. Nevertheless, the possession of marijuana is a crime. (p. 45)

Bruce's chapter also demonstrates the technique of condemnation of condemners, by subtly showing the hypocrisy of legal drug abusers who condemn those who use illicit drugs. In it, he creates an imaginary scene set in a jury room, where the jurors are deliberating on a verdict for a marijuana user. His female jurors discuss their own instrumental use of a variety of prescription drugs, including sleeping pills, amphetamines, and Demerol. One woman offers another, who complains of fatigue, some Demerol. Another juror asks the others to identify some pills given to her by a neighbor:

(An elderly woman juror, silent until now, turns and speaks)

Elderly woman: Come on ladies. We need a verdict. What are we going to do with this man?

First woman: Oh, yes—the dope addict. How does a person sink that low? (p. 47)

Feminist Approaches

Although there are a variety of feminist approaches,[8] they have in common two fundamental questions: "*And what about the women?*' In other words, Where are the women in any situation being investigated? If they are not present, why? If they are present, what exactly are they doing? . . . [and] . . . '*Why is all this as it is?*'" (Lengermann and Niebrugge 2010:194). Historically, comparatively little research has been done on drug and alcohol use among women (Sanders 2009). Feminists point out that this is a reflection of the general neglect of women's issues in criminology and the sociology of deviant behavior. Peralta and Jauk (2011) note that "men have long been the target and focus of research, prevention, and intervention without considering the gendered underpinnings of alcohol-use and alcohol-related problems despite evidence for the importance of gender" (p. 888). For example, in Pittman and Snyder's (1962) anthology, *Society, Culture, and Drinking Patterns*, the definitive collection of research and writing on alcohol abuse and alcoholism of its day, out of 35 articles, only two devote any space to women's substance abuse. One of these (A. Ullman 1962) discussed drinking among (college age) women, and he only devotes three pages to this topic. His reference section lists just two articles on the topic, one of which is a study of inmates in a correctional institution, and the other is his own article upon which his present chapter is based. The other article by Joan Jackson (1962) dealt primarily with the effects of the husband's alcoholism on the family. In a small section of 11 lines discussing the alcoholic wife and mother, Jackson noted that "there are no empirical studies of the alcoholic wife's effect on the family" (p. 475). It is only within the last few decades, with the advent of feminist sociology, that substance use and abuse by women has been studied. An example of a more recent edited volume dedicated solely to women's substance abuse is that of Gomberg and Nirenberg (1993). This volume includes not only research on alcohol use, but also studies of women and illicit drugs, tobacco, and eating disorders.

One interesting study, which illustrates Lengermann and Niebrugge's (2010) typology of feminist theories, including those of gender inequality, gender oppression, and structural oppression, is Maher and Daly's (1996) ethnographic research on women's role in the informal drug economy in the Bushwick neighborhood in Brooklyn over a 3-year period. Initially interviewing 211 female crack addicts, the

Simon Belcher/Alamy Stock Photo

Photo 1.3: Heroin addict cooking up before shooting up.

researchers focused on a smaller sample of 45 women whom they observed and repeatedly interviewed. Prior to using crack, most of the women had used heroin or powdered cocaine. On the average, their drug use extended over more than 10 years. Over 90% of them were homeless. The researchers found that "recent drug markets continue to be monopolized by men and to offer few opportunities for stable income generation for women. While women's *presence* on the street and in low-level auxiliary roles may have increased, we find that their *participation* as substantive labor in the drug-selling marketplace has not" (Maher and Daly:397; italics in original).

Sommers, Baskin, and Fagan (1994) studied how 30 women who had been violent criminals, drug abusers, and participants in deviant street subcultures left "The Life." All the women had used drugs. Eighty-seven percent were crack addicts, 70% used cocaine, and 10% were heroin addicts. What the researchers found is consistent with Ray's (1961) description of how addicts go through relapse and abstinence cycles. They first experience turning points, negative sanctions or experiences, which motivate them to reexamine their situation. The second stage in the process involves a public announcement that the woman has decided to quit her criminal involvement, and the third stage involves what Sommers et al. (1994) term "maintenance." At this juncture, the women tried to integrate themselves into a noncriminal identity and social world and worked to maintain this new self-image.

Not only research but also treatment modalities have been traditionally male-oriented and male-dominated, especially those using medical models, which have been influenced by Alcoholics Anonymous (Peralta and Jauk 2011; Sanders 2009). It is only since the mid-1990s that feminist approaches to treatment have been developed (Peralta and Jauk 2011). Sanders (2009) studied a nonprobability sample of 167 women involved in a women-only A.A. group by using a specially developed survey and accounts written by these women about their lives. Using both liberal feminist and phenomenological feminist approaches, she examined how women empower themselves as active participants in A.A.

Examining the situation of women and substance use in Australia from a feminist perspective, Stephens (1995) pointed out that whereas women's use of alcohol and other legal drugs is no longer constrained as it has been in the past, it still elicits different attitudes and social responses than substance use by men, a point also made by Sanders. The objective of her research was to understand why this is so, its pervasiveness, and its effect on women. She examined how the meanings of women's substance use have been socially and historically constructed and why they continue to persist.

Dutchman-Smith (2004) posed the question, "Is alcohol really a feminist issue?" Her complaint about some feminists (or what she calls "pseudo-feminists") is that, by focusing on women's binge drinking and their explanations for it (e.g., to overcome anxieties over not having the perfect body), they are infantilizing women. Women, she writes, drink for the same reason that men drink: to relax and to get drunk. Feminism, for Dutchman-Smith, is about, among other things, "the right of women to behave as wickedly (or as virtuously) as men. It's what we call equality, and it's non-negotiable." "The outrage over women's drinking habits," she writes, "represents an ongoing discomfort with women being adults and doing adult things. This discomfort masquerades as a concern for women's health and well-being. [Some writers] reduce feminist activism to whatever may benefit passive women with a permanent patriarchal framework, even though this tramples over what benefits women overall, which is to be regarded as fully grown human beings." A drinker herself, who admittedly sometimes drinks too much, she says that "after several drinks I do not think, 'that'll show the patriarchy.' I think, 'I'd like some chips and is there a quiz machine in here?'"

Other Perspectives

Although we primarily employ sociological theories in this book, they are not, of course, the only frameworks used to try to understand drug and alcohol use. As we shall see in Chapter 8, there are also psychological, genetic, physiological, medical, and lay explanations, such as that popularized by Alcoholics Anonymous. Although sociological theories explain alcohol and drug use as social behavior and examine how interaction and learning within reference groups and subcultures influence the individual's perception and actions, many of these other perspectives are more concerned with addiction, which they see as an individual issue. They therefore look for particular characteristics that may be involved in alcoholism and drug addiction. For example, some psychologists believe that there is an addictive personality and identify common personality traits among chronic alcoholics and addicts.[9] Geneticists look for inherited vulnerabilities among these populations. Physiological and medical researchers are most concerned with the consequences of heavy substance abuse such as the development of tolerance and the physical effects of long-term use.

Researching Drug and Alcohol Use

Sociologists who study addiction employ many of the standard methods used in the discipline. These include survey research, ethnographies, in-depth questioning, and case studies. Often, more than one of these methods is combined. So, for example, in-depth questioning is often used to supplement the participant observation of ethnographers and vice versa. Hoffer (2006) noted that his "interview data alone was sometimes insufficient to draw conclusions about what was happening" (p. 16). This was especially true when he obtained conflicting reports from dealers and customers. His own observations enabled him to reconcile conflicting statements.

Surveys have been employed extensively in addiction research, especially in the study of alcohol use and abuse (Jellinek 1962; Weinberg and Vogler 1990). Survey research is a relatively inexpensive way to gather large data sets, and it readily lends itself to computer analysis. Care must be taken, however, both in sampling and question selection and sequencing.

Ethnographies give an up-close, intimate picture of the people being studied, enabling the sociologist to understand their worldviews. Nels Anderson's (1923) study *The Hobo* remains the classic ethnographic example. Rudy's (1986) ethnography of Alcoholics Anonymous; Weinberg's (1994) research on gay male drinking; Bourgois's (1998a) study of heroin, cocaine, and crack users in East Harlem, his ethnography of heroin shooting encampments in San Francisco (2003), and study of drug use and violence among a network of Puerto Rican crack dealers in the Barrio (1998b); Pierce's (1999) study of young, white, middle-class heroin users; and Hoffer's (2006) study of heroin dealers are more recent examples. Though providing rich data, ethnographers are limited by the roles they take in the field and the challenges in organizing, analyzing, and interpreting qualitative data. Ethnographic research is labor intensive and time consuming and therefore a relatively expensive research method. It also requires a good deal of interpersonal skills to be accepted by those whom one studies.

Case studies are sometimes used by sociologists as a means of generating hypotheses and discovering fruitful avenues for further study. Highly labor intensive, this methodology presents problems of generalizing findings to a larger universe. Hoffer's (2006) study of two heroin dealers is an excellent example of the case study method. Hoffer was able, through the friendships he developed in the field, to understand from the inside the world of heroin dealers and users. He found, for instance, that "the heroin economy is based upon multiple small-scale organizations" (p. 105) rather than being controlled by some centralized authority. He was also able to observe how one heroin-dealing network evolved over time and how formal attempts at social control through urban renewal actually facilitated the growth and sophistication of this network.

In Chapter 7 we discuss some of the research done by psychologists (or social psychologists coming from the psychological side of the discipline) on individuals' perception of attractiveness and its relationship to the willingness to participate in risky sexual activities when using alcohol. Some of these studies use laboratory experiments, whereas others employ field experiments. Sociological researchers and social psychologists trained as sociologists are interested in some of the same behaviors, but they approach them through ethnographies, in-depth interviews, and survey research.

NOTES

1. Though the terms *drug abuse* and *alcoholism* are still widely used in popular culture and the media, they have been replaced in the professional lexicon (as presented in the *DSM-5*) by the terms *substance use disorders, alcohol use disorder, tobacco use disorder, cannabis use disorder, stimulant use*

disorder, *hallucinogen use disorder*, *opioid use disorder*, *inhalant use disorder*, and *sedative use disorder* (buppractice 2017; Horvath, Misra, Epner, and Cooper 2016; SAMHSA 2015b).

2. According to SAMHSA, addiction is "the overpowering physical or emotional urge to continue alcohol or other drug (AOD) use in spite of adverse consequences. In the context of AOD, addiction is a cluster of chronic disorders that spring from multiple, interacting etiological influences and that vary considerably in their onset, course, and outcome" (Verhoeven 1993).

3. The term *junkie* was first used in the 1920s, whereas *drug abuse* (and by extension *drug abuser*) came into common usage between 1965 and 1970. Another term, *dope fiend*, can be traced back to between 1890 and 1895.

4. Some writers would not consider Goffman to be a pure symbolic interactionist. For example, Rod Watson (2009) writes, "Goffman's use of similes and other tropes, is then, a major part of his 'machine for making formal properties,' in the tradition of his teacher E. C. Hughes and others in the 'symbolic interactionist' genre of sociology (though Goffman himself cannot really be conceived as a symbolic interactionist *tout court*" (p. 105). By this, Watson does not mean to deny the symbolic interactionism in Goffman but rather to indicate that he is a "complex case" who was also influenced by Talcott Parsons and W. Lloyd Warner and includes other perspectives within his theoretical framework. Watson notes that he is taking Goffman at his own word from an interview with Jef Verhoeven (1993) in *Research on Language and Social Interaction*. In that interview, Goffman presents himself as a complex case, influenced not only by Warner and Parsons but also by A. R. Radcliffe-Brown, and rejecting academic labels such as *symbolic interactionist*.

5. This section on sociological theories is an expanded and revised version of a discussion that first appeared in Thomas S. Weinberg (2012).

6. *Bread* is the term for money in the *cats'* argot, and "a 'hustle' is any non-violent means of 'making some bread' which does not require work" (pp. 4–5).

7. See Chapter 2 for a discussion of the legalization of marijuana.

8. Lengermann and Niebrugge (2010) identify a number of feminist perspectives, which they organize under four larger issues.

a. Gender difference: "Women's location in, and experience of, most situations is different from those of men in the situation" (cultural feminism, existential or phenomenological feminism, feminist institutional theory)

b. Gender inequality: "Women's location in most situations is not only different but also less privileged than or *unequal* to that of men" (liberal feminism, rational choice feminism)

c. Gender oppression: "Women are *oppressed*, not just different from or unequal to, but actively restrained, subordinated, molded, and used and abused by men" (psychoanalytic feminism, radical feminism)

d. Structural oppression: "Women's experiences of difference, inequality, and oppression vary by their social location within capitalism, patriarchy, and racism" (socialist feminism, intersectionality theory) (p. 199).

9. The authors know individuals who appear to have addictive personalities. One such man, for example, has gone from one addiction to another. He is a self-acknowledged alcoholic, who participated in the Alcoholics Anonymous program. Later, he became a cocaine user. During

that period, when he was in his sixties, he started to cross-dress, a behavior that, for many men, is addictive (for examples, see Bullough and Weinberg 1988). His economic downfall came when he began frequenting casinos and gambling. As he told one of us, it was his entire fault. Another man, a former addict and recovering alcoholic, would commonly devour huge amounts of food and developed a need to continually buy specialty clothing items.

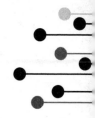

CHAPTER 2

Alcohol, Tobacco, and Other Drugs

From a sociological perspective, there is little difference among addicted drug users, no matter what their drug of choice: heroin, cocaine, crack, methamphetamines, alcohol, and so forth. In fact, as we will see later in this chapter, many users combine more than one drug, including alcohol, and it is not unusual for an individual to have multiple addictions. Despite chemical differences among various substances, drug users, especially those who are addicted, act pretty much the same way. There are very little behavioral differences between, say, heroin addicts and alcoholics.[1] Becoming a user of illicit drugs or an addict or alcoholic is part of an interactive process, whereby the individual makes sense of his or her behavior and eventually sees the world through the addict or alcoholic role.

The world of addiction is complex, characterized by multiple relationships, with its own argot, norms, expectations, and perspectives. Addicts and alcoholics actively participate in this world by adopting its view. Both heroin addicts and alcoholics center their lives around their favorite substances, engage in secondary deviance to support their addictions, alienate others close to them, and so forth.

Many nonsociologists, however, would not agree with sociological perspectives on drug and alcohol use. Among these others are politicians, government officials, and law enforcement personnel, who are selective in what they consider dangerous drugs and drug abusers. In the following section, we look at the different ways in which alcohol, tobacco, and various other drugs have been officially categorized, with implications for how drug users are labeled and how the legal and medical systems process them.

The War on Drugs and the Federal Schedules

After taking office in January 1969, President Richard M. Nixon made what came to be called the war on drugs a priority. In fact, in an address to bipartisan leaders in Congress, on June 17, 1971, he stated, "America's public enemy number one in the United States is drug abuse. In order to fight and defeat this enemy, it is necessary to wage a new, all-out offensive" (Nixon 1971a). Well before this, however, President Nixon began an antidrug campaign, starting with Operation Intercept,

Photo 2.1: Operation Intercept caused huge traffic jams at the U.S. border to Mexico.

from September 21, 1969, to October 11, 1969, which attempted to stop drugs from entering the United States at its borders. The operation was a failure, for it only confiscated about 160 pounds of marijuana, just slightly more than had been seized before the program began (Golgowski 2013).

In 1970, with the support and encouragement of the Nixon administration, Congress passed the Comprehensive Drug Abuse Prevention and Control Act, which contained as Title II the Controlled Substances Act, which we discuss in more detail in Chapter 9 ("The Comprehensive Drug Abuse Prevention and Control Act of 1970"). This legislation established federal schedules, or categories within which different types of drugs were listed, according to what was seen as their currently accepted medical use and their potential for abuse. The following list of scheduled substances is found on the website of the U.S. Drug Enforcement Administration (http://www.justice.gov/dea/druginfo/ds.shtml).[2]

Schedule I

Schedule I drugs, substances, or chemicals are defined as drugs with no currently accepted medical use and a high potential for abuse. Schedule I drugs are the most dangerous drugs of all the drug schedules with potentially severe psychological or physical dependence. Some examples of Schedule I drugs are heroin, lysergic acid diethylamide (LSD), marijuana (cannabis), 3,4-methylenedioxymethamphetamine (ecstasy), methaqualone, and peyote.

Schedule II

Schedule II drugs, substances, or chemicals are defined as drugs with a high potential for abuse, less abuse potential than Schedule I drugs, with use potentially leading to severe psychological or physical dependence. These drugs are also considered dangerous. Some examples of Schedule II drugs are cocaine, methamphetamine, methadone, hydromorphone (Dilaudid), meperidine (Demerol), oxycodone (OxyContin), fentanyl, Dexedrine, Adderall, and Ritalin.

Schedule III

Schedule III drugs, substances, or chemicals are defined as drugs with a moderate to low potential for physical and psychological dependence. Schedule III drugs abuse potential is less than Schedule I and Schedule II drugs but more than Schedule IV. Some examples of Schedule III drugs are combination products with less than 15 milligrams of hydrocodone per dosage unit (Vicodin), products containing less than 90 milligrams of codeine per dosage unit (Tylenol with codeine), ketamine, anabolic steroids, and testosterone.

Schedule IV

Schedule IV drugs, substances, or chemicals are defined as drugs with a low potential for abuse and low risk of dependence. Some examples of Schedule IV drugs are Xanax, Soma, Darvon, Darvocet, Valium, Ativan, Talwin, and Ambien.

Schedule V

Schedule V drugs, substances, or chemicals are defined as drugs with lower potential for abuse than Schedule IV and consist of preparations containing limited quantities of certain narcotics. Schedule V drugs are generally used for antidiarrheal, antitussive, and analgesic purposes. Some examples of Schedule V drugs are cough preparations with less than 200 milligrams of codeine or per 100 milliliters (Robitussin AC), Lomotil, Motofen, Lyrica, and Parepectolin.

The first thing to notice about these schedules is the use of the term *abuse*. The term itself is vague, subjective, and not scientific, which is why the *Diagnostic and Statistical Manual of Mental Disorders, Fifth Edition (DSM-5)* no longer uses the term. Whether a substance is being "abused" depends on the perspective of whoever is viewing this behavior. Even a more scientific sociological definition of substance abuse focusing on whether use has affected the user's health, behavior, and social relationships is problematic, because many of these problems only show up much later in the abuser's deviant career. There are, for example, what are called "functioning alcoholics," who go to work, take care of their families, and do not seem, at least for years, to have any health or relationship issues. The same can be said for occasional users of other drugs, such as tobacco, heroin, cocaine, marijuana, methamphetamine, and the like. It is only in retrospect that we may say that the person was a substance abuser. Eventually, substance abuse catches up with the individual. Heroin users may overdose; develop hepatitis, AIDS, or other problems because of their use; and usually alienate those closest to them. Tobacco and alcohol abusers develop cardiovascular problems, cancer, liver problems, and so forth. Second, if we look closely at these schedules, it becomes apparent that two very common drugs with no currently accepted medical use and a high potential for "abuse" are not listed anywhere in the schedules. These drugs are alcohol and tobacco. Like heroin and other opiates, they also present a high risk of dependence or addiction, a situation in which increasing amounts of the substance are required to achieve the same effect. Ultimately, added increments of the drug are no longer effective in satisfying the user's needs, and at that point, he or she has developed a tolerance. As with all addictive substances, withdrawal results in a variety of symptoms. The question is why aren't alcohol and tobacco included in the schedules? They would appear to fit well into Schedule I, the most restrictive of the schedules. Although as documented in Chapter 5, there may be some health benefits to moderate use of alcohol, neither alcohol nor tobacco has any currently accepted medical use, and both have a high potential for abuse and addiction. In Chapter 8, we examine the consequences of heavy alcohol use. Alcoholism is a societal problem affecting millions of people. Not only is heavy alcohol use implicated in deaths from accidents and interpersonal violence, but also prolonged use has a high probability of eventuating in cardiovascular disease, liver cirrhosis, alcoholic paresis, and death.

The harmful effects of tobacco use have long been recognized. In fact, by 1939, researchers concluded that smoking was linked to cancer and cardiovascular disease (History.com n.d.). In 1965, Congress passed the Cigarette Labeling and Advertising Act, which required the warning "Caution, Cigarette Smoking May Be Hazardous to Your Health" to be placed on all cigarette packages sold in the United States (R. J. Reynolds Tobacco Company n.d.). This was later followed by supplementary legislation requiring additional warnings on a rotating basis. Today, ads for cigarettes and "smokeless tobacco" in magazines also must include these warnings.

On April 1, 1970, President Nixon signed legislation banning cigarette ads from television and radio (History.com n.d.). Since that time, concerned about the possible harmful effects of secondhand smoke, many jurisdictions have banned smoking from public places such as restaurants and bars and even outdoor venues such as parks. Colleges and universities have also barred cigarette smoking from their campuses. Airlines, which once permitted smoking in all parts of their planes, gradually reduced the number of smoking seats and flights during

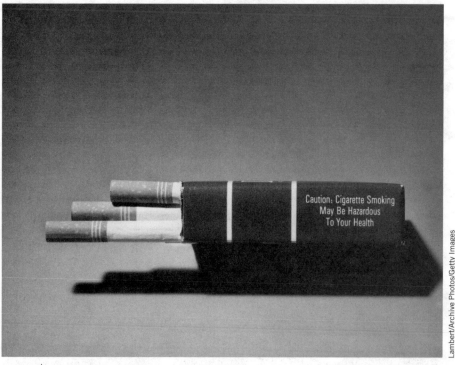

Caution: Cigarette Smoking May Be Hazardous To Your Health

Lambert/Archive Photos/Getty Images

Photo 2.2: Warning label on the side of a cigarette package in 1966.

which smoking was permissible, until finally prohibiting it altogether. The Centers for Disease Control and Prevention (CDC) estimates that every year more than 480,000 Americans die from cigarette smoke. This figure includes those who are nonsmoking victims of secondhand smoke (CDC 2014). Smokeless tobacco (chew, snuff, and snus) has been linked with a variety of cancers including mouth, tongue, gum, cheek, and throat as well as esophageal, pancreatic, and stomach cancers (American Cancer Society n.d.).

A third fact to notice about the federal schedules is the diversity of substances included in Schedule I. Along with heroin and other opiates, hallucinogens[3] such as LSD, peyote, and marijuana, are included in the list of drugs. However, the content of these schedules is not written in stone. For example, inclusions have been modified since the schedules' inception. Since the Comprehensive Drug Abuse Prevention and Control Act was passed in 1970, "approximately 160 substances have been added, removed, or transferred from one schedule to another" (U.S. Department of Justice, Drug Enforcement Administration, Office of Diversion Control 2016), so it is quite possible that in the future marijuana may be removed from Schedule I. We discuss this possibility later in this chapter.

A fourth difficulty in understanding the rationale behind the federal schedules is related to the third observation just noted. Substances in them are not classified by their chemical properties; rather, they are listed according to their medical usefulness and perceived potential for abuse and dependence. Thus, chemically similar drugs are often listed in different schedules. For example, heroin is listed in Schedule I, but morphine, its precursor, used to reduce pain, is found in Schedule II along with methadone, used to treat heroin addiction.

There are two main reasons why alcohol and tobacco do not appear in the schedules. The first of these is economic. Both drugs contribute billions of dollars to the American economy. In 2011, for example, the beverage alcohol industry contributed over $41 billion in revenue to state and local governments in the form of a variety of taxes and other fees. Additionally, Americans spent over $162 billion on alcohol in 2011. The alcohol industry spends a huge amount of money marketing their products. According to David Jernigan (2008), "Alcohol companies spend close to $2 billion every year advertising in the United States alone. From 2001 to 2007, they aired more than 2 million television ads and published more than 20,000 magazine advertisements."

The World Health Organization reports that in 2012–2013 (the most recent years for which they have data) federal revenue from excise taxes on cigarettes alone was $34,025,700,000 (World Health Organization 2015). In 2011, tobacco companies spent about $8.8 billion in marketing cigarettes and smokeless tobaccos. These figures do not include marketing expenses for cigars or pipe tobaccos (Federal Trade Commission Cigarette Report 2013). The World Lung Foundation (2012), citing the fourth edition of the *Tobacco Atlas*, reports that globally "in 2010, the combined profits of the six leading tobacco companies was U.S. $35.1 billion."

Given the huge profits enjoyed by the alcohol and tobacco industries, it is not surprising to note that they have a powerful presence in government. They use their financial resources to gain favor in Congress, rewarding representatives who support favorable legislation and opposing bills that might interfere with their businesses. The Center for Responsible Politics, for instance, reports that from 2015 to 2016, the National Beer Wholesalers Association contributed more than $3.52 million and the Wine and Spirits Wholesalers of America contributed $1.26 million to various campaigns (OpenSecrets.org, Center for Responsible Politics 2016). For the 2016 election cycle, the top 20 contributors to the alcohol industry gave a total of $23,424,228 to both Democrat and Republican politicians and "outside spending group" campaigns (OpenSecrets .org 2016). The top recipients of this largess for 2015–2016 were Hillary Clinton (D-presidential candidate; $541,193), Representative Mike Thompson (D-California; $231,091), Senators Charles Schumer (D-New York; $208,900) and Marco Rubio (R-Florida; $193,450), and Representative Paul Ryan (R-Wisconsin; $192,508) (OpenSecrets.org 2016).

In 2013, the tobacco industry spent $25,136,100 on lobbying. The five biggest contributors were the Altria Group ($10,190,000), Philip Morris International ($8,300,000), Lorillard, Inc. ($2,770,000), Reynolds American ($936,337), and the Vector Group ($590,000). These contributions pale in comparison with the $72,907,172 spent by tobacco interests in 1998 campaigns (OpenSecrets.org, Center for Responsible Politics 2014). Thus, even though there are some restrictions placed on alcohol and tobacco products, for the federal government to put them in any of the schedules would be akin to killing the proverbial goose that laid the golden eggs.

The second reason why alcohol and tobacco do not appear in the federal schedules is cultural. Both have long histories of popular acceptance as legitimate substances. In Chapter 6, we discuss the place of alcohol in popular culture and show that its acceptance has been embedded in our way of life. Much the same can be said for tobacco. Tobacco has a long history in the New World, dating back to pre-Columbian times. In fact, carvings made somewhere between 600 CE and 900 CE showed Mayans using tobacco (Marjorie Jacobs Community Learning Center 1997). In the early 16th century, the Spanish introduced tobacco to Europe (Wikipedia 2014a), and by 1612, the settlers in the Jamestown, Virginia, colony were growing tobacco as a cash crop and their main source of income (Marjorie Jacobs Community Learning Center 1997). Like alcohol, tobacco in all its forms has become integrated into American popular culture. Depictions of people smoking pipes and cigarettes were painted by European artists such as Edouard Manet, Vincent Van Gogh, Henri De Toulouse-Lautrec, Paul Cezanne, and Pablo Picasso, among others. Pop art and modern art also depict tobacco but currently often highlight its negative effects (Wikipedia 2014b).

Cigarette ads were ever-present in magazines from the 1890s until today.[4] They served to create an image of the cigarette smoker as sophisticated, glamorous, or masculine. Television and radio advertisements for tobacco, until they were banned by legislation signed into law by President Nixon in 1970 (History .com n.d.), presented positive cultural images of smoking. Virginia Slims, for example, used the slogan "You've come a long way baby" to promote a sophisticated feminist image of the female smoker who used their product. Marlboro showcased the "Marlboro Man," a very masculine looking cowboy model, to promote their product, conjuring up an image of the virile, active, take-charge cowboy icon. In the new millennium, ads have changed, however. One antismoking ad uses former smokers who talk about and graphically show how cancer caused by smoking has affected their lives. In one ad, a throat cancer survivor tells viewers to be careful shaving with a stoma. In another, a young woman, her face disfigured by surgeries necessitated by cancer, is shown lying in bed. Her death is then announced. In a commercial debuting in late summer 2014, a different tactic is employed. Pictures of several young people smoking are shown. These pictures apparently have been posted by these people to social media accounts. The narrator says disapprovingly that this is free advertising for "big tobacco" and gives a Twitter address for more information.

Antismoking commercials do not, however, necessarily reduce smoking. In fact, New York City's Department of Health released data in September 2014 showing that smoking in that city had increased since 2010 by 16% and that more than 1 million residents were smokers. In response, New York City planned to initiate a new antismoking ad campaign called "Imagine for Life" ("Increase in Smokers" 2014).

Photo 2.3: Paul Hurst plays gangster "The Gouger" Mizoski in 1931's *The Secret Six*, an example of how cigars were linked with criminals.

Movies from the 1920s well into the '60s had numerous scenes in which people were smoking. In the early movies, cigarettes were shown as a sophisticated behavior of upper-status "society" characters. Later, young actors were seen smoking as a sign of rebellion. These media certainly had a role in shaping social attitudes toward tobacco, a fact that was not lost on the cigar industry. As Jackson Toby, drawing on an article by Keith Monroe in *Harper's* magazine, relates, when movie stereotypes of cigar-chomping villains and gangsters appeared, "in 1940 the cigar industry counterattacked, founding the Cigar Institute of America and hiring a top-flight advertising man" (Toby 1971:73).[5] Photographers were offered monthly prizes for published photos of people, especially celebrities, smoking cigars. Additionally, movie producers were encouraged to have heroes smoking cigars in their movies by promising them to distribute publicity posters for those films to the 25,000 cigar counters in the country. As Toby puts it, "Heroes started smoking cigars, and cigar sales boomed" (Toby 1971:73).

"Good Drugs" and "Bad Drugs": The Media, Labeling, and the Changing Image of Marijuana

The example just discussed illustrates that the media have a powerful influence on the acceptance or rejection of substances, essentially defining for us what are "good drugs" and "bad drugs." In fact, some substances like tobacco and alcohol are not labeled as drugs at all. The late comedian and social commentator Lenny Bruce succinctly captured this distinction in his book, *How to Talk Dirty and Influence People*. He writes that "so I do not understand the moral condemnation of marijuana, not only because of its nontoxic, nonaddicting effects as contrasted with those of alcohol, but also because, in my opinion, caffeine in coffee, amphetamine, as well as all tranquilizers—from Miltown to aspirin to nicotine in cigarettes—are crutches for people who can face life better with drugs than without" (Bruce 1963:61). Bruce goes on to condemn the labeling process and to note the role played by the media and entertainment in that process: "Judging from the newspapers and movies, one would believe that drug users are sick, emotionally immature, degenerates, psychos, unstable. They are not right in the head. They are *weirdos*. So, I would assume, they belong in jail with all the other crazy people" (Bruce 1963:61).

Is There a Drug Epidemic? Trends in Drug Use

Alcohol and Tobacco

Although a National Institute on Alcohol Abuse and Alcoholism report indicates that the apparent per capital ethanol consumption of persons 14 years of age or older has declined in the United States from 1970 to 2007 (National Institute on Alcohol Abuse and Alcoholism 2009), alcohol is still widely consumed. Citing the Behavioral Risk Factor Surveillance System survey, the CDC reports that "more than half the U.S. adult population drank alcohol in the past 30 days. Approximately 5% of the total population drank heavily, while 17% of the population binge drank" (CDC n.d.-a). The national Youth Risk Behavior Survey (YRBS), conducted on 9th- through 12th-grade students in public and private schools every 2 years during the spring semester, showed a decrease in the percentage of teenagers reporting both having had at least one drink of alcohol on at least one day in the 30 days preceding the survey from 1999 to 2011 (50% to 38.7%) and a decrease in binge drinking, as defined by having had five or more drinks of alcohol in a row within a couple of hours on at least one day in the 30 days prior to the survey from 1997 to 2011 (33.4% to 21.9%) (CDC n.d.-b).

Despite the recent increase in smoking in New York City, tobacco use seems to be decreasing. This reduction is especially notable for young people. The percentage reporting smoking in the month before the survey in 2012 was half of that reported by teenagers in 2002 (National Institute on Drug Abuse 2014). The CDC reports a decline in smoking for high school students from 27.5% in 1991 (the first year data were collected on this age group) to 18.1% in 2011 and a decrease in the percentage of adults who are cigarette smokers from a high of 42.4% in 1965 to 19.0% in 2011 (CDC 2016a).

Marijuana

We can currently see a delabeling and relabeling process developing as this chapter is being written in early 2017. Marijuana, once labeled as a dangerous and gateway drug to other illicit substances and thereby residing in Schedule I, is rapidly coming to be viewed as a substance with important medical uses. As of this writing, 29 states plus the District of Columbia have legalized the medical use of marijuana. The most recent states to do so are Arkansas, Florida, North Dakota, Ohio, and Pennsylvania, all in 2016. States that have legalized marijuana for medical uses are Alaska, Arizona, California, Colorado, Connecticut, Delaware, Hawaii, Illinois, Maine, Maryland, Massachusetts, Michigan, Minnesota, Montana, Nevada, New Hampshire, New Jersey, New Mexico, New York, Oregon, Rhode Island, Vermont, Washington State, and the District of Columbia (Wikipedia 2014c). In New York, the drug may be ingested in various ways but may not be smoked. As was noted in Chapter 1, several of these states, Alaska, California, Colorado, Maine, Massachusetts, Nevada, Oregon, Washington State, and Washington, DC, now also allow the recreational use of marijuana by adults. Of course, by federal law, marijuana is still illegal for medical or any other use in these states, but as more states decriminalize the drug, and their profits soar from its sales, this could change. Perhaps eventually marijuana may be moved to Schedule II or III or even completely removed from these listings as the relabeling process continues.

One interesting development in the continuing marijuana saga involves what sociologist Erich Goode (2014:111) calls its "illegal instrumental use" by professional football players in the National Football League (NFL). An Associated Press (2014) article commented on the dilemma faced by officials of the NFL, whose players use marijuana as the drug of choice to self-medicate concussions and other injuries: "As attitudes toward the drug soften, and science slowly teases out marijuana's possible benefits for concussions and other injuries, the NFL is reaching a critical point in navigating its tenuous relationship with what is recognized as the analgesic of choice for many of its players" (p. B5).

There was a time when marijuana cultivation and its use were not illegal in the United States. This all changed with the passage of the Marihuana Tax Act in 1937. We examine the social and political factors leading to this law in greater detail in Chapter 9, "History of Drug Use in America and Attempts to Control It." Briefly, according to Howard S. Becker, the law came about through the efforts of Harry J. Anslinger, the director of the Federal Bureau of Narcotics, now the Drug Enforcement Agency. As part of that campaign antimarijuana news stories were planted in newspapers by the Bureau (Becker 1963),[6] which also sponsored a movie, *Reefer Madness*. The movie, which purports to dramatically document the moral degeneration of youth caused by smoking marijuana, was widely viewed in the 1930s. Nowadays, it is presented as a curiosity, often to raise money for pro-marijuana campaigns.

The movie opens with clippings of newspaper articles and screaming headlines about marijuana-related crimes, followed by "Dr. Carroll," the high school principal, talking about a marijuana-related murder involving high school students in his community. As he talks to a parent group, the film shows newsreels about heroin trafficking and then segues into scenes of police harvesting marijuana plants, while Dr. Carroll, who calls marijuana "a deadly narcotic," somberly intones, "More vicious, more deadly, even than these soul destroying drugs, is the menace of marijuana" (Gasnier 1965/1936).

In Chapter 10, we examine in more detail the arguments surrounding marijuana use. We also look at the relationship between marijuana and the opiates, especially heroin, a connection often made in claims that marijuana is a gateway drug to more serious addictions. The two drugs are often conflated as they were in *Reefer Madness*.

Heroin

As we have seen in Chapter 1, the use of heroin, the prototypical dangerous street drug, appears to be spreading. In response to an increase in heroin use, on June 24, 2014, New York governor Andrew Cuomo signed a bill to address what was seen as a "heroin, opioid and prescription drug abuse epidemic" (New York State 2014). Has heroin use now become an epidemic? According to Joan F. Epstein and Joseph C. Gfroerer (n.d.), "Efforts to estimate the prevalence of heroin use have a long history with precise estimates remaining difficult to determine." However, using the Community Epidemiology Work Group (CEWG) and the Drug Abuse Warning Network (DAWN) as their data sources, they note that "numerous reports have suggested a rise in heroin use in recent years, which has been attributed to young people who are smoking or sniffing rather than injecting" (Epstein and Gfroerer n.d.).

Nora D. Volkow (2014), director of the National Institute on Drug Abuse (NIDA), states that "the numbers of people starting to use heroin have been steadily rising since 2007."[7] She speculates that this may be the result of users shifting from abusing prescription painkillers, which are less readily available and more expensive. Sources of information used by NIDA include Monitoring the Future (MTF) survey, a yearly survey of teenagers conducted by the University of Michigan's Institute for Social Research and funded by NIDA, and the National Survey on Drug Use and Health (NSDUH) of the Substance Abuse and Mental Health Services Administration (SAMHSA), an ongoing survey of the civilian, noninstitutionalized population of the United States aged 12 years or older. Similarly, John Wihbey (2014) writes, "In general, the usage of heroin, its availability and the number of persons arrested for trafficking have grown in recent years. Between 2002 and 2010, the number of persons who reported using heroin over the past year grew by 50%, from 400,000 to more than 600,000, according to the Substance Abuse and Mental Health Services Administration." A recent survey from SAMHSA's NSDUH reports that from 2007 to 2012, there was an increase in known intravenous heroin users from 373,000 to 669,000 (Rawlings 2013). Given the evidence provided by reliable sources, it is probably safe to say that heroin use has grown. Whether this increase constitutes an "epidemic" is a matter of opinion, although as we have seen in Chapter 1, there has been a dramatic increase in heroin overdoses in some places, such as upstate New York. What about other drugs? There are indications that the use of methamphetamine has decreased. According to the NSDUH, there were 731,000 users in 2006 and only 440,000 in 2012. However, the number of marijuana smokers has increased. "In 2012, 18.9 million people used marijuana—7.3% of the population—up from 14.5 million in 2007. The number of daily users, now 7.6 million Americans, is growing as well" (Rawlings 2013).

Nonmedical Use of Pharmaceuticals

The nonmedical use of pharmaceuticals appears to be increasing. The PDMP Center of Excellence at Brandeis University considers their use to be a "growing national epidemic" in which "addiction, overdoses and deaths involving nonmedical prescription drug use, especially narcotic pain relievers, have risen dramatically over the last decade" (PDMP Center of Excellence, Brandeis University n.d.). Citing a NSDUH study, the report authors note that "of the 3.1 million individuals 12 or older estimated to have used an illicit drug for the first time in 2009, 28.6% initiated use with prescription drugs, second only to those initiating with marijuana (59.1%)" (PDMP Center of Excellence n.d.).

According to SAMHSA (2011a), the total emergency department (ED) visits for nonmedical use of pharmaceuticals increased by roughly 100,000 visits per year from 536,247 in 2004 to 1,079,683 in 2009. "Representing about a quarter of all drug-related ED visits and over half of ED visits for drug abuse or misuse, an estimated 1,079,683 ED visits in 2009 involved the nonmedical use of prescription drugs, over-the-counter medicines, or other types of pharmaceuticals. Over half (53.6%) of ED visits resulting from nonmedical use of pharmaceuticals involved multiple drugs, and 17.8 percent involved alcohol" (SAMHSA 2011b).

Multiple Drug Use

Some users may have a particular drug of choice, but many people use multiple drugs, often at the same time. This is not a new phenomenon. Writing about this behavior more than four decades ago, Emil Pascarelli, a physician who started a methadone maintenance program at Roosevelt Hospital in New York City in 1968, observed that

> what we are beginning to come up against is not merely drug addiction, but *multiple* drug addiction. It is a phenomenon of the 1970s; most of the people who come into the methadone maintenance program are multiple addicts. In addition to shooting heroin, about 70–80 percent smoke marijuana because it is cheaper and easier to get; they take "ups" and "downs," anything they can get. As the present generation matures, multiple addiction will become an increasingly serious problem. (Pascarelli 1972:5)

Dr. Pascarelli was prescient. According to a 2009 Drug Abuse Warning Network report, 576,752 emergency room visits involved multiple drugs (SAMHSA 2011b). Also, 519,650 emergency room visits (56.1%) involved alcohol mixed with other drugs. Of these combinations, cocaine was involved in 29.4% and marijuana in 24.1% of the visits. Heroin was mixed with alcohol in 8.3% of the cases, stimulants in 3.4% of the ER visits, and methamphetamine mixed with alcohol accounted for 2.3% of these visits (SAMHSA 2011c). According to Jane Carlisle Maxwell (2006), "Abuse of prescription drugs is often in combination with other prescription drugs and alcohol, usually 'to get high.'"

In summary, from a sociological point of view, how we think about, classify, respond to, and regulate the use of drugs, including alcohol and tobacco, is complex, reflecting the interaction among economic, political, and sociocultural realities. As we have seen in this chapter, the chemical composition and effects of the various drugs appears to be of less significance than these other factors.

NOTES

1. In a personal communication, Ben Woodrow, a retired educator who has had extensive experience with both alcoholics and drug users, provided a street-wise, tongue-in-cheek explanation of the difference between alcoholics and heroin addicts, reflecting the perceived chutzpa of the latter: "An alcoholic will steal your wallet and immediately leave town. An addict will steal your wallet, hang around, and help you look for it."

2. This list of drugs presented on the DEA's website is not complete and is apparently provided by the agency simply as examples. Morphine is not listed here but is in fact contained in Schedule II.

3. The term *hallucinogen* is a value-laden one, whose implications are very negative. Some writers, such as Humphrey Osmond, who has used these drugs and is therefore favorably disposed toward them, coined the term *psychedelics* to refer to LSD, psilocybin, mescaline, peyote, and other "mind-altering" drugs (see Aaronson and Osmond 1970), whereas the psychiatric profession often uses the terms *psychomimetic* or *psychotomimetic*, noting the experiential similarity described by users to how psychotic patients describe their experiences.

4. For an interesting collection of cigarette advertisements from the 1880s up through the 2000s please see http://www.vintageadbrowser.com/tobacco-ads

5. The source cited by Dr. Toby is Monroe 1955.

6. Using content analysis of the number of antimarijuana articles prior to and after the passage of the Marihuana Tax Act, as cataloged in the *Reader's Guide to Periodical Literature*, Becker concluded that the FBN had played a major role in generating antimarijuana publicity leading to the law's passage. In an analysis of Becker's data and that of other writers who either support or refute Becker's position, Galliher and Walker (1977) concluded that there is not enough evidence to warrant his contention.

7. As one of her important sources, Dr. Volkow cites Substance Abuse and Mental Health Services Administration, *Results from the 2012 National Survey on Drug Use and Health: Summary of National Findings* (Rockville, MD: Author, 2013).

Drinking Alcohol
The Alcohol Culture

Ideological Alcohol Culture

Culture is the human-made environment and consists of ideological, behavioral, and material customs. This definition applies to the manner in which alcohol is consumed in the United States, because eating and drinking does not only consist of ingesting a solid or liquid substance. Humans surround eating and drinking with theatrical performances, which are commanded by public opinion and become folkways, mores, and laws.

A folkway is a custom that carries no sanction, either positive or negative. A more is a custom that carries an unofficial negative or positive sanction enforced by the general consensus of the majority of citizens. Therefore, failure to drink alcohol is criticized in American culture by labeling a nondrinker as a "teetotaler" and a municipality or other area in which alcohol is prohibited as an area that is "dry." Yet, even as failure to use alcohol is criticized, excessive drinking of alcohol is negatively sanctioned by the mores as well as the law.

About 70% of Americans drink alcohol, whereas 30% prefer not to drink. The average American drinks only 9.4 liters of alcohol per year. This equals 470 pints of beer or 31 glasses of wine. Fifty-three percent of American alcohol consumers prefer to drink beer. Spirits make up 31% of alcohol consumption, and wine is least favored with only 14%. Nevertheless, 31% of all deaths of 15- to 29-year-olds in the United States are alcohol related. If viewed by states, it appears that states with a high percentage of evangelical Protestant adherents have a lower rate of alcohol use, and especially binge drinking, than states that are mainly Catholic, such as states in the Northeast, the Northern Plains, and the West Coast (Holt, Miller, Naimi, and Sui 2006).

Drinking and Stress Relief

There is evidence that behavior concerning alcohol is the product of beliefs concerning alcohol, inasmuch as all behavior is a priori determined by beliefs. One of the most widespread beliefs about the use of alcohol is the view that drinking alcohol alleviates job stress as well as life stresses in general. Because this is widely accepted, many companies provide employees with counseling by social workers, psychologists, or psychiatrists through employee assistance programs.

These efforts seek to help employees overcome their alcohol or drug problems. The effectiveness of these programs has not been determined (Weiss 1978).

There is an assumption that job stress causes drinking and leads to alcohol abuse. This approach has been repeatedly investigated, leading to the conclusion that job stress is not necessarily connected to the use of alcohol. In fact, many workers deal with job stress all the time but do not use alcohol. It has even been reported that some employees involved in high-stress jobs drink less than those not so employed. The reason for this decline in drinking alcohol lies in the lack of time for socialization on the part of high-stress workers. This means that those who work a great deal have less opportunity to engage in social drinking than those who have more time. Indeed, many who drink too much will claim that their job is driving them to drink; however, such a claim may well be a post hoc rationalization (Weiss 1978).

Job stress can mean several things. It can mean conflict on the job with supervisors or fellow employees. It can also refer to failure to succeed in the job, or it can mean an overload of responsibilities. An excessive number of hours at work will provoke the use of alcohol as a means of relieving the pressure on the job, which carries over to leisure time. Research has concluded that job overload is more likely than any conflict or failure to succeed as a cause for using alcohol (Neff and Husaini 1982).

Drinking beliefs are largely responsible for the difference between heavy and light drinking. These beliefs are the result of peer pressure, cultural norms, and early socialization. Of course, "work overload" may also be a belief in that the same amount of work is viewed as too much by some workers and is accepted as normal by others. Those experiencing work stress tend to believe that alcohol helps them relax, forget about the job, and allows them to "unwind." Yet there are many who do not suffer from work overload who also drink to unwind (Peyser 1982).

Although beliefs about alcohol influence drinking, drinking in turn shapes beliefs. Seeking to alleviate stress, the drinker tells himself or herself that alcohol leads to that relief. Because, according to Shakespeare, "nothing is either good or bad but thinking makes it so," this interactive phenomenon works for the consumer of alcohol.

This means that unless there is a belief that alcohol alleviates stress, the connection will not be made, so that highly stressed individuals will nevertheless refrain from alcohol use.

Heavy drinking is often related to the need for friendship and communion. Many a drinker began a drinking career in a bar where he or she met others whom the person already knew or who befriended him or her there. In the course of the camaraderie among drinkers at the same bar, night after night, the moderate drinker slowly graduates into a heavy drinker, as he or she spends an inordinate amount of money and time in the company of their peers. Friends who believe that drinking alcohol after work is an important means of relaxing and enjoying leisure time will influence each other to do the same.

The excessive use of alcohol, leading to alcohol dependency or alcoholism, differs from moderate use of alcohol, because moderate drinking will indeed relieve stress, whereas alcoholism, designated a disease by the American Medical Association, creates vast amounts of stress and physical disability in addition to social rejection.

Drinking and Religious Beliefs

Beliefs about the use of alcohol are related to religious beliefs. In fact, some religious denominations prohibit the drinking of alcohol altogether, whereas others frown on its excessive use. Mormons, Buddhists, Muslims, Free Methodists, and some others denounce the use of alcohol and promise eternal damnation to those who drink it. Other religions teach that alcohol is a food and its use is an important part of daily life. Religion is one of the most important determinants concerning the drinking of alcohol.

Alcohol use causes about 75,000 deaths every year in the United States and many more in other countries. Excessive drinking of alcohol is the third ranking preventable death after smoking and overweight. Alcohol use is also responsible for child abuse, domestic violence, teen pregnancy, and marital infidelity. Its most egregious consequence is alcoholism, including binge drinking, which is defined as drinking more than five drinks on one occasion. These dangers have led some religious denominations to ban the use of alcohol altogether. Because 87% of Americans claim that religion is important in their daily lives, it is instructive to discern whether religion has any influence on the consumption of alcohol (Mokdad, Marks, Stroup, and Gerberding 2004).

Despite the claim by 87% of Americans that religion is important in their lives, 67% of Americans said in a 2010 survey that religion is losing its influence on them (Pew Forum on Religion and Public Life 2010). Because some denominations preach doctrines that prohibit the use of alcohol by means of the so-called hellfire hypothesis, such religions suppress the use of alcohol with the result that some of these preachments become counterproductive. This refers to Sigmund Freud's observation that suppression can lead to neuroses and that neurotic persons will then use alcohol to numb the guilt that accrues from religious teachings. This view is supported by some research, which reports that binge drinking and alcoholism is found to be high among some denominations that prohibit drinking alcohol altogether (Kutter and McDermott 1997).

A high proportion of Jews drink alcohol. Nevertheless, the rate of binge drinking and alcoholism is unusually low among the Jewish population in the United States and in Israel. Whereas alcoholism endangers about 7% of the American population, the Jewish alcoholism experience involves less than 1% of the Jewish population (Schmidt and Popham 1976).

The phenomenon of Jewish sobriety was already known to the mathematician and philosopher Immanuel Kant, who wrote in 1789, "It is the consequence of the siege passed down from generation to generation, and including the desire to hold on to one's senses and a distaste for the irrational that sets a limit to Jewish drinking" (Glazer 1952).

Because excessive drinking and public drunkenness lead to public censure, Jews are more likely to avoid such criticism because traditionally Jews were always under attack and sought not to add to the general hostility imposed on them by the Christian majority. Therefore, Jews have indulged in alcohol drinking within a family setting or within a religious ceremony. Both environments lead less to alcoholism than is true of drinking in a bar amid one's drinking friends (Glad 1947).

Jews have some alcohol protective characteristics that reduce the chances of alcoholism to a minimum. Included are family drinking and sacramental drinking as on the Sabbath and at the Passover meal. These measures are augmented by peer drinking. That means that Jews, like other Americans, are more likely to associate at holiday time or in other social situations with others of the same ethnicity. Therefore, the absence of heavy drinking of alcohol by Jews creates boundaries for all who participate, in that hardly anyone will exceed the expectations of the reference group, that is, a group whose norms are used by an individual as a guide to one's own values, opinions, and conduct (M. Davis 2012). This means that one's reference group, whether the family or any other group, becomes a control group influencing positive and negative judgments as to what is or is not legitimate. Therefore, what one drinks, with whom one drinks, and when and where one drinks are all associated with one's reference group. Age and gender,

Roger Ressmeyer/Corbis/VCG via Getty Images

Photo 3.1: A Jewish family celebrating the Passover Seder, where wine is consumed for symbolic and ceremonial reasons. Many beliefs about the use of alcohol are related to religious beliefs.

the two most basic status roles, are also important conditions making one eligible for drinking alcohol. Evidently then, the reference group sanctions the use of alcohol as well as eating and many other behaviors (Maloff, Becker, Fonaroff, and Rodin 1979).

The major consequence of Jewish failure to abuse alcohol is that the most sophisticated and extensive studies concerning Jewish alcoholism result again and again in the finding that only 1% of Jews abuse alcohol, whereas in the general American population 46% do not drink alcohol at all, 31% drink alcohol in moderation, and of the remaining 23%, only 13% drink five drinks or more on any one occasion. Assuming that there are about 240 million adults over the age of 18 in the United States, this means that 31 million Americans drink five or more drinks on one occasion. This is far more than is true of Jewish drinking despite the evidence that 77% of Americans either do not drink alcohol at all or are moderate drinkers (U.S. Department of Justice 2002).

Jews view alcohol problems as non-Jewish, so that the definition of the situation structures Jewish drinking. This means that people control their alcohol consumption by referring to social norms that prescribe how much alcohol people like them usually consume. Moreover, members of any group contrast themselves with members of other groups whose norms they reject. Therefore, Jews assume that moderate drinking is an out-group characteristic and moderation is an in-group characteristic. Snyder (1978) has observed that alcoholism is absent among groups in which drinking is included in socialization and is part of rituals central to the moral symbolism of those groups. This hypothesis was tested by Beeghley, Bock, and Cochran (1990). Their research concerning alcohol use among converts found that "the impact of religiosity on alcohol use is most powerful among those whose exposure to moral messages against alcohol consumption is greatest." Therefore, they also discovered that those who are least affected by prohibitionary norms are least affected by moral messages against alcohol consumption. This also means that those who changed religious affiliation from a denomination not much concerned with the use of alcohol to a fundamentalist denomination, which prohibits its use, will reduce if not eliminate alcohol consumption. This supports the reference group–socialization theory.

Not everyone agrees that alcohol consumption is primarily the product of reference group socialization. There are those who view alcohol abuse or alcoholism as a disease related to genetic etiology. This view has been widely disseminated by the media and is understood as a form of medicalization, which seems to remove responsibility for alcohol abuse from the drinker. In fact, the term *biomedicalization* has been used to describe conditions within the individual, which are therefore viewed as the root causes of alcohol abuse.

The American Society of Addictive Medicine (ASAM; 1990) has defined alcoholism as "a primary, addictive disease with genetic, psychosocial and environmental factors influencing its development and manifestations." ASAM further defines a disease as an involuntary disability, thereby denying individual responsibility as well as the reference group theory as causes of alcohol abuse.

The effort to reduce alcohol abuse to a biomedical disease deemphasizes the social aspects of drinking alcohol and therefore relies on increased technology and medication. As a result, research grants supporting the biomedical approach to the use of alcohol have become substantially higher than those that support sociopsychological approaches to drinking. Because all science is impacted by politics, the money spent on biomedical research cannot be used to investigate such issues as underage drinking and the most dangerous of activities influenced by alcohol, for example, drinking and driving. Investigation of the beverage industry is another issue that needs funding and the support of those seeking to deal with the American problem of alcohol abuse (S. Cohen 1993).

Alcohol abuse is most prevalent among adolescents. Beginning in the ninth grade at age 15, a considerable number of American children drink alcohol. In the ninth grade, 63.4% use alcohol. This increases with age. In the 10th grade, 71.1% use alcohol, and in the 11th grade this rises to 77.8%. In the 12th grade, 79.6% of high school students drink (U.S. Department of Justice 2004).

In 2009, one quarter of high school students were binge drinking, which is defined as drinking five or more alcoholic drinks in a row within 2 hours. The likelihood of binge drinking increases as students reach higher classes and attain an older age.

Behavioral Alcohol Culture

Innumerable young Americans believe that masculinity requires alcohol abuse. High school and college students younger than 21 years old constantly abuse alcohol as a means of proving their masculine prowess or, in the case of adolescent girls, as a method used to gain entry into the popular in-groups in their schools.

This is largely due to the constant advertisements for alcohol consumption directed at young people who are not legally entitled to drink alcohol. According to the National Minimum Drinking Age Act of 1984, all states of the union wishing to receive state highway funds must prohibit the use of alcohol for those not yet age 21. The law allows underage drinking for religious purposes if the drinker is accompanied by a parent, spouse, or guardian. Alcohol may also be used if prescribed for medical reasons. Because the armed forces admit those only 18 years old or older, it seems to many that this law is unfair, inasmuch as an 18-year-old may die for his or her country but may not drink a beer (U.S. Congress 1924).

Advertisements targeting young people are designed to promote positive beliefs about alcohol, which in turn leads to higher alcohol consumption. The advertisements include broadcasts, printed messages, and outdoor signs, especially at sporting events. Some youths are already heavy drinkers and are therefore encouraged by advertisements to continue to drink because the advertisements create the impression that alcohol is legitimate and "fun"

(Tapert et al. 2003). Generally, alcohol producers claim to use self-regulation as a means of reducing the effect of alcohol advertisements on high school and college age students.

Georgetown University has organized a Center on Alcohol Marketing and Youth, designed to track the amount of advertising targeting underage drinkers. This center has found that the alcohol industry spent $5.5 billion in 2 years on advertisements on television, radio, and print. No law prohibits advertising aimed at the youngest people, including junior high and high school students. In fact, young people are much more exposed to alcohol-promoting advertisements than are adults. The center found that 12- to 20-year-olds were exposed to 48% more beer ads than adults and that they were targeted with 20% more distilled spirit ads than adults. There are also gender differences in targeting young people with alcohol ads. Girls have been targeted more than boys with these ads. A recent federal survey showed that girls' drinking and binge drinking has outstripped that of boys (Johnston, O'Malley, and Bachman 2003).

The 15 television shows with the largest audience of teens aged 12 to 17, and clearly under the drinking age, all had alcohol ads. The alcohol companies did also air "responsibility ads" warning against drinking and driving and encouraging the use of designated drivers. Nevertheless, underage youths were 96 times more likely to see an ad promoting drinking alcohol than to see a responsibility ad (Center on Alcohol Marketing and Youth 2003).

The alcohol industry also targets minority youths more than others. Advertising aimed at minority youth is substantially greater than that directed at others so that Hispanic and African American youths see 66% more beer ads than is true of white young people.

This widespread advertising of alcoholic drinks directed at children has its consequences, including that 61% of high school seniors have used alcohol. One third of them are "current drinkers," and the likelihood of using alcohol increases between the start and end of high school. Whereas 3% of eighth graders report binge drinking, this rises to 16% for 12th graders. There has, however, been a significant decline in alcohol use by youngsters over the last decade (National Institute on Drug Abuse 2016).

One of the most publicized deaths caused by binge drinking was that of Scott Krueger, who had just arrived on the campus of the Massachusetts Institute of Technology when he moved into a fraternity house. There he was challenged to drink 10 beers and then take several shots of hard alcohol. He did so and passed out and died shortly thereafter at age 18. Likewise, Benjamin Wynne at Louisiana State University pledged a fraternity that demanded he binge drink, which killed him (Suleiman 1997).

In addition to the dangers related to binge drinking, the use of alcohol can cause risky sexual behavior. More than 600 studies have been conducted concerning the link between alcohol and sex. These studies have in part supported the common notion that drinking reduces inhibitions and is therefore responsible for risking disease as well as unwanted pregnancy. It is generally believed that drinking increases the likelihood of sexual activity, a belief supported by an overwhelming number of studies (see Chapter 7) (M. Lynne Cooper 2002).

Nevertheless, a third intervening variable may explain the relationship between drinking alcohol and sexual behavior. Poor impulse control can lead to one of these forms of conduct or to both of them. This is common among students who live in fraternity houses, which condone and in fact encourage excessive drinking and sexual adventures. Adolescents who live in single-parent homes or in conflict-ridden families are likewise at risk of getting involved in excessive use of alcohol and risky sexual conduct. Because many people believe that drinking alcohol decreases or eliminates inhibitions, there are those who deliberately induce others to drink so as to gain sexual access. The intention and wish to have sex is therefore the catalyst for excessive drinking (M. Lynne Cooper 2002).

It is well known that there are those who exhibit usually unacceptable behavior, not because they have consumed alcohol, but because they drank alcohol in order to later blame alcohol drinking for actions they intended in the first place. Behavior attributed to alcohol consumption is often determined by preexisting beliefs. This view can be tested by giving volunteers drinks that do not contain alcohol, although the volunteer is led to believe he or she drank alcohol. The consequence is that the believer will conduct himself or herself as if he or she had consumed alcohol without having touched one drink. This refers to risky sex as well as other forms of behavior (Hull and Bond 1986).

Drinking alcohol may be a harmless behavior. However, there can be little doubt that drinking while driving is dangerous, as a statistical summary indicates. This summary includes that in their lifetime, three out of ten American drivers are involved in at least one accident involving drunk driving. At least one half, and possibly 75%, of drivers whose license has been suspended for drunk driving continue to drive without a license.

For many years, 41% of traffic deaths in the United States have been alcohol related. This affects young people more than older people, for traffic crashes are the leading cause of death among those age 2 to 33 (National Highway Traffic Safety Administration [NHTSA] 2003).

Nine percent of those injured in traffic crashes were injured in alcohol-related crashes. By contrast, in those crashes that did not involve alcohol, only 0.6% resulted in death and 31% in an injury. Forty-four percent of those killed in alcohol-related deaths did not drink themselves but were the victims of a drunken driver. Of these, 22% were passengers in a car driven by a drunken driver, 13% were pedestrians, and the others were struck by a drunken driver while driving their own vehicle. These alcohol-related crashes vary considerably by gender, age, and race. Thus, 78% of people killed from alcohol-related accidents were males. Fifty-seven percent of alcohol-related traffic deaths were among those 21 to 29, followed closely by those 16 to 20 years old. The majority of those who died in these fatal crashes had a blood alcohol concentration (BAC) of 0.15, nearly twice the BAC allowed by law. Alcohol-related traffic deaths reflect the proportion of the races in the American population (NHTSA 2003).

Photo 3.2: Wreckage from a DUI crash.

Accidents resulting from drunk driving take place every 45 minutes in the United States. Because about 159 million drunken driving trips are undertaken every year, about 275,000 people are injured each year by drunk drivers. About 1.46 million people are arrested each year for driving under the influence of alcohol. The number of women involved in alcohol-related accidents is increasing. In the 1980s, only 9% of people arrested for drunk driving were women. In the 21st century, 29% of drunken driving arrests involved women (Nakate n.d.).

Thomas A. Gilray, a 29-year-old sheriff's dispatcher, drove his pickup truck at more than 80 miles an hour, striking two men and a parked vehicle. Both victims suffered traumatic brain injuries. One victim also had a broken neck and spent 2 months in a coma. Gilray had been drinking at a "Dyngus Day" festival, resulting in a BAC of 0.12 (Tocasz 2013).

Drunken driving is not the only life-threatening behavior related to alcohol consumption. Drinking too much is ipso facto, by the fact itself, related to a shortened life span. The evidence is that drinking six or more drinks at one sitting, within a short time, adds to the risk of death. The risk of death includes suicide, homicide, and vehicle fatalities. Those who need to drink excessively are also likely to suffer from blurred vision, heart disease, kidney failure, liver problems, and a host of difficulties involving all organs in the viscera.

Babies who depend on their mother's milk are also at risk if the mother drinks alcohol while breastfeeding. For that reason, pharmacies sell a kit called Milkscreen designed to test the amount of alcohol in a mother's milk. In addition, those who walk about drunk risk falling into the street and getting hit by a vehicle or being robbed and/or assaulted. Moreover, those who drink a lot of alcohol may become increasingly aggressive as their inhibitions are weakened.

All of this leads to an increase in mortality of about 10 additional deaths or a 9% increase in mortality at age 21. A substantial number of deaths at this age are due to alcohol consumption (Birkmeier and Hemenway 1990).

The Centers for Disease Control and Prevention (CDC) has published fact sheets concerning alcohol use and health. Accordingly, *binge drinking* is defined as four or more drinks for women or five or more drinks for men on a single occasion. It is further recommended that pregnant women not drink any alcohol and that those under age 21 also refrain from drinking. Evidently, recovering alcoholics can never drink alcohol again.

There are both short-term and long-term risks associated with the use of alcohol. Short-term risks include traffic accidents, drowning, falls, burning, and unintentional shootings. Thirty-five percent of violence against partners, in the main women, are common consequences of drunken behavior, as is the maltreatment of children on the part of both mothers and fathers. Other short-term risks associated with alcohol consumption are sexual assault, unprotected sex, sex with multiple partners involving the risk of acquiring a venereal disease, and unwanted pregnancy. Even alcohol poisoning is a consequence of excessive drinking. Alcohol poisoning suppresses the central nervous system, which can cause loss of consciousness, coma, respirational depression, and death (CDC 2016b).

Long-term consequences of excessive drinking of alcohol include dementia, stroke, and cardiovascular problems. Psychiatric problems, including anxiety, depression, and suicide, can result from excessive drinking. These symptoms of excessive drinking also lead to unemployment and family dissolution.

Some alcohol consumers develop cancer of the mouth, throat, and esophagus, for the risk of cancer increases with increasing use of alcohol. The most common of these diseases is cirrhosis of the liver, which is among the 15 most common causes of death in the United States. This means that in 1 year there are upward of 16,000 liver disease deaths in the country. Excluding homicide and suicide, there are nearly 26,000 alcohol-related deaths in the United States. Fifteen million Americans are affected by alcohol abuse and dependency, although the average American drinks only 13 beers or 152 ounces of alcohol per year. Alcohol abuse is unevenly distributed among the states. Wisconsin suffers the greatest amount of alcohol abuse, with 11.3% of the population involved. The lowest rate of alcohol abuse, according to the CDC, is North Carolina, where only 5.9% of citizens are involved (CDC 2016b).

Child abuse is yet another result of alcohol-induced behavior. This does not mean that there are no sober adults who also abuse children. It is, however, evident that child abuse and alcohol are associated in several ways. This kind of behavior is widespread; it has been estimated by Child Protective Services that 763,000 children are victims of maltreatment in the United States every year (U.S. Department of Health and Human Services 2010).

A considerable number of investigators have concluded that parents who use alcohol are more likely to abuse children than is true of those who abstain. This is particularly true of families who live in neighborhoods with a large number of alcohol outlets such as bars and liquor stores. Such maltreatment is widespread, and it has been estimated that 60% of parents in America use corporal punishment such as spanking. In addition, 5% of parents kick or hit children with their fist or an object. Up to 30% of parents neglect children, and nearly 8% are guilty of sexual abuse (U.S. Department of Health and Human Services 2010).

Rates of child abuse, and particularly physical abuse, are higher among heavy drinkers than among those who drink occasionally or not at all. Children of heavy drinkers are twice as likely to be beaten and three times as likely to be neglected than is true of other children. In families in which both parents abuse alcohol, the risk to children increases sixfold (Berger 2005).

Density of alcohol outlets also affects the amount of child abuse in a community. There is a positive relationship between child abuse and the number of alcohol providers within a short distance of family residences. The reverse is also true. The fewer the alcohol outlets per 1,000 persons, the less the child abuse. Higher density of bars is related to higher amounts of child maltreatment, even if other measures of social disorganization such as poverty, immigrant status, or minority oppression are included. Alcohol contributes independently to child maltreatment. Higher taxes on beer, wine, and other alcoholic beverages as well as a reduction of the legal BAC while driving are also related to a lower rate of child abuse and child homicide (Freisthler 2011).

Although alcohol use is indeed related to child maltreatment, it should not be overlooked that some cultures approve of beating children, so that even those who do not drink alcohol will engage in assault on children as was practiced widely in German homes and schools prior to the middle of the 20th century.

Another danger to children related to alcohol abuse consists of drunken driving by adults with children in their car. This occurs among people who drink a great deal as well as those who do not drink often but who become intoxicated on some occasions. Wedding receptions, christenings, birthday parties, office parties, Christmas celebrations, and other similar events regularly endanger children and adults subject to intoxicated drivers. Such drivers also maim and kill children run down in the street, as drivers become unable to recognize the dangers of driving in traffic (Coohey 2003).

Use of bars places an economic strain on families and tends to deprive children. For example, a beer consumed at home costs about $0.69. A beer bought in a bar costs about $4.25. In addition, parents who spend a good deal of time in bars meeting their friends may well leave children unattended, alone and neglected. These problems are even more pronounced among single parents who carry the burden of child-rearing alone. Single parents who cannot afford the cost of a baby or child sitter and also drink in a bar may well be tempted to spend the time drinking and leave children to fend for themselves. Yet nothing is more conducive to child endangerment than lack of supervision. Parents who spend time in bars are supported in this behavior by other parents equally engaged in socializing in bars, so that all act as reference groups for one another.

Parents have been known to drink a good deal of alcohol while their children participate in sports events such as baseball and football games. On numerous occasions parents have become violent while observing their children play at these games and have assaulted officials and each other.

In Payson, Utah, a 38-year-old father ran onto a football field and hit a 13-year-old boy under the chin in order to prevent the child from gaining a touchdown against his son's team (Alberty 2012).

In Burnsville, Minnesota, a basketball commissioner was attacked by two men during a sixth-grade game. The dispute had to do with officiating during overtime. Jeff Shand had his jaw dislocated and suffered a concussion and dental damage. The assailant was then subdued by other parents at the game by kicking him in the groin (P. Walsh 2010).

In Warren County, New Jersey, a shoving match at a wrestling contest ended with an assault on coach Dan Shamsudin by Robert Spezza. Shamsudin was accused of delaying tactics resulting in the defeat of Spezza's son and his son's team. These three examples can easily be expanded into hundreds of such incidents caused by drinking alcohol as parents watch their children at play ("Details Emerge From Fracas" 2010).

Material Alcohol Culture

The alcohol culture involves material expectations. This means that alcoholic drinks are served in a variety of glasses, bottles, or containers depending on the substance of the drink. Beer is usually bought in beer bottles or cans and may be consumed directly from the container. It may also be served in a beer glass at any bar. Wine is dispensed in wine bottles, but it is uncommon to drink wine directly from the bottle unless it is used by some "down and out" alcoholics. Otherwise, wine is served in wine glasses both at home and in restaurants. These wine glasses differ markedly from beer glasses and glasses used to serve nonalcoholic drinks or mixed drinks.

Eighteen containers used to serve alcohol can be identified. First is the beer mug. Second is the brandy snifter. There are also cognac glasses, which cost between $0.70 and $1.86. The word *cognac* is derived from a town in western France. The most expensive brandy cognac glasses have printed designs embedded in the glass and are advertised as a means of "impressing your friends." Then there is the champagne flute. The flute is a narrow, tall glass costing between $0.70 and $2.40. Champagne glasses may also carry a printed logo advertised as "personalized." The word *champagne* relates to a province in France. The cocktail is named after the tail of a cock or rooster. A number of legends surround the origin of *cocktail*, all to the effect that the tail feathers of a rooster were included in a drink consisting of alcohol, sugar, water, and "bitters." The collins glass costs between $22 and $78 for a set of six. A collins consists of 2 ounces of alcohol and 2 ounces of sour mix, topped by some club soda. The collins can also include juice from half an orange or lime. A collins glass differs from the cordial glass and the highball glass. A cordial is served in a cordial glass costing between $2 and $10. A cordial may also be called liquor. It has low alcohol content and is consumed after a meal. It is sweet and may be substituted for dessert. Cordials may be flavored with nuts, fruit herbs, or juices of various kinds.

Hurricanes are served in glasses that cost about $3. This drink is popular in the Bahamas and in New Orleans. It consists of coffee liqueur, rum, Irish cream, orange juice, and some lime. Margaritas are served in yet other glasses as are old-fashioneds. A margarita glass costs between $2.38 and $95.00 for a set of six for those willing to spend a lot. A margarita is a Mexican cocktail consisting of tequila and an orange-flavored liqueur with orange and salt at the rim.

The French contributed the parfait glass and the pousse café glass. Then there is the punch bowl and the red wine glass. The sherry glass is unique and so is the shot glass. Whiskey sour is served in a shot glass, and white wine is served in a white wine glass.

Alcoholic drinks are much more expensive in a bar than if taken at home. A bottle of beer bought in a grocery store in the form of a 24 pack will cost about $0.64 per bottle. A beer ordered in a bar or restaurant will cost at least $4. Wine and mixed drinks are even more expensive. A "top shelf" margarita can cost $8, although on the average a margarita costs $6, as do most mixed drinks. Wine costs about $4 per glass and is much cheaper if bought in a liquor store, depending, however, on such attributes as age, brand, and location.

Another aspect of the material alcohol culture is the bar. The bar is a designated room reserved for the serving and consumption of alcoholic beverages. The name *bar* is derived from the counter that divides the room between the server or bartender and the customers who consume the alcoholic beverages delivered at the bar. Customers are usually seated on high stools or at tables where waiters or waitresses serve them. Bars are differentiated by social class and therefore by the cost of drinks. For example, there are bars in New York City that charge $8 for a beer, $9 for cider, $10 or more for a glass of wine, and $28 to $85 for a bottle of wine, although some bottles of wine can cost $500 or more.

All of this leads to the conclusion that drinking alcohol involves a number of cultural phenomena designed to produce an alternative status system derived from spending money and having "inside" information in a manner similar to that of professionals, who use language to assure themselves a boundary between those on the inside and those not "in the know." Language is the most important criterion of a subculture, and the drinking community is indeed a subculture. Therefore, expensive restaurants and drinking establishments use French or Italian labels in an effort to attract wealthy customers who imagine that food and drink carrying French words enhance the consumers' social standing. The alcohol culture is rooted in beliefs leading to behavior.

The material alcohol culture depends of course on the production of alcoholic drinks from grains and grapes grown worldwide but particularly in Europe and the United States. In the United States, the alcohol industry generates $115 billion in annual sales. Anheuser-Busch, the largest of the beer brewers, reported a net income of $10.51 billion in 2010 ("Anheuser-Busch Profit Up" 2015:1).

The alcohol production market is concentrated in a small number of companies. This has come about as numerous companies merged so that nearly all mass-produced beer is made by only one company, AB InBev and SABMiller, which merged in late 2016. There are eight other alcohol producers in the United States that produce spirits (e.g., whiskey, vodka). These producers provide at least 70% of all alcohol consumed in the United States each year (J. Greenfield and Rogers 1999).

There is a heavy concentration of drinkers in America. Those who drink more than four drinks a day consume 42% of the alcohol sold. Among these heavy drinkers are those young people who consume five drinks or more per day. These hazardous drinkers account for more than half the alcohol industry's sales and 76% of the beer market. Hazardous beer drinking begins in the eighth grade, increases during the college years, and then declines after age 25 (Johnston, O'Malley, and Bachman 2000).

Underage drinking among those not yet 21 years old accounts for 10% of the alcohol market. It has been reported that students from the seventh through the twelfth grade annually consume 1.1 billion cans of beer and about 35% of all wine coolers. These children are generally binge drinkers in that they consume five or more drinks in each session. Early drinking of alcohol is important to the industry, because those who drink a good deal in their youth are most likely to become heavy drinkers as adults. Early onset of drinking is also correlated with learning deficits and higher injury rates (Dawson and Grant 1997).

As we have already seen, a large number of Americans do not consume alcohol or drink seldom and in small amounts. As a result, many people, and particularly students, overestimate the amount of alcohol consumption on the part of their peers and often believe that they must drink a great deal in order to imitate the majority.

The alcohol industry seeks to lure young people into drinking more and has therefore developed strategies designed to attract youngsters. Included are "alcopops," which blur the line between soft drinks and alcohol. These drinks feature flavors such as lemonade and mask the 5% alcohol included. Likewise, malt liquors are sold in 40-ounce containers and have high alcohol content at low prices. These too are popular among students, as are so-called test tube shots, which are called "hot sex" and look like dynamite. In addition, there are drinks that change the color of the drinker's tongue. All of this is intended to drive consumers into hazardous drinking (Mosher 1996).

The alcohol industry advertises in magazines, on television, and in movies all aimed at young people. In addition, the alcohol industry sponsors rock concerts, sporting events, and community celebrations all with large youth audiences. Video games are also a target for alcohol advertisers. Jack Daniels, a whiskey label, advertises on the Real Pool video game, and Miller Beer uses video race car driving on its website. These ads convey the message that "everybody is doing it and so should you." These messages are augmented by testimonials by rap musicians, sports idols, and movie stars. Cartoon characters, animals, and other child-friendly communications are also used. The ads promise the drinker sex, excitement, glamour, acceptance by others, and "sophistication" (Kilbourne 1999).

Because Congress has mandated that warning labels must be included in alcohol advertisements, these labels are printed very small and are barely readable.

College campuses are usually surrounded by numerous bars, liquor stores, and other outlets for alcoholic drinks. These places are the centers of socializing for students and others. In addition, many gas stations, convenience stores, and food stores earn a good deal of their profit from alcohol sales. The prices of alcoholic beverages have declined so much that a can of beer can be had for $0.69 even as inflation has eroded the taxes on alcoholic drinks. In addition, there are so-called happy hours, during which bars, bowling alleys, and other establishments offer discount drinks and finger foods. These happy hours usually occur from Monday through Thursday when business is slow (Erenberg and Hacker 1997).

The political power of the alcohol industry increases the risks that excessive drinking pose for the community. That political power consists of industry associations whose prime goal is ever-increasing alcohol sales. To achieve this objective the alcohol producers use their huge financial resources to control the legislative process leading to the emasculation of all regulatory agencies. The first of these brewers associations was the U.S. Brewers Association founded in 1862 for the purpose of limiting federal taxes on alcoholic beverages (Hu 1950).

The alcohol industry was profoundly affected by Prohibition, leading the industry to make every effort to bring about repeal of the Eighteenth Amendment to the Constitution. The industry spent a great amount of money challenging the constitutionality of that amendment until it was repealed on December 5, 1933 (Ostrander 1957).

Repeal of Prohibition meant a great deal more for California than other states because it is the home of the grape (wine) industry. This became true when over $75 million of new money poured into the state after repeal and land values increased substantially. This led to more taxation of these new profits and subsequently to easing the tax burden on other industries.

The Twenty-First Amendment left all regulation of the alcohol industry to the states and not the federal government. This in turn gave the industry the opportunity to influence state legislators by supplying them with large contributions to their election campaigns. State governments profited from repeal in that control of revenues, together with sales taxes, gave the states an income of over $286 million or 30% of all revenue (Byse 1940).

Because of these large political contributions, state regulations concerning alcohol were generally written by the alcohol industry by way of "friendly" lawmakers. As early as 1936, one lawmaker alone, Artie Samish, received $200,000 from the alcohol industry. In 1939, an investigation of corruption among legislators in favor of the alcohol industry called the Philbrick Report disappeared, so that no evidence of these "payoffs" could be discovered thereafter (Philbrick 1939).

In Nebraska, a bill was introduced into the state legislature seeking to curtail alcohol purchases on a "dry" Indian reservation. The bill would have authorized the establishment of alcohol impact zones in areas affected by a great deal of alcohol-related crime. The bill was never reported out of a committee because seven of the eight members of the General Affairs Committee had received contributions from Anheuser-Busch. Because 4 million cans of beer are sold to the Oglala Sioux tribe each year, alcohol has been at the root of the reservation's health and crime problem. Yet the contribution by the beer industry of more than $120,000 to Nebraska political candidates easily outweighed the needs of the Oglala community (T. Williams 2012).

During the 2010 election cycle, the alcohol industry spent millions in contributions to federal-level candidates for political office. Nancy Pelosi, the leader of the Democrats in the U.S. House of Representatives, has been the top recipient of contributions from the Gallo Wine Company. Representative Mike Thompson collected $50,500 for his campaign in 2010 from the alcohol industry. Brown-Forman, which makes Jack Daniels and Southern Comfort whiskey, has contributed over $3 million to political candidates from 1990 to 2010. Then there is the Boston Beer Company, which makes Sam Adams Beer. They contributed $32,000 to Democrat candidates in 2010, and Colorado's New Belgium Brewery contributed $12,000 to Democrats in 2010. A far longer list of contributions by the alcohol industry could be constructed, showing that regulating that industry is almost nonexistent (McKinder 2011).

After the Second World War, consumption of alcohol rose considerably in the United States. This was due to an increase in population together with the then new suburban lifestyle and new marketing techniques, which told Americans that consuming alcohol was part of being a sophisticated business or professional man. (Women were not then included in the professional or business class.) The alcohol industry made itself popular by widespread advertising with a view of not only increasing sales but also preventing federal regulation. Much of this effort consisted of labeling the retail feature of alcohol distribution responsible for excessive drinking and its consequences.

By labeling alcoholism a disease, the alcohol industry has successfully diverted attention from its contribution to hazardous drinking and "blamed" the individual rather than the alcohol culture as promoted by the alcohol business. This has led both the American Medical Association and the American Psychological Association to promote the disease model, despite evidence that drinking is a behavior that is not transmitted by a virus or produced by infection.

The American Medical Association views alcoholism as a disease because alcoholism meets five central criteria needed to be considered a disease. These are a pattern of symptoms including craving or a compulsion to drink, loss of control, physical dependency, and tolerance or the need to drink more and more in order to get "high." Additional criteria are chronic progression, subject to relapse, and treatability ("Alcoholism Is a Disease" 1956).

A number of researchers, including physicians, have disputed this definition because drinking alcohol certainly depends on obtaining such drinks and using them.

Social Functions of Drinking

The word *alcohol* is probably derived from the Arabic *al-kul*, which Arab chemists used as early as the 17th century. In recent years, discussion of alcohol consumption has focused on its excesses with a view of labeling alcohol dependency a disease and an individual pathology. This view was first promoted by the temperance movement of the 1920s and 1930s, until it found acceptance by the medical community. Yet by the 1980s, this medicalization was challenged by social scientists who view alcohol use as a behavior resting on the alcohol culture that teaches it. That behavior consists of normal drinking as conducted at innumerable events celebrating the life cycle as well as the cycle of nature (McDonald 1994).

Drinking alcohol is socially integrating. This is true when alcohol is used within religious ceremonies and when it is the focus of socializing in bars, restaurants, and taverns. Social integration is also involved in home drinking, for alcohol is usually served in American homes to entertain guests and family (Barrows and Room 1991).

It is customary and popular to lump together all substances containing C_2H_5OH, or alcohol, because they all produce psychoactive effects. Yet it wasn't until the 19th-century temperance movement linked all alcoholic drinks together that drinking beer, wine, and spirits were viewed as one vice. Many nonindustrial, nonscientific communities do not view all alcoholic drinks as originating from the same source, so that some cultures do not view some truly alcoholic drinks as containing alcohol. Beliefs of this kind are derived from the observation that the same grain can become bread, beer, or whiskey, depending on the techniques applied to it. This indicates that the consumption of alcohol is predicated on a number of beliefs with differential symbolic implications in various cultures (Strunin, 2011).

The culture of drinking alcohol includes variations in ingredients, methods of preparation, patterns of association and exclusion, modes of serving and consumption, moral evaluation, expected behavior while drinking, and even styles of inebriation in that drunken behavior differs depending on the dominant culture.

Although numerous psychoactive drugs are used around the world, alcohol is the most common and most numerous drug used everywhere. This excludes the Muslim world, where alcohol consumption is prohibited.

Archeologists have discovered that alcohol was used in Neolithic culture, also known as the New Stone Age (9000 BCE to 3000 BCE). In ancient Assyria, Egypt, and Iran, the consumption of beer was widespread in pre-Islamic days. Then, as now, drinking alcohol had numerous implications. Ancient breweries have been excavated even as wine was introduced to early Bronze Age Greece. From there it spread to Italy and from there to North Africa and subsequently to the Greek colony Massalia, which is today's Marseilles in France (Dietler 1990).

This led to France becoming a major wine producer during the years when France was a Roman province called Gallia or Gaul from the 5th century BCE to the 3rd century CE. Distilled alcohol was then used for medical purposes until in the 16th and 17th centuries, it spread to Germany. It became commercial and increased in production due to its widespread use as grain-based alcohol was produced in northern Europe (Matthee 1995).

South Americans also feasted with alcohol as early as the 9th century. The Maya of Central America drank maize beer as well as a fermented drink made from honey and bark and spiked with hallucinogens. The Spanish conquest of Central and South America introduced distilled alcohol and the production of wine from grapes to the New World. Innumerable other examples could be cited, which reveal that the production and consumption of alcohol was ubiquitous and ancient with social, political, and economic consequences as alcohol spread around the world (Rice 1996).

Drinking alcohol is so widespread not only because of the pleasure it affords the drinker but also because it is used to construct the social world in which the drinker lives. Alcohol creates a social world of relationships in which each participant in the drinking rituals finds his or her place. Drinking alcohol leads to identity construction relative to age, gender, class, occupation, family, ethnicity, and religion. An excellent example of this is the Jewish tradition of drinking a glass of wine at the outset of the Sabbath on Friday night. The drink is preceded by a blessing over wine and a recital from Genesis 2:2 concerning the creation of the world. The whole family and guests participate in this ritual, thereby creating a strong family bond tying the generations to one another (T. Wilson 2005).

Drinking alcohol has many meanings in American society. Included are drinking places. For example, a common neighborhood bar is far less prestigious than a bar in an expensive hotel or club. The timing of drinking events is also of importance to those who participate. There is a vast difference between drinking beer at lunchtime and drinking a mixed drink at an evening cocktail party; the amount of alcohol consumed also makes a difference. Those who drink more than the norm for their reference group are rejected in favor of those who drink no more or less than their in-group dictates. Finally, the behavior of those who have ingested alcohol is determined by the group expectations, which become the norm for alcohol consumption among drinkers.

Gender is a most important means of determining status and role. Therefore, masculinity is associated with the availability of alcohol, leading to at least one definition of manliness, namely, "He can hold his liquor." Women have traditionally been the suppliers of the alcohol that men drink. Women are also expected to behave differently than men when intoxicated and to drink different drinks than men. In addition, class boundaries have been secured by the use of alcohol in that a variety of drinks are available to members of the upper class, leaving the lower classes to drink cheap beer (Gonzalez 2001).

Alcohol has also been an important means of creating social capital and prestige, leading to political influence and power. This occurs through the manipulation of hospitality designed to gain access to those already in power. The drinking may occur in the home or at lavish ceremonial meetings at which heavy drinking becomes a feature of the social ladder one needs to climb in order to gain political power. Those who do not drink, or at least host drinking events, are unlikely to be considered for political appointments or nominated for political office (Jennings et al. 2005).

Drinking alcohol also has economic consequences. Alcohol is an important segment of the domestic economy in the United States alone, because a significant amount of agricultural resources are devoted to the production of alcoholic beverages. In addition, the production of alcoholic beverages involves a large labor force. According to the Bureau of Labor Statistics, the beer, wine, and distilled alcoholic beverage industry employs about 166,000 workers who earn an average of $38,000 a year (U.S. Department of Labor n.d.).

Brief History of Drinking in America

Americans have participated in drinking alcohol ever since the Pilgrims landed on Plymouth Rock in 1620. The same may be said of the Massachusetts Bay Colony, founded 10 years later under the leadership of John Winthrop. Both groups regarded themselves as Puritans in that they sought to live a pure life based on the Bible as they understood it. Yet these opponents of every vice were wedded to alcohol, which they brought with them from England. In fact, the *Mayflower* carried a supply of beer.

In part, the use of beer was necessary because water was unpurified and tasted bad. It was considered good only for animals or for cooking but was otherwise avoided. Instead, the colonists consumed beer, which, together with ale, was produced in the homes of the immigrants (G. Wilson 1945).

The members of the colonies had each brought with them wheat, rye, and barley seed as well as malt from which they brewed beer. In America they also used corn. This interest in beer was derived from England, the motherland of the settlers where beer was always a necessity of everyday life (Freiberg 1929:18).

The English immigrants soon engaged in the profitable fur trade, which caused them to deal with the Native population. These Native Americans were introduced to alcohol by the newcomers and traded fur for drink. Thus, 4 pounds of fur traded for 7 gallons of liquor, and "Indians" who killed a wolf within the town boundaries were rewarded with 3 quarts of wine (Felt 1827).

The Puritans used corporal punishment for drunkenness. Eyewitnesses to such punishments relate that drunks were tied to a post and whipped, believing that "the punishment fit the crime." The Puritan view held that drunkenness transforms "God's image" into a beast, for horses are whipped and horses are beasts. This relates to Genesis 1:27, "And God made man in His image."

It was, of course, one of the features of Puritan life that government regulated all social, economic, and political activities and that religious views were dictated by the established church, which was also the government. Therefore, innkeepers needed a license to be in business. Such licenses were issued contingent on the assurance by innkeepers that they would prevent excessive drinking. That requirement was generally ignored, even as fines were collected from innkeepers for drunkenness on the part of patrons (Felt 1827).

By 1646, the number of taverns in Puritan territories had increased to such an extent that the prohibitions against drunken conduct had mainly broken down and could no longer be enforced. Drunkenness had become widespread and wine was now sold to the Indians, and laborers were paid in wine. All this even as dancing and shuffleboard games were still prohibited all over New England (Weeden 2011/1890).

It is evident that neither preaching, nor fines, nor physical punishment could curb drinking alcohol in New England. Drunkenness continued and increased. That increase was helped significantly when a large number of Germans arrived in the United States in the middle of the 19th century. So many Germans came after 1848 that Americans of German descent constituted one sixth, or 50 million, of the U.S. population in 2013. The first German immigrants came to America in the 17th century. However, they were few and came later than the English, who therefore promoted British culture in this country prior to the arrival of any other ethnic group. In addition, Scottish, Welsh, and Irish immigrants gave the English speakers in America a plurality (Emmerich, 2010).

The 19th-century Germans came equipped with beer. In fact, the first German brewery was founded in Pottsville, Pennsylvania, in 1828. That brewery still ships about 2.5 million barrels a year. That is also true of the Boston Beer Company, although Anheuser-Busch is larger than either of these. In 1840, a German immigrant, John Wagner, began to brew beer in Philadelphia. Two years earlier, some German immigrants to Pennsylvania brewed beer on a small scale, and others brewed beer in 1838 in Virginia.

By 1873, there were 4,131 breweries in the United States. The number of breweries declined sharply thereafter but recovered in the 21st century to about 1,500 breweries. The reason for the decline of breweries in the late 19th century was that at that time Americans favored whiskey over beer. Then, the 14,000 commercial distilleries operated successfully, for the average amount of whiskey ingested by Americans at that time was more than 7 gallons per adult per year. Later, when the Germans flooded Pennsylvania and other states, whiskey drinking declined and beer drinking resulted in the founding of the great German beer producers such as Schlitz, Busch, Pabst, Blatz, Miller, and Anheuser (Ogle 2006).

When the United States entered the First World War in 1917, the anti-German sentiment in the country not only led a good number of people with German names to change their name to an English-sounding name, but it also led to antagonism toward German beer, so that some of the Prohibition activists claimed that Pabst, Schlitz, Miller, and Blatz were "the worst of all our German enemies." Because in-group virtues are out-group vices, many Americans viewed the alcohol-consuming immigrants of the 1890–1920 era as dangerous and incapable of ever becoming true Americans. The result of these beliefs, which affected the Irish immigrants more than any other group, was an effort to simultaneously prohibit the use of alcohol in this country and to keep foreigners out (Okrent 2010).

Beliefs about Irish drinking were rooted in reality in that the rate of admission of Irish Americans to psychiatric hospitals for alcoholism was far greater than that of any other ethnic group. In addition, Irish Americans had a higher rejection rate due to alcoholism from army services during the First and Second World Wars than any other ethnic group. The American Drinking Practice Survey found the highest incidence of heavy drinking and other alcohol-related problems among Americans of Irish background. Irish Americans also spend more money on alcohol in relation to income than do other Americans, and Irish Americans are more often convicted of drunkenness than is true of any other ethnic group (B. Walsh and Walsh 1973).

During the First World War and during the decade thereafter, anti-Catholicism became most virulent in the United States. This was in part provoked by the belief that the Catholic clergy, consisting in the main of Irish immigrants or Americans of Irish descent, were sympathetic to the German cause. Catholics were accused of "collusion with the enemy," and some claimed that there existed an "Irish sabotage" (Esslinger 1967).

In addition, many Americans resented that the Irish president, Eamon de Valera, traveled throughout the United States on behalf of the self-proclaimed Irish Republic then under British rule. De Valera seemed to "knife our British ally in the back" in her death struggle against the "Hun," meaning the Germans. Protestant clergy denounced de Valera as having contributed to the loss of American lives by siding with Germany during the war. Then, on Thanksgiving Day in 1920, "the worst riot in the city's recent history" broke out in New York, as 6,000 Catholics stormed the elite Union Club within sight of St. Patrick's Cathedral for flying the Union Jack, the British flag, in front of their building ("Thousands Present at MacSwiney's Mass" 1920).

These and numerous other events annoyed the Protestant majority of the 1920s, who expected immigrants to conform to their culture and their expectations as truly American. According to that view, the American language, religion, literature, law, and government were all British, and therefore immigrants were to undergo "Anglo-conformity" (Marty 1972).

The number of Catholics in the United States grew from 2 million at the beginning of the 19th century to 17 million in 1920. This frightened Protestants, who feared an end to their lifestyle, dominance, and religious convictions. Yet in light of the American ethic, which held that "all men are created equal," it seemed far better to attack foreigners or new immigrants on the grounds of their dangerous habits rather than their origin or their religion. This allowed the "know nothings" and other bigots to claim that Irish alcoholism was a vast danger to the American way of life and that, therefore, they and other Catholics such as Italians who drank too much should be excluded from further migrating to the United States. Furthermore, it seemed to many a Protestant that the drinking of alcohol should be prohibited, thereby making America less attractive to the "drunken Irish." Under the leadership of the aggressive Women's Christian Temperance Union, these beliefs led to the quota laws restricting immigration and to prohibition of the manufacture, importation, or drinking of alcohol in the United States (M. Nelson 1968).

The Women's Christian Temperance Union's crusade against alcohol began in Ohio in 1873. That year, 32,000 Ohio women forced manufacturers and distributors of alcoholic drinks out of business. As the liquor trade was denounced across the nation, the Women's Christian Temperance Union evolved from the earlier groups that denounced alcohol. Women became active in the temperance movement not only because they sought to protect themselves and their families from the consequences of male drinking but also because women linked the right to vote to the temperance cause. Because women could not vote in the 19th century, they had no power to influence the legislatures of the several states or the federal government to outlaw alcohol. They therefore used physical violence to gain their ends, in that women forcibly destroyed the liquor stock of bars and liquor stores. Women physically assaulted saloons and used sit-in prayer to disrupt the liquor business.

Nineteenth-century American women were viewed as paragons of virtue, who were encouraged to denounce the alcohol industry and the drinking habits of men. However, women were excluded from all leadership roles and not even allowed to speak at conventions concerning the possible prohibition of alcohol in the United States. Thus, women were told, and most believed, that they were dependent on men and could not achieve anything outside the home without male permission (Bland 1951).

As the temperance movement grew, the issue of women's right to vote became more and more prominent, leading to the Seneca Falls, New York, convention of 1848, in which the participants demanded the right of women to vote. The speakers at that convention denounced the oppression of women at the hands of drunken men and the powerlessness of women (Banner 1980).

At first, the movement against the drinking of alcohol appeared to succeed, for the amount of alcohol consumed by Americans declined considerably between 1830 and 1845. In 1830, the average adult consumption of alcohol was about 7.1 gallons per year. In 1845, this had declined to 1.8 gallons, a decrease of 75% (Rorabaugh 1976).

After 1848, the temperance movement suddenly suffered a setback. Alcohol consumption rose once more as German and Irish immigrants entered the United States by hundreds and thousands and finally millions. The drinking habits of these new immigrants led Maine to pass a law in 1851 prohibiting the manufacture and sale of alcohol entirely. Thereby, Prohibition became a political movement.

As it became more and more evident that the Women's Christian Temperance Union movement could not succeed without the right of women to vote, women joined the Good Templars, an organization that allowed women to hold office and to speak to large crowds of Prohibition supporters. The anti-alcohol agitators succeeded in dividing the nation into drinkers and abstainers, and German and Irish immigrants and descendants of such immigrants were in the forefront of drinkers. The hierarchy of the Catholic Church also opposed Prohibition, as did wealthy investors who needed to protect their money. In addition, large cities opposed Prohibition as more and more immigrants crowded into the East Coast cities and later into Midwestern cities such as Buffalo, Cincinnati, and finally Chicago. This increase in alcohol consumption appeared to temperance women to be a direct threat to the safety of American families, leading once more to direct action (Dannenbaum 1981).

Some women entered saloons and used axes to destroy the establishments and liquor supplies. Others sat down in the saloons and knitted or prayed. Sometimes these women were arrested but were not convicted in any court, because the juries sympathized with their cause. Juries all over the country found women involved in trespassing and assaulting drinking establishments not guilty (Furnas 1965).

In 1913, Congress passed the Webb-Kenyon Act, which prohibited "wet" states from exporting liquor to customers in "dry" states. Four years later, in 1917, two thirds of the states had liquor laws, so that the Eighteenth Amendment was preceded by Prohibition in a number of states, which had already prohibited alcohol as early as the 1850s (Charrington 1920).

Congress passed the Eighteenth Amendment to the Constitution in 1917, and several states did so by 1919. The amendment prohibited the manufacture, transportation, and sale of intoxicating liquors. This amendment became effective by means of the Volstead Act of 1919 and lasted from January 1920 until its repeal by means of the Twenty-First Amendment 14 years later.

One of the reasons for passing the Eighteenth Amendment was that it seemed to many people that all the world's problems would be solved if liquor were prohibited. These "problems" were associated with immigrants and their drinking habits, who were accused of corrupting children and spreading venereal disease. Even more important was the fear on the part of native-born Protestant citizens that their social standing, power, and way of life were being challenged by the mostly Catholic immigrants of the 1920s. The immigrants were almost entirely city dwellers, whereas Prohibition was strongest in rural areas whose "clean" living was favorably contrasted with the overcrowding, filth, disorder, and crime in the cities. The Protestant majority believed that they were in no sense "ethnics" but that they were true Americans, whereas the Irish and other Catholic immigrants seemed to be forever foreign to this country. Yet Prohibition failed because it could not be enforced as cities grew and immigrants poured into the country in ever greater numbers. In several years of the early 20th century, more than a million immigrants arrived in the United States. The peak year of this flood of newcomers was 1907, when 1,286,000 people arrived, so that 13 million immigrants were living in the country in 1910, when the total U.S. population was 92.2 million (U.S. Department of Commerce 1910).

Prohibition and the Wickersham Commission Report

A considerable literature concerning Prohibition and crime exists and is augmented by stories, movies, television, and personal recollections. These crime stories are not the province of this book. However, the report of the Wickersham Commission is of great interest here, because that report dealt with the enforcement of the Prohibition laws by the National Commission on Law Observance and Enforcement as of January 1931, which was 11 years after Prohibition was first imposed. George Wickersham was the attorney general in the Hoover administration. According to that report, "Working men and their families are drinking in larger numbers in quite frank disregard of the declared policy of the National Prohibition Act." The evidence for this conclusion was the number of arrests for drunkenness in public, deaths from causes attributed to alcohol abuse, hospital admission for alcoholism, and drunken driving (Wickersham 1931).

The prohibition of alcohol never had a chance of succeeding because the law was not supported by the mores. Customs in all cultures consist of folkways, mores, and laws. A folkway is a custom, which is optional in that one may or may not want to deal with it. Wearing a tie is an example. A more is a custom supported by public opinion and may be evaluated positively or negatively. An example of a positive more is cleanliness. It is not illegal to fail to wash oneself, but it is surely viewed with disdain. Washing is positively evaluated. A negative more would be prohibiting the drinking of beer. Hardly any American supports such a law, and that is the real reason why Prohibition failed. The Wickersham Report was greatly influential in bringing about repeal of the Eighteenth Amendment during the first months of the Roosevelt administration on December 5, 1933. Franklin Roosevelt had campaigned for that repeal, not only because of the organized crime murders that exploded in American cities during the so-called beer wars, but also because investors in the alcohol industry sought to recover their losses caused by Prohibition. In 1931, the anti-Prohibition forces were buoyed by the formation of the Women's Organization for National Prohibition Reform. This organization included some of the wealthiest women in America, including Mrs. Pierre DuPont, Mrs. August Belmont (Shoenberg), Mrs. Coffin Van Rensselaer, and Mrs. B. Stuyvesant Pierrepont. The women represented the interests of their wealthy husbands, who organized the Association Against the Prohibition Amendment, which successfully lobbied Congress to pass the Twenty-First Amendment to the Constitution (Root 1934).

After Prohibition ended, there existed a vast erstwhile illegal industry, which had been producing and distributing alcohol for 14 years. This industry was not controlled in any manner because it was illegal. The "speakeasies" sold whatever they wanted, opened or closed at any hour, and provided food and entertainment as they wished. The industry paid no taxes, although both producers and distributors paid off police.

After the Twenty-First Amendment took effect, the states and federal government introduced all kinds of controls on the liquor industry. Government regulators considered whether food could be served in an alcohol establishment, whether women should be admitted to bars, whether a drinking establishment should be called a "saloon," and what kind of licenses bar owners needed to obtain. Most important to government regulators was the introduction of taxes (Fosdick and Scott 1933).

One method used by some states was to limit the sale of liquor to state-owned stores. Nine states operate state-owned liquor stores. These are Alabama, Idaho, New Hampshire, Oregon, North Carolina, Pennsylvania, Virginia, Washington State, and Utah. In addition, nine other states contract the management and operation of liquor stores to private firms for a fee (Zullo et al. 2013).

The argument in favor of state-run liquor stores stemmed from the manner in which only four corporations had seized the manufacture of liquor by the end of the 1930s. These four were producing four fifths of the distilled liquor in the country. This led to the anxiety that shortly only a few corporations would own all liquor stores, a possibility foreclosed by the state-run stores (Levine 1985).

Prior to Prohibition, the saloon furnished beer, wine, and spirits and sold off-premises buckets of beer and other drinks. After the end of Prohibition, there were no more saloons. Instead, beer was now sold in grocery stores and "drug" stores, and liquor stores were prohibited from selling food or even cigarettes. This meant that a separation between public drinking places and establishments selling bottled alcohol developed. This led to much more drinking of alcohol at home, so that off-premises usage began to account for the majority of alcohol sales.

Photo 3.3: A sign of the times: Prohibition 1929.

The effort to control the use of alcohol led to the proliferation of licenses for selling beer, wine, or spirits. These licenses were made available to restaurants and other eating establishments, where eating limited the amount of alcohol consumed. At the same time, most states allowed counties to prohibit the selling of alcohol; there are 200 counties in the United States as of 2013 that are dry.

Because it was evident that Prohibition could not work, private organizations have assumed the responsibility of attempting to deal with excessive alcohol consumption. The National Council on Alcoholism, Alcoholics Anonymous, and the National Council on Alcohol Abuse have sought to reduce drinking and its associated health problems and other dangers. One such effort was to reduce the consumption of "hard liquor" in favor of beer, although this distinction rests on the myth that beer is less addictive than whiskey (Harrison and Laine 1936).

The regulation of alcohol consumption after Prohibition did eliminate the influence of organized crime from the alcohol business, although the powerful alcohol-producing lobby has at all times fought every regulation attempted by government. This is why regulation does not address health and welfare concerns, for the enormous profits of a few large corporations defeat any effort to promote public health measures associated with alcohol consumption (Levine 1978:143).

Attempts to Limit Alcohol Consumption

Efforts to limit alcohol consumption without prohibiting it altogether include limiting the availability to drink alcohol by restricting opening hours where alcohol is sold, by raising the minimum drinking age, and by raising the price of alcoholic beverages. Efforts have also been made to teach high school students how much harm alcohol drinking can cause and to educate bar staff to limit the amount of alcohol they will sell to those evidently inebriated. This would also apply to those who serve alcohol at private parties. These measures have all been tried with little effect on drinking behavior, including drunk driving (Babor 2003).

Seeking to limit the dangers that drunk driving continues to cause year in and year out, the circuit court in Orange County, Florida, has ruled that the organizer of a teen party is liable for a drunk driver. The case is called *Davis v. Clark* and deals with the injuries suffered by 20-year-old Steven Davis, who was struck by a truck driven by Thomas Grutter, who was so drunk that he crossed the center line and ran into Davis. Grutter then fled the scene of the accident. The victim, Davis, suffered a severe break of his pelvis, jawbone, collarbone, spine, and both arms. He also had a collapsed lung. His testicles were severely injured, so that he could no longer produce testosterone. Because of his many injuries, Davis could no longer work as a lab technician.

Davis's lawyers sued the owner of the house where the party had been held, using Florida's Open House Party criminal law, which makes it illegal for adults to serve alcohol to minors at a house. The lawyers also sued the party organizers with the result that a jury awarded Davis $4.5 million in damages and future medical expenses (Davenport 2012).

Florida is, of course, not the only state in which drunk driving kills and maims thousands of Americans each year. The National Highway Traffic Safety Administration (2013) reports that in 2012, drunken driving killed 10,322 people in the United States.

The difficulty of preventing drunk driving is best illustrated by the report that an average drunk driver has driven drunk 80 times before first arrest. It has also been estimated that adults drank too much and got behind the wheel about 112 million times in 2010. This amounts to 300,000 incidents of driving and drinking each day (CDC 2011).

Because drunk driving and other negative consequences are associated with excessive drinking, the end of Prohibition saw new strategies develop, with a view of reducing, if not eliminating, alcohol dependence. Though the Women's Christian Temperance Union and others blamed alcohol for the problems associated with it, post-Prohibition strategies shifted from the substance to the person. This change in emphasis was also the reason for the development of Alcoholics Anonymous (Levine 1978).

At the end of World War II in 1945, activists established the National Council of Alcoholism. This organization proposed that alcoholism is a disease, thereby rejecting the morality issues, which were the driving force in the abandoned Prohibition argument. Nevertheless, the anti–drinking-and-driving movement became the new temperance crusade, promoted in the main by MADD or Mothers Against Drunk Driving. This organization was founded by the mother of a child killed by a drunk driver, who was subsequently treated with leniency despite his previous convictions on similar offenses. With the help of several grants from charitable foundations, this group succeeded in changing California law to give drunk drivers tougher and longer sentences (Vejnoska 1982).

Only a year after its founding, MADD had over 600,000 members and 360 chapters in 50 states and a full-time professional staff administering a budget of $10 million. Extensive media coverage began in 1985, and that year MADD became *Time*'s "Man of the Year" (Lightner 1985).

Subsequently, 230 new anti–drunk driving laws were passed on the local level, even as President Reagan signed into law legislation prohibiting drinking alcohol for those less than 21 years of age by withholding road construction funds from states not in compliance. Therefore, all states passed under-21 drinking laws (Cloward 1977).

Drinking and Occupations

Occupation is the most important criterion of social prestige in America. According to numerous studies, physicians are regarded by the American public as having more prestige than any other occupation, whereas shoe shiners come in last. Yet when drinking alcohol is considered, we discover that alcohol is used by all levels of workers from doctors to laborers.

In 2010, most (64.8%) full-time employed Americans consumed alcohol. Among all the employed, 29.7% reported binge drinking. In addition, 8.5% of alcohol users consider themselves "heavy" drinkers. This means that about 56.6 million drinkers and 16.5 million heavy drinkers were employed in 2010 (SAMHSA 2011d). The losses associated with this much alcohol drinking consist of lost productivity, health care costs, and legal and criminal consequences amounting to $223.5 billion a year (Bouchery et al. 2011).

Although drinking alcohol is nearly universal among all employed, those who work in manual occupations have higher rates of excessive drinking than those who do not work at physical labor. This is particularly true of farm workers and service industry employees as compared to those working in professional occupations. Excessive drinking is also associated with mining, construction, and oil and gas extraction work (A. Barnes and Brown 2013).

No doubt work stress influences alcohol use. Using the two dimensions of job demand and job autonomy, it appears that high-demand and low-autonomy work contribute excessively to work-related stress, leading to more and more alcohol dependency. Failure to allow some workers to make autonomous decisions is related to excessive use of alcohol. Likewise, workers who are not supported or helped and are not in contact with others are also associated with excessive drinking.

Although physical labor is more likely to produce alcohol abuse among such laborers, it is also clear that those in high-prestige occupations may well drink to excess, although less opprobrium is leveled against such drinkers. Physicians, who rank highest among all American occupations as considered by all public opinion polls, are nevertheless possible alcohol abusers. This raises the question of whether a doctor should be allowed to drink while on call. The American Medical Association has a policy concerning the use of alcohol while a physician is practicing medicine. However, the policy statement is vague and subject to a variety of interpretations. The statement finds it unethical to practice while "impaired." Yet it does not say what is meant by the word *impaired* but leaves that judgment to each member of the profession (American Medical Association n.d.).

Drinking alcohol assumes a different dimension in the case of the medical profession as compared to other occupations, because a doctor may be called to an emergency even if not on call. Though the medical profession leaves a good deal of discretion to practitioners as to the drinking of alcohol while on duty, emergency medical technicians are subject to license revocation if they drink alcohol at any time while on duty. This is also true for airplane pilots, who are required to abstain from alcohol 8 hours before any flight. The policy concerning drinking and driving is even less tolerant (Federal Aviation Association n.d.; New York State Department of Health n.d.).

Alcohol misuse affects about 6.2% of the 118 million working population of the United States, or somewhat more than 7 million people. This leads to considerable absenteeism, mental health problems, and physical danger in work situations involving machines (U.S. Department of Health and Human Services 1996).

Alcohol use is also related to family situations such as living as a couple, having children at home, being involved in family conflict, and family income. Those who have the support of relatives and friends tend to drink less than those who have to face all of these stressors alone. Men are more likely to abuse alcohol than is true of women in these family situations, and as age progresses, alcohol intake declines, although education, health, and smoking also relate to the use of alcohol (Head, Siegrist, and Stansfeld 2004).

Alcohol intake is related to all aspects of the drinker's life, including his or her work situation. Work strain has also been associated with the use of alcohol. Those who must make workplace decisions, as well as those subject to physical and psychological demands in the workplace, are more likely to use alcohol than those who are not so burdened. Number of hours worked, irregular work schedules, and harassment on the job all contribute to the use of alcohol (Richman et al. 2002).

Seventy percent of the adult population of the United States uses alcohol regularly, but only 10% of this drinking population is alcoholic. Five percent of the workforce are alcohol addicts, and an additional 5% are serious alcohol abusers. Over half of all managers report that excessive use of alcohol causes them serious problems on the job, and 18% of such managers expressed anxiety about their own drinking (Kiechal 1982).

There can be little doubt that the military is the most stressful employment, because it offers a good chance of being wounded or killed. It is therefore not surprising that a study of the U.S. armed forces during the Iraq war showed that 12.4% of active service individuals and 14.5% of the National Guard misused alcohol. As more and more soldiers are deployed in foreign countries and engaged in combat, the drinking increases. Thus, during the decade 1998 to 2008, heavy drinking in the U.S. armed forces increased from 15% to 20% (Thomas et al. 2010).

This indicates that alcohol is used in American culture to relieve stress and anxiety. Furthermore, the military condones heavy drinking, so that military personnel are induced to drink a good deal because the military provides an alcohol culture. Heavy drinking among military personnel is associated with violence, accidents, and poor work performance.

Alcohol abuse is also related to the occupation of sales personnel, lawyers, physicians, and those who work in alcohol-related industries such as brewers and bartenders. In all of these occupations, employers must deal with the alcohol abuser in some manner. There are those, mostly small employers, who demand immediate termination of employment for anyone drinking too much. Only 11% of American employers terminate an employee for drinking too much. The majority of large firms refer employees to counseling and treatment programs, and 11% take no action (Borstein 1984).

One reason for the toleration of drinking on the job by a majority of employers is the Vocational Rehabilitation Act of 1973. According to that law, employment discrimination against the handicapped is prohibited. Alcoholism is included in the definition of *handicapped*, which makes it nearly impossible to let go and dismiss an employee from his or her job due to alcoholism. It is therefore most important for employers to screen out alcohol abusers during the hiring process (Tersine and Hazeldine 1982).

A number of factors related to drinking alcohol in the workplace have been identified. The size of the firm is one such factor, as is the type of industry. The freedom to set one's own work hours, as well as lack of supervision and severe stress, are also involved as is competition and the presence of others with alcohol problems (Madonia 1981).

It is well known that salespeople have drinking problems in excess of the general population. At least 50% of sales managers indicate that alcohol abuse exists in their salesforce. Because the majority of salespeople drink, and because their percentage of alcohol users is significantly higher than the 70% of Americans who drink, the percentage of salespeople who have a drinking problem is also higher than in the general population. This may well be explained by the fact that in many sales situations the consumption of alcohol is necessary (Patton and Questell 1986).

Lawyers are reputed to drink more than the average American. This is not only a popular belief but is indeed a matter of fact. The principal reason for the extraordinary amount of alcohol consumed by lawyers is that a significant percentage of practicing lawyers are experiencing psychological distress symptoms a good deal greater than is found in the general population. The symptoms have been traced directly to law practice, because law practice leads to anger and hostility. In sum, the environment surrounding lawyers is conducive to the creation of substantial psychological distress. The symptoms of this distress include compulsiveness, social isolation, interpersonal difficulties, anxiety, and depression (Shanfield, Andrew, and Benjamin 1985).

It is significant that married lawyers or those living with a significant other were less likely to be depressed, anxious, or otherwise in need of psychological counseling than those living alone. This is, of course, not only true of lawyers but agrees with numerous studies to the effect that alcoholism and other signs of emotional distress are less frequent among those who are happily married than among those who are marital failures or live alone (Schneidman 1984).

The nature of the trial lawyer's profession produces anger and the aggressiveness needed to win. The need to win leads to an aggressive personality with consequences for the lawyer's friends and family. Many lawyers cannot turn off the aggression when dealing with family. Their hard-driving behavior continues at home and leads to all kinds of resentment and pushback. This puts lawyers in a dilemma. Aggression is needed to be successful in litigation, but it is viewed as obnoxious if not utterly unacceptable in private life. The dilemma can be accommodated by drinking alcohol. In turn, alcohol use promotes anger. In American culture, a good deal of deviant behavior is legitimized by claiming that alcohol caused the unacceptable conduct. Therefore, getting drunk may appear to many lawyers and others as the means by which angry and even violent behavior can be rationalized (Billings 1979).

The American alcohol culture demands that most everyone drink alcohol on occasions concerning the life cycle: the observation of holidays; the entertainment of guests, friends, and relatives; and the consumption of food. This need to drink alcohol creates alcohol abuse in some of those who use it regularly, because fragile self-esteem can be absorbed by drinking alcohol or using another drug.

Among college students, the drug of choice is mainly alcohol, despite its negative consequences, such as failing grades, unplanned pregnancies, and even death. A number of researchers have concluded that the excessive use of alcohol among college students is caused by low self-esteem, a condition by no means absent from alcohol abusers older than normal college age. College students and others may well believe that drinking alcohol makes the drinker more socially desirable. Yet the negative outcomes of excessive drinking are even worse for those with low self-esteem than for those who have high or at least normal self-esteem.

Alcohol consumption in the United States is associated with social interaction and is symbolic of life cycle events. The failure of the temperance movement is therefore to be attributed to its opposition to American mores. The drinking of alcohol is also related to the construction of identity relative to gender, class, political power, and economic success.

Alcohol has been used in the United States since the coming of the Pilgrims and was enhanced by the German and Irish immigrants. Alcoholism is associated with a number of stressful occupations and with low self-esteem.

CHAPTER 4

Alcohol and Social Institutions

Alcohol and the Family

It is self-evident that any family may be affected by excessive alcohol use by any one of its members. Alone, the fact that those with alcohol-related disorders have higher costs for medical expenses in addition to the cost of the alcohol itself may cause economic hardships for those dependent on the alcohol user.

In addition, wives and children of heavy drinkers are more often in need of such medical services as psychiatric counseling because of the emotional damage caused by alcoholism in the family. It has also been found that the earlier a child uses alcohol, the greater the possibility of the child becoming alcohol dependent as an adult (Grant and Dawson 1997).

The rates of alcohol misuse appear to increase through adolescence. One study revealed that 8% of eighth graders, age 14, reported that they had been drunk one or more times in the past 30 days. The same was found among 21% of 10th graders and 33% of 12th graders (Johnston, O'Malley, and Bachman 1996).

A similar study conducted in New York State found that among 12-year-olds, 7% drank five or more drinks of alcohol in the month preceding that survey. Thirteen-year-old students reported that 13% had been involved in binge drinking, which reached 47% among 17-year-olds and 50% among those aged 18 (G. Barnes, Farrell, and Dwindle 1994).

The importance of parents for children can hardly be exaggerated. Parents exert a powerful influence on them during their early development, so that ineffective child-rearing becomes a major cause of deviant conduct. This means that poor or no supervision is a major cause for delinquent behavior including binge drinking of alcohol (Hirschi and Gottfredson 1994).

Parental support and control are the two ingredients leading to the development of a successful adult. The lack of both or one of these parental efforts will result in delinquencies of all kinds, including drinking alcohol. Parents who are involved in drinking large amounts of alcohol are also more likely than nondrinking parents to use physical violence by hitting each other and children. Such efforts at control cannot succeed because violence breeds violence and not compliance. There are also parents who explain peaceably why we should not drink more than a modest amount. In addition, there are those parents who monitor the whereabouts of their children at all times with a view of preventing deviant conduct. In sum, more support leads to better outcomes (G. Patterson and Stouthamer-Loeber 1984).

The outcome of control of adolescents by parents depends on the level of control exercised. Too much control as well as too little control are both ineffective, although physical violence is the worst of all means of dealing with children.

The principal reason for adolescent drinking is parental behavior. Children imitate the conduct of parents, so that the drinking patterns of parents are usually carried on by their children. This explains why some ethnic groups exhibit generations of hard-drinking folks, whereas others seem relatively sober for years.

Alcohol use is acquired through "modeling" in the sense that it is imitated and supported through beliefs leading to attitudes, which finally become personal conduct (Botvin et al. 1990).

Those who use a great amount of alcohol or other drugs frequently suffer from a lack of social skills that in turn lead to other problems including alcohol abuse. A number of investigators have found a link between deficient social skills and drug abuse, because alcohol abusers and other drug abusers believe that they can never succeed socially. Those who fail to make friends or otherwise notice a decrease in their social competence often increase their use of alcohol or other drugs. The reverse is also true. Increases in alcohol use lead to decreases in social skills and to a decrease in self-confidence and the ability to reach goals and complete tasks (Pentz 1985).

Parental alcohol use has consistently led to alcohol use among children and has also led to involvement in alcohol use by adolescents due to peer pressure. Furthermore, families with an alcohol-using adolescent are likely to be incapable of solving problems effectively. Such problems are often related to conflict concerning child-rearing practices, which in turn lead to alcohol use among older children or adolescents (Vicary and Lerner 1986).

Family disharmony influences early adolescent alcohol use in that adolescents with few social skills are more likely to use alcohol to deal with their social deficiencies. This means that alcohol is used to reduce stress for those who lack sufficient social skills to feel comfortable in social situations (Baer et al. 1988).

That families are heavily influenced by the excessive use of alcohol can be recognized when mothers who drink too much lose custody of their children. The involvement of the courts in deciding custody of children was already known in the 16th century when Henry VIII (1509–1547) established the Court of Wards and Liveries in England for the sake of promoting custody standards for the protection of children (J. Jacobs and Goebel 1962).

The courts routinely awarded custody to the father whenever a dispute arose concerning the mother's fitness to raise her children. The reverse was not considered until 1839, when mothers were finally awarded custody on the grounds that a father drank too much or otherwise abused his children.

In the United States, equality of parental rights was recognized with a view of maintaining the best interests of the child. It has been an assumption of American law that natural parents have a right to keep their children unless not fit to do so. In more recent years, legislatures have given courts considerable discretion in cases involving custody disputes between natural parents and third parties such as grandparents, other relatives, and/or social service agencies with reference to proof of neglect by one or both of the natural parents (*Wengert v. Wengert* 1950).

All this bears on excessive drinking by both parents or one parent. Parents who have been charged with such conduct may lose custody of their children if the court determines that such alcohol abuse infringes on the best interests of the child. Most state courts will refuse a mother's custody of her children if she has been guilty of alcoholism. In *Usery v. Usery* (1961), the husband sued the wife for divorce on the grounds of her alcoholism. The court then awarded the children to the wife, a decision that was reversed by the court of appeals, and the children were awarded to the father even though he too had a history of excessive drinking, mitigated by his membership in Alcoholics Anonymous. The mother admitted to frequent bouts of drinking and coming home late from local taverns.

Lichtenberg v. Lichtenberg (1942) involved a mother who brought the children to bars with her. She fought in these bars when she was drunk, came home intoxicated and very late, and was convicted several times of drunk and disorderly conduct. She was therefore denied custody in favor of her husband, after the court determined that her conduct had a direct bearing on her children's emotional and physical well-being.

In *Harris v. Harris* (1960), the mother took barbiturates and walked around the house in the nude while drunk, in the presence of her children. The court therefore denied her custody.

There are also cases in which the court awards child custody to third parties if both parents are deemed unfit to raise their child because of alcoholism. This was demonstrated by *Hall v. Hall* (1964), in which a divorce was granted because of the father's conduct while drinking. Because the mother was exhibiting an alcohol problem, child custody was given to an aunt and uncle. Yet the court of appeals reversed that arrangement and located custody in the chief juvenile probation officer with instructions to leave the child with the mother under supervision of the probation department.

In some cases, the courts have allowed mothers with severe drinking problems to keep their children. An example is *McKenzie v. McKenzie* (1957), in which the husband was granted a divorce on the grounds that Mrs. McKenzie drank to excess. She had left her young children out alone at night and was found later on the kitchen floor utterly drunk when a stranger returned her children. She had hallucinations caused by drinking, leading her to punish the children for no reason. Nevertheless, the court allowed her custody of the children because she had joined Alcoholics Anonymous.

In *Floyd v. Floyd* (1963), the grandparents were awarded custody of the children because the mother drank excessively. Here the court disregarded the fact that the mother had been a member of Alcoholics Anonymous for several years and had not had a drink for 2 years. The court denied any therapeutic value to her association with Alcoholics Anonymous and also denied the children the presence of their mother. The court defended its position by claiming that the mother's past behavior was more important than any effort at rehabilitation.

The dilemma produced by alcohol-induced conduct by a mother does not change the need of children for their mother. Therefore, the courts are placed into the uncomfortable position of either delivering the children into the hands of a neglectful or even abusive parent or depriving children of the most important relationship need by all who live.

It is no secret that alcohol abuse is more common among men than women. In fact, men exceed women in this regard at a rate of almost 3 to 1. It has also been confirmed by repeated studies that alcohol abuse declines with age so that 30- to 44-year-olds are less likely to suffer from alcohol abuse than those 18 to 29 years old. This trend continues, so that as age advances the rate of alcohol dependency declines. Nevertheless, alcohol abuse constitutes a significant public health problem with major implications for the family (Steinglass and Moyer 1977).

All kinds of deviant behavior decline with maturity and with the assumption of responsibility for a family. This is true of alcohol abusers as well as abusers of other drugs. This means that substance abuse increases as adolescents break away from their families but declines when the same adolescents marry and assume adult responsibilities. It is also significant that divorce generally leads erstwhile abusers to return to their old habits (Wren 1997).

Because parents are the most influential role models for their children, it is not surprising that this also pertains to drinking alcohol. It is evident, therefore, that parents who seek to curb the drinking behavior of adolescent children need to first consider their own use of alcohol or other drugs.

This is important because studies have shown that those who drink alcohol before the age of 15 are 4 times more likely to develop alcoholism than those who begin at age 21. Sixty-four percent of high school seniors report that they have been drunk, and nearly one third of all seniors say they have had five or more drinks in a row (Harckham 2000).

Although maturity leads to a decline of alcohol abuse among the young, there are numerous adults, including those sometimes labeled "elderly" or old, who abuse alcohol. In fact, alcohol-related medical problems put more older people into the hospital than heart attacks and cost taxpayers more than $230 million annually for hospital bills paid by Medicare. This happens because approximately 8% to 12% of people over 65 years suffer from alcoholism. This constitutes about 4 million citizens, although the number of seniors involved in alcohol abuse is probably larger but not reported, because many older people live alone, do not work, and have few friends (Miller 1993).

In addition to these reasons for failure to report alcohol problems among the old are the shame, guilt, and denial associated with alcoholism in many families. This "coverup" mentality is particularly evident with reference to women alcoholics, whose children and grandchildren will hide the drinking habits of mothers and grandmothers at all costs lest the family be shamed. Furthermore, it is a common aspect of alcohol abuse that the abusers deny their behavior and minimize their alcohol abuse. All this militates against gaining a reliable picture of senior alcoholism in this country and elsewhere.

Often the old are allowed to continue their drinking habits without interference by doctors or others, because middle-aged adults often believe that the old should not be deprived of their ingrained habits because they won't live much longer and therefore ought to have a right to enjoy their alcohol. This is a common reason for failure to deal with drinking by seniors. Yet the evidence is that those who can succeed in decreasing or eliminating their alcohol dependency feel a great deal better than before and lead a much more enjoyable old age than alcohol users (Miller 1993).

Widespread alcohol abuse across all ages and both sexes cost the American economy more than $1.4 billion in 2010. According to the Department of Health and Human Services, there are 10 sources of these costs. Deaths due to drugs and alcohol caused a loss of about $409 million in 2010. Workforce productivity loss amounted to $188 million, and treatment admission cost $47 million. Deep intervention led to an expenditure of over $1 million, but medical expenditures reached a staggering $303 million. Then there are the costs of crime and law enforcement caused by alcohol abuse. These amount to $120 million related to crime and $223 million to state and county corrections. Motor vehicle accidents cost the economy over $53 million a year, and child and social welfare amount to a cost of $54.5 million. Fire protection represented an additional cost of $9.5 million in 2010 (Mayhew 2010).

There is a group of Americans who do not seek alcohol nor do anything that would bring alcohol into them. Yet these people are affected by alcohol consumption just the same, because they are the unborn children of drinking mothers. Innumerable studies agree that alcohol use during pregnancy is associated with health problems that adversely affect the mother and fetus. "Thus, with respect to growth deficits, there is no safe level of drinking during pregnancy. Alcohol exposure during gestation causes growth deficits among the offspring at birth and during infancy" (Day and Richardson 2004:28), and heavy drinking by a pregnant mother leads to fetal alcohol syndrome, which is best understood as a developmental and neurobehavioral abnormality. A nursing mother should not drink alcohol because the baby absorbs as much alcohol as the mother.

Alcohol and Religion

Every year there are about 75,000 alcohol-related deaths in the United States. After smoking and overweight, alcohol abuse is third among preventable deaths in the country. In addition, alcohol abuse causes domestic violence, child abuse, random sexual relationships, and teen pregnancy.

It is therefore of interest that religion affects alcohol consumption. Because Buddhists and Muslims are prohibited from drinking alcohol, followers of these religions are seldom involved in alcohol-related problems; however, Muslims frequently resort to such drugs as hashish or cocaine. Neither Judaism nor Christianity prohibits the use of alcohol, although excessive drinking is rejected. Alcohol is used in ceremonies in both religions. Judaism views alcohol as food and elevates drinking alcohol to an important aspect of family life. There are a number of religions in which alcohol plays a role as a means of attaining mystical experiences (Chatters 2000).

In the 21st century, about one half of Americans are adherents of a religious group. Of these, 22% are Roman Catholics and 51% are Protestants; other Christians, such as Mormons, make up another 5% of the American population, so that Christianity has a following of about 78%. About 16% of Americans are unaffiliated, and 6% belong to small religious groups including Jews, Muslims, Hindus, and Buddhists (Pew Forum on Religion and Public Life 2013).

Alcohol is consumed by approximately 70% of the American population. Those who drink the least are evangelical Protestants, so that states with the highest proportion of such believers have the least amount of binge drinking. States with the highest proportion of Catholics have the highest number of binge drinkers. States with a high proportion of Jews, such as New York, New Jersey, and California, have a lot of alcohol drinking but a low rate of binge drinking and fewer alcoholics.

Religion may suppress alcohol consumption if a denomination includes doctrines condemning alcohol use altogether. It is also possible that those who participate in a religious community will find some support and a sense of belonging to a group, which absorbs the need for "drowning one's sorrow" in alcohol. Painful emotions and memories can lead to drinking alcohol as a means of reducing the misery. Membership in a religious group can also do this and thereby forestall excessive use of alcohol (Goldberg 1977).

Among those Americans who consider themselves "born again," both recent and lifetime disorders associated with alcohol are uncommon. Likewise, Jews have a low rate of such disorders, although a high proportion of Jews drink alcohol in family settings and at religious gatherings (Bock, Cochran, and Beeghley 1987).

One study has shown that Protestant adolescents are less likely to use alcohol than is true of Catholics. Fifty percent of Protestant adolescents and 69% of Catholic adolescents involved in that study used alcohol. In fact, Catholics had the highest prevalence of alcohol drinking during adolescence, compared to any other religion and compared to those without any religion. Among Latter-day Saints or Mormons, there is a significant reduction in alcohol drinking between the 94% who attend church services weekly and those who do not attend on a weekly basis. Among all others there appears to be no significant difference between those who attend church weekly and those who do not attend that often (Merrill, Folsom, and Christopherson 2005).

It is no secret that college students generally drink more alcohol than others who are of college student age but not so enrolled. National data indicate that 66.4% of full-time college students ages 18 to 22 drink alcohol as compared to 54.1% of nonstudents of the same age. This amount of drinking impairs academic performance; damages social relationships; and leads to unsafe sexual activity, blackouts, and unforeseen injuries (O'Malley and Johnson 2003).

The influence of religion on the level of college student drinking is visible. An interest in religion, however expressed, has been linked to a decrease in the amount of drinking by college students. Frequency of prayer has been linked to a decrease in alcohol consumption as has internalization of religious values (Von Dras, Schmitt, and Marx 2007).

It is evident that alcohol and the companionship the "bar scene" provides give alcohol consumers a sense of belonging and a good deal of social support. This is also true of church attendance, so that it is not surprising that those who attend religious services on a regular basis are less likely to use alcohol than those not so inclined. The same may be said of those who believe there is a God as compared to atheists. Religious practice, including observation of rituals and ceremonies, similarly reduces alcohol use. In sum, it is legitimate to hold that there is an inverse relationship between alcohol use and religiosity in whatever form it may appear (Nelms et al. 2007).

All humans have to deal with stressful life events. Therefore, alcohol is popular among those who are at the margin of the adult status-role, having left adolescence behind most recently. Alcohol and the situations in which alcohol is consumed provide social support to many who are marginalized for any reason. Religion and the situations in which religion is practiced also provide social support for

Photo 4.1: The Archbishop of Washington, Cardinal Theodore McCarrick, discusses "Bringing Spirituality Into a Busy Life" at a Washington nightclub.

adolescents and others, so that those associated with religion are less in need of visiting bars and nightclubs in order to find others with whom to consume alcohol. It is evident, therefore, that involvement in religion is a significant predictor of the frequency of alcohol use and that religiousness is related to lower use of alcohol among college students (Nelms et al. 2007).

Another group of alcohol users who have gained a good deal of attention for their alcohol dependency have been the clergy. Unlike students, who usually are not responsible for the lives of others, clergy are by definition most responsible for entire congregations. Therefore, alcohol-dependent priests and ministers are particularly marginalized for conduct that is either condemned or at least viewed as detrimental to the status-role of the clerical calling. It has been proposed that clergy drink alcohol because they seek to make themselves feel more powerful. Research has demonstrated that even light drinking allows the alcohol user to view himself or herself as being more powerful and that those who drink heavily are more likely to believe that they have great influence over others than is true of nondrinkers. Likewise, those who seek to influence others indirectly drink alcohol only modestly (McClalland 1971).

Sorensen (1973) concluded from a study of alcoholic and nonalcoholic clergy that clergy who were frustrated in their power needs were more likely to drink heavily than those who had no such needs. According to Sorensen, priests who have been limited in their involvement with social movements drink heavily, so as to compensate for their loss of power subsequent to limitations imposed by higher authority. Alcoholic priests also seemed more intent on influencing their superiors and parishioners and having their power recognized. Because these power needs are usually frustrated, such priests have a greater proclivity for becoming alcoholics than those not needing power.

Because alcohol addiction is of major concern to Catholic clergy, the American Catholic community has established two facilities for the treatment of alcohol-dependent male and female religious in the United States collectively called Guest House. The facility for female religious is located in Lake Orion, Michigan, and that for male patients is located in Rochester, Minnesota. These patients may be priests, deacons, seminarians, and others. The function of this residency is to provide behavioral health and addiction treatment. The treatment is gender specific and seeks to treat all who apply, including those who cannot pay for their stay at Guest House. Religion is very much in evidence at Guest House and is viewed as a source of resistance to addiction (Wikipedia 2017a).

Roy Barkley's (1990) *The Catholic Alcoholic* deals with the harm alcohol can do to the individual, the family, and society. Its author claims that many readers have recovered by reading this book, a claim hard to support.

Religion has impacted Alcoholics Anonymous (A.A.) since its inception in Akron, Ohio, in 1935. This can be observed despite the insistence of A.A. members that theirs is not a religion. That belief is promoted on the grounds that A.A. does not support a particular theology or denomination. However, from a sociological point of view, it could be argued that A.A. is indeed a religion, because it exhibits conditions that are the essence of religious groups everywhere. Thus,

A.A. separates the mundane, the ordinary, from the spiritual, the otherworldly, or, as A.A. calls it, "a higher power." A.A., like all religions, includes fellowship such as communion among members designed to give the believer support and encouragement. Like all religions, A.A. provides a written guide to living called "the Big Book" and views some persons as founders, namely Bill W. and Dr. Bob. These persons and objects are held in high regard and are referred to with respect similar to that found among all religious folk concerning their founders, prophets, objects, and books. A.A. also has ceremonies, meetings, and activities as well as a doctrine called the Twelve Steps, just as Christianity is based on the Nicene Creed and Judaism on Maimonedes's Principles of Faith (Gellman 1964).

A.A. provides its followers with a system of meaning, which is true of all religions. A.A. also interprets the relationship of man to man and man to the universe, as is true of all religions, even as a system of norms and values is proclaimed by A.A. in a manner similar to all religions. Finally, A.A. practices conversion in a manner similar to religious conversions. All this leads to the reasonable conclusion that A.A. is a religion (Petrunik 1972).

Alcohol and Education

Alcohol use begins at a time when almost all adolescents attend school. Therefore, it is evident that school-based efforts to reduce the risks associated with drinking alcohol should have more success than any other method. Alcohol consumption starts among some children at the young age of 10 when children are enrolled in grades four to five. By the time children reach the ninth grade, at least one half have had experience with drinking alcohol, and at college age very few have not been involved (Kosterman and Hawkins 2000).

Programs designed to intervene in drinking alcohol by young students have mainly focused on middle schools on the grounds that children younger than middle school age are seldom involved and that those old enough to attend high school can no longer be reached. Of particular concern are young students who engage in binge drinking and those who "act out" because they are drunk. Because nearly 40% of children start drinking alcohol in the eighth grade, such intervention can have an influence on alcohol abuse, however defined. Drinking alcohol is regarded as a male status symbol in many areas of the country but particularly among so many students who know little if anything about the risk factors alcohol brings with it (Komro, Perry, and Veblen-Morrison 2008).

To be successful in preventing alcohol abuse and its consequences among high school students and those younger, a program must focus on peer pressure to drink and to drink to excess. Such intervention needs to counteract the belief that alcohol use is "cool" and to show that it is not common among the very young. Social skills that help a student to resist pressure to drink alcohol need also to be taught by means of role-playing in small groups. This is best achieved by using peers to influence others to resist alcohol use. Such intervention must be repeated grade after grade over years in order to be effective (Perry et al. 2002). In Chapter 13, we discuss such programs that focus on youth, whose goal is to prevent them from being involved in substance abuse. We evaluate the effectiveness of the Just Say No campaign and the Drug Abuse Resistance Education (D.A.R.E.) program in its various iterations, such as the original program and the newer keepin' it REAL curriculum.

Nationwide, about one half of high school seniors consume alcohol every month; of this group, one third are drunk once a month. This means that intervention at the middle school level is not very effective and that alcohol education should begin in grade school before most children have ever used alcohol. Such early intervention is needed because alcohol can cause considerable damage to growing young people such as impairment of key brain functions (Squeglia, Jacobus, and Tapert 2009).

Because popular culture confounds masculinity with drinking alcohol, high school and college sports coaches have a good deal of influence on school athletes. This is almost universal, because American schools elevate sports achievement above academics both in secondary schools and in colleges and universities. The Centers for Disease Control and Prevention estimates that 63.2% of high school students have used alcohol and that 17% have consumed five drinks or more consecutively in what is commonly called binge drinking. Moreover, 20% had ridden in a vehicle with a driver who had been drinking, and 7.8% had themselves driven under the influence of alcohol (Kann et al. 2016). Most high school students believe that there is no harm in drinking alcohol, although alcohol is associated with four of the primary causes of death among individuals 10 to 24 years old. These are motor vehicle crashes, unintentional injuries, suicide, and homicide. In addition, the risk of contracting sexually transmitted diseases

Irfan Khan/Los Angeles Times/Getty Images

Photo 4.2: High school students see the results of drinking and driving.

increases considerably among those who use alcohol regularly. In schools, alcohol use is directly related to physical fighting, damage to school property, and poor academic achievement. Such students are also far more likely to run away from home, to steal, and to engage in vandalism. Those who begin drinking before age 15 are also more likely to become lifelong dependents on alcohol (Johnston, O'Malley, and Bachman 2005).

These consequences of drinking alcohol are found to be more frequent among high school athletes than among the majority of high school students. Coaches are evidently aware of this, for 80% of high school coaches report that they have talked to students about drinking. In view of the masculinity-alcohol connection, such talk has been largely ineffective despite suspensions and expulsions from athletic events. There are also programs and educational materials devoted to alcohol education, all without much success (U.S. Department of Justice 1998).

There are some schools in which coaches are required to talk to athletes about the dangers of drinking. Unless required to do so, few coaches want to deal with this issue for a number of reasons. One of these reasons is that a good number of coaches underestimate the number of alcohol-related problems associated with their students. Furthermore, it takes a number of alcohol-related events to make coaches and others aware that alcohol abuse exists within the American culture (Dobosz and Beaty 1999).

Among college students, alcohol drinking becomes a much more dangerous condition than is true of high school students. This is because college students have more money to spend than high school students and therefore can buy more alcohol. No doubt the more money college students can spend, the greater their use of alcohol, a phenomenon also found in the general population. For example, a 10% increase in the income of college students leads to a 3.4% increase in alcohol sales. In fact, some students spend over $500 a month on alcohol, and a large proportion of college students spend $100 to $200 on alcohol per month (B. Martin et al. 2009).

Consequently, the cost of drinks affects alcohol consumption. Because most college students are not wealthy and do not have large financial resources, any increase in the cost of a beer or other drink will reduce the number of binge drinkers and others. Bar owners in college towns are, of course, aware of this and therefore likely to lower prices and reward college customers with drink specials at unusually low prices (Hingson et al. 2009).

Academic performance is also affected by the use of alcohol. Students with an A average consume about 3.4 alcoholic drinks per week, whereas those who average grades of D to F drink nearly 10 drinks per week (Presley, Meilman, and Lyerla 1996).

There are those who believe that the federal drinking age should be lowered from 21 to 18, because the current prohibition leads to a great deal of hidden drinking, which a lower age would reveal. The federal government does not have such a law but instead has withheld highway construction funds from any state unwilling to maintain such a law.

Many college students believe that all college students drink a great deal. This is no doubt an unrealistic estimate, despite the fact that there is a culture of drinking alcohol on American campuses. It is therefore important to reach students with media that students use such as Facebook, Snapchat, and YouTube.

Because sports and alcohol consumption are both regarded as indications of masculinity in American culture, major sports events, and particularly important football games, become occasions for excessive alcohol consumption on the campuses of such football universities as Syracuse, Ohio State, and Oklahoma. This is also true of other major sports events such as basketball games. Such alcohol abuse can occur at home, in a bar, or at a stadium. American culture condones celebratory drinking, which is endorsed by public opinion and advertised by alcohol producers (see Chapter 6 for examples of commercials for alcohol) (Rabow and Duncan-Schill 1995).

Celebratory drinking leads to increased alcohol abuse among already heavy drinkers. That, in turn, leads to rioting, including the destruction of property and assaults on campuses and in the streets.

Not all college students regard themselves as sports fans. There are, however, some students and many others who may be called sports fanatics, who smash windows, set cars afire, throw rocks and bottles at police, and obstruct traffic. Colleges where a majority of students are sports fans also are more likely to damage others than is true in schools that do not invest heavily in sports (Falk 2005). No better example of this dictum was the scandal resulting from the excessive devotion to football at Pennsylvania State University in 2011.

Although men consume more alcohol than women, a significant number of female college students also engage in alcohol abuse. This fact may seem to negate the masculinity hypothesis but instead reinforces it, because most female drinking on college campuses is related to seeking acceptance by male students, who include in their desire for masculine status dominance over women. Women, seeking to please "the big men on campus," therefore consume alcohol in excessive fashion, despite the strong possibility of risky sexual behavior (see Chapter 7 for a discussion of alcohol and risky sexual behavior).

For both men and women students, impulse control is a deciding factor in alcohol abuse on campus. Those with strong impulse control are evidently more likely to abstain from drinking altogether or to drink moderately. This is illustrated by the finding that the average student consumes 5.7 drinks on the day of an important game and 8 times as many students drink alcohol on such a day than would do so on a normal day (Martens, O'Connor, and Beck 2006).

Alcohol and Government

There is hardly an area of American life that is not targeted by some government agency anxious to regiment the American public. It is therefore not surprising that bureaucrats are involved in regulating the alcohol consumption of American citizens, including occupational alcohol use.

There are federal regulations concerning alcohol use in so-called safety-sensitive jobs, which reputedly reduce the negative effects of drinking alcohol shortly before or while working. A digit dial telephone survey revealed that more than 15% or 19 million of the American workforce had used alcohol directly before work and that 7% or nearly 9 million of the workforce had used alcohol during the workday and worked under the influence of alcohol; more than 11 million worked with a hangover (Frone 2006).

The U.S. Department of Transportation (DOT) regulates workplace alcohol intake by some workers who operate trucks, ships, and railroad trains. The DOT also regulates alcohol intake for pilots and air traffic controllers. The Nuclear Regulatory Commission regulates alcohol consumption among operators of nuclear power plants. These regulations concern the period prior to beginning work, during which alcohol intake is prohibited, and the percent of blood alcohol concentration (BAC), which may be cause for dismissal, fines, or loss of license (U.S. Department of Transportation 2012).

Although there are confirmed alcoholics working in numerous jobs around the country, low-level drinkers are also seen as a danger to working people. Low-level drinkers may have no more than a little beer at any time, but they are nevertheless a danger to those working in their vicinity without being recognized. Numerous studies have shown that there is no safe level for alcohol exposure within safety-sensitive occupations. Furthermore, there is a residual effect resulting from drinking alcohol, which is that so-called hangovers can cause nausea, headaches, and fatigue leading to unsafe behavior (Holloway 1995).

In 1987, the U.S. Transportation Research Board, a division of the National Academy of Sciences, recommended that the DOT specify zero as the required level of alcohol among all commercial transportation operators. This recommendation is based on the evidence that, even 8 to 9 hours after moderate or heavy drinking, impairment continues.

In 1986, the U.S. government developed the Drug Free Workplace Program designed to test employees with safety-sensitive functions for the use of illicit drugs. This was to be administered by the Department of Health and Human Services. This program was applied with greater urgency after the 1990 conviction of three Northwest Airlines pilots for flying drunk. The three were convicted of flying under the influence a Boeing 727 with 91 passengers onboard from Fargo, North Dakota, to Minneapolis, Minnesota. This case was particularly egregious, because all three members of the flight crew—the captain, the first officer, and the flight engineer—were intoxicated. The three were the first to be convicted of the 1986 law directed at the use of prohibited substances and alcohol in the flight industry ("Prison for Three Northwest Pilots" 1990).

In 1991, Congress enacted the Transportation Employees Testing Act, which made alcohol testing mandatory for transportation employees with safety functions. This led the DOT to develop detailed guidelines for implementing workplace alcohol and drug testing. Those guidelines became part of the Code of Federal Regulations, which describes the procedures by which alcohol and drug tests are to be conducted. The Federal Aviation Administration adopted rules that require airlines to test flight crews, including flight attendants, flight instructors, and air traffic controllers, for alcohol misuse. Consequently, testing on randomly selected employees is therefore the principal method of preventing dangers arising from alcohol use by air traffic employees. Supervisors are trained to detect alcohol misuse by such employees. Such suspicion may be based on appearance, behavior, breath, body color, or impaired speech (Li et al. 2007).

An increase in the price of alcoholic drinks may in part help to reduce drinking behavior and have an impact on promoting the safety of air travel. The cost of alcoholic drinks is determined by the tax imposed on alcohol by all states of the union. Such taxes range from a beer tax of 2% in Colorado to 8% in the District of Columbia; a number of states charge a 7% sales tax, and others impose a tax of 4% to 5% for beer. Table wine and spirit taxes are a good deal higher (Tax Foundation 2009–2010).

In view of the numerous automobile crashes that result from drunk driving, as well as such other alcohol-related negative consequences as unwanted pregnancies, cirrhosis of the liver, alcohol dependency, poor grades, marital conflict, and others, it is of interest whether an increase in the price of alcohol as well as the amount of nonworking hours has a positive effect on the consumers of alcohol.

The evidence suggests that increases in the weekly hours of work are inversely associated with binge drinking. People whose free time has been reduced engage

AAron Ontiveroz/The Denver Post/Getty Images

Photo 4.3: Shopping for wine in a Colorado supermarket.

in less binge drinking than they performed before their work hours were increased. Likewise, an increase in taxes on alcohol reduces some drinking (Liang and Huang 2008).

Federal excise taxes on beer, distilled spirits, and wine have increased minimally since the 1990s, so that in real, inflation-adjusted value, taxes have declined since then. This means that a $35 tax on a barrel of beer in 1991 is equivalent to a $9 tax in 2013. Because all states tax beer and wine, and some also tax distilled spirits, taxes also impinge on the price of alcohol, although hardly any state has increased such taxes in years. However, prices of alcoholic beverages have increased more than taxes in recent years (Kinkel 2005).

After the repeal of Prohibition, some states began to monopolize the distribution of alcohol for off-premises consumption. This is done either by allowing only state-run stores to sell alcohol or by licensing alcohol retailers and wholesalers. Thus, exclusive state-run alcohol distribution raises the price. States also influence beer prices by limiting promotions such as happy hour specials, selling beer by the pitcher, or allowing free sampling of alcoholic drinks. Some states also prohibit quantity discounts. States that adopted these policies based them on the argument that these measures limit excessive drinking (Chalupka, Saffer, and Grossman 1993).

A number of economists have studied the relationship between price and alcohol consumption. These studies reveal that a 1% increase in price results in a 0.3% decrease in consumption, with corresponding decreases in consumption as prices increase. It is not surprising that price increases affect moderate drinkers more than abusive drinkers, who are evidently less responsive to price increases than normal consumers. These studies also find that college-age drinkers are most affected by price increases, because adolescent consumers seldom have the money to meet higher prices. Because drinking habits are formed at a young age, it is probable that increases in price by means of higher taxes would limit the number of young adults who abuse alcohol, thereby also reducing the number of adults who acquire alcohol abuse at a young age (Young and Bielinska 2006).

Increases in beer taxes also reduce fatal motor vehicle crashes, particularly among youths. Several studies have confirmed that drinking and driving can be reduced by increasing taxes on alcohol, so that injuries and deaths from motor vehicle accidents are also reduced. Furthermore, increases in alcohol prices also reduce domestic and youth violence, particularly the severe violence committed by some men on women. This is also true of the probability of assault of any kind, including bar brawls and other violent conduct (Markowitz 2000).

At one time, 18 states had established state-owned liquor stores, in part because they sought to control excessive drinking after Prohibition ended. These states were Alabama, Idaho, Iowa, Maine, Maryland, Michigan, Mississippi, Montana, New Hampshire, North Carolina, Ohio, Oregon, Pennsylvania, Utah, Vermont, Virginia, West Virginia, and Wyoming.

About two thirds of these states had established government monopolies, whereas one third used the private license system. A number of these monopolies have been abolished in recent years, so that private liquor stores could enter that business.

In Alabama, all liquor stores are state run. In 16 other states, there are partial state operations and some private alcohol sales (Wikipedia 2017b). This means that in a number of states wine and beer can be sold in grocery stores, whereas spirits are sold only in state-operated stores. The argument in favor of state-run liquor stores that state control of alcohol reduces deaths and traffic fatality rates is not supported by the data. Statistics show 87,798 alcohol-attributable deaths (AAD) in the United States between 2006 and 2010, or an age-adjusted alcohol-attributable death rate of 27.9 per 100,000 inhabitants of the country. Ranking the states' death rates related to alcohol from highest to lowest, New Mexico exhibited a death rate related to alcohol of 51.2 persons per 100,000, whereas New Jersey had a death rate related to alcohol of 19.1 per 100,000. Neither of these states has state-operated liquor stores (Wikipedia 2017b). Alabama's age-adjusted AAD is between that of New Mexico and New Jersey at 31.1 per 100,000 population ("Alcohol-Related Deaths" 2014).

Binge drinking, which is undoubtedly dangerous, is also unaffected by any state-run monopoly. It is more common in New York than in states bordering New York.

Those who argue that state monopolies create income for those states that use this system overlook the evidence that citizens will generally buy their liquor in a nearby state without a state monopoly, because monopoly states charge more than private stores facing competition. A study of the prices of alcohol in Pennsylvania, traditionally a monopoly state, found that average wine and beer prices are lower in all states bordering Pennsylvania and that the state loses about $3.5 million annually because citizens buy their liquor elsewhere (Commonwealth Foundation 2011).

It is for that reason alone that raising taxes on alcohol is not an effective way to raise money. For example, in Kentucky, a 2009 alcohol tax increase led to a reduction of income from that alcohol tax of 55%. Another example is the decreased income from alcohol raised by the federal government. When federal excise taxes were raised on the sale of beer, wine, and liquor, the tax raised $2.4 billion less than Congress had forecast (Congressional Research Service 2015).

Alcohol taxes are regressive. This means that such taxes impact the poor much more than the wealthy. The working poor are most affected by such tax increases, for over one third of all alcohol consumers in the United States come from families with an income of less than $50,000 annually. The poorest of all Americans, those making $20,000 or less a year, pay 18 times the alcohol tax compared to incomes of $200,000 per year.

Jobs are lost when alcohol taxes are increased. Unemployment in the nation's hospitality industry is above the national average. Evidently, therefore, raising taxes will increase unemployment. It has been estimated that if the federal government raises taxes on alcohol as was done in 1991, then 160,000 hospitality jobs are at risk. This is true because hotels, restaurants, and liquor stores gain their income from the sale of beer, wine, and spirits. These taxes hurt low-income hotel and restaurant workers the most because they are the targets of layoffs when business income declines. In Massachusetts a sales tax increase led to the loss of 800 jobs (American Beer Institute 2013).

Alcohol and Public Opinion

Because the use of alcohol is widespread in the United States, even as its abuse has caused a great many social and health problems, it is evident that Americans face a true dilemma concerning its use. Alcohol is present at almost all American celebrations from birthdays to weddings, holidays, and even ordinary dinners. Yet alcohol use has led to car crashes with resulting deaths and maiming, drowning, snowmobile accidents, falls, unintentional injuries, crime, homicides, assaults, domestic violence, risky sex, liver cirrhosis, poor school and work performance, and many other consequences. These consequences of alcohol use have led legislatures to pass many laws attempting to reduce, if not eliminate, these dangers. These measures receive a great deal of support from the American public, with particular emphasis on increased alcohol education as well as laws pertaining to drinking and driving (Wagenaar 1993).

Public support for restricting some advertising of alcoholic beverages is also high. Media such as television and billboards have been favorite targets of alcohol advertisers, although support for banning alcohol on television sporting events has been less popular. There is considerable support for the notion that drinking should be prohibited in public places (Wagenaar et al. 2000).

Surveys have shown that 42% of Americans favor state ownership of liquor stores, although the majority who hold that view live in states that do not have state-owned liquor stores. Only 37% of Americans favor tax increases on liquor unless the purpose of the tax increase is to deal with problems resulting from the use of alcohol. In that case 82% of those surveyed favor a tax increase on alcohol (Crow and Bailey 1995).

It is by no means surprising that any survey of public opinion concerning the use of alcohol is affected by the respondent's drinking behavior. Those who score high on drinking alcohol are less supportive of all measures seeking limits to alcohol consumption. Women are more supportive of alcohol control policies than are men. This is also true of those who view themselves as politically conservative.

Benefits and Costs of Alcohol

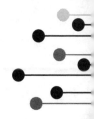

Benefits of Alcohol

Alcohol and the Life Cycle

Drinking alcohol is an ancient tradition practiced among the Greeks and Romans, who even labeled one of their gods Bacchus or Liber, the god of wine. These ancient peoples celebrated weddings and other events by becoming intoxicated, a condition viewed as an important means of enjoyment and recreation.

In American culture alcohol plays a role throughout life, and it may even begin before birth if a pregnant woman drinks. Because alcohol can endanger the fetus, there has been a public health campaign against the use of alcohol by pregnant women. This campaign consists of warnings by physicians and a label placed on every container of alcoholic beverages sold in the United States (Abel 1998).

Nevertheless, the Centers for Disease Control and Prevention (CDC) has shown that the drinking rate for pregnant women is 15.1%, of whom 7.6% engage in binge drinking. This can result in a child developing fetal alcohol syndrome, which can include facial deformities or mental retardation, as well as a low IQ or prematurity. Even aggressive behavior among school-age children may be the result of maternal use of alcohol. It is significant that 10% of pregnant women who use alcohol are college graduates (CDC 2008).

The failure of some pregnant women to protect their fetus from alcohol is related to the belief that alcohol improves the enjoyment of social gatherings such as weddings, from which pregnant women are hardly excluded and are therefore tempted to introduce their unborn child to alcohol.

Alcohol is present at almost all American weddings with various results. There are some weddings at which alcohol is consumed that feature anxiety and hostility by both sides. Alcohol removes all of this as the guests toast each other and the bride and groom with alcohol. These toasts begin with a toast to the bride delivered by the best man. Then anyone else may toast the bride or groom by tapping their glass with a spoon or fork, followed by whatever the guest wishes to say.

As the drinking continues and the bride becomes as drunk as others, some revelers participate in a "keg stand," which consists of having the standee lay his hands on a keg of beer while two or more strong men lift up his legs until he stands on the keg on his hands. This procedure may involve the bride or groom, so that at some weddings the bride is hoisted on the beer keg in her wedding gown. Some

Photo 5.1: Alcohol and the life cycle: pouring champagne at a wedding.

weddings also include other guests such as Grandma in the keg stand. This conduct is predicated on the assumption that drunken behavior is "fun." In American culture participating in such fun is required of those seeking to belong, even if not everyone would privately agree. The culture and peer pressure decide what is enjoyable and what is boring or even despicable.

Some weddings include open bars, so that all drinking is at the expense of the father of the bride or anyone else willing to pay. There are some weddings at which a cash bar is maintained after the open bar has been in use for 3 or 4 hours. All this drinking leads to a great deal of intoxication by the wedding guests as well as the bride and groom. Semi-open bars allow the guests only a limited number or kind of drinks and require that some drinks are at the expense of the wedding guests.

An open bar involves the chance that some wedding guests will indulge in behavior leading to accidents or risky sexual conduct. At a New York wedding some guests left the wedding in a speedboat. The driver of the boat was drunk and drove the boat into an abutment, killing two passengers (Mishane 2013).

Some people become belligerent when drunk, so that there are weddings at which fights between the guests lead to an undignified brawl and the destruction of the wedding party. A wedding photographer recalls how fighting broke out between two sides of the family at a wedding at which inordinate amounts of alcohol were consumed. The wedding ended when the police were called (Friedman 2005).

The *New York Times* reported that at one wedding a 2-year-old got hold of a bottle and then drank a large portion of wine as no one observed her. She died a few hours later ("Alcohol Kills Baby" 1930).

Not only fighting, but also rape, has occurred as a result of excessive drinking at weddings. This comes about because the eventual victim is so drunk that she cannot defend herself if attacked. Most victims who are drunk take the risk of associating intimately with someone not well known to them or under circumstances that make the victim vulnerable. Moreover, those who drink a great deal are likely to allow rapists to furnish them with a drink or more until their victimization is assured (Namibia 2012).

For some people, weddings are a danger because they are recovering alcoholics who cannot attend without risking a resumption of their destructive alcohol intake. Such people may feel pressured to attend the wedding of a close relative or friend, only to end up drinking to excess again.

Drinking alcohol is not confined to the young. The old also drink alcohol in the company of family and friends. This is not surprising because the old are as much in need of companionship as are other Americans. This means that the old, who are usually retired, need to adjust to life without work routines and are therefore more in need of companionship than those still working.

Not everyone drinks alcohol. Like so much human behavior, alcohol consumption is related to differential association in that people drink because others in their reference group do so, even as some abstain for the same reason. The old in American culture, generally deprived of association with younger people, are confined by American age stratification to association with others of their age, either through private friendships or by means of community centers or nursing homes. The old drink alcohol with those they know and those who will tolerate them. Because the United States exhibits an unusual degree of age segregation, drinking alcohol among them is subject to differential reinforcement in the sense that each person drinks alcohol as much or as little as his or her reference group demands. Nevertheless, confirmed drinkers and certainly alcoholics will sustain drinking mainly because of the effects of the alcohol itself (Akers et al. 1979).

Alcohol Profits

A second benefit of alcohol use is the profits earned by the alcohol industry and the political establishment. In 2014, about $110 billion was earned in wages paid to the nearly 4.6 million employees engaged in the production, distribution, and sale of alcohol. In that year, the alcohol industry contributed $475 billion to the U.S. economy (Distilled Spirits Council of the United States [DISCUS] 2017). Taxes on alcohol products are a major source of income for local, state, and federal government. In 2010, state and local taxes on alcoholic beverages amounted to $41 billion. When federal taxes on alcohol consumption in the United States are included, in 2014, taxes were 54% of the price of an average 750 milliliter 80 proof bottle of distilled spirits (DISCUS 2017).

Restaurants and bars make most of their income from the sale of alcohol. In Las Vegas, Nevada, the Tao Las Vegas earns 75% of its income from alcohol. This is not possible for all such establishments because, in states other than Nevada, there are numerous limits on the amount of profit from alcohol allowed a restaurant, the result of laws restricting the hours during which alcohol may be bought and served and the prohibition of public intoxication. In Nevada, there are no restrictions on the time or days during which alcohol may be sold (White 2017).

Most states require that someone evidently inebriated may not be served more drinks. In some states, alcohol cannot be sold on Sunday, and in other states laws determine where bars may be placed in restaurants that serve children. The average profit earned from the sale of alcohol in restaurants is 30%. Worldwide alcohol sales have increased so much that it has been estimated that due to population increases, by 2018, global sales will reach $1.3 trillion (Morley 2011).

The consumption of alcohol requires the cooperation of numerous employees of the alcohol industry. Included are those who sell alcohol and those who drive the trucks that deliver drinks to bars and restaurants. According to the Bureau of Labor Statistics, the mean income of sales personnel and truck drivers in the alcohol industry is $33,100. Sales representatives earn about $55,770, and their supervisors earn slightly more at $57,670. Laborers in the alcohol industry only earn about $28,650, and machine operators receive about $34,000 to $41,000. Managers in the alcohol-producing industry earn about $100,000. The chief executives in the industry earn about $145,320.

A good deal less is earned by those who serve alcoholic beverages. The 538,000 bartenders in the United States earn an average of $21,630, and servers and hosts of both genders earn no more than about $20,000 to $32,000 annually (U.S. Department of Labor 2012).

Alcohol and Health

Mortality

Because drunk driving and numerous physical disabilities are associated with excessive consumption of alcohol, the benefits of drinking alcohol are generally overlooked. Yet a considerable number of scientific studies reveal that moderate consumption of alcohol reduces the chances of acquiring a number of diseases and increases longevity among the consuming population (Ford 1988).

Because heart disease is the principal cause of death in the United States, it is important to note that drinking a moderate amount of alcohol results in a reduction of cardiovascular disease and particularly coronary artery disease, resulting in a decrease in heart disease from 40% to 60%. This is a conclusion reached by researchers at the National Institute on Alcohol Abuse and Alcoholism (T. Pearson 1996).

The Nutrition Committee of the American Heart Association notes that "the lowest mortality occurs in those who consume one or two drinks a day," and the World Health Organization Technical Committee on Cardiovascular Diseases holds that "the relationship between moderate alcohol consumption and reduced death from cardiovascular disease could no longer be doubted" (Wilkie 1997). A Harvard study found the risk of death from all causes to be 21% to 28% lower among men who drank alcohol moderately, compared to abstainers (Camargo 1997).

A worldwide study of the effects of moderate consumption of alcohol is significant. Women who drink one to two alcoholic beverages each day and men who drink two to four drinks a day have a lower risk of mortality than those who abstain. This conclusion was reached by analyzing 34 studies of 1,015,835 subjects around the world (Di Castelnuovo 2006).

These worldwide results indicate that despite differences in nutrition, the benefits of consuming alcohol in moderation are the same in all cultures. This is confirmed by reviewing a number of studies concerned with alcohol consumption and undertaken in various parts of the world. For example, a large-scale study in China found that middle-aged men who drank moderately had a nearly 20% lower mortality rate than abstainers (Yuan 1997).

Likewise, a British analysis of 12,000 male physicians found that moderate drinkers had the lowest risk of death from all causes over 13 years. A cancer research center in Honolulu found that persons with moderate alcohol intake "appear to have a significantly lower risk of dying than non-drinkers." An Italian study of 1,536 men aged 45 to 65 found that about 2 years of life were gained by moderate drinkers (one to four drinks per day) in comparison with occasional and heavy drinkers. A 14-year study of nearly 3,000 residents of an Australian community found that abstainers were twice as likely to enter a nursing home as people who were moderate drinkers. Drinkers also spent less time in hospitals and were less likely to die during the period of the study (McCallum, Simons, and Simons 2003).

General Health

A nationwide survey in the United States found that daily moderate drinkers experienced significantly less acute hospitalization than was true of abstainers or binge drinkers. Another study of nearly 20,000 participants found that moderate consumption of any alcohol, whether beer, wine, or spirits, was linked to better health compared to abstinence (Artalejo 2001).

A Dutch study of alcohol consumers concluded that moderate drinkers under stress were less likely to be absent from work than were either abstainers or heavy drinkers and concluded that abstinence is at least as unhealthy as excessive drinking (Vasser 1998).

Exercise and moderate drinking of alcohol slow down the health deterioration that occurs with aging. This is a conclusion reached by a study involving 2,500 people aged 65 and older who were followed for 8 years. Those who drank alcohol regularly but not to excess had fewer difficulties with their daily activities and physical functions (Wang 2002).

Heart Disease

Because heart disease is the leading cause of death in the United States, it is significant that drinking alcohol in moderation leads to a reduction in cardiovascular disease. The National Institute on Alcohol Abuse and Alcoholism (NIAAA; 2015) has found that moderate drinking is beneficial to heart health.

This is an important finding because heart disease kills about 1 million Americans every year. The Nutrition Committee of the American Heart Association concurs with this finding and published that "the lowest mortality occurs in those who consume one or two drinks per day" (T. Pearson 1996:3023).

Moderate alcohol consumption is associated with better endothelial function. The endothelium is a single layer of cells that line the blood vessels. Such drinking also has a favorable effect on cardiovascular disease (CVD). Another study showed that those who never drank alcohol were of greater risk of having high levels of CRP, or c-reactive protein, and IL-6, or interleukin 6, than those who drank moderately. CRP and IL-6 are predictors of heart attacks (Price 2004).

A study of 18,455 men from a physicians' health study revealed that those originally consuming one drink a week or fewer who increased their consumption to up to six drinks per week had a 29% reduction in CVD compared to those who did not increase their consumption. Men originally consuming one to six drinks per week who increased their consumption moderately had an additional 15% decrease in CVD risk (Sesso et al. 2000).

Alcohol promotes good health because it increases HDL or "good" cholesterol and decreases LDL or bad cholesterol. Alcohol also decreases thrombosis, commonly called blood-clotting, by reducing platelet aggregation. Alcohol reduces a blood-clotter called fibrinogen, but it increases the process by which blood dissolves. Furthermore, alcohol reduces coronary artery spasms in response to stress, increases coronary blood flow, reduces blood pressure, reduces blood insulin levels, and increases estrogen levels (Dairdron 1989).

Stroke

A review of 26 research studies found that consuming two alcoholic drinks a day is associated with a reduced risk of stroke. An American Stroke Association study of over 22,000 men found that light and moderate alcohol consumption significantly reduces the overall risk of stroke. A study published by the *Journal of the American Medical Association* found that consuming one or two drinks a day can reduce the risk of stroke by about half. It also found a protective effect of alcohol occurring among both men and women. This supports the National

Stroke Association's Stroke Prevention Guidelines regarding the beneficial effects of moderate alcohol consumption and the report by the American Heart Association that shows abstainers' risk of stroke to be double that of those who drink in moderation (Sacco 2001).

Diabetes

A review of 15 studies concerning diabetes and alcohol consumption found that moderate drinkers are less likely to have type 2 diabetes than abstainers and heavy drinkers. Teetotalers and heavy drinkers have an equal chance of getting the disease, according to this review conducted in the United States, Japan, Korea, Germany, Finland, the Netherlands, and the United Kingdom. Involved were 369,862 men and women followed for 12 years. These subjects were 30% less likely to develop the disease than either abstainers or heavy drinkers (Kopper 2005).

Among women aged 40 to 70 years, moderate drinking of alcohol was associated with a lower risk of developing type 2 diabetes in a large study conducted in the Netherlands for 6 years. The authors also reported that these results pertain to older women as well (Beulens et al. 2005).

Alzheimer's Disease and Dementia

Research on 7,460 women aged 65 and older found that those who consumed up to three drinks a day scored significantly better than nondrinkers on global cognitive functions, including such things as concentration, memory, abstract reasoning, and language. The investigators adjusted or controlled for such factors as educational level and income that might affect the results, but the significant positive relationships remained (Espeland et al. 2006).

Graham McDougall (2004) presented a paper at the meetings of the National Congress on the State of Science in Nursing Research titled "Older Women's Cognitive and Affective Responses to Moderate Drinking." McDougall found that moderate drinking among older women can benefit memory, according to research funded by the National Institutes of Health. Moderate drinkers performed better on instrumental everyday tasks and had stronger memory self-efficacy and improved memory performance. The performance memory tests included such topics as remembering a story or route, finding hidden objects, implementing intentions, and connecting random numbers and letters. In all cases, the group who drank scored better than those who did not drink. Women who drank alcohol in moderation also performed better on attention, concentration, psychomotor skills, verbal associative capacities, and oral fluency.

Similar results have been found in studies around the world including Japan, Italy, and the United Kingdom. An Italian study of 15,807 men and women 65 years old or older showed that only 19% of drinkers were mentally impaired, compared to 29% of abstainers. This relationship continued even when education, age, and health problems were considered (Zuccala 2001).

Scholars from the School of Aging Studies at the University of South Florida and the University of Alabama discovered that drinking alcohol reduces the risk of cognitive decline and dementia in later life. The scholars identified abusing alcohol and abstaining as equally responsible for cognitive decline and dementia (Andel 2005).

Arthritis

A longitudinal study in Sweden and two other studies also conducted in Scandinavia revealed that drinking alcohol is associated with a reduction in rheumatoid arthritis. Two independent case control studies of rheumatoid arthritis were used. The Swedish study used 1,204 cases and 871 controls, and the Danish study used 444 cases and 533 controls. Among alcohol consumers, the quarter with the highest consumption levels had a decreased risk of rheumatoid arthritis of 40% to 50%, compared to the half with the lowest alcohol intake (Kallberg et al. 2009).

A study by Dr. James Maxwell, of the University of Sheffield in England, of 1,877 men and women found that drinking alcohol reduced both the risk and severity of rheumatoid arthritis. Nondrinkers were 4 times more likely to develop rheumatoid arthritis than people who drank alcohol on more than 10 days a month. The risk of developing rheumatoid arthritis decreased according to the frequency of alcohol consumption (J. R. Maxwell et al. 2010).

Cancer

An analysis of data from 12 prospective studies that included 760,044 men and women, who were tracked for 7 to 20 years, found that moderate drinkers are about 37% less likely to develop kidney cancer than are abstainers (J. Lee et al. 2007). Likewise, Morton discovered that nine international studies show that drinking alcohol reduces the risk of non-Hodgkin lymphoma by 27%. The protective effect of alcohol did not vary with the consumption of beer, wine, or distilled spirits (Morton et al. 2005).

A cohort (people born the same year) of 35,156 women aged 55 to 69 years studied over a 9-year period found that alcohol consumption was associated with a significantly lower risk of developing non-Hodgkin lymphoma, compared with abstaining, and the amount of alcohol consumed, rather than the form (such as beer, wine, or distilled spirits), was significant. Alcohol evidently protects against this cancer (Chiu et al. 1999).

Alcohol reduced the risk of Hodgkin lymphoma for both men and women but more so for men, whose risk was lowered by 53% in a population-based case control study in Germany (Nieters 2005).

A study of women identified through the Cancer Surveillance System, a population-based cancer registry in Washington State, found that higher levels of alcohol consumption were associated with lower risk of developing thyroid cancer (Rossing 2000).

The Common Cold

Research has found that moderate drinkers are more resistant than abstainers to five strains of the common cold virus. Those who consume up to three drinks daily had an 85% greater resistance. Those who drink one to two drinks daily had a 65% lower risk, and those who drink fewer than one drink daily had a 30% lower risk than abstainers (S. Cohen 1993).

The foregoing indicates that the use of alcohol in moderation decreases the chances of becoming the victim of almost any disease. Therefore, it is necessary to define moderation. Medical researchers define moderation as one to three drinks a day. Drinking only half that amount is associated with very little health benefits. Very large individuals can consume more than that and may be able to consume four to five drinks a day and still benefit. Yet the same would be excessive for small individuals, so that it is recommended that women imbibe only 30% of male consumption. Recovering alcoholics cannot drink even one drink, which is also true of some who have allergic reactions to alcohol (Mulkamal 2003).

A drink can, of course, be very small or very large, so that two or more drinkers may consume widely disparate amounts of alcohol, although each drinks only one drink. Therefore, it is necessary to keep in mind that a standard drink is one 12-ounce bottle or can of beer, a 5-ounce glass of dinner wine, or one shot of 1 to 1.5 ounces of liquor such as vodka, tequila, or rum (Huang et al. 2002).

U-Shaped Curve

Alcohol is the cause of a good deal of illness as well as death and injury on the highways. In addition, alcohol causes many relational problems leading to spouse and child abuse, loss of employment, and poverty. Furthermore, it has been estimated that there are about 88,000 alcohol-related deaths in the United States each year. All this seems incongruous if compared to the benefits of drinking alcohol just discussed. Therefore, it is evident that there is a U-shaped curve associated with the consumption of alcohol. This means that those who drink one or two drinks a day benefit from the preventive power of alcohol and reduce the risk of suffering disease by about 30%. Yet those who drink five drinks or more each day may be binge drinkers, who risk their health and the chance of injury or death by reason of accident. Risky sexual behavior is also associated with heavy drinking. This includes unprotected sex, acquisition of a social disease, and sexual assault.[1] Excessive drinking by pregnant women can lead to stillbirths and defects in a child, which last for a lifetime. Excessive use of alcohol can also cause alcohol poisoning, which leads to the suppression of the central nervous system and loss of consciousness (American Academy of Pediatrics 2000).

We are therefore confronted with the evidence that moderate consumption of alcohol is beneficial, whereas excessive drinking leads to an early death and to diseases of all kinds, notably cirrhosis of the liver, cancer, heart disease, and dementia. The dilemma confronting alcohol users is that some moderate drinkers become binge drinkers and alcoholics, so that anyone drinking alcohol risks the possibility of alcohol abuse. We cannot therefore predict who will be able to maintain a low level of alcohol use and who will become an abuser.

The Bar Scene

Dealing With Loneliness

Another benefit of alcohol is the connections one may make at a bar. A bar is a site where alcoholic beverages are served. Some bars are attached to nightclubs, where food and lavish entertainment are offered the patrons. Other bars or taverns have no entertainment and very little food. The customers who make these bars possible are mostly single adults, who are driven by loneliness to seek the company of other women and men, even if the contacts available in drinking establishments are only superficial.

According to the U.S. Census, 96 million adults in the United States have no spouse. For every 100 single women there are 88 single available men, mostly concentrated in the older ages. This means that 43% of Americans over the age of 18 are single. Single is defined as someone who has never been married or is divorced or widowed. Sixty-one percent of singles have never been married, 24% are divorced, and 15% are widowed. Thirty-one million single Americans live alone, making up 27% of American households. In 1970, only 17% of Americans lived alone. Forty-six percent, or 52 million singles, maintain a household of which 11.6 million, or 9.9 million mothers and 1.7 million fathers, live with their children.

Seventeen percent of single adults are 65 years old or older, and of these, 766,000 were caring for their grandchildren. In over 6 million households, single adults live together without benefit of marriage, and in 2009, of these, half a million were same-sex couples. As a result, there are nearly 1,000 dating services in the United States that employ 4,300 people and have an income of $489 million annually.

This means that the bar is a vital institution in 21st-century American life, for at least one of its functions is to be "the other" dating service (U.S. Department of Commerce, Bureau of the Census 2009).

Jessica Olien (2013), a writer and contributor to the *Atlantic* and other magazines, describes how she moved from New York City to Portland, Oregon, where she knew no one. She made every effort to connect to people by playing golf, dating, going to bookstores, and visiting bars. Nevertheless, she experienced the horrors of loneliness because she could not connect. Her research on loneliness led her to the conclusion that people who suffer inadequate social interaction are twice as likely to die prematurely as those who have satisfying contacts. She writes that social isolation impairs immune functions and promotes arthritis, diabetes, and heart disease. Olien recorded that 40% of adults were victims of this condition, up from 20% in the 1980s.

John T. Cacioppo (2008), of the University of Chicago Psychology Department, found that loneliness is stigmatized in the United States. It is common that people who are often invited to large and loud cocktail parties and other social events are nevertheless lonely, because the people who surround them mean nothing to them. The key to social satisfaction is relationships with a few relatives and friends on whom we can rely and who can rely on us.

Of course, bars seldom fulfill the need for meaningful relationships. Nevertheless, they relieve the symptoms of loneliness temporarily. This is true of the thousands of salespeople who travel this country day after day, for months and years. There are about 1,800,900 traveling sales representatives in the United States. Their average annual income is about $60,530 (U.S. Department of Labor 2017a), so that some earn a great deal more than that, whereas others can hardly make ends meet. Traveling from city to city and staying in countless hotel rooms is a guarantee for loneliness after the day's work is done. These travelers are indeed ready to visit bars, particularly because bars are an integral part of most hotels.

Those who work in the transportation industry are also absent from home a great deal and need human interaction after work hours. For example, there were 97,900 flight attendants (U.S. Department of Labor 2017b) and nearly 38,980 airplane pilots (U.S. Department of Labor 2017c) working in this country. Many fly long distances without a chance of seeing home for some time. Then there are thousands of long-distance truck drivers who also spend most of their time on the road. This means that high mobility is another catalyst bringing Americans to bars so as to avoid the pain of being alone.

Both women and men are attracted to bars, although there are more men involved in the bar scene than women because more men are single and because more men have traveling occupations.

A poll conducted by *Ask Men,* an online magazine, found that 64% of women go to nightclubs and bars to meet men, 21% want to "see what happens," 12% seek to "have fun," and 3% come with male friends on a date. The majority, seeking a man, wear clothes deemed sexy or revealing. Some will dance alone on the dance floor after arriving with several girlfriends, thereby seeking attention from men without acknowledging this (Muller 2014).

There are also women in bars and nightclubs who aggressively approach men of interest to them. These women ask men to dance or they initiate a conversation with them. Such women will dance around a group of men or on the stage, thereby gaining attention. These women will also arrive with a group of other women but once in the bar will make every effort to talk only with men in an effort to go home with a man. Those who frequent bars report that there are some women in bars who dress provocatively but nevertheless seek to make an "innocent" impression.

Normally, men and women meet each other by dancing together. Men are more direct than women and more likely to say, if asked, that they seek sexual encounters in bars (Muller 2014).

Men attend bars with a view of finding a sexual relationship. They are therefore advised that the portrayal of power and success make men more attractive to women. Such a portrayal is best achieved by arriving at a bar with a number of friends who appear "cool" and interesting. The bar scene is also a place where rejection and affront occur. Many women become rude and insulting because they are confronted by numerous men night after night as they listen to yet another "line" intended to arouse their interest in yet another man seeking to seduce them. Indeed, bars can be cruel places where many men are treated "like a skunk at a picnic." There are both men and women who feel uncomfortable in the bar scene and who give away their discomfort, leading to certain rejection.

To avoid all this, some men visit "strip clubs." These clubs feature women in the nude or near nude. Strip clubs allow male visitors to imagine that they have control over beautiful women when, in fact, the strippers and bar owners control everything.[2] Strip clubs feed the imagination of men who seek to pretend that they have attained dominance over desirable women. Men spend a great amount of money to participate in this kind of entertainment, which may even include so-called "lap dancing." Such strip clubs may be labeled "fantasy islands" (Burton 2014).

Because bars serve alcohol, there are those who become belligerent under the influence of too much drink and too little self-control. This can lead to fighting in bars. For example, some bar patrons may take advantage of someone who has left his or her place at the bar to visit the restroom. When the person returns, he or she may find that someone else has taken their place and their $10 cocktail has been tossed out (Hein 2006).

Fights over the attention of women are not uncommon in bars. These fights are often provoked by women, who view such fights as evidence that they are most attractive. This mating ritual is reminiscent of the mating rituals by all animals from peacocks to elephants and is a reminder of how much human behavior is influenced by biological imperatives as explored by Edward O. Wilson (1975) in his groundbreaking book *Sociobiology*, which includes evidence that even in humans, mating behavior is indeed biologically grounded.

Social Stratification

Some bars cater to people with special interests, who congregate not only to enjoy a drink but also to gossip. Rehoboth Beach in Delaware is a wealthy community where 20% of the population has an annual income of $150,000 or more. So-called Washington insiders frequent bars in Rehoboth Beach, as do other prominent people. These bars offer entertainment consisting of dance music performed by live musicians and popular singers. These bars cater to women and men of all ages, including senior citizens. There are also "sing-along" bars in Rehoboth Beach and similar communities, as well as bars that feature piano players. Then there are bars that cater to the "leather culture." Some who participate in the leather culture are homosexuals. Others are interested in a variety of sexual activities or are wearing leather because they are "bikers" or bicycle riders (Naff and Marzullo 2007).[3]

Although neighborhood taverns are not nearly as common as they were before the 21st century, they do still exist. These bars serve local residents inexpensive beverages. Neighborhood bars are visited by people who know each other and spend years visiting these bars in their nonworking hours. Many of these bars were visited by families, although the majority of the customers were men. Before television these bars were the principal entertainment available to factory workers and others with similar incomes. Unlike the superficial relationships formed in popular bars in the 21st century, these older bars promoted permanent friendships and camaraderie not known in the current bar scene. Many of these taverns served home-cooked meals where local politics were discussed. To keep these taverns from disappearing, two Buffalo, New York, men, Marty Biniasz and Eddie Dobosiewicz, founded Forgotten Buffalo, which leads tours of local sites including taverns. Nevertheless, these bars are declining in number due to alcohol sold in stores, clubs, restaurants, and hotels. Most cities require that owners acquire a tavern license. These licenses are expensive and are curtailed, so that the neighborhood bar may soon be a relic of the past (Keen 2012).

College students are another segment of the America population who frequent bars. It is widely believed by college students that alcohol is a means of removing inhibitions regarding encounters with the opposite sex. This belief is

Photo 5.2: A neighborhood pub, the Admiral Duncan in Orlando, Florida.

Michael Tubi/Corbis via Getty Images

also common among those who frequent so-called high-class cocktail lounges, because those who participate in these encounters believe that the environment of the lounge or bar gives the sexual intentions of the participants an air of respectability. The belief that alcohol needs to be present in order to succeed in making contacts with those one wishes to meet and impress has given rise to numerous drinking establishments in college towns or in neighborhoods where colleges are located. Surveys have shown that alcohol is viewed as a social facilitator among college students, who generally do not like the taste of alcoholic beverages but drink solely to be an acceptable member of their peer group (Roebuck and Spray 1967).

College students visit bars for the same reasons older people go there. Students want to escape loneliness and boredom. They seek to have "fun," whatever that may mean, and to associate with friends with a view of meeting the opposite sex. It has been observed that, in the presence of alcohol, women more often initiate courtship sequences than men, although their approaches are more subliminal and skillful than the means used by men.

Because the use of alcohol is so common within the academic community, many colleges teach alcohol education courses. These courses have had little success in reducing the drinking habits of students. In fact, there is no evidence that any administrative effort to reduce alcohol consumption by students has ever succeeded (Ingalls 1984).

For many years homosexuals have segregated themselves in gay bars in an effort to meet those whose sexual orientation could be assumed the same. The word *gay* is derived from French and has been used as a means of escaping the stigma associated with *homosexual*.

Gay and lesbian bars insulate homosexual women and men from the disparaging comments to which lesbian women and gay men were exposed in "straight" bars. Homosexuals of both genders include about 3.8% or 9 million Americans. This number depends in part on various definitions of homosexuality, lesbianism, transgender, and other criteria.

Prior to June 28, 1969, homosexual bars were targeted by police who raided such establishments because homosexuality was illegal. Furthermore, homosexual bars were visited by male prostitutes whose activities were also subject to police action. The public generally supported these police assaults on the gay lifestyle, so that the mores were in accord with the law, and homosexuality was rejected as a threat to all viewing themselves as "normal." Then, during the early morning of June 28, 1969, and on several days thereafter, homosexual men fought the police who were raiding the Stonewall Inn, located in the Greenwich Village neighborhood in New York City. The police were accustomed to beating and assaulting those arrested and did so as customers of the Stonewall Inn were shoved into police wagons. This time, however, a large crowd outnumbered the police. The crowd fought the police by throwing garbage and other objects at the officers. As the riots proceeded, more and more people joined the rioters until the police finally withdrew. The outcome of these riots was that within 2 years there were gay rights organizations in every American city. In June 1999, the U.S. Department of the Interior declared Christopher Street where the Stonewall Inn was located a historical landmark, and on June 1, 2009, President Barack Obama declared June Gay and Lesbian Pride Month. There can be little doubt that a major civil rights revolution in the United States was begun at a bar to be forever associated with the constantly more and more inclusive democracy of the United States (Stryker 2008).

Homosexual bars cater directly to gays and lesbians and have become the lifeline of those not accepted elsewhere. The fact is that despite the loosening of restrictions and prejudices concerning homosexuality, there are still many stereotypes and antagonisms facing the homosexual community. Because the majority of homosexuals are men, gay bars cater mainly to men (Fuchs 2004). This includes the distribution of condoms in some homosexual bars with a view of reducing the ever-threatening AIDS infection. At one time an organization called Gay Men's Health Crisis received almost $800,000 a year from the Health Department of New York State, augmented by another $150,000 furnished by the City of New York and used to distribute condoms in homosexual bars (Kirby 1999:625).

The bar scene seldom provides more than an opportunity for establishing brief and superficial relationships. For that reason they are most suitable for those who travel a great deal or who have no permanent attachments, a condition facing more and more Americans.

The Bartender

The bar scene revolves around the bartender. Sometimes called "mixologists," the bartenders, mostly men, earn between $14,000 and $47,000 a year, including salary and tips (Payscale 2017). They mix drinks for customers at the bar and make up drinks for those who are served by female or male servers. No formal education is needed to enter this occupation, although it is necessary to learn how to create the numerous drinks demanded. This involves knowing the language used to access a variety of mixed drinks such as a bloody Mary.

Most states have a minimum age requirement of 18 to bartend, whereas some restaurants have higher age limits. The bartender is responsible for checking the age of anyone who appears to be less than 21 years old, for all states prohibit the consumption of alcohol among those not that old.

Bartending involves setting up a bar by filling up glass cabinets, loading ice machines, and organizing tools such as bottle openers, shakers, pitchers, and cutlery. Bartenders also handle cash, process credit cards, and, most important, keep customers happy. This means that bartenders have social skills needed to listen to customers who seek to unburden themselves by telling the bartender their troubles. Bartenders have been compared to psychotherapists, who succeed in helping customers live with their anxieties by listening to them.

Such interaction is not always pleasant. Bartenders must sometimes refuse to serve a customer who appears to be inebriated and who cannot drive safely.

The law prohibits bartenders serving alcohol to those evidently drunk, lest they become a danger to themselves and others. In fact, the bartender and the bar may face liability if someone leaves the bar incapacitated and then injures someone or causes a wreck (Kokemuller 2016).

Costs of Alcohol

Alcohol, Organized Crime, and Violence

When the Puritans landed in Plymouth in 1620, they brought with them a considerable amount of beer, which was safer to drink than water. Moreover, the Puritans were by no means opposed to the drinking of alcohol. On the contrary, New England had numerous taverns in the 17th century. Historian Samuel Eliot Morison (1930) noted that alcohol was used as an inducement by towns to acquire unpaid workers for house raisings and that, believing that alcohol was one of the necessities of life, churches provided it to the poor. Although popular opinion holds that the Puritans were joyless fanatics, Morgan (1966) observed that they enjoyed both food and beer.

It is therefore evident that drinking alcohol was never a crime in the United States until the manufacture, distribution, and consumption of alcohol was criminalized by the passage of the Eighteenth Amendment to the U.S. Constitution, effective January 17, 1920. Repealed by the Twenty-First Amendment in 1933, Prohibition, as that experiment was commonly called, set in motion one of the most violent epochs in American history. Not only was the production and use of alcohol a crime, but Prohibition led to a large number of extraordinary crimes, as organized gangs conducted innumerable murders, beatings, and destruction of property in the United States. The story of the Mafia and the rejection of Prohibition by a majority of American citizens has been told many times. Books, movies, and television seem to never end in depicting murder and bloodshed surrounding the effort to sell alcohol to the American public, whose mores would not support what the law demanded.

Immediately after the Volstead Act was passed in October 1919, Giovanni Torrio, also known as Johnny Torrio, organized a Chicago-wide syndicate for the operation of breweries and the distribution of alcohol by means of truck convoys. The Volstead Act was named after a Minnesota member of the House of Representatives, Andrew Volstead, who introduced the enabling act needed to make the Eighteenth Amendment effective. Organized crime recognized at once that prohibiting the consumption of alcohol in the United States would become a source of enormous wealth for those able to furnish the American public the opportunities to drink alcoholic beverages. In short, the law was defeated as soon as it was passed (Sandbrook 2012).

The Eighteenth Amendment created a vacuum quickly filled by organized criminals able to give citizens what they wanted. This means that the mores would not support the views of the Anti-Saloon League and the opinions of the Women's Christian Temperance Union. These organizations succeeded in having laws passed contrary to the habits of the American people, which were therefore not enforceable. The well-known outcome of the discrepancy between the law and public opinion was the beer wars between numerous murderous criminals willing to risk their lives for the sake of the huge profits to be gained by supplying citizens with alcoholic drinks. It has been estimated that at least 5,000 men were murdered in connection with the fighting over a claim to supply an area with alcohol (Lippmann 1931).

These killings came about as numerous gangs sought to dominate at least part of the Chicago territory in which alcohol could be sold to so-called speak-easies. The media have called the organized crime syndicates "the underworld." That underworld existed during the Prohibition years not only because the public wanted to consume alcohol but also because politicians protected the crime bosses. An example of the protection of professional criminals during the 1930s was the career of Jacob "Mont" Tennes, who began by owning one gambling saloon and became immensely wealthy as he acquired wire services for the dissemination of gambling news. This was possible because politicians protected him and others from prosecution. In fact, the Chicago police were also corrupt and accepted payoffs from bootleggers and gamblers who controlled an empire of crime during Prohibition years. The police also promoted the interests of such major criminals as Al Capone, by arresting only small liquor distributors, thereby eliminating competition and giving Capone a monopoly on the alcohol business. It was also customary for the police to fail to record arrests of powerful crime bosses and their followers, so that hardly anyone had a criminal record. All of this led to gang killings arising over all kinds of business disputes (Landesco 1943).

No doubt the most notorious of these murders was the St. Valentine's Day Massacre. This horror consisted of the slaughter of seven men in a brick garage in Chicago when four men, dressed as Chicago police, burst into the garage, lined up the seven victims, and using submachine guns, murdered them by firing 90 bullets into them. The killers were loyal to Al Capone, who sought to be the crime boss of Chicago. The victims were loyal to George "Bugs" Moran, who rivaled Capone. As a result of this massacre, Moran lost his power and never again participated in the beer wars. Capone then became the sole beneficiary of organized crime in Chicago, although the massacre alerted the public to the menace of organized crime and led to the eventual downfall of Capone (O'Brien 1929).

In view of the evidence that the consumption of alcohol has been popular in the United States since colonial days, it seems incongruous that alcohol consumption would be criminalized in the 20th century. The effort to use the law to suppress the consumption of alcohol was an outgrowth of the temperance movement, which began at the beginning of the 19th century. Then the women who organized against the use of alcohol sought to persuade men not to drink. These women believed that just about all the ills of this world were caused by "demon rum." They were, of course, particularly concerned with the frequent assaults on wives and others by drunken men. They believed that Christianity could alter drunken behavior and preached religion to no effect. Therefore, in the middle of the 19th century between 1846 and 1855, 13 states passed prohibition laws as the "army of God" became violent and demanded action on their behalf by the U.S. government (D. Williams 1966).

A number of activists organized in order to carry on the fight against alcohol. Included were the Prohibition Party, the Women's Christian Temperance Union, the Anti-Saloon League, the Lincoln-Lee Legion, the Union Temperance Society, the U.S. Temperance Union, and the American Temperance Union. These groups published a newspaper called *American Issue* and succeeded in gaining the support of some politicians (Benton 2003).

The most successful of these groups was the Women's Christian Temperance Union (WCTU). It was organized in Ohio in 1874 and promoted a crusade, which consisted of women praying in the streets and singing hymns in front of saloons. Some even broke open kegs of beer and let it flow down the street. This agitation led to the closing of some beer halls and generated a membership of 150,000 (Gordon 1898).

The leader of the WCTU was Frances Willard, who was elected president and stayed in that office until her death in 1898. Like so many other politicians, she needed to hold an office in order to collect the "psychic income" derived from holding an office. Although Willard believed she was succeeding in her effort to banish alcohol from the United States, she did not live long enough to see the failure that Prohibition provoked. Indeed, the WCTU still exists, although it has lost its influence and power. In fact, the very word *prohibition* brings to mind the Mafia, so that organized crime and not the WCTU is remembered in connection with that word (Messinger 1955).

The beer wars and other crimes committed by criminal organizations during the years of Prohibition are not the only examples of crimes related to the consumption of alcohol. Numerous studies over many years have shown that a disproportionate number of crimes are committed by people who have recently consumed alcohol (Cook and Moore 1993).

Parker and colleagues (2011) have shown a positive relationship between youth homicide and the availability of alcohol in the 91 largest U.S. cities. The National Council on Alcoholism and Drug Dependence (NCADD; 2015) reports that two thirds of the victims of an intimate, such as a current or former spouse or boyfriend or girlfriend, say that alcohol had been involved in that incident, and according to that report 40% of all violent crime victimization is related to alcohol consumption. Also, 37% of all violent offenders in American jails say that they had consumed alcohol at the time of their arrest (NCADD 2015). In addition, it is well known that many crime victims have used alcohol at the time of their victimization (Hutchinson et al. 1959).

Sociologists and criminologists have for years found positive correlations between alcohol use and crime, because alcohol impairs reasoning and reduces inhibitions. This means that alcohol acts as a catalyst rather than as the cause of crime. Of course, there are those who commit crimes such as theft and burglary because they need the money to buy alcohol (DiJulio 1996).

Some neighborhoods in American cities exhibit a high density of alcohol outlets and a high crime rate. These are usually poor neighborhoods that do not have the resources to prevent the establishment of numerous taverns, liquor stores, and bars. Poverty, high-density alcohol distribution, and crime are positively correlated (Gruenewald, Ponicki, and Holder 1992). This positive and statistically significant impact of alcohol availability and crime rates leads to the conclusion that, if public policy were to limit alcohol outlets in any neighborhood, the crime rate would decrease. This could be achieved by means of zoning laws and tax increases (Chaloupka, Grossman, and Saffer 1996).

Over many years, criminologists have found that alcohol is involved in one half to two thirds of homicides, in more than one half to two thirds of serious assaults, and in more than one fourth of rapes. In fact, over one half of everyday violence involves alcohol. Alcohol is also a consistent predictor of wife assault. Representative samples of wife assaults involving alcohol vary from 20% to 80%, depending on the amount of alcohol consumed. The heavier the drinking, the greater the chances of wife assault. Those who are assaultive are likely to abuse alcohol, and those who abuse alcohol are likely to be assaultive (Hotaling and Sugerman 1986).

Explanations for the relationship between violence and alcohol include emphasis on the pharmacological effects of alcohol on the nervous system. Excessive consumption of alcohol impairs cognitive and physiological responses that would otherwise redirect aggression. Then there is social learning as a reason for aggression involving alcohol. That means that some men and women use alcohol as an excuse for deliberate acts of aggression, which they had considered ipso facto. There are also some who suffer from an antisocial personality disorder leading them to assault not only their family but also strangers. Such violence is found in road rage situations and other confrontations involving targets not previously known to the aggressor, who is constantly involved in violent behavior (National Research Council 1999).

The use of alcohol and its production was criminalized by Prohibition in 1919. Yet long before this federal effort became law and failed, Prohibition existed in numerous towns and counties in this country, thereby criminalizing otherwise law-abiding citizens who made "moonshine" whiskey because they needed the income. This was and still is most common in the Appalachian region of the United States. There the production of whiskey has been part of the mores for centuries, although it is viewed as illegal by the state and federal government, which seek to collect a whiskey tax. Despite police efforts to suppress moonshining, this has not succeeded, because a law seeking to collect a tax or prohibit the manufacture of homemade whiskey is not supported by the communities that often rely on the income from illicit alcohol to bolster their minimum-wage jobs in construction, lumbering, and other poorly paid enterprises (Massey 2007).

The early European settlers of Appalachia came from the Ulster region of Ireland. These Protestants were the descendants of Scottish Presbyterians encouraged by King James I to leave Scotland and populate Ireland in an effort to reduce the influence of the Catholic population. In America these immigrants and their descendants continued to make whiskey as they had done in Europe. Yet here the state deemed them criminals, because they continued that tradition. By the 18th century, a host of laws criminalized private alcohol production among the 400,000 Ulstermen who had come to the United States. In addition to the tradition of whiskey making, these former Scots also had a tradition of seeking to escape government interference in their lives (Dabney 1974).

By the early 19th century, Appalachia was exporting 4 million gallons of legal whiskey, of which half went to New Orleans. The small farmers who made moonshine depended on that effort to make a living because the corn they raised cost far too much to get to market (Stewart 2004).

More than 10 years before the Volstead Act became law, numerous states had already outlawed the production and distribution of liquor. By 1917, there were 26 dry states, which prohibited the making of liquor. Then, after the repeal of Prohibition, illegal liquor disappeared from New York, Chicago, and Los Angeles but became the province of the mountain men of the South. These men worked hard to provide for their families, a practice necessary because of the low wages paid in Appalachia (Griffin and Thompson 2002).

The principal lesson here is that laws that contradict the mores cannot be enforced. This fact seems never to be understood by legislators, law enforcers, and other politicians, who seek political advantage from getting tough on crime without considering the voters.

Interpersonal Violence: Assault and Rape

According to the evidence, drinking is more likely to involve interpersonal crime than property crime. These crimes usually escalate from verbal abuse by both the offender and victim, both of whom are drinking. Alcohol increases the risk of being a crime victim, particularly if the eventual victim is consuming alcohol. It is common to blame alcohol for all kinds of criminal offenses, even without justification.

On an average day, about 6.5 million convicted offenders are under the supervision of criminal justice authorities. Of these, around 40% were using alcohol at the time of their offense. The most common substance used by these drinkers is beer, and wine is the least frequent source of alcohol used by offenders. These statistics reflect crimes known to the police. There are, however, many crimes that are never reported to any authority and those not reported because the victim is involved. This involvement frequently means that the victim had been drinking as the crime occurred. Alcohol consumption can lead to misperceptions of the significant other's intent and therefore may appear as permission to become sexually aggressive when that is not what was intended (L. Greenfield 1998).

Some users of alcohol become loud and verbally aggressive and therefore precipitate violence. This scenario often precedes wife beating, as an argument escalates when the husband resorts to physical assault because he is targeted by verbal

Photo 5.3: Alcohol and domestic violence.

abuse. Although it is unusual for only the wife to have been drinking before a physical attack occurs, it is common that both husband and wife were drinking or that the husband alone was consuming alcohol. Research has shown that at least three fourths of domestic assaults involve alcohol, whereas that was only true in 31% of assaults involving strangers (Kantor and Straus 1989).

Among women who drink, many do so because they are living in a violent relationship from which they cannot escape. They therefore use alcohol to submerge the pain and humiliation that they must deal with constantly. Alcohol is therefore not the cause but the consequence of violence in such relationships.

Those who assault women or otherwise behave constantly in an aggressive fashion need to be in control of others and seek power as a result of a distorted view of masculinity, either rooted in childhood experiences or taught in American culture by means of the media, sports fanaticism, violent video games, and numerous other inducements, leading some men to believe that violence proves their manhood. It is likely that such conduct is compensation for insecurities about being a man. Men who need to dominate others all the time have an excessive need to prove they are tough and in charge. Many men who exhibit such conduct have had abusive fathers. Furthermore, American society has traditionally devalued female qualities and made masculine attributes the American ideal (Taubman 1986).

Lemle and Mishkind (1989) hold that male heavy drinkers are obsessed with manly virtues and have real doubts about their efficacy as males. According to these writers, heavy drinkers, when under the influence of alcohol, have power and domination fantasies derived from unconscious feelings of deficiency. Alcohol abuse becomes a means of asserting power and feeling "like a man."

Although patriarchy has been challenged most successfully since Betty Friedan (1963) published *The Feminine Mystique*, many Americans continue to see men as legitimate controllers of women and therefore entitled to impose violence upon wives and significant others. This means that some men are socialized to believe they have the right to dominate women, including by using violent means. It is therefore not only alcohol that leads to domestic violence but also the belief that violence is a legitimate means of dealing with others, particularly wives. Such beliefs are much more prevalent among those who have little education and work in minimum-wage jobs. In fact, a study has shown that men who assault women often suffer from verbal deficits so that they use violence because they cannot express themselves (Dutton and Stachan 1987).

Because approval of violence is a significant determinant of wife assault, that attitude, not alcohol alone, leads to physical attacks. Heavy drinkers seek to forget worries, pain, and distress. They therefore become particularly angry if interrupted at home while drinking. Furthermore, violent men believe they can "get away with it" as long as they assault their helpless wives. Many of these attackers are most polite and friendly to everyone else, and particularly strangers, who may well be capable of defending themselves (Fagan, Barnett, and Patton 1998).

Assault is most common among chronic alcohol abusers, rather than among those occasionally intoxicated. Chronic alcoholics exhibit a form of psychopathology leading to dysfunctional relationships with family and friends. Many of those who become chronic alcoholics are the children of alcoholic parents and were themselves the targets of alcohol abuse and violence in their families of origin. Some alcoholics also fail to restrain their immediate needs and wishes and will use violence to get what they want at once.

Violent abusers will often isolate their wives and make them dependent on their demands. These men keep their victims from family and friends, so that they have no support, no information, and no advice. In this isolation strategy, the men are generally helped by the women they are beating, because the women don't want to talk about their mistreatment and don't want to exhibit the signs of violence visible on their face and bodies. Social isolation explains to some extent why victims cannot escape, and it also serves the perpetrators' escape sanctions for their atrocities. This indicates that as social isolation decreases and social support increases, the frequency of assault declines (L. Kelly 1996).

Violence against women is also related to beliefs supporting violence. For centuries, almost all cultures the world over considered wives the property of their husbands and taught that husbands were legally superior to wives. The belief that women were the property of their father and later their husband supported wife beating, with masculinity confused with masculine aggression. Likewise, sexual assault and sexual harassment, as well as wife assault, have been recognized as efforts to prevent a drop in masculine status (DeKaseredy and Kelly 2003).

Status in the United States depends primarily on occupation. Any inspection of occupational prestige in America shows that physicians are regarded as most prestigious, followed by professors, lawyers, dentists, architects, engineers, and psychologists. These and other occupations depending on higher education are well regarded by the American public, whereas laborers and others whose work is attainable without much education, and who earn little, rank low in the view of the majority of Americans. Sociologists agree that occupation is the most important criterion for calculating status and role in America. Consequently, those who believe they have little standing in this arrangement may feel angry at their situation and consider themselves relatively deprived. This, in turn, can lead to heavy drinking and to violence against wives and children among those who feel that their masculinity is threatened by their low standing (Goyder 2005). That threat has recently been amplified, as more and more women exceed the number of college-graduated men. Furthermore, as of 2010, about 23% of women earn more than their husbands (New 2012).

Assault is a serious felony. Therefore, women who risk the possibility of becoming the victims of this crime need to know that assault is positively associated with heavy drinking and with the frequency with which it has occurred in the past. Drunken assaults are more frequent in common-law and other unions of short duration and may be predicted if the aggressor indulges in name calling and other put-downs. Violence that begins early in a relationship has a good chance of continuing (Aldaronda and Kantor 1997).

Assault may also have a sexual content. Thirty percent of sexual assaults occur while the perpetrator is under the influence of alcohol, particularly when the victim is also intoxicated. This means that the attacker is no longer inhibited, even as the woman is no longer capable of defending herself. Alcohol use is not the cause of sexual assault, although there is a high correlation between consumption of alcohol and sexual assault. It is reasonable to believe that attackers might think about violent conduct but cannot carry it out unless they first consume alcohol. Alcohol may be regarded as a permission device allowing those who choose to assault another person to do so by furnishing the aggressor with an excuse to commit violence (Cunradi et al. 1999).

It is also important to consider that someone who is drunk is impaired sexually and must therefore make an extra effort to commit sexual assault. Therefore, people who assault others when drunk are not doing so because they are drunk but despite being drunk. It is commonly accepted that all sexual contact without permission constitutes sexual violence. This pertains to those who consumed alcohol, even if the perpetrators seek to use alcohol as an excuse for their behavior. The use of alcohol cannot be an excuse for imposing sexual contact on an unwilling target.

Sexual assaulters are more likely to have experienced abuse in their childhood than other men (National Center for Victims of Crime 2012). Therefore, these men were more often delinquent in their adolescence and have male friends who view forced sex as acceptable. Most of these men began dating at a young age and have had early sexual experiences.

Not all assaults are of a sexual nature. The FBI's Uniform Crime Reports includes 376,154 aggravated assaults in 2015, the most recent year for which crime statistics are available (2015, Table 29, "Estimated Number of Arrests," https://ucr.fbi.gov/crime-in-the-u.s/2015/crime-in-the-u.s.-2015/tables/table-29). That number is not extraordinary. Inspection of assault statistics in previous years shows similar results. Many of these assaults occur in bars and under the influence of alcohol (Abbey et al. 1994).

Women in bars and other alcohol-serving establishments are seen by some men as morally impaired because they drink. This belief, in turn, allows some men to imagine that they are entitled to assault a drinking woman, inasmuch as the aggressor imagines that the drinking woman has lost her right to respect and honor because she likes alcohol. The fact is that aggressors drink a great deal so as to later justify their conduct by pointing to their inebriation and that of their victim as excuses for violence, including intent to rape (Koss and Dinero 1988).

It is therefore evident that women who drink excessively in the company of men take a risk, which is not necessarily absent even if the male date is well known to them. This means that there are common stereotypes concerning women who drink alcohol. Many Americans believe that women who consume alcohol are sexually more available and promiscuous than sober women. Sexually assaultive men generally describe women who use alcohol as "loose" women, who are immoral and are therefore appropriate targets. This attitude leads some men to deliberately get a woman drunk so that they can rape her and then blame the victim (Abbey et al. 1996).

Because rape is an underreported crime, accurate statistics concerning this felony cannot be produced. Nevertheless, researchers estimate that about one fourth of all American women have been sexually assaulted and 18% have been raped. Of these, at least one half involve the consumption of alcohol by both the perpetrator and the victim. It is a popular myth that rape is conducted by strangers, who seize the victim in hidden places where there are few chances of escape. There may be such rapes. However, 80% of rapes are committed by people who know each other and are in the presence of alcohol (Abbey et al. 1996).

Crimes committed by those who drink a great deal may well originate with the need to steal money so as to buy alcohol. Alcohol can deprive the drinker of good judgment, including his or her ability to control one's aggression. Standards of behavior and aggression usually differ between sober and drunk conduct, particularly while driving. This means that driving drunk is a devastating crime practiced continuously in the United States.

Drinking and Driving

In 2015, 10,265 people were killed by drunken drivers in the United States. In addition, 345,000 were injured. Every 51 minutes someone is killed, and every 90 minutes someone is seriously injured by drunk drivers. Drunk driving costs $132 billion a year. Of the 1,132 children aged 0 to 14 killed in traffic accidents in

2015, about 209 or 16% were killed by alcohol-impaired drivers (CDC 2017b). Of these, about one half were riding with an adult drunk driver. In 2015, 1,089,171 people were arrested for drunk driving (FBI 2015, Table 29, "Estimated Number of Arrests," https://ucr.fbi.gov/crime-in-the-u.s/2015/crime-in-the-u.s.-2015/tables/table-29). That is 1% of the self-reported episodes of drunk driving, which do not come to the attention of the police (CDC 2017b).

The risk of crashing while drunk is greatest among drivers ages 21 to 24. That constitutes 34% of all such accidents, although that age group accounts for only 6.7% of the population of the United States (Census Scope 2000).

In view of these statistics, numerous states have adopted so-called zero-tolerance laws aimed at eliminating drunk driving on the part of those under the age of 21. These laws require states to revoke the license of any underage driver whose blood alcohol concentration (BAC) exceeds the limit of .02. For those over age 21, the BAC limit is .08. That is, of course, a harsher penalty than that enforced previously in most states (Carpenter 2004).

These zero-tolerance laws have reduced the amount of binge drinking by about 13% among men 18 to 20 years of age, with no effect for those somewhat older, aged 21 to 24 years. These laws are also effective with regard to crime, for the number of arrests of those affected by zero-tolerance laws rose significantly. Zero-tolerance laws are responsible for a significant reduction in property crime, which indicates that heavy drinking is responsible for many nuisance and property crimes. These property crimes are disproportionately the responsibility of young men in the age range of 18 to 20, which is the same as the age range most involved in binge drinking. Vandalism and violent crime are equally inflated in the same age range (Carpenter 2004).

In part, dangerous drivers are removed from the opportunity to drive when zero-tolerance laws are in effect. This reduction is the consequence of both the rate of arrest and the probability of arrest, which affect driving under the influence of alcohol and other crimes commonly called "nuisance crimes," including vandalism.

Recently, efforts have been made by the courts to break the cycle of alcohol use consisting of arrest, release, and rearrest. These efforts affect those who drive under the influence of alcohol, as well as those who drive having used other drugs. Such driving is a crime and has traditionally been punished by imprisonment. Now, Florida and other states have founded special drug courts to deal with all the problems associated with drunken driving and that affect public health. This means that a good number of alcohol and drug offenders are now processed by these courts, whose mission it is to deal with the root causes of this criminal behavior. Offenders adjudicated by these courts receive detoxification treatment, counseling, vocational education, group meetings, urine testing, and weekly court appearances to monitor their progress (Resig 1998).

These drug courts began in Miami and then spread across the nation, so that by 1999, over 400 such courts operated nationwide. By 2005, there were more than 1,600 drug courts in almost all states, and another 500 were added by 2007. Today, the 50 states have established 2,600 drug courts dealing with

150,000 persons each year. Those who are socially stable, in that they have a job and live within a family, are more likely to succeed from drug court programs than those who are not working and who live alone. The fact is that the majority of those who come before these courts are not stable citizens (Mackinem and Higgins 2008).

Generally, the courts do not succeed in curbing drunk driving. Those who are heavy drinkers are usually so addicted that the programs offered by the courts are ineffective. The law is effective with those who are not yet addicted but are sensitive to the threat of physical consequences in that state. Those who pay no attention to court-ordered programs have no reason to give up drinking alcohol.

Lower-class citizens live in a subculture that encourages drinking alcohol and has the proclivity to take risks. Another lower-class characteristic is the willingness to exchange safety for immediate gratification. This attitude is particularly confirmed by the fact that young men in American culture are encouraged to drink beer and other intoxicants. The peer pressure to consume alcohol is very strong in such communities, as is the pressure by the police and the law to abstain from alcohol when driving. It is required that others be allowed to drive once the individual becomes impaired by alcohol and unable to safely operate his or her car (Ross 1992).

A study made by the Gallup polling organization discovered that single white males are more likely to drink and drive than others, particularly when these men are high school- or college-educated citizens. Those with more formal education are more often involved in drinking and driving than those who have less education, possibly because the latter have fewer financial resources and cannot afford a lot of alcohol. Statutes prohibiting drinking and driving appear to affect mostly those who drink little and seldom attempt to drink and drive whereas the most confirmed alcohol consumers are hardly affected by the prohibition. There is then a subculture of DUI offenders on whom laws have little impact (Bertelli and Richardson 2008).

Problem drinking is clearly associated with recidivism. This means that alcoholism is hardly affected by punitive measures, which will not deter the confirmed alcoholic. Those who abuse alcohol and other drugs are so dependent on these substances that they cannot change solely because the behavior is punished (Yu 2006).

Drunk drivers who have been repeatedly arrested and are recidivists are familiar with the drinking and driving laws. A study by Baum (2000) discovered that drunk drivers are acquainted with the laws concerning the BAC permissible when driving, just as are most people in the general population. Heavy drinkers know how much one may drink in order to stay within the limits imposed by law. The same study found that there is a significant difference between violators of the driving-while-intoxicated laws and the moderate drinker. Violators are far more likely to refuse to leave their car behind when it is time to go home. These drinking drivers believe that the dangers of drunk driving are overrated and that everybody drinks and drives. The wider community disagrees with these beliefs and exhibits a different perception of this offense than is found among less sober citizens.

Drunk drivers exceed the number of drinks consumed by sober drivers. In one study, those who knew their limit drank an average of 3.19 drinks. Drunk drivers drank a good deal more. These differences were also visible in the perception of being caught while drunk driving. The perceived likelihood of arrest led DUI offenders to believe that they would probably not be arrested or convicted. Those who drank an acceptable amount were more likely than offenders to believe that excessive drinking would lead to arrest. There are also open-container laws in all states. Here again, the general public is more aware of these laws than the DUI population. In addition, the general population favors alcohol checkpoints far more than do those who drink and drive. DUI offenders believe that there are far too many checkpoints. Furthermore, those who drink a great deal are less aware than the general population that the police will stop drinking drivers. These errors in perception are due to the fact that the greater the problem with drinking, the greater the number of predriving drinks (Goodfellow and Kilgore 2014).

Alcohol and Tax Fraud

Excise (from the Latin *ex caedere*, "to cut") tax fraud is another crime associated with the consumption of alcohol. An excise tax is a tax on the purchase of a designated quantity of any item the IRS wishes to tax. That may be gasoline or wine. An excise tax is paid by the manufacturer or retailer and is either a state or federal tax as imposed by the state department of taxation or the federal IRS. A number of criminal organizations have developed schemes allowing them to avoid these taxes. These schemes target not only alcohol but also cigarettes, gasoline, and other items (Tax Law Firm 2011).

Excise taxes are normally passed on to consumers, so that the price of alcohol is partially related to the size of the tax. In California the excise tax per gallon of liquor is $3.30, and in Colorado it is $2.28. In Minnesota the excise tax is $5.03. The most heavily taxed states are New York, where the excise tax is $6.44, and Florida, with an excise tax of $6.50 (Siegel et al. 2013).

Federal excise taxes on alcohol amount to $13.50 on a gallon of distilled spirits, $18.00 on a gallon of beer, and $3.50 on a gallon of wine. This translates into $2.14 for a bottle of whiskey, $0.33 for a six-pack of beer, and $0.22 for a bottle of wine (Congressional Budget Office 2016).

Unpaid excise taxes may amount to $5 billion to $10 billion per year. These taxes are collected more than once as the product moves from the wholesaler to the retailer to the customer. This invites fraud at several collection points in the process of eventually sending the money to its final destination, the IRS.

Tax fraud related to excise taxes is also produced by the differences in price of alcohol between the states. When the tax in one state is less than the tax in a bordering state, then it becomes profitable to organize the smuggling of alcohol from one state into another. Alcohol is a legal substance so that there is normally no reason for authorities to look for any illegal activity related to its use. In fact, it is to be expected that consumers would buy alcohol or any other substance in a state with lower prices than in one with higher prices. This becomes detrimental to states that have a common border with states with lower tax rates. Alcohol is easily transported and widely used. Therefore, it is most likely the target of smugglers who pay no taxes at all.

The tax differences between the states concerning alcohol are considerable. There are states that charge only $.02 per gallon of beer and others that charge $0.77. Since the states do not coordinate alcohol taxes, this condition will continue.

An example of such tax fraud occurred in Oregon, where the defendant pleaded guilty to filing 70 fraudulent excise tax returns during a 3-year period. The fraud was committed by William Myers, owner of the Side Pocket Food Company. Myers defrauded the IRS of $879,000 between October 1, 2008, and August 31, 2011. The company purchases bulk alcohol and distilled spirits from manufacturers and then blends it for bottling liquor such as whiskey and vodka under different brand names. Myers claimed that no federal excise taxes were owed, even though he collected the taxes from his customers. He then spent the money on a house, a car, business expenses, and credit card bills (Tomlinson 2012).

Christopher Eiras was arrested by agents of the Bureau of Alcohol, Tobacco, Firearms and Explosives (ATF) on 70 charges of submitting false liquor reports in 2011 and 2012, in a manner resembling the bootleggers of the 1930s. He was convicted and jailed, but the charges were later dropped (Pulliam 2014).

Likewise, Alton Trowell, Christie Comkowycz, and Dalton Ridlon were arrested after trying to sell moonshine on Facebook. Unfortunately for them, their prospective customer was an undercover detective (Axelbank 2016). Similarly, Michael Freeman sold moonshine at the Gator Bowl game in Jacksonville, Florida. Agents of the ATF bought vodka and moonshine during the game, along with hot dogs (Lyons 2012). Numerous other citizens were also arrested in Florida for selling moonshine. This led a number of citizens to comment on the Internet that the police seem not to care about rapists, murderers, burglars, and an assortment of violent criminals but rather jail innocent citizens trying to make a few dollars to boost their income.

There can be little doubt that tax collectors are the most unpopular of Americans and that those who chase after illegally produced alcohol are running counter to the mores of almost all Americans. Prohibition was a failure because alcohol is popular in this country. Therefore, moonshining will continue in spite of law enforcement, because it appears as a petty offense to the American public, and its enforcers appear more like persecutors than prosecutors.

NOTES

1. See the discussion in Chapter 7, "Alcohol and Sexual Behavior," especially the sections "Drinking and Disinhibition" and "Risky Sex."

2. On this idea, see Ruby Pearson, "Backroom 'Dance'," in *Selves, Symbols, and Sexualities: An Interactionist Anthology*, eds. Thomas S. Weinberg and Staci Newmahr (Los Angeles: Sage, 2015), 237–242.

3. On gay leather bars and other drinking establishments in the gay male world, see Thomas S. Weinberg, *Gay Men, Drinking, and Alcoholism* (Carbondale: Southern Illinois University Press, 1994). See also the discussion and ethnographic examples in Chapter 7.

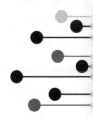

CHAPTER

6

Alcohol in Popular Culture

In this chapter, we look at the many ways in which alcohol has become part of popular culture. Alcoholic drinks have long been a part of the human experience. Alcohol has been used for at least 10,000 years and is the most widely consumed substance worldwide (Goode 2008:177). In fact, "alcohol has played a central role in almost all human cultures since Neolithic times (about 4000 BCE). All societies, without exception, make use of intoxicating substances, alcohol being by far the most common" (Social Issues Research Centre 1998:6). In 2013, archaeologists digging in the ruins of a Canaanite palace located in northern Israel and dating from 1700 BCE discovered 40 large ceramic wine jars in a storage room. They "announced . . . that they had found one of civilization's oldest and largest wine cellars. The storage room held the equivalent of about 3,000 bottles of red and white wines, they said—and they suspected that this was not the palace's only wine cellar" (Wilford 2013:A5). The use of wine, however, dates from further back, at least 8,000 years ago, and "makes its appearance in the first written story we now possess, the four-thousand-year-old Sumerian *Epic of Gilgamesh*" (Burk and Bywater 2008:1).

Historically, alcohol has served several purposes, including those of religion, communion, recreation, and escaping from problems. These functions, of course, overlap. Over the course of many centuries, alcohol has become strongly embedded in popular culture. This can be seen through a perusal of various cultural elements including art (sculpture and painting), literature (novels, short stories, and poetry), music (including both drinking songs and songs with drinking as part of their theme), television, movies, popular magazines, commercials and advertisements, games, jokes, and comedic routines. The examples provided in this chapter are by no means exhaustive; each of these categories could fill a large volume. They are used only as illustrations of the ways in which alcohol has become intertwined with popular American culture.

Depictions of Drinking and Alcohol in Art

One of the earliest representations of alcohol use is found in a Roman sculpture, the *Barbarini Faun*, which dates from about 220 BCE. It is thought to have been copied from a Greek statue. Janson (1971:119) describes the sculpture in the following way: "A drunken satyr is sprawled on a rock, asleep in the heavy-breathing, unquiet manner of the inebriated. He is obviously dreaming, and the convulsive gesture of the right arm and the troubled expression of the face betray the passionate, disturbing nature of his dream."

Much early European art revolved around religious themes. One fresco by Michelangelo Buonarroti depicted the result of heavy alcohol use as part of a biblical story. His painting *The Drunkenness of Noah* (1509) illustrates the following passages from Genesis:

> And Noah the husbandman began, and planted a vineyard. And he drank of the wine, and was drunken; and he was uncovered within his tent. And Ham, the father of Canaan, saw the nakedness of his father, and told his two brethren without. And Shem and Japheth took a garment and laid it upon their shoulders, and went backward, and covered the nakedness of their father; and their faces were backward and they saw not their father's nakedness. (Jewish Publication Society 1917:11)

By the 17th century, drinking and drunkenness had become a common theme in European art. One example is *The Bacchanal of the Andrians* (1523–1526), by the Flemish baroque artist Peter Paul Rubens. The painting depicts a drinking party in a rural grove of trees. The central figure in the foreground is a nude female, passed out from drinking. Male participants, some of whom are also nude, hold aloft goblets of drink, while a clothed couple dances. Another Flemish baroque artist is Adriaen Brouwer, whose genre paintings, such as *The Bitter Potion* (also called *The Bitter Tonic* or *The Bitter Draught*) from about 1635 and *Drunken Peasant in a Tavern* (c. 1624), depict scenes of peasants drinking and smoking.

During the same time period, Dutch artist Jan Steen captured drunkenness in two paintings, *The Dissolute Household* and *The Wine Is a Mocker*, both completed from 1663 to 1664. In the former work, the central figure is the woman of the house, leaning back in a chair; her arm is outstretched, holding an empty wineglass to be refilled. Her right foot is stepping on a Bible. The latter painting shows a woman passed out from drinking, as two men attempt to load her into a wheelbarrow. She is surrounded by smiling observers, obviously amused by her plight.

A more serious depiction of the dangers of drinking is Englishman William Hogarth's *Gin Lane*, his response to the Gin Act of 1751. His print illustrates a chaotic, nightmarish scene, in which cadaverous poor people drink themselves to death, a baby tumbles over a railing, a man fights with a dog over a bone, and a corpse is loaded into a coffin (J. Jones 2012).

La Bacchante, a work by French realist Gustave Courbet, painted between approximately 1844 and 1847, portrays a woman passed out after drinking, an empty goblet by her side. Francesco Vinea, a 19th-century Italian artist, made a number of paintings showing drinkers in taverns and wine cellars. Among these works are *In the Wine Cellar* (1889), *A Good Vintage*, *Merriment in the Tavern*, and *A Jolly Proposal*. Vinea's paintings are lighthearted, showing people

Photo 6.1: A partial scene from William Hogarth's _Gin Lane,_ painted about 1751.

Culture Club/Hulton Archive/Getty Images

celebrating and enjoying themselves. Another artist during this time was Peder Severin Kroyer, a Danish painter, whose 1888 work _Hip Hip Hurrah_ depicts a group of well-dressed men and women at an outdoor banquet table, lifting their wineglasses in a toast.

In the 19th century, absinthe, a bitter, high-alcohol-content drink, became popular among Parisians. Their affair with absinthe was documented both in paintings by contemporary artists such as Degas (_L'Absinthe,_ 1875–1876), Manet (_The Absinthe Drinker,_ 1859), Picasso (_Woman Drinking Absinthe,_ 1901; _The Absinthe_

Drinker, 1901; *Two Women Seated in a Bar*, 1902), and Toulouse-Lautrec, who was himself an absinthe drinker. Additionally, absinthe drinking was depicted in advertising signs of the day (Adams 2005).

Paintings portraying drinking and drinkers seem to have disappeared by the early 20th century, at least in the United States. Some modern European artists, such as Leon Zernitsky, a Russian, occasionally produce paintings with alcohol-related themes (e.g., *Champagne and Love*). The modern artistic depiction of drinking and alcohol appears in commercial forms such as posters and advertisements in magazines. Many of these illustrations are simple photographs of the product being advertised, sometimes arranged with other objects as a still life. In other cases, alcoholic beverages are shown in a more creative way. For example, a recent issue of *Imbibe* magazine has an advertisement for Fernet-Branca, a bitter Italian liqueur. Under the heading "Shockingly Unique," there is a photograph of an attractive woman standing outside a tavern. A well-dressed man and woman are looking at her in shock, because she is holding an alligator on a leash. *Whiskey*, another alcohol specialty magazine, contains an advertisement for KA VA LAN, a malt whiskey. In the photograph, the bottle is superimposed on a verdant forest scene, complete with moss-covered rocks and a babbling stream. Another ad, for Buffalo Trace, a Kentucky straight bourbon whiskey, is titled "Stand Strong." Accompanying a photograph of the bottle is a drawing of two bison in a western scene.

Movies and Television

Drinking scenes are ubiquitous in movies, from the upper-status cocktail parties depicted in the drawing-room comedies of the 1930s to the toga parties of 1978's *National Lampoon's Animal House*. Movies have had a strong influence on popular culture, even adding to our knowledge base.[1] For example, most middle-aged men, having reached maturity in the 1960s, will immediately recognize the phrase "shaken, not stirred" as referring to the preference of James Bond, Agent 007, for preparing a Vodka martini.

Serious movies have also been made about the hazards of alcohol. One, *The Lost Weekend*, made in 1945, starred Ray Milland as an alcoholic writer. The film follows his character, Don Birnam, through a weekend binge during which he steals money, is ejected from a bar, is knocked unconscious after falling down the stairs, is hospitalized, and escapes and returns home, only to experience terrifying hallucinations. The film ends on a hopeful note, as Don appears to be coming to grips with his alcoholism with the support of his girlfriend Helen (Jane Wyman). *Days of Wine and Roses* (1962) follows the drinking careers of Joe and Kirsten Clay from social drinkers to alcoholics. Joe eventually recovers after a stint in rehabilitation and help from Alcoholics Anonymous. Kirsten does not.

A more recent comedy film, *The Hangover* (2009), follows a series of misadventures of four men who go to Las Vegas for a bachelor party. When they awake

Photo 6.2: A scene from *The Hangover*.

in their hotel suite the next morning, they have no memory of what happened the night before. Their rooms are in disarray; there is a tiger in their bathroom and a baby in a carrier. One of the men, a dentist, is missing a tooth, and the bridegroom is missing. The film then shows them trying to reconstruct the prior evening, through a series of ever wackier situations. Truth be told, their collective amnesia was not attributable to alcohol, although they had been drinking heavily. The brother of the bride-to-be had put Rohypnol, an amnesia-causing drug, into their drinks, thinking that it was LSD.[2]

Drinking establishments are represented in many films. For example, Gilley's, a western bar established by country singer Mickey Gilley, was the primary setting for the action in 1980's *Urban Cowboy*, starring John Travolta and Debra Winger. The 1989 movie *Roadhouse* revolved around the attempt of "cooler" (the head bouncer) James Dalton, played by Patrick Swayze, to establish order in a Missouri country/western bar.

Other movies revolve around the lives of bartenders as they practice their trade. One of these is *Cocktail* (1988) in which the main character, played by Tom Cruise, learns not only how to mix drinks but also how to take advantage of his good looks and talents to impress women. *Coyote Ugly* (2000) follows a young woman named Violet, played by Piper Perabo, as she auditions to become one of the female bartenders/entertainers at a New York City bar.

Bars and taverns have played a central role in at least one very popular television show. *Cheers* (1982–1993), a long-running comedy set in the eponymous

Boston drinking establishment "where everybody knows your name," is probably the most prominent of these. Another sitcom set in a tavern was *Archie Bunker's Place* (1979–1983), a spinoff of the 1970s show *All in the Family* (1971–1979) (Wikipedia 2016a). Other television programs in which bars and taverns have a recurrent, though not necessarily central role, include Boss Hogg's roadhouse the Boar's Nest in *The Dukes of Hazzard*, the Bada Bing in *The Sopranos*, the Brick from *Northern Exposure*, the Drunken Clam from the cartoon comedy *Family Guy*, and the Long Branch Saloon from *Gunsmoke* (Wikipedia 2016b). The Esquire cable network, Esquire HD, has a new show, *Best Bars in America*, that features comedians Jay Larson and Sean Patton, who visit and drink (often several drinks) at a variety of taverns featured in *Esquire* magazine's annual list of the best in the country, while discussing the establishments' histories and specialties with their bartenders.[3] There is even a television show, *Bar Rescue*, in which expert Jon Taffer attempts to help tavern owners salvage their troubled businesses and return to solvency.

The Andy Griffith Show (1960–1968) featured Otis Campbell (played by Hal Smith), the Mayberry town drunk. In the show, Otis was almost always heavily intoxicated and would let himself into a cell to sleep it off. In one episode, he even tells new deputy that one of the cells is his "home" on Fridays and Saturdays. Never a belligerent drunk, Otis was played for laughs. One of the best known drunks was comedian Foster Brooks (1912–2001), who portrayed a "loveable lush" in television cameos and celebrity roasts.

July 9, 2013, marked the debut of Comedy Central's *Drunk History*. Based on a web series created by Derek Waters and Jeremy Konner, the program has inebriated people recounting important moments in history, which are then acted out by celebrities, who imitate the slurring speech patterns of the drunken narrator (Goodman 2013).

The Discovery Channel had an ongoing reality series *Moonshiners*, which followed men in the Carolinas and Virginia who made illegal alcohol. It was renewed for three years in 2013. A spinoff of that series, *Tickle*, followed one of the men featured in *Moonshiners*.

Commercials

Alcohol commercials have been a part of advertising almost from the beginning of television. Early commercials from the 1950s and '60s often used jingles and songs in an effort to make sure viewers remembered their product. For example, Rheingold beer, a beverage brewed in New York City and New Jersey, was a popular drink on the East Coast. Its theme song was set to the tune of Emil Waldteufel's "Estudiantina Valse" ("The Students' Waltz"):

> *My beer is Rheingold, the dry beer*
> *Think of Rheingold whenever you buy beer*

It's not bitter, not sweet,

It's the dry flavored treat,

Won't you try extra dry Rheingold beer?

Schaefer beer also created a memorable musical commercial:

Schaefer is the one beer to have when you're having more than one.

Schaefer flavor doesn't fade even when your thirst is done.

The most rewarding flavor in this man's world,

For people who are having fun.

Schaefer is the one beer to have when you're having more than one.

In the 1950s, cartoon characters Bob and Ray Piel were spokesmen for Piel's beer. It was rumored that although people remembered Bob and Ray, they forgot what they were advertising.

Modern television commercials for alcoholic beverages emphasize the fun aspect of social drinking, showing youthful men and women imbibing in glamorous settings at posh parties, on beaches, or camping in magnificent wilderness settings. A commercial for Ciroc, an upscale vodka, is set in Las Vegas, with attractive 30-somethings smiling and drinking, while in the background, Frank Sinatra croons, "Luck Be a Lady."

Masculinity is a strong theme in some of these commercials, especially those for beer, as they are directed primarily toward men. One Samuel Adams commercial proclaims, "Declare your independence from common beer." The secondary message is that of exclusivity: Only the most knowledgeable drinkers choose Samuel Adams. A similar implication is made in the Dos Equis beer commercial noted in Chapter 8, in which "the most interesting man in the world" chooses that particular beer.

Alcohol and Music

There are two kinds of music involving alcohol: songs sung when drinking and songs about drinking. The latter, found in many country songs, often deal with the negative aspects of drinking.

Songs Sung While Drinking

One classic drinking song many people sing in England, Ireland, and the United States, "Show Me the Way to Go Home," was written by Irving King in 1925. "King" was actually two collaborators, James Campbell and Reginald Connelly (Wikipedia 2016c). This song has been recorded by many artists, including Emerson, Lake & Palmer and Jefferson Starship, and has been included in a number of television programs like *Family Guy*, *The Monkees*, and *Duckman*. The lyrics are as follows:

Show me the way to go home

I'm tired and I want to go to bed

I had a little drink about an hour ago

And it went right to my head

Whereever I may roam

On land or sea or foam

You will always hear me singing this song

Show me the way to go home

A number of polkas have been written and sung about beer. One of the more popular songs is "In Heaven There Is No Beer," sometimes called "In Heaven There Ain't No Beer," which has been recorded by a number of polka bands. The first line of the song is

In heaven there is no beer

That's why we drink it here

And when we are gone from here

Our friends will be drinking all the beer

"The Beer Barrel Polka," also known as "Roll Out the Barrel," an upbeat paean to beer, is another well-known song about alcohol, originally written by Czech composer Jaromir Vejvoda in 1927, with lyrics written in 1934 by Vaclav Zeman. As recorded by Will Glahe, the song was number 1 on the Hit Parade in 1939 (Wikipedia 2016d). The chorus of the song is as follows:

Roll out the barrel, we'll have a barrel of fun

Roll out the barrel, we've got the blues on the run

Zing boom tararrel, ring out a song of good cheer

Now's the time to roll the barrel, for the gang's all here

A popular drinking song written and performed by country artist Roger Miller is the "Chug-a-Lug" song. It details a young man's first experiences with wine and moonshine. The singer notes that his experience was not completely pleasant because the alcohol burned his "tummy" and made his ears ring (CowboyLyrics.com n.d.).

Songs About Drinking

There are hundreds of songs about drinking,[4] which fall into several categories. Some of these are folk songs, many of which have traveled in various forms from the British Isles. Others are homegrown, often told as stories, primarily found in the country/western genre. In the following discussion, we look at some of these as illustrative of the various ways in which alcohol appears in popular music.

Alcohol Anthropomorphized

In some songs, alcohol is depicted as a seductive woman, leading the user down a path of self-destruction. Such is the case in "Nancy Whiskey," a story song originating in the British Isles. Recorded by a number of artists, including the Canadian country/folk duo Ian and Sylvia, it is the first-person tale of a weaver who falls in love with whiskey, to his detriment. A few lines of the song suffice as an illustration:

As I went down through Glasgow City, Nancy Whiskey I chanced to smell

I went in, sat down beside her, seven long years I loved her well

The more I kissed her, the more I loved her, the more I kissed her, the more she smiled

Soon I forgot my mother's teaching, Nancy soon had me beguiled

Now, I rose early in the morning, to slake my thirst, it was my need

I tried to rise but I was not able, Nancy had me by the knees

Country group Highway 101's song "Whiskey, If You Were a Woman" has a slightly different take on alcohol as a seductress. In it, a woman plaintively wishes that her man was cheating on her with another woman, rather than with whiskey, because she could compete with another human, but she has no chance in separating him from his alcoholism. "Oh whiskey, if you were a woman," she sings, "I'd fight you and I'd win / Lord knows I would."

Alcohol as a Means of Coping With Difficulties

In some songs, alcohol is seen as a way of escaping one's sorrows and personal problems, although never effectively. Jimmy Buffett's "Margaritaville" is about a man coping with a broken relationship by drinking margaritas, noting, "It's that frozen concoction that helps me hang on."

Merle Haggard recorded an album in 1980 titled *Back to the Barrooms* that contained a number of drinking-related songs. One of his songs not included in this collection is "Tonight the Bottle Let Me Down," which expresses the drinker's frustration with the ineffectiveness of alcohol in numbing his pain. It begins "I've always had a bottle I could turn to / And lately I've been turnin' every day." The singer goes on to say that the wine—"his one true friend"—has lost the desired effect on him, and now he is hurting again in "old familiar ways."

Negative Effect of Alcohol on Lives

A number of songs relate how alcohol, and especially the bar life, destroys people's lives. In one song, Emmylou Harris tells the story of a woman who has seen better days, but in the evening she becomes "The Queen of the Silver Dollar," where "she rules this smokey [*sic*] kingdom / Scepter is a wineglass and a barstool is her throne." A rhythm and blues song, "Bad, Bad Whiskey," performed by Buddy Guy and Junior Wells, complains that "Bad, bad whiskey / Made me loose [*sic*] my happy home." In "I'm Gonna Hire a Wino to Decorate Our Home," sung by David Frizzell, the singer's wife comes up with a creative idea to keep the singer at home and away from the bar. She is going to hire a "wino" to turn their house into a tavern, so that he will "feel more at ease" and he "won't have to roam," thus avoiding the hazards of the bar life and its threats to their marriage.

Magazines

There are numerous specialized magazines for consumers of beer, wine, and distilled spirits. Examples are *Wine Spectator*, *Wine Enthusiast*, *Imbibe*, *Liquid Culture*, *Food & Wine*, and *Whiskey*. These publications include articles about notable people in the alcohol industry, reviews of products and accoutrements, and other entries of interest to their readership. There is even an online magazine, *Modern Drunkard Magazine*, the standard of which bears the banner, "Standing Up for Your Right to Get Falling Down Drunk Since 1996." As one may surmise from this statement, *Modern Drunkard Magazine* takes a humorous perspective on a very serious issue. Standard features include Wino Wisdom, You're a Drunk, Skid Row Poetry, Comics, Booze News, Product Reviews, Drunk of the Issue, and Drunkard Video. Additionally, this online publication provides links to many other like-minded pro-alcohol sites such as Mydivebar.com, The Southport Drinker, NYBarfly .com, DrinkinHand.com, Liquorsnob.com, SorryIGotDrunk.com, BeerTutor.com, OneMoreBeer.com, UselessDrunk.com, and Beerbellie.com ("Staying fit one beer at a time"), a site promoting a book that purports to help people lose weight while drinking.

Alcohol and Literature

Literature

Drinking, alcohol, and drunkenness have been part of English literature for centuries. These themes can be traced back at least as far as Geoffrey Chaucer's *The Canterbury Tales*. In a number of those tales, "Prologue," "The Miller's Prologue and Tale," The Reeve's Tale," "The Cook's Tale," "The Pardoner's Tale," and "The Squire's Tale," for example, alcohol is mentioned:

> 637 *And for to drynken strong wyn, reed as blood;*
> 638 *Thanne wolde he speke and crie as he were wood.*

639 And whan that he wel dronken hadde the wyn,

640 Than wolde he speke no word but Latyn.

(Internet Sacred Text Archive 2011: "Prologue")[5]

12 The Miller that for-dronken was al pale,

13 So that unnethe upon his hors he sat,

14 He nolde avalen neither hood ne hat,

15 Ne abyde no man for his curteisie.

(Internet Sacred Text Archive 2011: "The Miller's Prologue and Tale")[6]

230 Ful pale he was for dronken, and nat reed.

231 He yexeth, and he speketh thurgh the nose

232 As he were on the quakke, or on the pose.

242 This millere hath so wisely bibbed ale

243 That as an hors he fnorteth in his sleep,

244 Ne of his tayl bihynde he took no keep.

(Internet Sacred Text Archive 2011: "The Reeve's Tale")[7]

343 That muchel drynke and labour wolde han reste;

344 And with a galpyng mouth hem alle he keste,

345 And seyde, It was tyme to lye adoun,

346 For blood was in his domynacioun.

352 Ful were his heddes of fumositee

353 That causeth dreem, of which ther nys no charge

354 They slepen til that it was pryme large

(Internet Sacred Text Archive 2011: "The Squire's Tale")[8]

Drinking and drunkenness also appear in the works of William Shakespeare. For example, the following statement by the Porter from *Macbeth*, Act II, Scene II, is often cited (Hylton n.d.):

Macduff: Was it so late, friend, ere you went to bed,

That you do lie so late?

Porter: 'Faith sir, we were carousing till the

second cock: and drink, sir, is a great

provoker of three things.

Macduff: What three things does drink especially provoke?

Porter: Marry, sir, nose-painting, sleep, and

urine. Lechery, sir, it provokes, and unprovokes;

it provokes the desire, but it takes

away the performance: therefore, much drink

may be said to be an equivocator with lechery:

it makes him, and it mars him; it sets

him on, and it takes him off; it persuades him,

and disheartens him; makes him stand to, and

not stand to; in conclusion, equivocates him

in a sleep, and, giving him the lie, leaves him.

Othello, Act II, Scene III, provides another example of references to drinking (Hylton n.d.):

Iago: Some wine, ho!

(Sings)

And let me the canakin clink, clink;

And let me the canakin clink

A soldier's a man;

A life's but a span;

Why, then, let a soldier drink.

Some wine, boys!

Cassio: 'Fore God, an excellent song.

Iago: I learned it in England, where, indeed, they are

most potent in potting: your Dane, your German, and

your swag-bellied Hollander—Drink, ho!—are nothing

to your English.

Cassio: Is your Englishman so expert in his drinking?

Iago: Why, he drinks you, with facility, your Dane dead

drunk; he sweats not to overthrow your Almain; he

gives your Hollander a vomit, ere the next pottle

can be filled.

Perhaps the character most exemplifying drinkers in Shakespeare's plays is Sir John Falstaff, a hearty man, womanizer, voracious eater, and drinker of sack, a sweetened imported wine, who appears in *The Merry Wives of Windsor* and in both King Henry IV plays. In *King Henry IV,* Part 2, he extols drink's virtues:

A good sherris sack hath a two-fold operation in it. It ascends me into the brain; dries me there all the foolish and dull and curdy vapours which environ it; makes it apprehensive quick, forgetive, full of nimble fiery and delectable shapes, which, delivered o'er to the voice, the tongue, which is the birth, becomes excellent wit. The second property of your excellent sherris is, the warming of the blood; which, before cold and settled, left the liver white and pale, which is the badge of pusillanimity and cowardice; but the sherris warms it and makes it course from the inwards to the parts extreme: it illumineth the face, which as a beacon gives warning to all the rest of this little kingdom, man, to arm; and then the vital commoners and inland petty spirits muster me all to their captain, the heart, who, great and puffed up with this retinue, doth any deed of courage; and this valour comes of sherris. So that skill in the weapon is nothing without sack, for that sets it a-work; and learning a mere hoard of gold kept by a devil, till sack commences it and sets it in act and use. (Hylton n.d.)

American literature of the 19th and 20th centuries is full of references to drinking, drunks, and drunkenness. Many of the most prominent authors, some of whom themselves had drinking problems, included heavily drinking characters in their novels. For example, Herman Melville first published his novel *Moby Dick* in 1851. One of his minor characters, Dr. Bunger, is accused by a patient of being drunk: "'Oh, very severe!' chimed in the patient himself; then suddenly altering his voice, 'Drinking hot rum toddies with me every night, till he couldn't see to put on the bandages; and sending me to bed, half seas over, about three o'clock in the morning'" (Melville 1930:633). Melville (1930) also writes about the importance of beer to Dutch whalers:

The quantity of beer, too, is very large, 10,800 barrels. Now, as those polar fisheries could only be prosecuted in the short summer of that climate, so that the whole cruise of one of these Dutch whalemen, including the short voyage to and from the Spitzbergen sea, did not much exceed three months, say, and reckoning 30 men to each of their fleet of 180 sail, we have 5,400 Low Dutch seamen in all; therefore, I say, we have precisely two barrels of beer per man, for a twelve weeks' allowance, exclusive of his fair proportion of that 550 ankers of gin. Now, whether these gin and beer harpooneers, so fuddled as one might fancy them to have been, were the right sort of men to stand up in a boat's head, and take good aim at flying whales; this would seem somewhat improbable. Yet they did aim at them, and hit them too. But this was very far North, be it remembered, where beer agrees well with the constitution; upon the Equator, in our southern fishery, beer would be apt to make the harpooner sleepy at the mast-head and boozy in his boat; and grievous loss might ensue to Nantucket and New Bedford. (p. 642)

In Mark Twain's novel *Adventures of Huckleberry Finn*, published in 1885, Huck's father, Pap, is the town drunk. Jack London's (1913) autobiographical novel, *John Barleycorn*, describes his drinking career beginning at the age of 5. Although documenting his heavy drinking,[9] London (1913) denies that he is an alcoholic, writing, "But mine is no tale of a reformed drunkard. I was never a drunkard, and I have not reformed."

F. Scott Fitzgerald's (1992) novel about wealthy youth in the Roaring Twenties, *The Great Gatsby*, first published in 1925, has many drinking scenes. In Ernest Hemingway's (1929) novel *A Farewell to Arms*, his protagonist, Lieutenant Frederic Henry, an American ambulance officer for the Italian army during the First World War, is a heavy drinker. He drinks a variety of alcohol—wines of all types, especially white Capri; brandy; cognac; and vermouth. Eventually, Henry develops jaundice from his drinking:

"There is no doubt about it," the house surgeon said. "Look at the whites of his eyes, Miss."

Miss Gage looked. They had me look in a glass. The whites of the eyes were yellow and it was the jaundice. I was sick for two weeks with it . . .

[Miss Gage] "I suppose you can't be blamed for not wanting to go back to the front. But I think you would try something more intelligent than producing jaundice with alcoholism."

"With what?"

"With alcoholism. You heard me say it." (Hemingway 1929:152–154)

John Steinbeck, another American author, wrote the novel *Tortilla Flat*, first published in 1935. It is the story of the close friendship of a group of "paisanos," ethnic Mexican men living in a poor part of town, who drink heavily.

Poetry

There have been many poems written about drinking and intoxication. For example, W. B. Yeats (1916) wrote "A Drinking Song":

Wine comes in at the mouth

And love comes in at the eye;

That's all we shall know for truth

Before we grow old and die.

I lift the glass to my mouth,

I look at you, and I sigh.

Charles Bukowski (1977), an American poet, wrote "Beer," a rather depressing comment on how he coped with disappointment "waiting for things to get better." The first line of his poem sets the mood: "I don't know how many bottles of beer I have consumed while waiting for things to get better."

Recently, a number of organizations such as Best Teen Poems, Family Friend Poems for Teens, and Family Friend Poems have encouraged teenagers to write about their feelings about drinking, their own and that of their family members.

Drinking Games

Games traditionally are one way in which people encourage others to imbibe large quantities of alcohol (along with continuous toasts). The simplest game is called Chug-a-Lug, probably after Roger Miller's song referenced earlier. In it, people compete to see who can finish a large quantity of beer in the shortest time. The idea is to keep swallowing the liquid without stopping to take a breath. Onlookers urge the competitors on by chanting as they drink. There are endless variations of this game. For example, a container may be passed around a circle of drinkers, who try to drain the beer as quickly as possible, or individuals may be timed as they separately compete. This has traditionally been a favorite game of fraternity men.

Beer pong, sometimes called Beirut, is a simple game. Ten cups filled with beer are set up in a triangle at either end of a long table, often a ping-pong table. Two teams take turns attempting to land a ping-pong ball in the other team's cups. When that happens, the team in whose cup the ball has landed must drink the beer in it, and the cup is then removed from the table. The winner is the team that first eliminates all its opponent's cups. The game has been commercialized. Companies sell "professional" beer pong tables, all ready for the beer cups, for about $100. Another device looks similar to a portable basketball hoop. A stand, about 6 feet tall, holds a backboard with cups arranged vertically in a circle. The object, of course, is the same—to land a ping-pong ball into a cup of beer. Spencer Gifts, for example, sells tables, cups, balls, and T-shirts with beer pong sayings.

One company, Late for the Sky, has developed a number of drinking games based on Monopoly, including Beer-opoly, Wine-opoly, Cocktail-opoly, and Brew-opoly. Almost any game can be turned into a drinking game, requiring only motivation and creativity. There are numerous card games, coin toss games, ball and cup games, and so forth. The object of all of these is the same: to "legitimately" get very drunk in the spirit of fun and fellowship.

Drinking games have entered the high-tech age of the 21st century. Tinder, a dating app that can be downloaded on a smartphone, is used by groups of women as the center of a drinking game, whose rules may change. For example,

Photo 6.3: Beer pong.

One Friday in January, 11 women in their mid- to late 20s gathered around a long table at a bar in Brooklyn to play. At first glance it looked antisocial: heads bowed while one player punched her phone in the air and announced that she had spotted a guy posing with an unidentified child in his dating profile. "Kid in the picture, and he hasn't specified it's his sister's. Drink!" With loud cheers, the party suddenly turned boisterous as the women called out other rules that mandated a sip. (Stampler 2014:45)

Jokes

There are many jokes about drinking and drunkenness in American popular culture, illustrating a number of topics. One popular theme begins with the phrase, "A drunk walks into a bar . . ." The drunk in the joke is usually portrayed as confused and disoriented, but sometimes he is not as discombobulated as he first appears and is able to coax drinks out of the bartender or other patrons. Other jokes involve encounters between drunks, drunk drivers, and the police. Still other themes involve the drinker's often shaky relations with his spouse, infidelity, attempting to pick up other patrons at the bar, bragging about one's physical or sexual prowess, confiding one's troubles with the bartender, dealing with hangovers, making bad decisions while intoxicated, and trying to stop drinking. Many of these jokes can be found on the Internet at sites such as Funny Jokes (http://www.free-funny-jokes.com/funny-bar-jokes.html), Bars and Bartending (http://barsandbartending.com/bar-jokes-2), and pubcurmudgeon (http://www.pubcurmudgeon.org.uk/misc/djokes.html).

This brief discussion looks at the myriad ways in which alcohol has been integrated into our culture. These examples are admittedly selective. The idea is not to comprehensively review all of the possible contributions in each category but rather to illustrate how important alcohol is in American culture and social life. Through literature, music, games, jokes, television, movies, advertisements, and the like, alcohol is all around us. For many people, alcohol is well integrated into their everyday lives. They are not necessarily alcoholics, yet beverages are seen as important elements in their activities. This view is encouraged and supported in the multiple ways documented in this chapter. For some people, the provision of alcohol is an indispensable accoutrement to even casual entertaining, a point made in the following quotation:

> I expect to be offered a drink when I go visiting. I hate to go visiting and not even be offered a drink. I may refuse the drink, but I at least expect to be offered one. If somebody doesn't want to offer me a drink—I just feel that they [sic] don't know how to entertain. (Weinberg 1994:22)

NOTES

1. For a comprehensive treatment of alcohol in the movies, see Norman K. Denzin, *Hollywood Shot by Shot: Alcoholism in American Cinema* (New York: Aldine de Gruyter, 1991).

2. Rohypnol is a sedative that depresses the central nervous system. Also known as "roofies," it is often termed a date rape drug. See http://www.drugfree.org/drug-guide/rohypnol.

3. See http://tv.esquire.com/shows/best-bars-in-america.

4. See, for example, Songfacts, "Songs About Alcohol" (http://www.songfacts.com/category-songs_about_alcohol.php), and Wikipedia, "Category:

Songs About Alcohol" (http://en.wikipedia.org/wiki/Category:Songs_about_alcohol).

5. The modern English translation is "And drinking of strong wine as red as blood. Then would he talk and shout as a madman would. And when a deal of wine he'd poured within, Then would he utter no word save Latin."

6. The modern English translation is "The miller, who with drinking was all pale, So that unsteadily on his horse he sat, He would not take off either hood or hat, Nor wait for any man in courtesy."

7. The modern English translation is "For pale he was with drinking, and not red. He

hiccoughed and he mumbled through his nose, As he were chilled with humours lachrymose; This miller had so roundly bibbed his ale, That, like a horse, he snorted in his sleep, While of his tale behind he kept no keep."

8. The modern English translation is "That labor and much drinking must have rest; And with a gaping mouth all these he pressed, And said that it was time they laid them down, For blood was in the ascendant as shown; The fumes of wine had filled each person's head, Which cause senseless dreams at any time. They slept next morning till the hour of prime."

9. "My alcoholic reminiscences draw to a close. I can say, as any strong, chesty drinker can say, that all that leaves me alive to-day on the planet is my unmerited luck—the luck of chest, and shoulders, and constitution. I dare to say that a not large percentage of youths, in the formative stage of fifteen to seventeen, could have survived the stress of heavy drinking that I survived between my fifteenth and seventeenth years; that a not large percentage of men could have punished the alcohol I have punished in my manhood years and lived to tell the tale. I survived, through no personal virtue, but because I did not have the chemistry of a dipsomaniac and because I possessed an organism unusually resistant to the ravages of John Barleycorn. And, surviving, I have watched the others die, not so lucky, down all the long sad road."

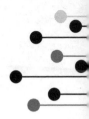

CHAPTER 7

Alcohol and Sexual Behavior

A Book of Verses underneath the Bough,
A Jug of Wine, a Loaf of Bread—and Thou
Beside me singing in the Wilderness—
Oh, Wilderness were Paradise enow!
                              —Khayyam 1889/1120

Candy is dandy, but liquor is quicker.
                              —Nash 1931

The opening quotations illustrate two very different perspectives on alcohol and sex. Omar Khayyam's almost 1,000-year-old verse equates alcohol with love and romance, whereas Ogden Nash's crass and pragmatic doggerel written in the early 1930s sees alcohol as a tool for seduction. Not much has changed in a thousand years or 86. On one side, couples often understand a romantic dinner, perhaps in an upscale restaurant with candlelight and a bottle of premium wine, as foreplay, helping them to "get into the mood." On the other side, the disinhibiting effects of alcohol are well known, and this quality is often exploited by both men and women, especially in single bars and large house party situations.[1]

The effects of alcohol on sexuality have been well known for centuries. One example, cited in Chapter 6, comes from Shakespeare's *Macbeth*, in which, in response to Macduff's question, "What three things does drink especially provoke?" the Porter replies, "Marry, sir, nose-painting, sleep, and urine. Lechery, sir, it provokes, and unprovokes; it provokes the desire, but it takes away the performance: therefore, much drink may be said to be an equivocator with lechery: it makes him, and it mars him; it sets him on, and it takes him off" (Hylton n.d.). Thus, alcohol, as a disinhibitor ("candy is dandy, but liquor is quicker"), may free people from societal constraints to seek sexual contact, but because of its depressive effects, too much alcohol makes sexual performance difficult.

Drinking and Disinhibition

The disinhibiting effects of alcohol on one's sexual behavior are succinctly summed up by a statement on a woman's T-shirt sold in a mall specialty store.

The front of the red-sequined black shirt declares in red lettering, "Wine Makes Me Take My Clothes Off."

A number of studies have explored the relationship between alcohol use and disinhibition, especially among high school and college student populations.[2] These studies take a variety of approaches. Both qualitative theory building and quantitative methodologies are used. Most of the attempts to understand alcohol use and disinhibition use laboratory experiments, but others are carried out in the field in naturalistic settings such as bars or parties. The laboratory studies use different designs, depending on what theory they are testing and what consequences they are examining. Some research, for example, looks at the relationship between drinking and risk taking, as in the failure to practice safe sex. Other researchers are interested in whether drinking makes people less discriminating in their choice of partners (the "beer goggles" thesis). Because of these different approaches and goals, findings are not always consistent from one study to another.

In a widely cited meta-analysis of research covering a period of 10 years, M. Lynne Cooper (2002) found that alcohol use was consistently related to the decision to have sex, including risky sex. In a qualitative study using a symbolic interactionist framework, Vander Ven and Beck (2009) analyzed 469 drinking stories from college students, combining them with 32 interviews obtained at three university sites, in order to understand "getting drunk and hooking up." Drawing on the theoretical work of C. Wright Mills's paper "Situated Actions and Vocabularies of Motive," Scott and Lyman's seminal work "Accounts," and Sykes and Matza's "Techniques of Neutralization,"[3] they investigated drinking and sexual behavior as a social process, rather than as a simple individual decision made outside of a specific social context. They noted that "alcohol may . . . be used as a proverbial 'safety net' for college students, where alcohol is consumed to excess *before* a potential questionable sexual encounter because the student knows that *if* anything happens, it can be effectively attributed to the alcohol. . . . In some cases, college students may be actively seeking out reasons that others will accept *before* an act occurs" (Vander Ven and Beck 2009:630; italics in original). These students are responding to a widely held belief that sexual encounters are a not unexpected outcome of intoxication among their peers and may even be "natural." As Vander Ven and Beck (2009) observe, "Because it seems as though a dominant vocabulary of motive exists on the college campus, it is reasonable to posit that it influences the attitudes of those within the collegiate subculture. Many of the respondents viewed drinking to excess as a reasonable motive for questioned alcohol-related coupling" (p. 641).

Vander Ven and Beck's thesis is supported by the quantitative research of Bersamin et al. (2012) who investigated the relevance of college drinking settings to the likelihood of students having sexual intercourse with a stranger. They identified six settings: Greek fraternity and sorority parties, residence hall parties, campus events, parties at off-campus houses or apartments, restaurants and bars, and outdoor settings. They examined the situational-specificity hypothesis, which "suggests that drinking behaviors and patterns are a function of environmental cues. Cues unique to each environment influence alcohol expectancies as well as memory associations, which, in turn, may influence alcohol use patterns. . . . Unique setting characteristics may exist that increase students' risk for alcohol-related sexual behavior regardless of drinking behavior or other individual characteristics" (Bersamin et al. 2012:275).

In their web-based and mailed questionnaires, responded to by a random sample of 14,280 undergraduates at 14 public California universities, these researchers found that having sexual intercourse with a relative stranger after drinking was significantly related to the type of drinking setting. "Specifically," they conclude, "the results indicated that Greek parties, followed by residence-hall and off-campus parties, are high-risk settings for having alcohol-related sexual intercourse with a stranger relative to other locations" (Bersamin et al. 2012:279). A sociological explanation for these findings is that the normative social expectations of these settings are more permissive to sexual behavior than those in other drinking venues.

Devos-Comby, Daniel, and Lange (2013) examined the effects of dating and being in a committed relationship on alcohol consumption and preliminary sexual outcomes in "natural drinking groups" (NDGs), defined as "a collection of two or more people organized to share a social activity centered in drinking who are bonded by friendship or other interpersonal relationships" (p. 2392). Their self-selected sample consisted of 302 undergraduates, who answered an online questionnaire on their most recent NDG drinking experience. The researchers found that over one fifth of their sample reported having had casual sexual contacts (also known as "hookups") with others in their NDG during or right after drinking. As they had earlier hypothesized, this held only for those students who were not in committed relationships. They speculated that the percentage of students reporting having had casual sex related to drinking would have been higher if they had included sexual partners from outside the NDG. Devos-Comby et al. (2013) conclude that "when sexual contact occurred with a partner without a dating relationship, no or little prior desire to have a sexual relationship characterized these encounters, corroborating their casual nature; this perhaps attests that intoxication, more than prior desire, may trigger these sexual contacts" (p. 2397).

Risky Sex

Related to the finding that young people are more likely to engage in sex when they have been drinking is the issue of sexual risk-taking behavior. These risks include rape and having unprotected sex, which may lead to unwanted pregnancies and sexually transmitted infections (STIs). In a systematic review and meta-analysis of 12 quantitative studies that examined the effects of alcohol on risk taking, Rehm et al. (2011) found that "random effects analysis indicated a significant positive association between BAC [i.e., blood alcohol concentration] and the intention to engage in intercourse without a condom, demonstrating that the higher the BAC, the more pronounced the intention to engage in unsafe sex" (p. 53). Neither gender nor the type of community studied significantly modified this relationship.

Agius et al. (2013) studied the sexual behavior and alcohol use of late-secondary students in Victoria, Australia. They were especially interested in the relationship between binge drinking, which they defined as having five or more drinks on a given occasion, compulsive drinking (being unable to stop drinking), and having risky sex (i.e., having multiple partners, not using a condom, later regretting alcohol-related sex). The data for their paper came from a large, longitudinal questionnaire study of young people in Australia and the United States. They found an association between alcohol use and sexual behavior, with binge and compulsive drinkers being more likely than others to report both having had sex in the previous year and regretting having had it due to alcohol. "In line with the hypotheses," they write, "the study found excessive alcohol use continued to show statistically significant associations with sexual behaviour and indicators of risky sex, after controlling for demographic, school and family factors" (Agius et al. 2013:80).

Researchers have examined three alternative theories of why intoxication may result in risky sex. These are alcohol myopia theory (Steele and Josephs 1990), alcohol expectancy theory, and alcohol as an aphrodisiac (Lyvers et al. 2011a). Alcohol myopia theory asserts that when drinking, people focus on the most salient information, ignoring more distal cues. For example, when intoxicated, the perceived attractiveness of a potential sexual partner may override cues about that person's STI status, or potential for violence, or concerns about pregnancy. Alcohol expectancy theory states that people's behavior while drinking is a function of their expectations. These expectations are not simply individual beliefs; they are built into different drinking settings, as the work of Vander Ven and Beck (2009) and Bersamin et al. (2012), discussed earlier, suggests. Consider for a moment an example of alcohol-related behavior that does not involve sexuality—the different expectations and behaviors of guests at an upper-middle-class cocktail party and patrons of a biker bar or roadhouse, in which fights frequently occur. Drinkers in both settings may be equally intoxicated, but the expectations for behavior, and hence the behavior itself, are radically different.

Alcohol as an aphrodisiac posits that alcohol stimulates sexual desire. According to Lyvers et al. (2011a), this thesis has received the least research support. They do, however, cite a few studies that indicate that alcohol may stimulate dopamine release, which might "promote sexual desire" (Lyvers et al. 2011a:100).

Gilmore, Granato, and Lewis (2013) were interested in developing strategies for prevention or intervention programs to reduce possible alcohol-related sexual risk behaviors such as noncondom use. Their applied research is therefore somewhat different from the other studies. They were interested in the possible relationships among protective behavioral strategies (PBS) for drinking (e.g., eating before drinking, keeping track of how much one has drunk, alternating non-alcoholic with alcoholic drinks, and so forth), condom-related PBS, and condom use and alcohol-related sexual activity. Their random sample consisted of 436 college students. Though they acknowledged both alcohol myopia and alcohol expectancy theories, and speculated about the ways in which PBS may modify behaviors explained by those alternative theories (e.g., PBS may reduce the effects of alcohol myopia by making safety cues more salient during drinking and may also reduce alcohol expectancies by increasing one's belief that one has control over one's alcohol-related behavior or by reducing the risk of drinking to intoxication), they do not specifically test these theories in their research.

Gilmore et al. (2013) used a number of measures in their quantitative study, a modified drinking PBS scale, a condom-related PBS scale, and questions on condom use and alcohol use prior to engaging in sexual behavior. They concluded that "consistent with previous research, drinking PBS were related to actual drinking behavior, and this was true for sex-related drinking behavior (i.e., drinking prior to sex) as well. This suggests that drinking PBS are not only related to drinking behavior, as indicated by previous research . . . but they are also related to sex-related drinking behavior. . . . Contrary to our hypotheses, we did not find an association between drinking PBS and condom use or condom use while drinking" (Gilmore et al. 2013:477). Though interesting, their findings do not, unfortunately, differentiate between alcohol myopia and alcohol expectancy theories and could be used to support both perspectives, as they speculated.

Alcohol Myopia

In a study reported in the *Journal of Substance Abuse*, Lyvers et al. (2011a) examined the alcohol myopia theory in a naturalistic study of 72 heterosexual young adults solicited at a campus pub and at campus parties. A breathalyzer was used to test the subjects' BAC. They were then shown photographs of highly attractive unfamiliar models of the opposite sex and asked to rate their intentions of having sex with them, given the opportunity to do so. The attractive pictures were used as impelling cues. The subjects were also given information about the models that served as inhibitory cues with three levels of risk: a slightly risky STI scenario, a more risky STI scenario, and a very high STI risk scenario. Lyvers et al. (2011a) found that "in the naturalistic settings of a campus pub and campus parties, BAC was significantly positively correlated with self-reported likelihood of young adult men engaging in risky sex with highly attractive unfamiliar models even at the highest risk level, whereas in young adult women the relationship was significant only at the slight risk level. Men gave significantly higher risky sex intent ratings than women at all three levels of risk" (pp. 104–105). The authors, however, are reluctant to attribute their findings to alcohol myopia theory because the positive relationship between BAC and risky sexual intentions was present even when the risk was high (e.g., the partner is said to be HIV positive and protection was not available). "This result appears contrary to alcohol myopia theory," they write, "unless one assumes that the impact of extremely high attractiveness is so great for men that even what would seem to be strong inhibiting cues are overridden in the intoxicated state" (Lyvers et al. 2011a:105). They feel that an alternative explanation, alcohol expectancy effects, cannot be ruled out.

J. Walsh et al. (2014) studied the use of alcohol (and marijuana) and the probability of condom use by college women. They asked a sample of 483 female freshman university students to keep 12 monthly accounts of their most recent sexual activities with casual and romantic partners. They concluded that "after controlling for partner type, we found no associations between drinking and condom use, contrary to what might be predicted by alcohol myopia theory" (J. Walsh et al. 2014:154). However, they did find some evidence supporting expectancy theory: "Alcohol consumption and expectancies interacted such that associations between drinking and HED [i.e., heavy episodic drinking] and condom use were marginally more negative for those women holding strong expectations that alcohol use would lead to sexual risk-taking" (J. Walsh et al. 2014:154).

Expectancy Effects

The idea that one's expectancies of the effects of alcohol affect one's behavior is the most sociological of the theories proposed to explain risk taking. As noted, this perspective is given some support by the J. Walsh et al. (2014) study, the qualitative research of Vander Ven and Beck (2009), and the quantitative investigation of Bersamin et al. (2012).

Ham et al. (2013) examined the ways in which drinking context affects alcohol outcome expectancies (AOE)—the belief that one will experience certain effects as a result of drinking alcohol—and alcohol use frequency. Their review of previous research indicated the importance of social context for both prior alcohol use and anticipated alcohol consumption. To understand why alcohol-related behaviors vary across social contexts, the authors used the situational specificity hypothesis, according to which "drinking behavior varies across contexts because of the association between certain cognitions regarding the effects of alcohol and cues presented by a situation" (Ham et al. 2013:622). Their sample consisted of 334 college student volunteers recruited from undergraduate psychology courses in a southeastern public university. Subjects were given a modified version of the Comprehensive Effects of Alcohol Scale and the Drinking Context Scale. They found that AOEs differed by context. Moreover, "positive AOE related to enhanced sexuality were greater when considering the effects of drinking in personal-intimate drinking contexts compared to negative coping drinking contexts" (Ham et al. 2013:627). They also found that this effect of enhanced sexuality was higher in convivial settings than in personal-intimate contexts. The authors note that "consistent with expectancy theory, participants who endorsed positive AOE related to enhanced sexuality or tension reduction in convivial contexts also reported they were more likely to use alcohol in such contexts. For college students, many convivial drinking contexts (e.g., parties, clubs, and concerts) might serve a purpose of meeting a potential sexual partner" (Ham et al. 2013:629).

Beer Goggles

Alcohol clouds one's judgment, increasing the likelihood of engaging in risky sexual practices. It also makes one less discriminating in one's choice of sexual partners, as Mickey Gilley's song "Don't the Girls All Get Prettier at Closing Time" acknowledges. The singer makes the point that as he increases his consumption of alcohol over the course of an evening in a bar, his judgment of women's attractiveness becomes impaired, as they "all begin to look like movie stars."[4]

The ability of alcohol to enhance the perception of attractiveness of potential sexual partners, so humorously described by Mickey Gilley, has been called "beer goggles." Researchers have seriously considered whether this, in fact, really happens. Neave, Tsang, and Heather (2008) studied an opportunistic sample of 103 university students in a laboratory setting. To control for the possible confounding effect of expectancies, some mild deception was used in their study design. Their male and female students were given either alcohol or a placebo. Some of them were correctly told that they would be given alcohol; others were told that they would be given alcohol but were not; another group of students, who were told they would not receive alcohol, were, in fact, given alcohol; and a fourth group of students was correctly told that they would not be given alcohol. Students were then asked to rate the attractiveness of male or female faces, which had previously been rated for attractiveness by a different sample. No significant differences were found among groups in ratings of attractiveness. Neither the ingestion of alcohol nor the expectancy of receiving alcohol influenced the subjects' opposite-sex face attractiveness ratings.

Other researchers, however, *have* found a relationship between drinking and perception of attractiveness of potential sex partners. For example, B. Jones et al. (2003) conducted three experiments in the naturalistic settings of campus bars and licensed eating areas. They used different opportunistic samples for each experiment, with each sample having 80 participants. Half of each sample reported having been abstinent for the day; the other half self-reported alcohol consumption. The subsamples were composed of equal numbers of men and women. As in the Neave et al. (2008) study, the subjects were asked to rate the attractiveness of male and female faces. The researchers found that "there was an opposite-sex alcohol consumption enhancement of facial attractiveness ratings but no own-sex enhancement" (B. Jones et al. 2003:1073). In the second experiment, a new subsample was asked to rate faces for distinctiveness, and in the third study, another subsample was told to rate wristwatch faces for attractiveness. No alcohol-related enhancement was found in either of those two studies, causing B. Jones et al. (2003) to conclude that "thus the enhancement effects of consuming alcohol *appear to be specific* to judgements of the attractiveness of opposite-sex faces" (p. 1073; italics added).

In their second study, reported in *The Journal of Social Psychology*, Lyvers et al. (2011b) specifically examined the issue of beer goggles. Eighty social drinking, heterosexual college students (41 men and 39 women) were recruited from a campus pub and campus parties. After testing their BAC, the students were categorized into three groups: nonintoxicated, moderately intoxicated (BAC = .01%–.09%), and highly intoxicated (BAC = .10%–.19%). They were then presented with 30 photographs of the faces of "moderately attractive" men and women, previously ranked by another sample. The researchers found that both intoxicated samples gave significantly higher attractiveness rankings to the faces than did the sober sample. The relationship between level of intoxication and attractiveness ratings did not differentiate between male and female subjects. They conclude that "consistent with predictions, the present results indicated that perceived attractiveness of unfamiliar opposite sex faces was positively associated with alcohol intoxication, confirming the 'beer goggles' phenomenon" (Lyvers et al. 2011b:110).

Halsey et al. (2010) offer an explanation for why acute alcohol consumption appears to increase attractiveness ratings of faces. In their study, 64 self-selected students, who were classified as either sober or intoxicated, were shown pictures of faces on a computer. The faces were presented either singly or in pairs. The students were asked to rate the faces for symmetry, first by comparing the paired pictures and then by looking at the single faces. Halsey et al. (2010) found that the sober participants were better able to recognize and more likely to prefer the symmetrical faces than were the intoxicated subjects, leading them to suggest that alcohol may play a role in perceived attractiveness by reducing one's ability to perceive asymmetry, thus enhancing the ratings one gives to the opposite sex.

It seems clear from the literature that alcohol serves as a disinhibitor, allowing drinkers to engage in sexual activity. What is not so obvious are the mechanisms through which decisions are made to do so. As we have seen, researchers disagree about whether alcohol myopia or alcohol expectancies affect decisions to have sex, especially risky sex. Additionally, the role of attractiveness of potential sexual partners as a proximal cue in alcohol myopia is open to debate. Some writers find a relationship between BAC and attractiveness ratings, whereas others do not. Part of the problem of assessing these findings is inherent in the methodologies used. The laboratory studies, for example, suffer from artificiality, and hence their generalizability to the real world is problematic. Moreover, they are vulnerable to demand characteristics, and their use of deception, as in a balanced placebo design, can be discovered by subjects as Neave et al. (2008) note.

Field experiments (e.g., the two studies by Lyvers et al. [2011a and 2011b] and the B. Jones et al. study [2003]) in naturalistic settings such as bars and parties avoid the issue of limited generalizability posed by laboratory experiments. Additionally, researchers are able to screen out potential participants who have figured out the study design beforehand. Yet there are still fundamental problems with these kinds of studies. They use convenience samples, which may not be representative of the universe they are studying. Importantly, showing subjects photographs of faces is fundamentally different from their interacting face-to-face with real people. These studies ask about *intentions* and do not look at actual behavior. As a classic study by LaPiere (1934) demonstrated, people's attitudes and expressed intentions do not always translate into their behavior. Aronson,

Wilson, and Akert (2013) point out that the relationship between attitude and behavior is affected by many variables.

Survey research on these issues also has inherent problems, including methods of recruiting subjects. Some studies, for example, Devos-Comby et al. (2013) and Ham et al. (2013), used self-selected samples. Even those studies such as those of Agius et al. (2013), Bersamin et al. (2012), and Gilmore et al. (2013), which used random samples, face issues common to all surveys, including misinterpretation of questions, concealment, and exaggeration.

Alcohol and Sexual Assault

One cannot discuss the consumption of alcohol and risky sex without also examining one of the most dangerous risks of drinking, sexual assault. It is estimated that about 25% of American women have been the victims of sexual assault, and about half of these attacks involved alcohol use by the assaulter, the victim, or both (Krebs et al. 2007; Maryland Collaborative 2016; S. Ullman and Najdowski 2010). Abbey (2002) notes that in one of her earlier studies, both the victim and the assaulter had been drinking alcohol in 81% of the sexual assaults. About one half of all sexual assaults are committed by men who have been drinking (Abbey et al. 1994). This problem particularly affects college students (Abbey 2002; Brown, Hendrix, and Svriuga 2015; Krebs et al. 2007; Research Institute on Addictions 2014; U.S. Department of Justice 2008).

Photo 7.1: Signs against sexual assault, Harvard Yard, Harvard University.

In *The Campus Sexual Assault (CSA) Study*, Krebs et al. (2007) reviewed the literature on substance use and sexual assault involving college students. They noted that although these studies clearly demonstrate a strong relationship between substance use and sexual assault, they do not differentiate between sexual assaults that occur during victim incapacitation and those involving physical force. Accordingly, their own study distinguished among several categories of sexual assault, including those occurring when the victim was incapacitated by alcohol. Krebs et al. (2007) used a web-based survey to collect data from random samples of 5,466 women and 1,375 men undergraduates enrolled at two large universities. They found that 13.7% of the women reported having been sexually assaulted since entering college. More than half of them (7.8%) had been assaulted when they were incapacitated after having voluntarily consumed alcohol or other drugs, and 0.6% were certain that this had happened when they had been given a drug without their knowledge. Krebs et al. identified a number of statistically significant factors that increased a woman's risk of experiencing sexual assault when incapacitated. These variables include the frequency with which women reported getting drunk since entering college (which was also positively associated with being a victim of physically forced assault), the frequency with which they reported being drunk during sex, and having been unknowingly given a drug.

Eighty-nine percent of incapacitated assault victims reported drinking alcohol, and 82% said they were drunk before the sexual assault. The number of sexual partners a woman had since entering college also increased the risk of being a victim of both physically forced and incapacitated sexual assault.

Krebs et al. (2007) also examined the context of sexual assault. They found that the frequency with which the women attended fraternity parties was statistically significant. In fact, 28% of the incapacitated victims and 14% of the physically forced sexual assault victims said that their assailant was a fraternity member. The U.S. Department of Justice (2008) notes that getting drunk is accepted in many fraternities and sororities and that heavy drinking at Greek parties is the norm. Fifty-eight percent of incapacitated victims indicated that they were at a party when they were assaulted. In addition to fraternity and other parties, researchers identify bars, dormitory rooms, apartments, and parents' homes as common settings for alcohol-related sexual assaults (Abbey 2002; Maryland Collaborative 2016; Research Institute on Addictions 2014). Over 60% of victims said that the assault had occurred off campus. The assailants were not complete strangers; most women had seen or talked to them prior to the assault.

Researchers have proposed a number of explanations for alcohol-related sexual assaults, being careful to note that drinking itself does not cause this behavior and that it is the assailant, not the victim, who is responsible (Abbey 2002; Abbey et al. 1994; Maryland Collaborative 2016). Explanations for alcohol-related sexual assaults may be classified into two broad categories: the personality characteristics of the assailant and the norms defining alcohol use and the social expectations for alcohol-related and sexual behaviors. Assaulters are seen as more hostile toward women than nonassaulters and lacking in empathy. They are also more traditional than other men in their attitudes toward gender roles (Abbey 2002), more likely to see male-female relations as adversarial, and more likely to approve of force in interpersonal relationships (Abbey et al. 1994; Research Institute on Addictions 2014). They also engage in antisocial behavior and have positive attitudes toward impersonal sex (Maryland Collaborative 2016; Research Institute on Addictions 2014). Additionally, these men accept male dominance and aggression as normal and believe in rape myths (Research Institute on Addictions 2014). They are also more likely than men who do not engage in sexual assault to drink heavily (Testa and Cleveland 2017).

The social norms/social expectations explanations address the interaction between general ideas about sexuality and situationally based alcohol expectancies. The Research Institute on Addictions (2014) identifies a number of social norms regarding alcohol and sexuality that influence sexual assault. Among these is a college culture that "promotes" a culture of binge drinking and casual sex. Both men and women college students believe that alcohol increases the likelihood that a date will eventuate in sexual intercourse (U.S. Department of Justice 2008). Moreover, alcohol-related sexual assault is influenced by the norms of the larger society, including a hookup culture, a sexual double standard, and a belief that intoxicated rape is not really rape because it doesn't fit the stereotype of violent rape (Research Institute on Addictions 2014).

Testa and Cleveland (2017) recruited 994 freshmen men at a large public northeastern university by e-mail to participate in a longitudinal (5-semester) study of their behavior and attitudes. They were directed to a secure Internet site to fill out a 30-minute questionnaire during each semester. Topics covered included sexual aggression, heavy episodic drinking, bar and party attendance, hookups, measures of self-control, antisocial behavior, hostility toward women, and attitudes toward impersonal sex. They found that men who engaged in heavy episodic drinking were more likely than others to have engaged in sexual assault, but this behavior was completely explained by characteristics they shared with other heavy drinkers, such as impersonal sex orientation, antisocial behavior, and low self-control, rather than by drinking. In fact, when the researchers substituted party or bar attendance for heavy episodic drinking as independent variables, they found that frequency of attendance in these settings increased the risk for predatory sexual behavior. However, when they entered hookups into their analysis, frequency of attendance in these settings became insignificant and hookups became significant predictors of sexual aggression. Testa and Cleveland (2017) conclude that "casual sex may be an even more proximal driver than drinking settings" (p. 7). As they and others note, parties and bars may simply be used by predators as settings in which to encounter vulnerable women for casual sex. Women who are drinking are easier prey for their sexual advances. Men with these intentions may use the disinhibiting effect of alcohol as a justification for their behavior (Abbey 2002; Abbey et al. 1994; Maryland Collaborative 2016; Research Institute on Addictions 2014).

People and Places: Drinking Contexts and Sexuality

The (mostly quantitative) research already discussed looks at drinking contexts either as reported by subjects in questionnaires or as part of field experiments conducted in the naturalistic settings of college pubs, sororities and fraternities, and dorm parties. In this section we review ethnographic research, which provides us with a more intimate look at how alcohol and sexuality are related. Ethnographers serve as participant observers, carefully documenting what they see and experience, yet always mindful of the effects their presence may have on the interaction they are viewing.

The Marketplace Bar

An early and now classic study of drinkers and drinking contexts comes from an English study, *The Pub and the People: A Worktown Study* by Mass Observation. Mass Observation was founded in 1937 by Tom Harrisson, Charles Madge, and Humphrey Jennings to document the lives of ordinary working people. Finally published in 1943, this volume was resurrected and republished in 2009.[5] Strongly influenced by American sociologists of the Chicago school, this work represents the efforts of many ethnographers who collected a vast amount of data. Most relevant to the present chapter is their observations of sexual interactions in the pub, including conversations about beer and sex, attempts of men to seduce women with drinks, and the role of prostitutes in the pub.

Sexuality, then as now, was an important inducement to visit a pub: "The pub is always full of youthful customers. Barmaids with sex appeal are a great draw" (Mass Observation 2009/1943:56). A local pubgoer, who was an ex-policeman, was engaged to ask "a few chaps" why they liked beer. Among the answers he recorded were some referring to the sexual powers of beer. One man claimed that after drinking he was able to satisfy his wife "with the maximum of efficiency." Another young man asserted that beer "gives me a good appetite and puts plenty of lead in my pencil" (Mass Observation 2009/1943:46). Summarizing these declarations, the authors write, "The factor that emerges here, that was not mentioned in the written material, is the effect of beer on drinkers' *sexual powers*. While convention forbids reference to this aspect of beer drinking on other occasions, there is an element of facetiousness in the pub replies that stresses this sort of reason, a very real one" (Mass Observation 2009/1943:47; italics in original).

Sherri Cavan's (1966) now classic monograph, *Liquor License: An Ethnography of Bar Behavior,* is a rich source of information on sex and drinking scenes. "The Marketplace Bar" chapter still seems fresh and current. In it, she succinctly notes that "other than liquor, perhaps the commodity most frequently handled in the public drinking place is sex, on either a commercial or noncommercial basis" (Cavan 1966:171). Cavan discusses three types of sexually oriented encounters:

Photo 7.2: The marketplace bar.

that of the pickup, the occupational behavior of B-girls, and the interaction between prostitutes and their customers.

The Pickup

The pickup is a mutually agreed upon sexual liaison originating in the sexual marketplace. Cavan (1966) is very good at describing in great detail these non-commercial encounters in heterosexual bars. These interactions are similar to, but less overt than, those between the "semiprofessional" women who will have sex for drinks and the men who fancy them, described in the Worktown study. Cavan observes the place of the bartender in facilitating contacts by serving as an inter-mediary through whom a man will send a drink over to a woman to whom he is attracted. The woman, in turn, may refuse the drink, accept it without acknowledging the potential suitor, or indicate her receptiveness to his overtures.

Cavan (1966) contrasts this socially controlled and ritualized mating dance with the attenuated proceedings in male gay bars: "Bar pickups among homosexuals may be differentiated from pickups among heterosexuals by the fact that in their basic form they typically appear to be more rapid and succinct" (p. 190). However, since her book was published in 1966, Cavan could not have foreseen the advent of the heterosexual singles bars in the mid-1970s described by Judith Rossner (1975) in her novel *Looking for Mr. Goodbar* and depicted in the popular movie inspired by it. In those settings sexual contacts were made for "one-night stands" much more quickly than in the relatively sedate drinking establishments she studied. Additionally, Cavan's observations about rapid pickups in gay male bars only described certain kinds of establishments. There are as many kinds of bars in the gay community as there are in the heterosexual world, each with its own culture, atmosphere, and norms, including those for making sexual overtures. The kind of quick eye contact acknowledgment of one's willingness to engage in sexual activities occurs most often in the discos or dance bars, the gay equivalent of the straight singles bar scene. It is much less likely to happen in the cocktail lounges and piano bars frequented by a well-dressed, older professional crowd.[6] A gay man described the way in which habitués of the Sultan, an upper-middle-class piano bar, typically set up contacts:

> At the Sultan I've met some people, but we do stuff like instead of giving our first names and saying, "Hope to see you again," we exchange cards. . . . And people say stuff like, "I would really like to get to know you better," and when people say that at the Cabin they mean, "Your place or mine?" typically. . . . So it's not primarily cruising in the sense of sex that night [for patrons of the Sultan] but more in the sense of really meeting people and maybe a relationship or whatever will develop from that. (Weinberg 1994:42)

Like the marketplace bars observed by Cavan, at the Sultan sending a drink through the bartender was common, and the recipient could respond similarly to the women in her study:

> Phil, Sully and I had gone out barhopping and stopped at the Sultan. Phil seemed to know everyone there and went from patron to patron, flirting with some men and sitting on the laps of others. Later, he was persuaded to get up and sing, which he did to enthusiastic applause. Toward the end of the evening, the bartender presented him with a drink, indicating that it came from one of two men in their sixties sitting at the end of the piano bar. Phil took the drink without acknowledging the source. About half an hour later, he went over to the men and chatted briefly and politely with them, indicating by his physical distance from them, the uncharacteristic lack of animation in

his facial expressions, and the time that had elapsed since the receipt of the drink that he was not interested in them. We left a few minutes later. (Weinberg 1994:43)

In other gay bars, a feeling-out process often occurs, with men initiating casual conversations with others to assess the possibility of a sexual encounter:

In the midafternoon, Jake took me on a tour of his favorite West Holly-wood bars. The first two of these were leather bars.[7] The first establish-ment we visited, the Falcon's Nest, had fewer than a dozen men present. We were standing at the bar with our drinks when a guy in his early thirties, wearing a cowboy hat, walked over, beer in hand. He began a conversation with us. When we left shortly afterward, Jake told me, "Did you see that he was hitting on you?" I told him that I had not. (Author's unpublished field notes)

Sometimes an invitation is made in a roundabout way, so that if the other man shows disinterest, an embarrassing situation is avoided:

The Roundup, another leather bar, was crowded, with a lot of men milling about. I noticed two young men entering the bar together, and assumed that they were lovers. A few minutes later, one of them came up to me and started a conversation. He told me a long and involved story about a friend of his who had picked up another man at the bar. He said his friend was lying on the floor, face up, while the other guy was crouched over him masturbating, when his friend felt something warm fall on his chest. The other man had defecated on him. "What do you think of that?" my new companion asked. I wasn't sure how to answer him, so I just said, "I guess you have to be careful when you take home someone you don't know." After a bit more chatting, he moved on. When I told Jake about my encounter he said, "He was feeling you out to see whether you would be interested in doing that." I said, "Are you sure? Isn't that other guy his lover?" Jake said, "No, they're just roommates." (Author's unpublished field notes)

B-girls

B-girls are employees of the bar who work on commission. Their role is to get men to buy them drinks at inflated prices.[8] As long as men keep the drinks com-ing, the women will pay attention to them. When a man stops buying, the B-girl turns her attention elsewhere. As Cavan notes, some men know the B-girl game and willingly engage in it, paying an attractive woman in drinks for her time and conversation. Other patrons may be naively unaware of the commercial nature of the B-girl–bar patron relationship and believe, at least at first, that they are par-ticipating in a legitimate pickup. The following passage from the present writer's unpublished field notes illustrates the more aggressive behavior of some B-girls, who do not wait for a man's approach:

> Jack had come to visit me in Paradise City and wanted to see Tijuana. We drove down there and walked around the touristy part of town. The place was sad looking, with unpaved streets and shabby storefronts. As we passed a bar, an outside puller grabbed my arm. "Come in guys," he said, "Nice girls, good drinks. Cheap." Jack wanted to go in; I was reluctant. We descended a long flight of steep steps into a dimly lit basement room. On a stage next to the bar, a fully clothed, chubby stripper was doing a desultory dance as if she were half asleep. As soon as we sat down at a table, two women came and sat down beside us. "Do you want a companion?" one asked in broken English. "No," I quickly lied, "I'm married. My wife would not approve." She turned her attention to Jack. Following my lead, he said, "My wife wouldn't like it either." They got up and left. I looked around the room, noting several rough looking patrons seated at the bar. "Drink up," I said, "and let's get the hell out of here." We polished off our watered down drinks, paid and left. The stripper was still doing her somnambulistic dance, fully clothed, as we went up the stairs.[9]

There does not seem to be an equivalent to the B-girl in the gay male bar scene.

Prostitution

The Pub and the People includes a discussion of pub-based prostitution. The authors distinguish between full-time professionals and semiprofessional or amateur pub whores. They note that "in Worktown, a town in which strangers are not common, and whose transient population is small, prostitution does not flourish: the full-time prostitute is a rarity. The small band of them that exists are to be found in a few town centre pubs. . . . One of these pubs in particular is regarded as their headquarters" (Mass Observation 2009/1943:266). A man who spent a considerable amount of money per week on prostitutes gave an ethnographer his detailed typology of the prostitutes to be found in the pubs of Worktown: "When I asked him how much they charged he replied there are types that will do it for free drinks, those are the type that are married or receiving some income from elsewhere, then there are those who manage to scrape enough together by backstreet methods, prices varying from 2s. to 5s., but the real professional type that take their clients home charge from 10s. to any price according to what they think a client can pay" (Mass Observation 2009/1943:266).[10] The women who will have sex for drinks are those referred to as semiprofessional. According to the writers, they are the most common type of pub prostitute.

As Cavan (1966) has noted, some drinking venues serve as home territory bars for prostitutes, whereas in other establishments, "the relationship between prostitution and the public drinking place is one in which prospective 'tricks' are merely channeled through the establishment, to make contact with the prostitute at some other location. . . . In other establishments either with or without the knowledge of the management, women may work as cocktail waitresses primarily for the purpose of making arrangements with patrons for afterhours employment" (p. 201).

The male bar prostitution scene was vividly described by John Rechy (1963) in his autobiographical novel, *City of Night*. Rechy's protagonist is a male prostitute who travels between New York, New Orleans, Chicago, and Los Angeles, selling his services in the cities' gay bars. His book is filled with vivid descriptions of these bars, the hustlers[11] who inhabit them, the friendships and relationships among them, and their dealings with the men whom they service. The following field notes describe two establishments frequented by hustlers. The first of these is upscale and discreet; the interaction in the second bar is less subtle:

> We had dinner in Numero Uno, an upscale bar-restaurant in which Jake told me wealthy Hollywood types met young men for sexual dalliances. I could believe this, since the parking lot was filled with exotic Italian sports cars, Lamborghinis, Masseratis and Ferraris. I did not notice any sexual undercurrent, though, as it was still early in the evening and the place was almost empty.

> Jake described the Phoenix as a hustler bar, which became apparent as soon as we entered. The patrons were grey haired men in their 50s and 60s and young muscular men in their early to mid twenties, dressed as I was, in tight t-shirts and jeans. Jake told me that the young men were looking for "sugar daddies," while their elders were looking for a sex partner for the evening. As the evening progressed, I noticed some of the men pairing off and quietly leaving. (Author's unpublished field notes)

Strippers and Strip Clubs

Strip clubs are another setting in which alcohol is combined with sexuality,[12] although this varies by political jurisdiction. For example, in San Francisco, total nudity is not allowed in bars that serve alcohol; in Ontario, Canada, complete nudity is legal in drinking establishments. Physical contact between strippers and patrons is perfectly acceptable in some jurisdictions but forbidden in others. In some places, for example, strippers give lap dances—a modern version of the "sensuous dancing" described by Cressey (1932) in *The Taxi-Dance Hall*—and private shows in a backroom, all perfectly legal.[13] In Paradise City, however, the city council passed a law requiring the strippers' stage to be at least 6 feet from the nearest patron, probably because of incidents like this:

> I was sitting at the bar, which formed the edge of the stage, sipping my drink. The place was nearly empty as it was still early. One of the strippers, an attractive brunette, stood right in front of me, squatted down

and thrust her pelvis inches from my face. The bartender hollered at her, "What do you think you're doing with that guy? You know that's not allowed." Without missing a beat, she retreated back to the middle of the long, narrow stage. (Author's unpublished field notes)

Although much of what goes on in strip clubs is fantasy or simulated sex, some strippers are also prostitutes, as a number of publicized arrests make clear. For example, a March 2012 article in the (Philadelphia) *Daily News* reported on a number of arrests of strippers for prostitution in several area clubs over a few months' time. The director of the sexual-trauma and psychopathology program at the University of Pennsylvania's Center for Cognitive Therapy is quoted as saying, "You can't truly separate stripping from prostitution. It's a continuum. . . . The prostitute and the stripper are so similar in their dynamic; that's why you see stripping flow into prostitution" (DiFilippo and Lucas 2012). A more recent article in the *Morning Call*, a Lehigh Valley, Pennsylvania, newspaper, gave details on a program for first-time offenders to which stripper/prostitutes had been admitted, after having been arrested in a prostitution sting at an Allentown club (Amerman 2014). In Midtown Manhattan in 2010, strippers were also arrested for prostitution after making arrangements for sex with an undercover detective (S. Jacobs 2010). In Tampa Bay, Florida, 16 strippers were arrested as prostitutes in August 2012 (Hijek 2012), and in Providence, Rhode Island, police investigated underage strippers and prostitution in one of the city's strip bars ("Police Continue

Photo 7.3: A strip club combines alcohol and sexuality. Some strippers also work as prostitutes.

Investigation" 2013). These are just a few examples of a widespread pattern of behavior in which alcohol, strip clubs, strippers, and patrons are intertwined.

Both the chemical effects of alcohol and the expression of sexuality are filtered through a cultural membrane. People's perceptions and behavior are structured by the meanings they have learned in interactions with others. We learn, for example, how to drink, including what, how much, where, proper drinking etiquette, and the like. The same process involves learning about sexuality: where, when, why, what, and with whom is sexual expression appropriate and permitted by one's culture. We learn about standards of attractiveness and sexiness as well.[14] Thus, from a sociological perspective, alcohol expectancy theory as an explanation for alcohol-related sexual behavior makes the most sense. People use the norms and values they have learned as a guideline for acceptable behavior. As Bersamin et al. (2012) and Ham et al. (2013) found in separate studies, the social context within which drinking takes place makes a difference in whether people act out sexually. The significance of social context has been noted in the Worktown, Cavan, and Weinberg ethnographies in which the writers note that different expectations for sexual behavior depend on the type of drinking establishment. Most importantly, these studies demonstrate that the norms and values of one's reference group are central to alcohol-related behavior.[15]

NOTES

1. See, for example, L. M. Cooper, "Alcohol Use and Risky Sexual Behavior Among College Students and Youth: Evaluating the Evidence," *Journal of Studies on Alcohol* 14 (2002): 101–117.

2. See, for example, Paul Agius et al., "Excessive Alcohol Use and Its Association With Risky Sexual Behaviour: A Cross-Sectional Analysis of Data From Victorian Secondary School Students," *Australian and New Zealand Journal of Public Health* 37(1) (2013): 76–82; Melina M. Bersamin et al., "Young Adults and Casual Sex: The Relevance of College Drinking Settings," *Journal of Sex Research* 49(2–30) (2012): 274–281; L. M. Cooper, "Alcohol Use and Risky Sexual Behavior Among College Students and Youth: Evaluating the Evidence," *Journal of Studies on Alcohol* 14 (2002): 101–117; Loraine Devos-Comby, Jason Daniel, and James E. Lange, "Alcohol Consumption, Dating Relationships, and Preliminary Sexual Outcomes in Collegiate Natural Drinking Groups," *Journal of Applied Social Psychology* 43 (2013): 2391–2400; Amanda K. Gilmore, Hollie F. Granato, and Melissa A. Lewis, "The Use of Drinking and Condom-Related Protective Strategies in Association With Condom Use and Sex-Related Alcohol Use," *Journal of Sex Research* 50(5) (2013): 470–479; Michael Lyvers et al., "Alcohol Intoxication and Self-Reported Risky Sexual Behaviour Intentions With Highly Attractive Strangers in Naturalistic Settings," *Journal of Substance Use* 16(2) (2011): 99–108; Michael Lyvers et al., "Beer Goggles: Blood Alcohol Concentration in Relation to Attractiveness Ratings for Unfamiliar Opposite Sex Faces in Naturalistic Settings," *Journal of Social Psychology* 151(1) (2011): 105–112; Nick Neave, Carmen Tsang, and Nick Heather, "Effects of

Alcohol and Alcohol Expectancy on Perceptions of Opposite-Sex Facial Attractiveness in University Students," *Addiction Research and Theory* 16(4) (2008): 359–368; Jürgen Rehm et al., "Alcohol Consumption and the Intention to Engage in Unprotected Sex: Systematic Review and Meta-Analysis of Experimental Studies," *Addiction* 107 (2011): 51–59; Thomas Vander Ven and Jeffrey Beck, "Getting Drunk and Hooking Up: An Exploratory Study of the Relationship Between Alcohol Intoxication and Casual Coupling in a University Sample," *Sociological Spectrum* 29 (2009): 626–648; Jennifer L. Walsh et al., "Do Alcohol and Marijuana Use Decrease the Probability of Condom Use for College Women?" *Journal of Sex Research* 51(2) (2014): 145–158.

3. C. Wright Mills, "Situated Actions and Vocabularies and Motives," *American Sociological Review* 6 (1940): 904–913; Marvin B. Scott and Stanford M. Lyman, "Accounts," *American Sociological Review* 33 (1968): 46–62; Gresham M. Sykes and David Matza, "Techniques of Neutralization: A Theory of Delinquency," *American Sociological Review* 22 (1957): 664–670.

4. Written by Baker Knight, it was recorded in 1976.

5. The authors are indebted to Dr. Rod Watson of Institut Marcel Mauss, Paris, France, for making us aware of this study.

6. For a description of this kind of bar see Thomas S. Weinberg, *Gay Men, Drinking, and Alcoholism* (Carbondale: Southern Illinois University Press, 1994).

7. Leather bars are frequented by men interested in sadomasochistic sex. Leathermen advertise their inclinations with key chains dangling on either the left side (meaning they are dominant) or the right side (denoting their preference for the submissive role) of their jeans. Their tastes are signaled by color-coded handkerchiefs worn in either the left or right back pockets. At the time of this study, the most daring establishments were in San Francisco, where actual sexual activity took place in the bars. Some partial nudity could be found in the Los Angeles area bars but not in the leather bars of Paradise City.

8. More often than not, these drinks are either watered-down or nonalcoholic drinks that appear to be alcoholic. Bartenders keep track of the number of drinks purchased for the B-girls and they are usually paid at the end of the evening.

9. This unpublished observation was part of a more extensive and focused study on gay male drinking. As a way of contextualizing interaction in gay drinking settings, establishments catering to heterosexuals such as singles bars and discos were also visited and field notes kept.

10. The "backstreet" methods mentioned in this quote refers to the practice of people having sex in the narrow alleys paralleling the streets after the streetlights go off.

11. *Hustler* is the term used by male prostitutes to describe themselves. Some of these men, like Rechy's protagonist, define themselves as heterosexual, whereas others have a bisexual or gay self-identity.

12. See, for example, Danielle Egan, *Dancing for Dollars and Paying for Love: The Relationships Between Exotic Dancers and Their Regulars* (New York: Palgrave Macmillan, 2006); Craves E. Enck and James D. Preston, "Counterfeit Intimacy: A Dramaturgical Analysis of an Erotic Performance," *Deviant Behavior* 9(4) (1988): 369–381; Rebecca A. Mestemacher and Jonathan W. Roberti, "Qualitative Analysis of Vocational Choice: A Collective Case Study of Strippers," *Deviant Behavior* 25 (2002): 43–65; Lara Catherine Morrow, "Cyclical Role-Playing and Stigma: Exploring the

Challenges of Stereotype Performance Among Exotic Dancers," *Deviant Behavior* 5 (2012): 357–374; Lisa Pasko, "Naked Power: The Practice of Stripping as a Confidence Game," *Sexualities* 5 (2002): 49–66; Carol Rambo Ronai, "Sketching With Derrida: Ethnography of a Researcher/Erotic Dancer," *Qualitative Inquiry* 4(3) (1998): 405–520; Carol Rambo Ronai and Carolyn Ellis, "Turn-ons for Money: Interactional Strategies of the Table Dancer," *Journal of Contemporary Ethnography* 18 (1989): 271–298.

13. For an excellent description of these interactions, see Ruby Pearson, "Backroom 'Dance,'" in *Selves, Symbols, and Sexualities: An Interactionist Anthology*, eds. Thomas S. Weinberg and Staci Newmahr (Los Angeles: Sage, 2015), 237–242.

14. On culture and sexuality, see Thomas S. Weinberg, "Introduction," in *Selves, Symbols, and Sexualities: An Interactionist Anthology*, eds. Thomas S. Weinberg and Staci Newmahr (Los Angeles: Sage, 2015), xiii–xxi.

15. On the impact of reference groups on drinking and sexual behavior, see Thomas S. Weinberg, *Gay Men, Drinking, and Alcoholism* (Carbondale: Southern Illinois University Press, 1994).

CHAPTER 8

Alcoholism

Perspectives on and Explanations of Alcoholism

Any serious discussion of drinking behavior inevitably turns to a consideration of alcoholism. Although no one can give a precise count of how many Americans are alcoholics, it is undoubtedly a serious problem. For example, according to the FBI's Uniform Crime Reports (UCR) for 2015, there were 10,797,088 arrests made that year for all crimes. Of that number, 1,089,171 arrests were made for driving under the influence (DUI) and 405,880 arrests were made for drunkenness (FBI 2015, Table 29, "Estimated Number of Arrests," https://ucr .fbi.gov/crime-in-the-u.s/2015/crime-in-the-u.s.-2015/tables/table-29). These two offenses account for almost 14% of all arrests. If we also consider arrests for disorderly conduct (at one time there was an offense called "drunk and disorderly"), we can add another 386,078 offenses, and arrests for vagrancy add 25,151 more to the total. Of course, not all of those arrested for these offenses are *alcoholics* as we define the term in this chapter. For some people, DUI or public drunkenness is a one-time, isolated event, whereas for others it is a chronic behavior. And although some people arrested for disorderly conduct may have been drinking heavily, the arrests of others may have had nothing to do with alcohol. Although vagrancy laws are theoretically applied to anyone who has no permanent address or visible means of support, they are frequently applied to derelicts, many of whom have drinking problems. Another difficulty in interpreting these data is that they are for the number of arrests, not the number of persons arrested, so that some of the total may be accounted for by multiple arrests of individuals. Nonetheless, the UCR data still give us a feel for the magnitude of the problem.

So what is alcoholism? It is a complex phenomenon, involving psychological, genetic, physiological, medical, and sociological issues. Therefore, how this question is answered depends on who you ask and their professional and personal perspectives.

Psychological Perspectives

Psychologists have identified common personality characteristics of obsessive-compulsive chronic alcoholics. Edward Podolsky (1960), for example, lists the following:

> 1. Compulsive rituals and obsessive fears. 2. Rigidly controlled emotional reactions. 3. Hypochondriacal trends. 4. Rigid perfectionism of an obsessive-compulsive quality. 5. Compulsive pseudo-attempts at suicide and homicide. 6. Compulsive doubts and vacillation. 7. With intensified fears, threats and frustrations he resorts to alcohol in an attempt to moderate these intolerable feelings, obsessive thoughts and compulsive activities. (p. 236)

In a later paper, discussing "the passive aggressive alcoholic personality," Podolsky (1964) notes that this personality type cannot tolerate failure and therefore drinks to reduce tension when success is important. Drinking increases his awareness of his inadequacies, and he drinks more to "attain the never-attained equilibrium." The alcoholic personality is a variation of the addictive personality. In a research report prepared for the National Academy of Science, Professor Alan R. Lang and his colleagues described the addictive personality as including, among other characteristics, impulsive behavior and difficulty in delaying gratification, feelings of social alienation, and strong feelings of stress (B. Nelson 1983). These observations, however, do not explain how these personality traits and related behaviors develop, nor do they show how they are related to alcoholism. Are they the product of socialization, or are they the result of inheritance or some interplay between them? There is, however, an alternative explanation for what appears to be an addictive personality, a characteristic that psychological theorists would locate *within* the individual. That explanation is reinforcement theory. According to this perspective, the individual responds to a stimulus (perhaps a drug like heroin) with a favorable result (a reward). This response is now reinforced. Manny's autobiography mentioned earlier (Rettig, Torres, and Garrett 1977) gives numerous examples of the pleasurable effect of heroin. His continued use of the drug appears to be a combination of seeking the high and avoiding withdrawal. It would appear that much of the addictive behavior of some individuals is an attempt to seek pleasurable experiences that then become reinforced, rather than the manifestation of an addictive personality.

There is a possibility that genetics may be relevant to the etiology of alcoholism, either by somehow affecting personality traits, and hence, behavior, or in the inheritance of a physiological sensitivity to alcohol. Marshall and Murray (1991) state, "Susceptible people differ from the population not in personality but in the way in which they metabolise alcohol" (p. 73). There is some evidence that there may be a genetic factor involved affecting the processing of alcohol. Some research also suggests that personality traits differentiating alcoholics from nonalcoholics are genetically transmitted. These possibilities are discussed in the following section.

Genetic Explanations

Some data indicate that vulnerability toward alcoholism may be inherited. One of the earlier writers about alcoholism and genetics, Marc A. Schuckit (1986), noted that "the importance of genetic factors in alcoholism is supported by family, twin, and adoption studies" (p. 991). He further observed that adopted-away sons of alcoholics had 4 times the risk of developing alcoholism than the offspring of nonalcoholics. Later, Schuckit (1992) noted that children of alcoholic-dependent parents demonstrate a decreased intensity to moderate levels of alcohol. However, these early family, twin, and adoption studies must be interpreted with care because most of them suffer from methodological problems ("The Genetics of Alcoholism" 2013). In these early studies the mechanisms implicated in alcoholism were not identified. Clearly, caution should be exercised in assuming a connection between individual genes and alcoholism. A cross-species study by Pandey et al. (2004) "suggests that genetic factors play an important role in the development and maintenance of alcohol-drinking behaviors" and that "higher innate anxiety levels play a crucial role in the initiation and maintenance of alcohol-drinking behaviors, and this may be related to the anxiolytic[1] action of ethanol" (p. 5022). One study noted that there is a confirmed association in variants of a specific gene (GABRA2) that differentiates between alcoholics and nonalcoholics. The authors found that variations in that gene affected impulsiveness (Villafuerte et al. 2012). Although this particular gene has now been identified, we still do not yet know how its effect on impulsiveness operates in the genesis and maintenance of alcoholism. Ducci and Goldman (2008) found that 40% to 60% of the variance in alcoholism between people was accounted for by genetic factors.

Physiological Perspectives

The physiological view focuses on the development of tolerance as a characteristic of alcoholism. By tolerance we mean a situation in which increasing amounts of alcohol are needed to attain the same physical state of intoxication. At some point, added increments no longer serve this purpose. By this time, the drinker goes through withdrawal if alcohol is totally removed. Recovering alcoholics report a number of withdrawal symptoms including panic attacks, anxiety, mild confusion, depression, insomnia, nightmares, sweating, shaking (delirium tremens, also called the "DTs" or the "shakes"), skin crawling, vomiting, cramps, severe headaches, dry mouth, and fatigue ("Readers Respond" 2012). These withdrawal symptoms are the same as those reported by heroin addicts.

Medical Perspectives

The medical profession focuses on the physical consequences of heavy alcohol use. These include cirrhosis of the liver, cardiovascular disease, and malnutrition. Additionally, alcoholics may experience "blackouts," situations in which they appear to be aware of what they are doing at the time but later have no memory of what has happened. In the following passage, a recovering alcoholic describes a blackout experience. It was this event that convinced him to contact Alcoholics Anonymous and begin recovery:

> I was driving home from this party . . . and it was very, very foggy, and I don't even remember getting in the car. . . . All I can remember is opening my eyes, looking at my friend . . . and she's yelling . . . for me to slow down . . . and I looked ahead of me and there was this big truck. . . . I closed my eyes and the next thing I remember is hitting the curb outside my house. [The next morning] we went out to look at my car and there was a big dent in it. And I asked her if I had hit a person and she said no, she didn't remember. . . . I was driving home in a car I didn't even know I was in. (Weinberg 1994:118)

Heavy drinkers often neglect their nutritional needs, basically drinking their dinner. At its extreme, heavy drinkers may experience alcoholic paresis, or what has been called "wet brain." Ultimately, the physical consequences of long-term chronic alcohol use may be death.

Alcoholics Anonymous and the Illness Concept of Alcoholism

According to Alcoholics Anonymous (A.A.), perhaps the most successful organization in helping alcoholics to abstain,[2] *alcoholism* is a label affixed to a person

Photo 8.1: The Big Book of Alcoholics Anonymous.

not by others but by oneself. Founded in 1935 by Bill Wilson, a stockbroker, and Dr. Bob Smith, a physician, A.A. serves to enable alcoholics to stay sober through mutual support and encouragement. It is important to note that the organization considers alcoholism to be an illness, one that progresses whether or not a person continues to drink. Therefore, according to A.A., alcoholics cannot and should not ever drink. They are never cured; they are forever recovering alcoholics. Alcoholics Anonymous recognizes what they call "dry drunks." That is, even if the individual is no longer drinking, his or her attitudes and reactions to situations are the same as they were when he or she was still drinking. The recovering alcoholic may even turn to excessive eating, shopping, gambling, or other drug use.

Sociological Perspectives

Sociologists view drinking as a social behavior structured by norms and values (Mizruchi and Perrucci 1962). Therefore, they see alcoholism as a deviation from the drinking patterns of the group to which the individual belongs. As part of the process of developing a deviant drinking "career" (Becker 1963; Goffman 1961), individuals may begin drinking more than their friends on any given occasion and increasing the occasions on which they drink. So, for example, if one's friends go out on Friday and Saturday evenings and have two or three drinks during the night, the prealcoholic may have four or five drinks and begin going out by himself or herself during the week as well. Eventually, the individual leaves the original group and finds another group whose drinking is similar to his or her own. This is often referred to as "the geographic cure."

Sociologists also look at the social consequences of drinking behavior. Alcoholics eventually may alienate their friends, become estranged from their families (Weinberg and Vogler 1990), lose their jobs, get arrested for public intoxication or driving while intoxicated, and so forth.

The sociological perspective is reflected in the Michigan Alcoholism Screening Test (MAST). MAST is a 22-item, self-administered test to help drinkers decide if they have a drinking problem. The items to which drinkers are asked to respond (and then score their responses) include questions about drinking behavior and its physical and social consequences. Some examples of questions that target the social consequences of drinking behavior are the following: Do you feel you are a normal drinker ("normal" is defined as drinking as much or less than most other people)? Have you ever gotten into physical fights when drinking? Has drinking ever created problems between you and a near relative or close friend? Have you ever lost friends because of your drinking? Have you ever gotten into trouble at work because of drinking? Have you ever lost a job because of drinking? Have you ever neglected your obligations, family, or work for two or more days in a row because you were drinking? Have you been arrested more than once for driving under the influence of alcohol? Have you ever been arrested, or detained by an official for a few hours, because of other behavior while drinking? Other questions focus on the physiological and medical consequences discussed earlier (Buddy T. 2012).

For sociologists, alcoholism is not just an individual phenomenon; it is also influenced by the social context. There are a number of societal aspects that lend themselves to creating an environment in which alcohol addiction is more likely to occur. The most obvious of these is the *presence of alcohol in the group*. It is difficult, for example, to become an alcoholic if one is a Muslim living in a country controlled by Islamic law. Similarly, members of the Church of Jesus Christ of Latter-day Saints living in Mormon communities do not use alcohol, nor do ascetic Protestants, for it is also prohibited by their religions. Interestingly, as Mizruchi and Perrucci (1962) note in their review of research done by Jerome H. Skolnick, Charles R. Snyder, and Straus and Bacon (Skolnick 1958; Snyder 1958; Straus and Bacon 1954), when individual members of these groups do drink as, for example, when young adults attend secular colleges and form friendships with non-Mormons or non-ascetic Protestants, they inevitably develop problems. Mizruchi and Perrucci (1962) explain this in terms of proscriptive and prescriptive norms. Prescriptive norms are not haphazardly arranged. Instead, they consist of organized spoken and unspoken understandings about the use of alcohol, prescribing, for example, who may use it and who may not; what type of beverage or beverages are consumed; how alcohol is to be used, including special rituals and on particular occasions; how much is appropriate to be consumed on any occasion; where and with whom it is drunk; the permissible and deviant uses of alcohol; and the consequences for deviant use. Groups in which drinking is not allowed have only proscriptive norms, so that when members of those groups do use alcohol, they have no guidelines (i.e., prescriptive norms) to follow in order to control their drinking. Hence, they get into trouble (Mizruchi and Perrucci 1962).

A favorable attitude toward the use of alcohol is a second characteristic lending itself to substance abuse. As we have seen in Chapter 1, we live in an alcohol-friendly culture. Alcoholic drinks are popular among Americans, with 70% consuming alcoholic beverages. Ads for whiskey, beer, and wine are ubiquitous on television and radio and in popular magazines. Most of these ads present drinking as glamorous, sophisticated, sexy, and popular. The young (mainly 20- and 30-somethings) actors in these advertisements are lean, beautiful, and obviously having the time of their lives while drinking. The sole exception to the youth rule in these advertisements is the Dos Equis beer commercial, starring a man in his 60s. However, he is introduced as "the most interesting man in the world" and is shown in flashbacks as a younger man, engaging in numerous adventures. At the end of the commercial he sits, dressed in a tuxedo, with two young and beautiful women fawning over him.

An indication of the importance of alcohol in American culture is the amount we spend on it. In 2011, this figure was a staggering $162 billion ("Behind Americans' $162 Billion Alcohol Tab" 2013). The use of alcohol is supported by the government. It is interesting that the two most destructive and addictive substances available (the other being tobacco) are not regulated within the federal government's schedules.[3] This is probably explained by the amount of revenue federal, state, and local governments receive from taxing the sale of alcohol. According to the Distilled Spirits Council of the United States (2017), "The beverage alcohol industry contributed over $21 billion directly to state and local revenues during 2010." Another $20.1 billion "came from indirect revenues such as corporate, personal income, property and other taxes generated by the beverage alcohol industry."

A third characteristic conducive to the development of alcoholism in a group is *the ability to administer the drug*. This is not as problematic for alcohol as it is for other drugs such as heroin, which ultimately requires injecting the substance. Nevertheless, Becker's (1963) observations about becoming a marijuana user also apply to the process of becoming a consumer of alcohol: One has to learn how to use alcohol, recognize the signs of intoxication, and interpret being drunk as pleasurable in order to continue its use. For some people, certain types of alcohol are just not palatable, which makes drinking more complicated than it might appear at first glance.

The fourth and fifth elements are the *existence of normal human problems*, for which there is *a perception that there are no other solutions than drinking*. A classic example is the case of the Aztecs who, after their advanced civilization was destroyed by the Conquistadores, became a nation of drunkards, abusing pulque, which had previously been a sacred beverage with severe punishments for those who became drunk while drinking it. According to Madsen and Madsen (1979), "The Spanish conquest destroyed the Aztec empire and reduced its proud citizens to servile members of a subordinate group. Widespread drunkenness was one of the earliest and most persistent responses to the shock of conquest" (p. 39). The Aztec experience clearly illustrates Emile Durkheim's (1966) concept of anomie. With their civilization and all its social institutions destroyed, the prescriptive norms regulating the use of pulque were also dissolved, thereby opening the way for a once sacred beverage to be used as a secular intoxicant.

To summarize this discussion, alcoholism is a social behavior influenced by the person's interaction with others. As David R. Rudy (1986) notes, "Becoming alcoholic and the type of alcoholic one becomes has as much to do with the responses of others—treatment agencies, psychiatrists, A.A., and friends—as it does with the drinking activities and life experiences of the persons labeled alcoholic" (p. xiv). We look at the effect of others on the alcoholic's career in the "Relapse and Abstinence Cycles" section later in this chapter.

Chronic alcoholics eventually develop medical and physiological problems. They also tend to exhibit particular personality characteristics and behavior, even when they are no longer drinking. Anyone who has ever counseled alcoholics can testify that they are often manipulative, impulsive, and angry people with low self-esteem who suffer from anxiety and depression (J. Davis 2004). What we don't know is how these traits are related to heavy drinking and alcoholism, if at all. Do they influence decisions to drink heavily, or are they the results of excessive alcohol use? If they *are* causally related, in what ways do they impact alcohol use?

As noted, researchers have identified genes that affect impulsiveness in humans (the GABRA2 gene) and anxiety-like behaviors and preference for alcohol among rats (the CREB gene) (Pandey et al. 2004).[4] We still do not know, however, the mechanisms through which anxiety or impulsiveness, even if genetically influenced, are related to alcoholism.

Becoming Alcoholic

Alcoholism can be seen as a career, during which the individual moves through a series of steps, phases, or stages (Jellinek 1962; Rudy 1986). The earliest formulation of the phases of alcoholism was put forth by E. M. Jellinek (1962), using an analysis of more than 2,000 drinking histories. He was quick to point out, however, that not all the symptoms he identified fit all addicts. Nor did all alcoholics follow the same phase sequence. Nevertheless, he asserted that his formulation held for the "great majority" of addicts.[5] Howard S. Becker (1963) developed a more general structure for understanding deviant careers within which the situation of the developing alcoholic can be understood. His stages include (1) commission of a nonconforming act, (2) the development of deviant motives and interests, (3) the experience of being caught and publicly labeled as a deviant, and (4) joining a subcultural group of like-minded people. It should be noted that not everyone follows this sequence; in fact, Becker's own experience with marijuana began after he had joined a group of jazz musicians and was motivated to try the drug. In the following paragraphs we examine Jellinek's formulation within Becker's larger framework.

Commission of a Nonconforming Act

The use of alcohol is different from the use of other drugs, because drinking is a socially acceptable activity, at least for those over a certain legal age for whom it is not deviant behavior. Nevertheless, many underage people begin by furtively experimenting with alcohol, and the earlier one begins drinking, the greater the likelihood that one will develop drinking-related problems (Weinberg 1994). Not all nonconforming acts are intentionally committed; no one, of course, starts out intending to become an alcoholic. Few young people are able to understand the possible long-range consequences of their behavior. Jellinek (1962) points out that, in the beginning, alcohol use is always socially motivated, whether or not the individual eventuates as an addict. Social motivations for the prealcoholic may include wanting to be accepted as part of a group, using alcohol as a social lubricant to alleviate shyness, and so forth. The person who becomes either an alcohol addict or a habitual symptomatic excessive drinker soon discovers a sense of relief in drinking, which does not characterize the normal social drinker. Gradually, says Jellinek, the individual's tolerance for alcohol increases and the use of alcohol for relief becomes constant. This observation falls into Becker's second stage: the development of deviant motives and interests.

Development of Deviant Motives and Interests

Finding relief in drinking becomes an important motive for alcohol use. By this time, social motives are no longer very important. As Jellinek (1962) observes in his discussion of his second phase, the prodromal phase, the drinker now becomes preoccupied with alcohol. When he or she attends a social gathering, his or her most important concern is whether there will be enough alcohol present. One way of assuring that enough alcohol will be available is to bring some: "I usually drink [at parties or friends' homes]. In fact, I will—if wine, for instance, is not likely to be, oh, accompany dinner, I usually can be counted on to bring some" (Weinberg 1994:106).

The problem drinker may "have several drinks in anticipation of a possible shortage" (Jellinek 1962:362). One man illustrates this strategy: "And if I go out dancing, I'll start before I go out and then when I get there [I'll continue drinking]. It's a little bit cheaper when you go out. It makes it fun going over there" (Weinberg 1994:106). This is the stage in which, according to Jellinek, the drinker experiences blackouts. He or she is now drinking surreptitiously. At this point, the individual is engaging in secondary deviance, which may help cover or facilitate the initial (i.e., heavy drinking) deviance (Lemert 1967). So, for example, he or she may hide alcohol, add water to whiskey consumed from the family's liquor cabinet, steal from family members, and even resort to violence to obtain money to support this habit.[6] This behavior characterizes Jellinek's third stage, the crucial phase: "And sometimes I'd be drinking at work, too. . . . I worked in a drug store with a large liquor department—one of the great ironies of my life—they put me in charge of that whole liquor room that was downstairs in a cage. And I could go down and break a half-pint of vodka and it would go into "breakage." Then I would drink the broken bottle" (Weinberg 1994:115).

During Jellinek's crucial phase, the alcoholic goes through periods of abstinence and relapse, begins to rationalize drinking, starts to socially isolate himself or herself, quits jobs, and becomes estranged from others. As Jellinek (1962) puts it, at this point the individual's *entire behavior becomes alcohol centered* (p. 364; italics in original). In Jellinek's fourth or chronic phase, the alcoholic is rarely sober. He or she experiences deterioration in thinking and physical problems become apparent. The DTs may be experienced, and tolerance to alcohol may be lost. By now it has become obvious to others that there is a problem, and he or she may become publicly labeled.

Experience of Being Caught and Publicly Labeled as a Deviant

Once someone is caught and exposed as a deviant, as when an arrest for DUI is reported in the local newspaper, there is a significant change in his or her public identity. As Erving Goffman (1963) put it, the person's identity is "spoiled." He or she is, in Goffman's words, no longer "discreditable" (i.e., hidden) and is now known or "discredited." The drinker's central life problem is no longer managing information about his or her alcoholism, but that of dealing with tension in interaction with others. The alcoholic has become, in a word, stigmatized. The drunk identity now becomes what Becker (1963) calls a new "master status," the most important position that people use to classify others. As part of the new label, one also inherits the "auxiliary status" traits of the drunk (e.g., dirty, disreputable, unreliable), which replace one's original auxiliary status traits attached to one's former social identity. As part of this process, the alcoholic may begin to reevaluate his or her self, behavior, and relationship to others, what Goffman (1961) has called the "moral career." As Jellinek (1962) notes in his description of the crucial phase, the alcoholic now "reinterprets his or her interpersonal relationships" (p. 364).

Joining a Subcultural Group of Like-Minded People

Deviant subcultures provide two major functions for individuals. First, they facilitate their behavior and needs by providing whatever it is that they require. Second, and more important, subcultures provide the explanations, rationalizations, neutralizations, attitudes, and ideologies that allow the individual to carry out his or her behaviors, while maintaining a reasonably positive sense of self. They provide reference groups within which the drinker's behavior is normalized. Bars, especially those serving specific populations such as gays (Weinberg 1994); neighborhood taverns or home territory bars, "which are used as though they were the private retreat for some special group" (Cavan 1966:205); and sports bars, whose patrons are avid followers of a particular sports team, are examples of drinking subcultures. Prus (1983) notes that such bars "can be seen as small communities, with friendships and animosities, exchanges and barters, politicizing and gaming, recreation and work, intimacy and distancing, gossip and reputations, and deviance and control" (p. 462). James P. Spradley (1988) captured the essence of skid road (from which the term *skid row* derives) bars by observing that they "are not simply places to drink, they are institutions where strangers with spoiled identities can meet and find security in their common humanity as tramps" (p. 256).

One of the most studied subcultures in which drinking is an important activity is that of skid row.[7] Sociologists have been interested in skid row subcultures for a long time. The earliest description of this world is Nels Anderson's 1923 ethnography *The Hobo*. Anderson knew whereof he wrote, having himself been an itinerant worker and a resident of skid rows. The skid rows of Anderson's day were viable communities with a variety of social institutions. He noted that most of the men in the West Madison area in Chicago, the setting for much of his observations, were younger than middle age and interested in seeking work. Moreover, "the hobo was seldom an illiterate person. Even when illiteracy was high among urban and rural workers, the hobo was a newspaper reader and an ardent follower of the sport page. He had a higher degree of mental curiosity and cosmopolitan interest than most workers" (Anderson 1923:xiv).

Writing about skid row a half century later, Howard M. Bahr (1973) noted that the numbers of what he called "tribes" of skid row men were declining. One of the central themes of Bahr's book centers on powerlessness. "One of the dominant arguments of the book," he wrote, "[is] the idea that one of the main distinguishing features of the skid row man, and a fundamental key to many of his problems, is his powerlessness. That powerlessness is identified as an inevitable consequence of disaffiliation" (Bahr 1973:13). That is, by avoiding stable relationships and the responsibilities they entail, men also relinquish control over their environment, which is derived from these relationships. Bahr described different types of skid row men. He observed that many of them do not fit the stereotype of the derelict or "wino." About one fifth of these men, he wrote, are teetotalers, and he observed that about 40% of them are employed.

Jacqueline P. Wiseman's (1970) symbolic interactionist study of alcoholic skid row residents focused on their treatment. Like Bahr, she noted their estrangement from conventional ties. "In addition to being without friends, the skid row alcoholic is almost completely without the social anchorage—the personal ties—that most middle-class men take for granted" (Wiseman 1970:9). This lack of social relationships and support systems makes relapse after treatment almost inevitable. As Wiseman (1970) pointed out, when the men are in rehabilitation, "the environment of friendship at the institution is *contrived* for the express purpose of offering the alcoholic a warm, supportive (therapeutic) community" (p. 227; italics in original). This is not reality for them when they come out into the streets.

Photo 8.2: Skid Row, downtown Los Angeles.

There is no niche welcoming them back. They have no resources. As Wiseman (1970) explained, "The Row men stop drinking while imbued with the rehabilitator's framework; they start drinking when they *see things differently* on the outside" (p. 229; italics in original). Failure to validate a new nonuser identity causes the individual to call into question his or her new self and leads to failure.

Spradley's (1988) classic work *You Owe Yourself a Drunk: An Ethnography of Urban Nomads* is a detailed description of the world of homeless, alcoholic men. In it he illustrates the complex relationships these men have with one another and social control agencies. In a chapter titled "A World of Strangers Who Are Friends," he describes the skid road subculture as "a world of implicit rules and definitions which these men use to understand and organize their own experience" (Spradley 1988:253).

One of the more interesting skid row institutions is what has been called "bottle gangs," which Spradley (1988) writes is "the most important primary group among tramps" (p. 1173). Bottle gangs consist of two or more men, usually no more than about five, who pool their resources to share a bottle of alcohol. This is not merely a way of affording a drink; rather, the act of consuming alcohol in this context is a ritual whose social motives include acknowledging and validating each other's social identities and affiliation with the group. This group, albeit temporary, has a structure, which includes role differentiation (e.g., the initiator of the group and the man who "makes the run" for alcohol) and rules defining who can participate, how much each man drinks, topics of conversation, and so forth.

Relapse and Abstinence Cycles

Like most substance abusers, many alcoholics go through periods of abstinence and relapse. The sociological question is what causes attempts at sobriety and what precipitates "falling off the wagon"? Alcoholics Anonymous members often talk about "hitting bottom," that is, reaching a point at which their alcohol abuse has destroyed their social relationships, their financial security, and, most of all, their self-respect.

An important paper by Marsh B. Ray (1961) explains the social psychological processes involved in relapse and abstinence cycles. Although written specifically about heroin addicts, it is appropriately applicable to other substance abusers, including alcoholics. There is little difference between alcoholics and other substance abusers such as heroin addicts. In fact, multiple drug use, including alcohol, is common. Like heroin addicts, alcoholics put their drug of choice above everyone and everything else.

At the extremes of their addiction, they engage in secondary deviance to support their habit, committing the same acts as crack addicts and heroin abusers (Lemert 1967; Weinberg 2012). According to Ray (1961), an attempt at abstinence does not necessarily begin with physical "drying out." Its impetus comes from the kind of interaction the individual has with others, an encounter that calls into question the addict's identity as an addict (e.g., alcoholic, crack cocaine user). What is important, according to Ray, is the kind of object the individual makes of himself or herself during this process. If, in the case of the alcoholic, he or she begins to see himself or herself as a sober person, motivation to remain abstinent will be present. Once individuals stop substance abuse, they enter a period in which they are constantly attempting to figure out where they fit in the drinking–nondrinking continuum. It is during this time that support from others for the abstinent identity becomes especially vital. For example, as noted, Wiseman (1970) has shown that the critical variable determining whether homeless men remain abstinent once they return to skid row after completing rehabilitation programs is the availability of support systems. Unlike many middle-class recovering alcoholics who have family support, most skid row–dwelling men do not. Their chances of having a successful outcome are therefore less likely, because they have a narrower "social margin," which "refers to the amount of *leeway* a given individual has in making errors on the job, buying on credit, or stepping on the toes of significant others without suffering such serious penalties as being fired, denied credit, or losing friends or family" (Wiseman 1970:223; italics in original). The alcoholic's newly acquired nondrinking self requires constant validation from significant others, which is not always forthcoming, even for middle-class recovering alcoholics, however, because those people on whom the alcoholic now relies are the very same ones he or she has disappointed numerous times before. Relapse may occur when the alcoholic's new identity as a nondrinker does not get validated by significant others.

The Family and Alcoholism

Alcoholics do not live in a vacuum. Their behavior profoundly affects those around them, especially their spouses, children, and parents. Jellinek has noted that during the crucial phase, alcoholics may drop friends and withdraw from interaction with their families, becoming increasingly isolated. By the time he or she is in Jellinek's chronic phase, the alcoholic is rarely sober, and drinking is no longer a social act; it is a solitary behavior.

Joan K. Jackson (1956) was one of the earliest writers to describe the effects of alcoholism on the family. She identified several stages families go through in an attempt to cope with and adjust to the husband and father's heavy drinking. Briefly stated, in the first stage, the wife attempts to deny that there is a problem. During this time the wife and family define the husband's drinking as normal and controllable, for episodes of drinking are sporadic, interspersed with "normal" periods. The second stage involves attempts to eliminate the problem. At this point, the wife defines her husband's behavior as "not normal" and makes a variety of attempts to control it. However, nothing that she does—drinking with him, hiding his alcohol, trying to understand him, nagging him—works. A period of disorganization marks the third stage. Here, the wife gives up trying to change her husband's behavior. In the fourth stage, the wife "attempts to reorganize in spite of the problem," as the husband loses the respect of his family (J. Jackson 1956:366). The wife becomes the head of the family, and the husband is ignored or treated as a wayward child. The fifth stage is characterized by efforts to escape the problem, and the family organization is continually disrupted as more crises occur. In the sixth stage, the wife reorganizes the family without her husband. The seventh and final stage, recovery and reorganization of the family, occurs when and if the husband achieves sobriety. There are still problems, however, for the wife may be unwilling to yield her status as head of the family. In a study of women participating in Al-Anon groups, Weinberg and Vogler (1990) found some of the same family dynamics reported by Jackson. A major difference was that the women they studied had participated for various lengths of time in an Al-Anon support group, and so once they had joined Al-Anon, they were able to cope better than the wives studied by Jackson. The women said that the group had strengthened them and helped them to put their husbands' drinking in perspective. Al-Anon served to alleviate guilt by teaching the women that they had no control over their husbands' drinking and that it was his problem, not theirs. Women who scored high on a Rosenberg-type self-esteem scale felt more negatively about their husbands' heavy drinking than those with low scores. The higher a wife's self-esteem, the less likely she was to feel that she had failed as a wife and the less concerned she was that others would find out. The less control over her husband's drinking, as measured on a modified Rotter internal-external control scale, the higher her self-esteem and the more likely she was to reject her husband (Weinberg and Vogler 1990).

Treating Alcoholism

Alcoholism has been treated in a variety of settings and by using a number of techniques and strategies. Some of the places in which treatment occurs include special wards in general hospitals; specialized addiction hospitals and for-profit rehabilitation organizations; mental hospitals; therapeutic communities (TCs); and voluntary, informal self-help organizations like A.A. Therapies include individual and group counseling, guided group interaction, the use of alcohol antagonists such as Antabuse as adjuncts to other treatments, and medically supervised alcohol withdrawal.

Therapeutic communities are based on a clinical model that assumes that drug and alcohol abusing behavior is a symptom of the individual's underlying problems, and the goal of the TC is to change his or her negative attitudes and behavior patterns. To do this, the individual is placed in a group situation separated from the outside world, where a structured environment and group pressure and support are used to promote positive change. The effectiveness of TCs has not been established, but modified versions of them, especially for special populations and multimodality approaches, show some promise (National Institute on Drug Abuse 2011).

Alcoholics are often treated by individual therapists. As part of a resocialization process, the therapist attempts to help the patient gain insight into his or her problems. This is usually a difficult and frustrating process, as the alcoholic resists delving into these matters, tries deflecting the therapist's questions, and continues drinking. Most internists and family practitioners, as well as other medical specialists, have alcoholics in their practices, because heavy chronic drinkers inevitably present with the kinds of health issues just discussed. Inevitably, the physician's attempts to treat the patient's illnesses are frustrated by the patient's resistance to stopping drinking. The major issue is that the alcoholic, although physically ill, does not fit into the traditional sick role. The sick role requires, in addition to medical validation, the individual to recognize that this role is temporary and undesirable and that it is necessary to get well. In order to get well, the patient *is supposed to want to get better* and to make every effort to do so by *following the*

Photo 8.3: Sobriety chips from Alcoholics Anonymous, marking periods of abstinence.

doctor's orders. From the physician's point of view, however, the patient does not want to get well, for the patient ignores his or her advice and continues drinking. Moreover, the alcoholic fails to give the traditionally expected deference to the doctor. It is not unusual for physicians to refer these patients to A.A. while focusing on treating their physical ailments.

Some sociological–social psychological principles have been shown to be effective in attitude and behavior changes. These principles can be found in most rehabilitation programs. The first principle is to remove the individual from his or her alcohol-using environment. As we have seen, becoming alcoholic is a process or career. Like any career, it has certain expectations for behavior, which are reinforced within the alcoholic's milieu. Wiseman's work, previously cited, illustrates this issue. Second, attitude research shows that it is easier to change someone's perspective within the context of a group with which he or she can identify than influencing the person in an individual situation (Asch 1940, 1956). So the important principle here is to integrate him or her into another group of former and recovering abusers whose goal is abstinence. This is a central function of A.A. A third principle is to provide the individual with opportunities to demonstrate adherence to the new group's norms and to conforming behavior. The alcoholic shows this by refraining from drinking and by participating in the activities of the group, including attending meetings, which is a critical part of participating in A.A., for example. The last principle is to reward the individual for his or her compliance with the program. The most important rewards for people are not material; they are symbolic, involving the validation of their progress from, and favorable feedback by, significant others. A.A., for instance, recognizes members' sobriety anniversaries.[8] Members are presented with medallions, chips, or coins to recognize sobriety, starting with the first day or 24 hours of sobriety. Coins of different colors represent varying times staying sober over months and years.

NOTES

1. *Anxiolytic* refers to preventing or reducing anxiety.

2. In a 1996 55th reprinting of *Twelve Steps and Twelve Traditions,* A.A. claimed to have over 100,000 members worldwide. The organization estimated that at that time over 2 million had recovered through their program. See Alcoholics Anonymous, *Twelve Steps and Twelve Traditions* (New York: Alcoholics Anonymous World Services, 1981), 15.

3. Schedules are the government's classification of drugs in five categories, depending on their potential for abuse and their medical value. Schedule I drugs have no currently accepted medical use and a high potential for abuse. Examples include heroin, lysergic acid diethylamide (LSD), marijuana (cannabis), 3,4-methylenedioxymethamphetamine (ecstasy), methaqualone, and peyote. Schedule II drugs have a high potential for abuse, although less abuse potential than Schedule

I drugs, with use potentially leading to severe psychological or physical dependence. They may have some currently accepted medical use in the United States. Drugs listed under Schedule II include cocaine, methamphetamine, methadone, hydromorphone (Dilaudid), meperidine (Demerol), oxycodone (OxyContin), fentanyl, Dexedrine, Adderall, and Ritalin. Schedules III through V have increasingly less abuse potential and also have accepted medical use. See Drug Enforcement Agency (DEA), "Drug Scheduling," U. S. Department of Justice. Retrieved August 18, 2013 (http://www.justice.gov/dea/druginfo/ds.shtml).

4. CREB is a protein. The acronym stands for cyclic AMP responsive element binding protein.

5. Jellinek's formulation has not been without criticism. For a comprehensive discussion of other writers' concerns and research attempting to verify the content of his phases, see David R. Rudy, *Becoming Alcoholic: Alcoholics Anonymous and the Reality of Alcoholism* (Carbondale: Southern Illinois University Press, 1986), especially 81–85.

6. For a dramatic example of the extent to which some alcoholics will go to support their drinking, see Rudy, *Becoming Alcoholic*, 22.

7. Nels Anderson, *The Hobo: The Sociology of the Homeless Man* (Chicago: University of Chicago Press, 1923); Howard M. Bahr, *Skid Row: An Introduction to Disaffiliation* (New York: Oxford University Press, 1973); James P. Spradley, *You Owe Yourself a Drunk: An Ethnography of Urban Nomads* (New York: University Press of America, 1988); Jacqueline P. Wiseman, *Stations of the Lost: The Treatment of Skid Row Alcoholics* (Englewood Cliffs, NJ: Prentice Hall, 1970). The term *skid row* is a corruption of the term *skid road*, which has its origin in the dirt pathways used to "skid" logs down from the hills to the river in logging camps. The term *skid road* is still used in Washington State.

8. See, for example, the following website that people can use to send sobriety congratulations to others and to record their own sobriety anniversaries: http://www.aahistory.com/newbirth.html.

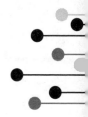

CHAPTER 9

History of Drug Use in America and Attempts to Control It

Origin of Hashish and the Persian Assassins

Hashish is made from the resin of the cannabis plant. This has been used for thousands of years as indicated by archeological discoveries as ancient as 9000 BCE (Samorini 1992). By 900 CE it had spread throughout Arabia, where it was consumed by eating it. Somewhat earlier, in 874 CE, an Iraqi peasant, Hamdan ibn Ashrat, popularly known as Quarmat, became the leader of the Ismaeli sect of Islam. The sect engaged in a bloody list of conquests by killing indiscriminately. This inspired the Ismaelis of Alamut or Eagles Nest in northern Persia or Iran to wage a campaign of murder and terror against all opponents of their faith.

In this spirit, the Ismaeli Muslims organized a sect whose leader was to be absolutely obeyed. They then moved into a mountain fort, ten thousand feet above sea level, where they were impregnable. Alamut then became the center of a group of young men who used hashish to give them hallucinations of various kinds. Under the influence of hashish, these men were capable of killing anyone at any time. These killers were therefore called Hashishin in Arabic, from which the word *assassin* is derived (Durant 1950).

It took until 1800 for the drug to be known in Europe. This came about when Napoleon's troops learned of this drug during their campaign in Egypt. Later, hashish came into use in Ireland, when in 1842, Dr. William O'Shaughnessy gave some hashish to Peter Squire, who then made an extract later known as Tilden's extract (Russell 2003).

Chinese Opium Wars

Opium came to the United States from China in the 19th century at a time when drug addiction had reached immense levels in that country. That addiction was principally caused by British and American efforts to introduce opium to China for the profits to be made (McCoy 1972).

In 1785, the first American ship reached China, beginning a trade with that country, which included sealskins, cotton, wood, and furs. Silver was also exported, but all of this represented a one-way trade in favor of China. Therefore,

American businessmen began to sell opium to the Chinese at a considerable profit. This had already been done by the British, who had defeated the Chinese in the First Opium War in 1839, caused by Chinese resistance to the importation of opium into their country. As a result of this British victory, more and more opium was imported into China, leading to more and more Chinese opium addicts. Therefore, it was estimated that by 1906, over 27% of the adult male population of China was addicted to opium ("Opium in China" 2015).

In 1856, the Chinese once more resisted British aggression, leading to a second opium war in which the British were supported by France. By then, Hong Kong, Shanghai, and a number of other Chinese cities had been occupied by Britain. American interests were accommodated after the so-called Arrow War, leading to the concession by the Chinese that opium was to be a legitimate article of commerce. Yet by 1880 Americans were no longer involved in the opium trade with China because of falling prices and considerable competition. In that year also, a treaty between China and the United States ended Chinese importation of opium into the United States and vice versa (Clyde 1940).

Prior to the 1880 treaty, some of America's leading families were making vast fortunes from selling opium. These families included the Delanos, Peabodys, and Cabots.

Although importing opium into the United States was prohibited in 1905, the introduction of opium into the United States by Chinese immigrants continued by those who were addicted before coming here. This means that by 1849, Chinese immigrants brought opium smoking to America with the California Gold Rush. This led to the view among the population of European descent that the Chinese were a "yellow peril" seeking to destroy America with drugs. One of the consequences of these beliefs was the passage of a California law in 1858 that prohibited the entry of "anyone of the Chinese and Mongolian races" to enter California. Then revisions in the U.S.-China Burlingame Treaty allowed the United States to suspend Chinese immigration. In 1879, California adopted a new constitution that allowed the state government to decide who may live in the state. It also banned Chinese from employment in any level of government in the state.

Chinese immigrants had been employed in building the transcontinental railroad, but when that project came to an end, Chinese immigrants were seen as cheap labor competing with Euro-Americans for jobs. After the Central Pacific Railroad had been built, the Chinese became competitors for jobs in industry and commerce, and soon a considerable hatred of Chinese immigrants developed. Chinese were depicted as subhuman, as inferior and dangerous. They were confined to living in Chinese ghettos (Chinatowns). Popular opinion viewed the Chinese as criminals, gamblers, savages, and prostitutes (Smith 1966).

Thereafter, the Chinese Exclusion Act of 1882 prohibited all immigration of Chinese laborers for 10 years. Renewed in 1892, it was made permanent in 1902 but repealed in 1943 (Kanazawa 2005). The act excluded Chinese from immigrating to the United States, because the government viewed the presence of Chinese as detrimental to order in areas were the Chinese had settled. The law provided a

THE ONLY ONE BARRED OUT.

Enlightened American Statesman.—"We must draw the line *somewhere*, you know."

Photo 9.1: Chinese Exclusion Act, 1882. "The Only One Barred Out." American cartoon.

fine of $500 for anyone bringing Chinese into the country and threatened 1-year imprisonment for such a violation. Chinese who came after November 17, 1880, were to be deported, and those who came before that date were given certificates of identification (Chinese Exclusion Act 1882).

Despite the popular rejection of the Chinese on the grounds that they imported opium to the United States, opium was legally sold in this country throughout the 19th century. Morphine also came into common use after the Civil War, and heroin was widely distributed at the end of the century (Howe 1955).

These drugs were chiefly distributed through five channels. These included physicians, who dispensed opiates directly to patients, and drugstores, which sold opiates over the counter to users who had no prescription. Grocery stores and pharmacies also sold opiates, which were ordered by mail, and innumerable "patent medicines" were reputed to cure almost anything but were in fact opium or morphine concoctions (Townes 1912).

Opium was legally imported and morphine was legally manufactured from the imported opium. Furthermore, opium poppies were legally grown in the United States. Opium was sold for $10 to $12 per pound (Lichtenstein 1926:123). During the Civil War, the Confederate states also produced opium, as did the Union. This continued until 1942, when Congress passed the Opium Poppy Control Act. That act was repealed in 1972, because its enforcement was transferred to other narcotics control measures.

Thus, during the 19th century, distribution of opium and other drugs reached into every farm, village, town, and city. Sales of opium increased during the century beyond the increase of the population, and that included laudanum, which is opium in alcohol. As a result, many druggists became rich by selling more and more opium products (Terry and Pellens 1928).

Eaton (1888) cites a survey of 10,000 prescriptions filled by 35 Boston drugstores in 1888, of which 1,481 contained opiates. Of all prescriptions filled three or more times, 78% contained opiates.

In 1878, the Michigan State Board of Health surveyed the state to discover how many citizens were using drugs. This report showed that in Huron, a village of 437 inhabitants, there were four "opium eaters" and one "morphine eater." Likewise, in the village of Otisville, with a population of 1,365, there were 18 opium eaters and 20 morphine eaters. In several communities around the state, children were also using these drugs (Terry and Pellens 1928).

Not everyone supported the use of opium. Many Americans viewed drug use as disreputable, a view that also included the drinking of alcohol. There were also those who considered both alcohol use and nonalcoholic drugs as immoral, an opinion that also denounced dancing, theatergoing, gambling, and sex. In the 19th century the use of drugs was seen as weakness of the will and of moral degeneration (Anonymous 1888).

An excellent example of the experiences of someone who used heroin in the 19th century is *The Hasheesh Eater* by Fitz Hugh Ludlow (2013/1857). It has been reprinted several times, the last edition in 2013.

Ludlow claimed that the cannabis user has a greater insight into beauty and truth, but he also calls the ends of such use a poisonous wilderness. The book was widely read and led to the establishment of hashish parlors all over the country. In 1876, visitors to the Philadelphia Centennial Exposition could buy hashish there.

Ludlow's book was given two different interpretations. The prohibitionists emphasized the addictive aspects of hashish and the horrifying hallucinations associated with its use. Those who supported the use of cannabis sought to reach the "mystical heights" Ludlow promised (Kalant 1971).

The Civil War (1861–1865) led to a considerable increase in the use of opium in the South and in the North. Indeed, opium had been used in both areas of this country before the war. So-called female complaints were treated with opium, so that addicts were primarily upper-class, Southern white women.

Once the Civil War began, doctors on both sides used opiates to deal with all kinds of pain and discomfort. The treatments included morphine powder, which was injected with the recently invented hypodermic syringe. The wounded were treated with that method, and nearly 30,000 ounces of morphine sulphate were dispensed to Union soldiers at the beginning of the war. This increased to 10 million opiate pills by 1865. Because pain continued for some time after a soldier was discharged, many became drug addicts in an effort to ease the pain. In addition, many relatives of the dead and wounded used drugs to live with the emotional consequences of the Civil War. The survivors of the fighting were often maimed and crippled and needed to relieve their suffering. For that they used drugs (Courtwright 1982).

By the 1880s, pharmaceutical companies produced hashish painkillers, marijuana and tobacco snuff, and marijuana cigarettes. During those years, synthetic drugs such as aspirin began to appear. At the end of the 19th century, chemists had isolated the active components of cannabis, leading to a number of breakthroughs in cannabis research. However, synthetic drugs were now becoming popular, leading to a system of controlled prescriptions.

Drug use was then identified with foreigners and undesirable immigrants, so that it became un-American to use opium, which became identified with Chinese immigrants. Cannabis was widely used in Mexico and from there migrated north to Texas and other southwestern states including California, where the importation of opium was banned in 1908.

Controlling Drug Use

Pure Food and Drug Act of 1906

In 1906, Congress passed the Pure Food and Drug Act. This act required that drugs including alcohol, cocaine, heroin, morphine, and cannabis be accurately labeled with dosage and contents. The purpose of these provisions was to prevent the further sale of these drugs as patent medicine capable of curing all that ailed anyone. These drugs continued to be legally available, although their use declined by 33% after labeling became the law (Musto 1999).

The Pure Food and Drug Act became law mainly due to publication of Upton Sinclair's (1906) novel *The Jungle,* in which Sinclair exposed the horrendous working conditions that faced immigrants forced to labor in the stockyards of Chicago. Included in the description of these nightmares was a considerable discussion of the filth and pollution of the meat delivered to unsuspecting consumers. Sinclair also described how some of the immigrants resorted to drugs to deal with their misery stemming from the exploitation they suffered at the hands of the meat industry bosses. The consequence of this publication was an uproar against the meat industry and its practices related to the consumption of meat, which included dead rats and other filth. Although no one cared about the suffering of the immigrants working in these houses of horror, people did not want to eat foul food. This led to the passage of the Pure Food and Drug Act, despite the almost universal denunciation of Upton Sinclair.

Opium Exclusion Act of 1909

In 1909, Congress passed the Opium Exclusion Act, the first national prohibition law. It prohibited the importation of opium for smoking and was therefore directed at Chinese immigrants. The private use and possession remained legal. By 1909, opium smoking had declined a great deal, but California went further and prohibited any possession of opium. These laws did nothing to halt the trade in opium, but instead they led to unprecedented crimes associated with smuggling drugs into the country (Gieringer 2006).

Harrison Narcotics Act of 1914

In 1914, the Harrison Narcotics Act was passed by Congress. This law required those who had been dispensing narcotics to register with the Bureau of Internal Revenue, pay a tax, and keep a record of the drugs used. It allowed physicians to prescribe narcotics for patients in the course of normal treatment, but not for addiction. The act had 12 sections detailing the means by which drugs could be distributed legally in the United States. The law forced dealers, pharmacists, and physicians to maintain records of drug transactions.

National Prohibition Act of 1919

Five years later, as discussed in Chapter 3, the antidrug lobby succeeded in making alcohol illegal in the United States. The National Prohibition Act of 1919 was the enabling legislation, which followed the adoption of the Eighteenth Amendment to the U.S. Constitution, making the manufacture, production, use, and sale of alcoholic beverages illegal in the United States. The law is generally known as the Volstead Act after Andrew J. Volstead, who chaired the Senate Judiciary Committee and who sponsored the legislation. This law was vetoed by President Woodrow Wilson. However, Congress overrode that veto, so that Prohibition went into effect on January 16, 1920. The ensuing crime wave led to organized opposition to the law, and the Eighteenth Amendment was finally repealed in 1933. Nevertheless, there are counties and towns where prohibition continues (Childs 1947).

The Geneva International Commission

In 1924, the United States participated in the Geneva International Commission on Narcotics Control. This commission was convened by the International Opium Commission, leading to the decision to limit the exporting of hashish to medical and scientific usage. Nevertheless, after the First World War, the U.S. government bought 300 tons of opium to be used in veterans hospitals (U.S. Congress 1924).

Marihuana Tax Act of 1937

Because several agencies participated in trying to control the trafficking in narcotics, a considerable amount of infighting among agencies developed. To put an end to this rivalry, Congress established the Federal Bureau of Narcotics (FBN) in 1930. This bureau was located in the Treasury Department. It was administered by a commission appointed by the president with a mandate to enforce the Harrison Act. President Hoover appointed Harry J. Anslinger the commissioner. At first the FBN, later called the Drug Enforcement Administration (DEA), dealt only with cocaine and opium. As the Depression of the 1930s deepened, the FBN began to enforce marijuana laws because the more expensive drugs were less popular than the cheaper marijuana. Moreover, marijuana was imported from Mexico, had a Spanish name, and was therefore far more likely to be viewed as dangerous by reason of its origin (Anslinger and Ourslee 1961). The Marihuana Tax Act, passed in 1937, was ineffective in reducing the use of marijuana. Twenty years after the act's passage, the drug was still being used by thousands of Americans. Between 1958 and 1968 drug arrests increased from 10,000 to more than 160,000. Furthermore, the percentage of persons arrested for drug possession under age 21 increased from 14% to 56% during that decade. The Marihuana Tax Act demanded that those who use the drug incriminate themselves by paying a tax on its possession. The U.S. Supreme Court invalidated this law in 1969 in *Leary v. United States* because it was plainly unconstitutional in view of the Fifth Amendment. It was repealed by Congress in 1970 and rewritten so that marijuana was no longer classified as being as dangerous as heroin. Therefore, the penalties were reduced ("Administration About-Face" 1969).

Nevertheless, there was and is good reason to consider marijuana dangerous, especially when used by children. This is by no means unknown. In fact, although not very common, according to the Substance Abuse and Mental Health Services Administration's (SAMHSA) report for 2014, published the following year, some children as young as 12 have had access to this drug wherever it is freely available to adults (SAMHSA 2015a).

Narcotics Drug Import and Export Act of 1951 (The Boggs Act)

Drugs of all kinds are distributed worldwide and reach the United States from numerous areas. For example, the German port city of Hamburg is known as a worldwide distribution center of drugs, as are the Bahamas and numerous other sources. This worldwide distribution of drugs led to the establishment of the Division of Foreign Control in the Prohibition Unit of the Treasury Department (Schneckebier 1929).

It became more and more evident that a good number of drug dealers escaped American police forces because the United States had no jurisdiction in foreign countries. Likewise, other governments were also limited in dealing with drug dealers who escaped to another jurisdiction. This dilemma led to the establishment of Interpol in 1914. Yet the United States did not join Interpol because J. Edgar Hoover, the FBI director, did not want any competition. Years later, in 1958, the United States did finally join Interpol (U.S. Department of Justice 1985).

In 1951, Congress passed the Narcotics Drug Import and Export Act, or Boggs Act, which increased penalties for all drug violations. This act lumped together marijuana and narcotics and provided the same penalties as for violation of the Marihuana Tax Act—payment of a tax and penalties of 5 years in prison and a $25,000 fine for the first offense.

Narcotics Control Act of 1956

In 1956, Congress passed the Narcotics Control Act, which increased the penalties even further. The states passed similar laws. These laws were passed because it was believed that there had been a major increase in drug use and because legislators thought such laws could prevent if not reduce the use of drugs.

The hearings concerning the proposed Narcotics Control Act led the congressional committee to accuse the Supreme Court of using a "too liberal" interpretation of constitutional safeguards. The committee was opposed to restrictions the Supreme Court had imposed on the use of telephone tapping. It was also opposed to allowing accused drug offenders the use of bail and viewed existing maximum penalties of 5, 10, and 20 years, depending on the number of offenses, too low. The committee even opposed drug rehabilitation efforts on the part of the medical profession and demanded that drug smugglers and those selling heroin be executed. The argument in favor of capital punishment for heroin sellers was that heroin leads to murder, robbery, and rape. The committee also favored abrogating the limitations on the right of federal drug agents to search and seize property. It even proposed that anyone convicted of a drug offense be prohibited from traveling outside of the United States (R. King 1972).

A statement by Representative Boggs, reported in the Congressional Record, claimed that there had been an immense increase in drug addiction between the late 1940s and 1950 (Schaffer Library of Drug Policy n.d.). This led to the inclusion of mandatory minimum sentences in these drug laws and the passage of similar drug laws in 17 states. In addition, 11 states increased the penalties already in force. The federal penalties were 2 years in prison for a first offense of drug possession, 5 years for a second offense, and 10 years for a third and subsequent offenses. In addition, a fine of $20,000 was imposed. The sale of drugs was punished with 5 years in prison for a first offense, 10 years for a second offense, and 10 years for the sale to a minor by an adult (Schaffer Library of Drug Policy n.d.).

This law was imposed based on the belief that the United States had more addicts than any other country, that drugs were shortening and destroying human lives, and that most crimes committed in metropolitan areas were caused by drugs. It was further claimed by supporters of this law that addiction was contagious and was spreading all over the country, so that addicts must be placed in quarantine and isolated in prisons. It was further claimed that Chinese-manufactured heroin was being sent to this country in order to enslave America.

In 1960, the U.S. Bureau of Narcotics arrested two drug dealers, one of whom was of French nationality. These arrests revealed that a "French Connection" was involved in smuggling drugs into the United States. Those arrested were convicted and jailed for 5 years and charged a $10,000 fine, which seemed ridiculous in view of narcotics dealers' profits of $20 million annually ("Imprisoned by U.S. in Narcotics Ring" 1958).

Rockefeller Drug Laws

The most notorious and cruel state law prohibiting drug possession was the 1973 law imposed by the New York State legislature at the request of then governor Nelson Rockefeller. Known as the Rockefeller drug laws, these laws were passed in response to President Richard Nixon's declaration of a "war on drugs." These laws imposed mandatory sentences on people convicted of even minor drug law violations by removing judges' power to consider each case individually.

The consequences of these laws were horrendous. Whole families were destroyed and the lives of citizens ruined. First-time offenders addicted to drugs were imprisoned without any help being offered, leading to the federal laws of the 1980s that sent millions of Americans to prison with mandatory sentences (Papa 2013).

These New York laws were finally repealed in 2009 during the administration of Governor David Paterson. The repeal allowed judges to send offenders to rehabilitation and counseling instead of sending them to prison. This came about because the war on drugs had failed, and its prohibition had become as odious as the prohibition of alcohol in the 1920s (Peters 2009).

Nixon's war on drugs was conducted by the Bureau of Narcotics and Dangerous Drugs (BNDD). This agency was the result of a merger between the Bureau of Narcotics in the Treasury Department and the Bureau of Drug Abuse Control in the Department of Health, Education and Welfare. The new agency, the BNDD, was placed into the Department of Justice. This agency dealt with international and interstate activities and located nine foreign offices in Italy, Turkey, Panama, Hong Kong, Vietnam, Thailand, Mexico, France, and Colombia.

Medicalizing Drug Use

After years of passing numerous laws punishing drug possession and sales with ever greater severity, some members of Congress and some state legislators were willing to consider some other measures designed to at least reduce, if not eliminate, the drug traffic and its use. This led to the passage of the Narcotics Addict Rehabilitation Act of 1966, which was largely punitive but also included provisions to allow drug addicts not charged with any crime to be subject to civil commitment for treatment. The announced purpose was to rehabilitate and help drug users to become useful members of society.

Porter Farm Act of 1929

The Narcotics Addict Rehabilitation Act of 1966 was not the first time Congress had at least given lip service to the possibility of assigning drug addicts to medical procedures. In 1929, Congress passed the Porter Farm Act, which led to the incarceration of drug addicts but also provided medical treatment, psychological counseling, vocational training, and hospital treatment.

The Porter Farm Act was unsuccessful, and it was therefore replaced by civil commitment as instituted by the Narcotics Addict Rehabilitation Act. Civil commitment to an institution was also enacted in New York, California, and Massachusetts. These commitments resembled the manner in which the mentally ill were committed. The outcome of these commitments was that the drug addict was locked into a cell in a mental hospital and given little or no treatment (Chapman 1963).

Some of the addicts incarcerated in mental hospitals were volunteers, who stopped the use of drugs while incarcerated but resorted back to using drugs as soon as they left the hospital. In California, the program included the opportunity to escape prison by volunteering for a civil commitment. This was not open to those who applied too late or who had committed a felony.

The federal and state laws provided that addicts who had completed a specified amount of time in a mental hospital were to be compelled to enter a halfway house upon release. There they were to be subject to periodic testing to determine that they remained drug-free. In case the addict reverted to drug use, he or she could be forced to return to hospitalization and more treatment, provided an order of the committing court was obtained.

This program was as unsuccessful as the punitive laws have been since they were first used to stem drug addiction. It is evident that nothing yet tried has stopped drug addiction, including alcoholism, in this country or elsewhere.

Comprehensive Drug Abuse
Prevention and Control Act of 1970

In 1970, Congress tried again by passing the Comprehensive Drug Abuse Prevention and Control Act. This law, like others before it, failed to give any consideration to differences in lifestyle and experiences among different segments of the American population. Race, ethnicity, class, gender, and religion affect human behavior, so that drug use has different meanings to a variety of people affected by any law. Yet equality before the law is one of the principal aspects of America. Is it then legitimate to treat different populations differently when it comes to enforcing the law among different ethnic groups? (Kleck 1981).

Legislators mistakenly assign penalties to behavior that is common to some segments of the population and is hardly known to others. This means that the law often reflects concern with one segment of the population, while failing to recognize others also living in the district but represented by a few. Criminal law is a reflection of the social conditions in a community (Kleck 1981) and generally represents the mores of a community. This means that the values of a society are codified in the law, because they are widely shared in the community and represent common interests (Chambliss 1969).

Researchers have argued that American drug legislation largely represents an effort of the white majority to reject minorities such as Chinese, African Americans, and Mexicans. The view of these writers is that the opium laws were aimed at the Chinese, who were seen as a threat to Protestant America; that the Marihuana Tax Act was aimed at Mexican and other South American immigrants; and that blacks were the target of laws pertaining to the Harrison Narcotics Act. These minorities were not welcomed by those who made these laws, because it was feared that the target population would become violent under the influence of the forbidden drugs and attack white society (Susman 1975).

All of this, therefore, pertains to the Comprehensive Drug Abuse and Control Act. It cannot be overlooked that alcohol, whether in the form of beer or scotch whiskey, can indeed be a dangerous drug. However, whiskey imported from Scotland is surely more acceptable to America's dominant legislators than marijuana, which comes from Mexico and is sold by "dangerous" South Americans.

The Comprehensive Drug Abuse and Control Act lowered penalties for possession, compared to previous legislation. This was done because many members of Congress found that their own children or those of the upper class were using drugs. It was therefore considered reasonable to lower penalties on youthful offenders who came from "good" families and were not related to lower-class criminals and "opium eaters" (Rosenthal 1977).

Methadone Control Act of 1973

The Methadone Control Act of 1973 regulated methadone licensing and established federally funded methadone clinics for dispensing methadone. The purpose was to treat opiate addicts by substituting methadone hydrochloride, which had been approved by the Food and Drug Administration in 1947. Methadone is a synthetic opiate used for detoxification and maintenance in patients who are opiate dependent, which is in the main heroin. It may only be administered by licensed practitioners, such as physicians. It has the advantage of blocking the craving for heroin. Yet this substance is also addictive and may result in dependence after repeated use. Furthermore, methadone has a number of adverse effects such as nausea, hypertension, and others ("Public Health Issue" 2000). In Chapter 13, we discuss methadone maintenance and one of the more successful programs, the Nyswander and Dole program.

In 1973, President Richard Nixon abolished all previous drug enforcement agencies in favor of the then new Drug Enforcement Administration (DEA). The DEA viewed marijuana as a minor problem and concentrated its resources on the enforcement of laws prohibiting the use of heroin and other drugs deemed dangerous. Those who wrote articles in *DE*, the magazine of the DEA, as well as those who testified before congressional committees, treated marijuana use as a minor nuisance not worthy of criminalization. Therefore, the focus of the DEA for the first 7 years of its existence was entirely on the so-called hard drugs (Page and Clelland 1978).

When Ronald Reagan was elected president in 1980, emphasis on hard drugs began to decrease and marijuana became the focus of the DEA, as President Reagan announced an end to permissiveness. This led the DEA to suddenly find all kinds of "scientific" evidence to the effect that marijuana was indeed a dangerous drug and that "new" findings made it essential that the use of marijuana be suppressed. Accordingly, the DEA published a list of terrible consequences reputedly arising from marijuana use. These included the assertion that those using this drug suffer from impaired learning and intellectual performance; that marijuana causes chest pain; that it creates traffic hazards because it diminishes driving ability; that marijuana causes the same lung problems associated with cigarette smoking; that it may cause brain damage and damage the immune system; that marijuana affects the endocrine system; and that the human reproductive system is adversely affected (Pollin 1980).

These warnings were published in *DE*, although no scientific evidence for these assertions was presented. Instead, the political situation had changed and the DEA sought to be aligned with the new conservatism.

The Drug Abuse Warning Network

During the Reagan administration, the reputed increase in drug use in the country continued to worry politicians and the public as the media depicted the violence associated with "crack" cocaine. This led to a public demand for more enforcement of the drug laws, so that in Washington, DC, alone, felony drug law prosecutions rose 500% between 1983 and 1987 (Coyle 1988).

Similar increases in drug law prosecutions were recorded in other American cities. Nevertheless, the anger of some citizens against drug dealers became so vehement in the 1980s that some people resorted to assault and arson because they believed the police could no longer protect them against drug pushers. In Detroit, a jury acquitted two men who admitted setting fire to a crack house. In some communities police had to protect drug dealers from citizens attempting to beat the dealers with baseball bats, pipes, and rocks (Wilkerson 1988).

The extensive use of drugs also impacts public health. It evidently affected the AIDS epidemic, which became most prominent in the media with stories about addicts who became infected while sharing dirty needles in "shooting galleries" (Moore 1979).

The effort by police to control drug use on the local level leads to the reduction of available drugs on that level in favor of increases in drugs obtained from drug cartels located mostly in South America. It is, of course, evident that controlling the importation of drugs by organized drug monopolies is more difficult than dealing with local sellers of drugs. Therefore, law enforcement is confronted with a dilemma. This may be understood by consulting the Drug Abuse Warning Network (Schelling 1971).

This network helps to feature the criminality of drug addicts, which is extremely high because a considerable amount of crime in many localities is committed by heroin users. This is because heroin users cannot work but are in need of money to feed their habit. This is further supported by using the National Institute of Justice Drug Use Forecasting System. This system collects data from numerous cities for new arrests. Using the results of urinalysis leads to the conclusion that nearly 80% of those arrested for a street crime test positive for drug use, mainly heroin. This does not mean that 80% of crimes are committed by drug users, because white-collar crimes and organized crime are not considered (Nurco 1985).

Those engaged in drug trafficking and in drug sales face some obstacles not known in normal business transactions. Unlike with other businesses, illicit drug sellers are constantly worried about arrest, as are drug buyers. Both are faced with high costs, because the sellers cannot advertise; use the courts to enforce contracts; sue anyone; or call the police if they are threatened, assaulted, or shot (Reuter and Kleiman 1986). The ethnography of Hoffer in Denver, Colorado, and Bourgois's research in East Harlem, discussed in Chapter 11, illustrate drug sellers' attempts to evade detection and arrest by police.

The other side of the heroin trade is that increased policing of drug suspects will overburden the courts, leading to the dismissal of numerous arrested dealers and users, as the courts, jails, and prisons become far too overcrowded. This means that the criminal justice system is not prepared to deal with a huge number of drug offenders, so that many are let go or let off with just a fine or no adjudication.

An additional obstacle to enforcement of the drug laws is that police are generally less active at a time when drug dealers are most employed. Many of the drug deals go on in private homes or bars, hotels, and offices. This means that drug dealing is pushed underground and therefore less likely to be visible to law enforcement.

Drug merchants have another advantage over the police departments seeking to control them and that is gang formation. This is particularly true of youth gangs as the most prominent drug merchants. These gangs fight each other for the profits to be gained from the drug business. As a result, there are at least an estimated 1,100 people killed in the American drug wars each year. Of these, Chicago alone experienced 507 drug-related murders in 2012 (Conroy 2012).

The number of Americans killed in the drug wars exceeds the number killed in the war in Afghanistan (Breslow 2015). This, and the considerable amount of drug-related homicide in South America, has led Latin Americans to ask the

United States to legalize the use of drugs and end the violence in a manner similar to the end of the Prohibition era related to alcohol in the 1930s.

Many U.S. citizens, of course, are also demanding an end to prohibition concerning drugs, so that the dispute between the enforcers of a rather puritan attitude toward drugs and those who want to use them has become an issue in American politics.

It has been estimated that the United States spends about $40 billion a year on the war on drugs, both at home and abroad. Meanwhile, the American public spends $100 billion annually on cocaine, heroin, marijuana, and methamphetamines. Since 2010, there has been a 40% increase in the amount of marijuana consumed in the United States, coupled with a decrease in cocaine use of 50%. Heroin use has remained steady over the years as the supply is delivered to the United States from poppy growers in Mexico and Colombia (Kilmer et al. 2014).

As a consequence of the drug business, an extraordinary number of Americans have been incarcerated. The Bureau of Justice Statistics reports that between 2001 and 2013, more than half of the prisoners in federal institutions were convicted of drug offenses. In 2013–2014, 98,200 people were imprisoned in federal facilities for possession, trafficking, or other drug crimes. At the same time, 210,200 inmates of state prisons were held for drug offenses. These comprised 16% of the state prison population. Twenty-five percent of female inmates and 15% of male inmates were serving time in state prisons for drug-related offenses (Carson 2014).

ZUMA Press, Inc./Alamy Stock Photo

Photo 9.2: Local police and DEA agents raid a drug house.

The cost of keeping one inmate in prison for 1 year is about $125,000. This may vary somewhat between states but not by much. In addition, there were 986,000 people on probation for drug offenses, or 25% of the 3,943,000 people on probation in 2013. Likewise, 33% of people on parole in 2013 had been in prison for a drug offense (Maruschak and Bonczar 2013).

Because of the war on drugs, people who are addicted cannot legally satisfy their need. Therefore, 16% of federal prisoners and 18% of state prisoners committed a crime in order to gain money for drugs. If those who were sentenced to prison were given treatment for drug addiction, the cost would be $20,000 less than imprisonment (Justice Policy Institute 2010).

All of this has been a terrible burden on the American taxpayer. Considering only marijuana offenses, we find that of 170,535 people in federal prisons and 1,244,311 in state prisons in 2014, 55% of federal prisoners and 21% of state prisoners were incarcerated on a drug offense. Of these, 12.4% or 11,630 federal prisoners had used marijuana and 12.7% or 33,186 state prisoners had done the same (Mumola and Karberg 2005).

The imprisonment of drug users and dealers has had little effect on the use of these substances by the American public. The reasons for this failure are first that drug transactions are continued by others whenever someone is jailed for this crime. This means that drug dealers are almost immediately replaced by another drug dealer after someone is jailed, so that the "replacement effect" defeats the purpose of incarceration. Moreover, new recruits to drug dealing are usually younger people, who are more attuned to violence than older dealers. Finally, the incarceration of drug users and dealers creates openings for those aspiring to make a profit from dealing drugs (Pew Center on the States 2009).

The U.S. State Department has repeatedly issued a warning for tourists planning to visit Mexico. This warning is based on the murder of 47,515 people slaughtered in drug-related violence in Mexico between December 1, 2006, and September 30, 2011. The number of U.S. citizens murdered in drug-related violence in Mexico rose from 35 in 2007 to 120 in 2011 and to 648 between 2011 and 2014. During those same years, 50,000 Mexican citizens have been murdered in the drug wars (H. Martin 2013).

A good deal of dispute has arisen concerning the possible spillover effect of the Mexican drug wars into the United States. Some claim that the United States is victimized by the Mexican violence, whereas others argue that there is no evidence for this contention. There is also a contentious debate as to the narcotics-related murder rate. The FBI Uniform Crime Report for 2015 shows 1,488,707 drug violations in that year (2015, Table 29, "Estimated Number of Arrests," https://ucr.fbi.gov/crime-in-the-u.s/2015/crime-in-the-u.s.-2015/tables/table-29).

The Marijuana Controversy

Despite the effort of the DEA to demonize users of marijuana, the American people have decided to move in the opposite direction and bring about the legal use of that drug. This effort was first promoted by supporting the use of medical marijuana for some cancer patients and HIV sufferers who were demonstrably able to alleviate the pain of these diseases by the application of marijuana.

In part, the use of marijuana as medicine came about as more and more Americans used alternative medicine instead of prescriptions by establishment physicians. Marijuana evidently alleviates some of the consequences of chemotherapy such as nausea, vomiting, and pain. As of this writing, Alaska, Arizona, Arkansas, California, Colorado, Connecticut, Delaware, Florida, Hawaii, Illinois, Maine, Maryland, Massachusetts, Michigan, Minnesota, Montana, Nevada, New Hampshire, New Jersey, New Mexico, New York, North Dakota, Ohio, Oregon, Pennsylvania, Rhode Island, Vermont, Washington State, and the District of Columbia have approved the legality of marijuana for medical purposes (Anna 1997; Wikipedia 2014c). Some states—Alaska, California, Colorado, Maine, Massachusetts, Nevada, Oregon, Washington State—and Washington, DC, now also allow the recreational use of marijuana by adults.

Nevertheless, the federal government threatened prosecution under the Uniform Controlled Substance Act of anyone using marijuana, no matter its benefits to the sick. The argument of the DEA bureaucrats was that marijuana was no more effective in alleviating the physical illnesses involved than other drugs (Anna 1997).

The argument of the DEA for maintaining the prohibition of marijuana was based on the belief that marijuana is a "gateway drug" leading users to become addicted to heroin and other dangerous substances. The DEA also claimed that legalizing marijuana will send the wrong message to children, who will interpret

Mike Theiler/AFP/Getty Images

Photo 9.3: Demonstrators for the legalization of marijuana in front of the White House, April 2, 2016.

legalization of marijuana as being a form of safe recreation. All these arguments have been challenged by medical researchers, physicians, and patients because of its effectiveness. Indeed, the government's position is not logical. It should therefore be understood that the DEA supports many bureaucrats afraid of losing power and income if forbidden substances become legal (Stempse 1998).

In 1999, the Institute of Medicine issued a comprehensive report by 11 independent scientists concerning marijuana. This report concluded that "scientific data indicate the potential therapeutic value of cannabinoid drugs, primarily THC, for pain relief, control of nausea and vomiting, and appetite stimulation; smoked marijuana, however, is a crude THC delivery system that also delivers harmful substances" (Joy, Watson, and Benson 1999:130). The report recommended the "short-term use of smoked marijuana (less than six months) for patients with debilitating symptoms (such as intractable pain or vomiting)," provided it met a number of conditions:

> failure of all approved medications to provide relief has been documented, the symptoms can reasonably be expected to be relieved by rapid onset cannabinoid drugs, such treatment is administered under medical supervision in a manner that allows for assessment of treatment effectiveness, and involves an oversight strategy comparable to an institutional review board process that could provide guidance within 24 hours of a submission by a physician to provide marijuana to a patient for a specified use. (Joy et al. pp. 130–131)

Furthermore, this report found no evidence that giving the drug to sick people would increase the use of the drug in the general population. The 11 scientists also concluded that marijuana is not a gateway to the use of heroin (Stolberg 1999). This entire controversy put physicians in a dilemma. Medical ethics demand that physicians ease the pain and suffering of their patients, even as the government seeks to penalize those who follow this humane procedure.

Marijuana is a product of the hemp plant, which grows almost everywhere. Among the numerous compounds found in marijuana are cannabinoids. These compounds have the positive effect of reducing pain, affecting neurologic and movement disorders, reducing nausea of chemotherapy patients, and alleviating glaucoma. The negative effects of marijuana are the possibility of compromising the immune system, as well as a number of other risks (Marmor 1998).

Another negative was that in the 1990s an ounce of synthetic marijuana called Marinol taken in the form of a pill cost $500 for 100 pills. By 2016, this cost was greatly reduced because marijuana is readily available and there is a good deal of competition for customers. The cost of producing cannabis is about $1 an ounce, which equals about 60 marijuana cigarettes. The average dose is one cigarette.

The agitation for decriminalizing the use of cannabis led a number of states to furnish voters with an opportunity to cast ballots in favor of making marijuana legal. This resulted in Arizona's citizens voting in 1994, 65% to 35%, to make marijuana legal. Likewise, California voters voted 56% to 44% to legalize marijuana (Lantis 1997).

This led to the passage in California of the Compassionate Use Act of 1996, allowing patients and primary care givers to grow and possess marijuana. This law allows physicians to prescribe marijuana when the patient suffers from cancer, anorexia, AIDS, chronic pain, spasticity, glaucoma, arthritis, migraine, or any other illness for which marijuana provides relief. No prescription or record keeping is required. This last provision means that, in effect, anyone can obtain marijuana in California by complaining about anything to a physician. It also means that California was the first state to defy the DEA (Lantis 1997).

The DEA responded by threatening to deprive any physicians of their registration if they help patients under the California drug law. The federal government also shut down the Cannabis Buyers' Clubs in California. Therefore, those who needed marijuana to survive were forced to buy marijuana on the black market where much of the supply is contaminated and dangerous. Despite the effort of the DEA to prevent the sale of drugs anywhere in the United States, voters in California decided otherwise.

The best example of the decriminalization of marijuana is Colorado Amendment 64, enacted in November 2012. According to this legislation, adults aged 21 or older can grow six cannabis plants privately and can legally possess all the cannabis from a plant they grow.

According to this amendment, driving under the influence is prohibited. The amendment also provides for the licensing of product manufacturing facilities and retail stores as well as testing facilities. Subsequently, Colorado enacted the Colorado Retail Marijuana Code. This allowed the first store to open on January 1, 2014. Coloradans supported the use of marijuana 54% to 43%. Sixty-six percent also supported making marijuana legal in private homes. More than 60% of Colorado residents also wanted laws regarding marijuana to be as well enforced as alcohol laws.

States allowing the production and use of marijuana for recreational purposes are Alaska, California, Colorado, Maine, Massachusetts, Nevada, Oregon, Washington State, and Washington, DC. Twenty-nine states and DC allow the use of marijuana for medical purposes, even as a majority of Americans support the abolition of federal drug laws in a manner similar to the abolition of the alcohol laws in the days of Franklin Delano Roosevelt.

The lesson learned is clear. In the American democracy, fanatic repression for any reason loses to the determination of the American people to live in freedom, even with the risks that drugs inevitably bring with them. One of these is violence, including bloodshed and homicide.

CHAPTER 10

Drugs in Popular Culture

Drugs have long been embedded in Western culture. Before the arrival of Europeans, the Native population had been using a variety of substances. The Aztecs, for example, used teonanacatyl, a hallucinogenic mushroom. The Jivaro and other South American Indian groups used a tea made from the banisteriopsis vine (*Banisteriopsis caapi*) variously called ayahuasca or yahe. The potion is a hallucinogen, causing users to see visions such as images of snakes and jaguars (Harner 1965). Some North American tribes used peyote, from which psilocybin is derived (La Barre 1989).[1] Before the Harrison Narcotics Act of 1914, a variety of substances containing cocaine or opiates were widely used, often without prescriptions. Examples include a variety of patent medicines, wines, syrups, powers, lozenges and tonics, tincture of opium, laudanum, and paregoric (Gomez 1984). This chapter looks at the ways in which a variety of drugs have been and are being viewed within popular culture, including art, literature, music, comedy, television, and movies. The examples used are not meant to be comprehensive but simply to illustrate the degree to which drug use has become part of our society. Additionally, we examine the relationship between the media and licit and illicit drugs and prevalent popular beliefs about drugs, such as the idea that marijuana is a gateway drug to heroin and other "harder" drugs.

Art

Depictions of drug use in art do not seem to be as prevalent as images of alcohol use, which we discussed in Chapter 6. There are, however, some images of psychedelic mushrooms in the art of the Olmec and Mazatec, Minoan figurines wearing opium poppies, and figures wearing crowns of opium poppies on Greek vases (Ancient-Wisdom n.d.).

An interesting Victorian-era work is *Opium Smoking—The Laskar's Room*, a pen and ink drawing made by Gustave Dore in 1872 (Victorian Web n.d.). The picture is dark and gloomy, with four figures in the shadows to the left and a solitary female figure in the center, reclining on a bed, her features lit by a candle, with which she is lighting a long pipe. It is an illustration of a scene in *The Mystery of Edwin Drood*, an unfinished novel by Charles Dickens, which is reproduced later in this section.

One of the earliest modern artists whose work was influenced by drugs, especially his LSD use, is Robert Dennis Crumb, who drew his psychedelic cartoons as R. Crumb. His work first appeared in *Zap Comix* in 1968, and his art was very popular as part of the underground comics ("comix") movement (Wikipedia 2016e)[2] in the late 1960s and '70s. Robbie is a more recent artist whose art is considered to be psychedelic.[3]

David Goldstein (2001) has collected examples of drugs in the comics, which draw from newspaper comic strips, editorial cartoons, and magazines mostly from the 1980s and cover a variety of substances.

Damien Hirst is a controversial modern artist whose paintings are assumed to represent drugs. His painting *Albumin, Human, Glycated* consists of 165 dots of various colors in 15 columns by 11 rows. It is said to represent various drugs (Quora n.d.).

Tracey Emin is a modern British artist, some of whose works are controversial. Her installation *The Bed* shocked its viewers. According to British sociologist Rod Watson,

> The Emin bed was an installation, with it is said, a real bed, real soiled underclothing, etc.—I don't know if the vomit was real! The installation was like a nightmarish real situation, and caused a real controversy here. One question was "but is it art?" I think it is, and that it is a brilliant piece (plus it made her rich!). It makes a real comment on the contemporary life of many people in many societies. It may be "autobiographical" in many ways, a self-comment on Emin's own early life, but it also, of course, stands on behalf of the drug and alcohol-fuelled scenes inhabited by so many in our society. One traditional role of art has always been to "epater le bourgeois," to use the famous French phrase—that is, to shock and outrage the respectable middle-class person! This installation surely does that—not for the sake of simply shocking respectable people, but also to make a comment on the society. To me, it challenges artists and art viewers to "get real"! To me, Emin is like an ethnographer in art.

> I do know that [Damien Hirst] and especially Emin, have struck a chord with the general public with their drug-themed work—even if the public doesn't like these works (but many, like me, do), there is a "recognizability" to these works—they do seem to reflect a popular recognition that they address what's going on in our society, whether or not one likes what's going on. (Watson, personal communication, February 17 and 18, 2016)

Literature and Poetry

As mentioned earlier, Charles Dickens provided a description of a contemporary Victorian opium den in his unfinished novel *The Mystery of Edwin Drood*:

Shaking from head to foot, the man whose scattered consciousness has thus fantastically pieced itself together, at length rises, supports his trembling frame upon his arms, and looks around. . . . He lies, dressed, across a large unseemly bed, upon a bedstead that has indeed given way under the weight upon it. Lying, also dressed and also across the bed, not longwise, are a Chinaman, a Lascar,[4] and a haggard woman. The two first are in a sleep or stupor; the last is blowing at a kind of pipe, to kindle it. . . . "Another?" says this woman, in a querulous, rattling whisper. "Have another?"

"Ye've smoked as many as five since ye come in at midnight," the woman goes on, as she chronically complains. . . . "Ah, poor me, the business is slack, is slack! Few Chinamen about the Docks, and fewer Lascars, and no ships coming in, these say! Here's another ready for ye, deary. Ye'll remember like a good soul, won't ye, that the market price is dreffle high just now? More nor three shillings and sixpence for a thimbleful! . . . Ye'll pay up accordingly, deary, won't ye?" She hands him the nearly-emptied pipe, and sinks back, turning over on her face.

He rises unsteadily from the bed, lays the pipe upon the hearth-stone, draws back the ragged curtain, and looks with repugnance at his three companions. He notices that the woman has opium-smoked herself into a strange likeness of the Chinaman. His form of cheek, eye, and temple, and his colour, are repeated in her. Said Chinaman convulsively wrestles with one of his many Gods or Devils, perhaps, and snarls horribly. The Lascar laughs and dribbles at the mouth. The hostess is still. (Dickens 1980/1870:3–5)

A somewhat similar description of a visit to an opium den is given by Dr. John Watson in Sir Arthur Conan Doyle's story "The Man with the Twisted Lip":

Through the gloom one could dimly catch a glimpse of bodies lying in strange fantastic poses, bowed shoulders, bent knees, heads thrown back and chins pointing upwards, with here and there a dark, lacklustre eye turned upon the newcomer. Out of the black shadows there glimmered little red circles of light, now bright, now faint, as the burning poison waxed or waned in the bowls of the metal pipes. The most lay silent, but some muttered to themselves, and others talked together in a strange, low monotonous voice, their conversations coming in gushes, and then suddenly tailing off into silence, each mumbling his own thoughts and paying little heed to the words of his neighbors. (Doyle 2009a:212–213)

Dr. Watson's friend and colleague detective Sherlock Holmes is perhaps the most well-known drug-using character in English literary fiction. His addiction

"IT WAS A PROSTRATE MAN FACE DOWNWARDS UPON THE GROUND."

Photo 10.1: Sherlock Holmes and Dr. Watson.

first appears in the very beginning of *The Sign of the Four* originally published in 1890. His associate Dr. John Watson narrates:

> Sherlock Holmes took his bottle from the corner of the mantelpiece, and his hypodermic syringe from its neat morocco case. With his long, white, nervous fingers he adjusted the delicate needle and rolled back his left shirt-cuff. For some little time his eyes rested thoughtfully upon the sinewy forearm and wrist, all dotted and scarred with innumerable puncture-marks. Finally, he thrust the sharp point home, pressed down the tiny piston, and sank back into the velvet-lined armchair with a long sigh of satisfaction. (Doyle 2009b:75)

Over the years of their personal and professional relationship, Dr. Watson attempted to help Holmes to withdraw from drug use. Although eventually

Holmes became abstinent, Watson was very sensitive to the fragility of his friend's abstinence. In "The Missing Three-Quarter" he observed,

> For years I had gradually weaned him from that drug mania which had threatened once to check his remarkable career. Now I knew that under ordinary conditions he no longer craved for this artificial stimulus; but I was well aware that the fiend was not dead but sleeping, and I have known that sleep was a light one and the waking near when in periods of idleness I have seen the drawn look upon Holmes's ascetic face, and the brooding of his deep-set and inscrutable eyes. (Doyle 2009c:589)

An important book about heroin use and users is *Junkie: Confessions of an Unredeemed Drug Addict* written by William S. Burroughs (W. Lee 1953) using the nom de plume William Lee. In his introduction to the annotated 2003 edition of the book, now titled *Junky*, Oliver Harris makes it clear that William Lee is really Burroughs and that the book is "both more and less than a record of Boroughs' early years on heroin. . . . Having things to say about marijuana, cocaine, peyote, yahe, and antihistamines, as well as opium and its derivatives, it's halfway to being a pharmacopoeia" (Burroughs 2003:x).[5] He says of Burroughs, "If you're looking for books by William Burroughs, there are over two dozen to choose from, most if not all of which make reference to narcotics and addiction. Junk and Burroughs go together, he's *the* addict-artist of the twentieth century" (p. ix).

One of the minor characters in Harper Lee's (2006/1960) now classic novel about life and race relations in 1930s southern Alabama, *To Kill a Mockingbird*, Mrs. Dubose, was medically addicted to morphine. The book's narrator, 7-year-old Scout, describes her appearance during one of her "fits": "She was horrible. Her face was the color of a dirty pillowcase, and the corners of her mouth glistened with wet, which inched like a glacier down the deep grooves enclosing her chin." Suddenly, Scout notices a change in Mrs. Dubose: "Something had happened to her. . . . Her head moved slowly from side to side. From time to time she would open her mouth wide, and I could see her tongue undulate faintly. Cords of saliva would collect on her lips; she would draw them in, then open her mouth again" (H. Lee 2006/1960:122–123). Scout's father, Atticus, explains to Scout and her brother Jem that what they had thought were fits were symptoms of Mrs. Dubose's voluntary withdrawal from morphine: "'Mrs. Dubose was a morphine addict,'" says Atticus. "'She took it as a pain-killer for years. The doctor put her on it. She'd have spent the rest of her life on it and died without so much agony, but she was too contrary—'" (p. 127).

In 1966, Jacqueline Susann's novel *Valley of the Dolls*, about the use and abuse of pills such as tranquilizers by women in the entertainment industry, was published. Two of these drugs first appeared in the 1960s. The first of these, Librium, was approved by the FDA in 1960. Valium, a more refined drug, was produced by Hoffman-La Roche in 1963 (A. Cooper 2013). A year after her book was published, a movie based on it debuted.

Drug themes also appear in poetry. A prominent example is Alfred Lord Tennyson's (2015/1832) poem "The Lotus-Eaters," inspired by Homer's *Odyssey*. Contemporary drug-related poetry can be found on the Internet. Examples include Deep Underground Poetry's (2017) collection "Drug Poems," which includes writers' perspectives on drug use and addiction to alcohol, medications, and illicit drugs, and Digital Poet's (n.d.) musings.

Music

Although not as extensive as music related to alcohol use, there is still a body of recordings relevant to the use of illegal drugs, going back to the early 20th century. One of the earliest songs referencing the use of illicit drugs is "Minnie the Moocher," first recorded by Cab Calloway and his orchestra in 1931 (Wikipedia 2015a). The lyrics include the following lines (MetroLyrics 2016a):

She messed around with a bloke named Smoky,

She loved him though he was cokey.

He took her down to Chinatown,

And he showed her how to kick the gong around.

In the song, *cokey* means that he is a cocaine user. According to the Urban Dictionary (2009), to "kick the gong around" was 1930s slang for smoking opium. It comes "from Chinese opium dens of the last century where customers struck a gong to make the attendant come and bring them a pipe."

Cocaine appears in a number of songs, going back at least to 1927's "Dope Head Blues" recorded by Victoria Spivey and Lonnie Johnson (YouTube 2011). In 1929, The Memphis Jug Band recorded "Cocaine Habit Blues" with Memphis Minnie and Hattie Harth (YouTube 2009). The lyrics acknowledge that "cocaine habit mighty bad / It's the worst old habit that I ever had," but the singer still acknowledges that it gives her pleasure: "I love my whiskey, and I love my gin / But the way I love my coke is a doggone sin" (elyrics.org n.d.). "Cocaine Blues" was written by T. J. Arnall and William Lee and recorded in the late 1940s by both W. A. Nichols's Western Aces and Roy Hogsed and the Rainbow Riders (YouTube 2013). It was later recorded by Johnny Cash. It tells the story of a man who says that he shot "his woman down" after taking "a shot of cocaine" (MetroLyrics 2016b). Singer/songwriter J. J. Cale wrote "Cocaine," which became a big hit for Eric Clapton when he recorded it in 1980 (Sweeting 2013).

LSD is referenced in a number of songs. "Just Dropped In (To See What Condition My Condition Was In)," written by Mickey Newbury, was a hit for Kenny Rogers and the First Edition in 1968. Its lyrics describe what can only be an LSD "trip" (lyricsfreak 2016). "White Rabbit," performed by Jefferson Airplane, references the use of drugs including pills, smoking a hookah, and "some kind of mushroom," presumably a hallucinogen. The lyrics were written by Grace Slick:

"Slick got the idea for this after taking LSD and spending hours listening to the Miles Davis album Sketches of Spain" (Songfacts 2016a).

Marijuana appears in 1970's "One Toke Over the Line" by Mike Brewer and Tom Shipley. According to Shipley, "When we wrote 'One Toke Over the Line,' I think we were one toke over the line. I considered marijuana a sort of sacrament. . . . If you listen to the lyrics of that song, 'one toke' was just a metaphor. It's a song about excess. Too much of anything will probably kill you" (Songfacts 2016b).

The Rolling Stones' song "Mother's Little Helper" is about Miltown, a minor tranquilizer licensed for the short-term relief of anxiety (Inglis-Arkell 2015). It appeared in 1966 on their album *Aftermath* around the same time as Jacqueline Susann's book *Valley of the Dolls* and the movie based on it. The book, movie, and song reflected what was going on in society in the late 1960s. In an article originally published in the *Atlantic Monthly* in August 1966, Bruce Jackson reported on his observations of pill use at a party of middle-class adults: "Sometimes the pill-takers meet other pill-takers, and an odd thing happens: instead of using the drug to cope with the world, they begin to use their time to take drugs. Taking drugs becomes *something to do*. When this stage is reached, the drug-taking pattern broadens: the user takes a wider variety of drugs with increasing frequency. For want of a better term, one might call it the white collar drug scene" (B. Jackson 1970b:256–257; italics in original). The behavior of those adults observed by Jackson fall under sociologist Erich Goode's (2014) category of illegal recreational use, because their drug taking is motivated by the search for pleasurable experiences. The women in Susann's novel are engaged in either legal instrumental or illegal instrumental drug use, depending on their source of drugs, because they use pills to cope with their situation.

Comedy

Drug-related comedy is found primarily in standup routines, record albums, and movies. The undisputed kings of this genre are Tommy Chong and Richard "Cheech" Marin. Chong began his entertainment career as a musician. After being fired from his band, he worked the lights for strippers in a nightclub he co-owned with his brother. Finding the usual strippers' routines boring, Chong began writing skits for them, including comedy sketches. He met Richard Marin when he was recommended as a possible straight man for Chong's show.

After performing some successful comedy skits at a Battle of the Bands contest as a warmup for their band, which never did get a chance to perform because Tommy and Richard took up all of their allotted time, they suddenly realized that they were now a comedy team and no longer musicians. On the rainy ride home from the contest, they came up with the name for their act, Cheech (Marin's nickname) & Chong (Chong 2008).

Cheech and Chong continued to polish their act, adding new characters and skits. Their act was seen by record producer Lou Adler, who produced their first

Photo 10.2: Tommy Chong and Cheech Marin with a prop bag of marijuana.

album *Cheech & Chong* in 1971 (Chong 2008). That album and their subsequent productions contained a number of drug-related cuts as well as other comedy skits. Although this is not the place for a detailed discography,[6] a few examples from their earliest albums may serve to give the reader some idea of their kind of drug-related humor. In "Acapulco Gold Filters" on the *Cheech & Chong* album, Cheech and Chong imagine what a commercial for legalized marijuana would sound like. The product spokesman keeps intentionally flubbing his lines and adding new ideas, so that he can prolong recording and continue smoking. The cut contains a jingle: "No sticks, no seeds that you don't need / Acapulco Gold is badass weed." In "Dave" on the same album, a nervous Dave is locked out of the house. Because he is holding marijuana and is afraid of being caught by the police, he frantically keeps trying to get his partner to let him in. When he knocks, his friend asks, "Who's there?" Dave responds, "It's me, I've got the stuff." His friend, obviously stoned, doesn't recognize Dave's voice. When Dave says, "It's Dave, let me in," his friend responds, "Dave's not here." Dave continues to ask to be let in, and his partner keeps asking, "Who's there?" As Dave, now frightened and frustrated, continues to identify himself, his friend keeps telling him, "Dave's not here." When Cheech and Chong originally recorded this skit, Cheech was outside, wearing a heavy overcoat in 100-degree weather, lending authenticity to "Dave's" frustration (Chong 2008).

Their second album, *Big Bambu*, released in 1972, was unique. It was made to look like a giant-size pack of rolling paper, Bambu, which is an actual brand. Inside the album is a giant rolling paper, with the faces of Cheech and Chong printed on it. That album includes "Rebuttal: Speaker Ashley Roachclip," who attempts to defend the use of marijuana but is so high that he keeps messing up his rejoinder and forgetting what he wants to say. Eventually, his rebuttal deteriorates into obscenities. "Let's Make a Dope Deal," is a stoner's take on the popular television game show. When a contestant picks the wrong door, out comes "Officer O'Malley of the FBI. You're busted!" The third album, *Los Cochinos*, released the following year, introduces narcotics officer Sergeant Stedanko, who appears in two of their movies, as a bumbling, comical character played by Stacy Keach.

The late Richard Pryor talked about his addiction to cocaine in his standup routines (Pryor 2013a) and later incorporated his setting himself on fire while high from freebasing cocaine into his act (Pryor 2013b, 2013c). His track "Freebase" appears in his 1982 concert film, *Richard Pryor: Live on the Sunset Strip*. Referring to that incident, Pryor said, "One thing I learned was that you can run *really fast* when you're on fire!" (McFly 2013).

Magazines

Unlike alcohol, for which there are many periodicals for wine connoisseurs, beer drinkers, and whiskey users, as discussed in Chapter 6, magazines for recreational drug users are limited. The major source of information for marijuana users is the venerable magazine *High Times*. Founded in 1974 by Thomas King Forcade, it was supposed to be a one-issue parody of *Playboy* with cannabis plants as centerfolds, but it was so well received that it "has become a stoner-American institution" (Abrahamian 2013). On its website,[7] *High Times* presents readers with cannabis-relevant news, videos, reviews of marijuana variations, stories about celebrities, links to other sites and advertisements for drugs and drug paraphernalia, recipes, a "headshop" where they sell clothing and other items, and popular events such as their Cannabis Cup trade show. According to the website,

> The HIGH TIMES Cannabis Cup is the world's leading marijuana trade show, celebrating the world of ganja through competitions, instructional seminars, expositions, celebrity appearances, concerts and product showcases. Hosted in states that have legalized medical and recreational marijuana, the Cannabis Cup stands as the foremost gathering place for the cannabis community to network and celebrate. Going strong for nearly three decades, HIGH TIMES Cannabis Cups are the most established and trusted in the marijuana industry, continually fighting for the political legitimacy of the plant. ("Cannabis Cup" 2015)

Movies and Television

The depiction of drug use in movies goes back to the silent film era: "Douglas Fairbanks Sr.'s Detective Coke Anyday knocked out smugglers with injections from his lightning-fast needle in a 1916 Sherlock Holmes spoof called *The Mystery of the Leaping Fish*" (Gomez 1984). Movies and television shows can be divided into two categories: those whose plots revolve around drugs and their distribution and use, and those in which the drug culture is a subplot or peripheral element. These broad categories can be further broken down into dramas and comedies with pro- and antidrug views. These opposing attitudes toward drugs reflect several themes: (1) the drug user as innocent victim, seduced and destroyed by predatory pushers and the power of drugs; (2) the drug dealer or pusher forced into trafficking by circumstances beyond his or her control; (3) the drug user as harmless and goofy and drug use as a pleasurable experience; (4) the drug subculture; and (5) drug use and the police.

Drug User as Innocent Victim

Two of the earliest movies, whose concern was with the evils of drug use, came out in the mid-1930s. They were *The Cocaine Fiends*, released in 1935, and *Reefer Madness*, released the following year.[8] The opening statement of *The Cocaine Fiends* sets the tone for the film:

> Among the many evils against which society struggles, one of the most vicious is the traffic in dope. . . . In every community where the menace develops all the forces which society can mobilize, including social agencies, doctors, law enforcement officials and government band together to stamp it out. . . . Without such activity the dope evil would run rampant.

The statement continues, noting that an enlightened public is needed to join the fight against "dope," the presumptive goal of the film.

In the beginning of the movie, Nick, a drug pusher, avoids the police by hiding in a roadside café in a small rural town. There he charms Jane Bradford, an innocent woman who runs the café along with her mother. When Jane becomes stressed after dealing with the police who come looking for Nick, he gives her some "headache powder," which miraculously cures her pain. He convinces Jane to come back to the city with him, promising her marriage. While living in the city, Nick continues to feed Jane's habit with the headache powder. When she is told that what she has been receiving is really dope, she screams, "Dope! You mean I've been taking dope?" She confronts Nick but quickly realizes that she needs dope. She is an addict and gradually becomes tough and adjusted to her new life. She takes on a new persona, "Lill," the gangster's "moll."

Meanwhile, Jane's brother, Eddie, goes to the city to look for her. He takes a job as a carhop to support himself. Fanny, a coworker, introduces him to dope, but, like his sister, he doesn't realize what it is. Inevitably, both Eddie and Fanny get fired because they can no longer handle their jobs. They move into a rooming house, where they have trouble making ends meet. They are confronted by their landlady, who accuses Eddie of being a "hop head." "Hop head. Hop head!" he shouts. "I'm a hop head. I'd sell my soul for just one shot." Neither he nor Fanny has any money for drugs, so she leaves the room and goes out into the streets to prostitute herself to support their habits. While on the street, she is recognized by Dorothy, the daughter of a wealthy businessman, who gives her some money. Although she is a minor character in the movie, Dorothy's presence becomes critical to the plot's denouement.

Returning home with the money, Fanny is told by Eddie that he doesn't love her. She is distraught, and after he leaves to get drugs, she turns on the gas and asphyxiates herself.

When Jane finds her brother in an opium den, the apparent source of the criminals' drugs, she convinces him to go back home, telling him that it is too late for her to do so. She goes to find Nick for money to send Eddie home, only to discover Dorothy held captive in an apartment for the apparent pleasure of the "boss" of the drug ring. Dorothy promises Jane $1,000 if she helps her to escape. Armed with a gun, Jane confronts Nick and the boss, who arrive at the apartment. She shoots and kills Nick in self-defense. It turns out that the boss is none other than Dorothy's apparently respectable father. Jane tries to cover for him, but the police have been watching him and know he is the head of the drug ring. Jane is arrested and Dorothy and her friend Dan, whom she finds out is an undercover vice squad detective, declare their love for each other.

Reefer Madness, originally *Tell Your Children*, is the story of the pitfalls of smoking marijuana, as narrated by the high school principal, Dr. Carroll. In the movie, an adult drug dealer, Jack Perry, befriends high school students and introduces them to marijuana at parties in the apartment of his friend, Mae. Mae is herself a drug pusher, but her clients are adults. Two of the central characters in the movie, Bill Harper and Mary Lane, are innocent high school sweethearts. Mary's brother, Jimmy, is taken with Jack, whom he sees as older and sophisticated. Jimmy drives Jack to his boss's office, where Jack gets a supply of marijuana. He gives Jimmy a reefer. After smoking it, Jimmy drives recklessly, hitting a pedestrian. Fortunately, the man survives.

Bill, who becomes a frequent visitor to Mae's apartment, gets hooked on marijuana. One of the other characters in the film, Blanche, is attracted to Bill. Another one, Ralph Wiley, is smitten by Mary. During one of his visits to the apartment, a marijuana-intoxicated Bill joins Blanche in a bedroom, where they may or may not have engaged in sex. Meanwhile, Mary makes her first visit to the apartment, looking for Jimmy. Ralph, who is there, gives Mary what she thinks is a cigarette but is really a marijuana reefer. Ralph takes advantage of Mary's intoxication, attempting to rape her. Bill, still stoned, comes out of the bedroom, sees what is happening, and attacks Ralph. At that moment, Jack arrives at the apartment, pulls Bill off Ralph, and attempts to hit him with his gun. During their struggle, the gun goes off, killing Mary. Jack knocks Bill out, puts the gun in his hand, wakes him up, and convinces Bill that it was he who shot Mary.

Bill is arrested and set for trial. Meanwhile, Ralph is undergoing an attack of conscience. He is also showing signs of insanity. He believes that Jack is out to kill him, which is actually the case, because Jack's boss has told him to get rid of Ralph. When Jack arrives at Mae's apartment, Ralph kills him with a fireplace poker.

At Bill's trial, Blanche testifies, exonerating him. As she is led out of the courtroom by a matron, Blanche breaks away, runs, and dives out a window to her death. Ralph is brought before the court, by this time totally demented, and is sent to an asylum for the rest of his life.

Both of these early movies have the same theme, albeit buried within different plots: drugs and drug pushers are evil corrupters of innocence and youth, causing moral decay (especially sexual promiscuity) and death.

Drug Dealer or Pusher Forced Into Trafficking

One of the classic perspectives in criminology is called strain theory. This framework assumes that most people are decent and law abiding. When they engage in deviant behavior, it is the result of having been put into an untenable position. A familiar example of strain theory is Robert K. Merton's (1957) anomie theory, which sees crime and deviance as an attempt to achieve culturally approved goals when the culturally approved means are inaccessible. In his article "Crime as an American Way of Life," Daniel Bell (1953) refers to (organized) crime as a "queer ladder of social mobility." In their opportunity theory, Richard A. Cloward and Lloyd E. Ohlin (1960) add to strain theory the idea that the form taken by deviance is structured by the available criminal opportunities. So, for example, if someone is in a financial crisis, which cannot be resolved by legitimate means, if drugs are available, the individual may focus on drug dealing as a way of surviving. This is the premise of two popular television shows, *Weeds* and *Breaking Bad*. The themes were so similar, in fact, that Vince Gilligan, the creator of *Breaking Bad*, said that had he known about *Weeds* earlier, he would never have developed his own project ("Vince Gilligan" 2012). The protagonists in both series begin dealing drugs to solve their financial problems. The central character in *Weeds* is a young, middle-class housewife, Nancy Botwin, left widowed with two small children. In order to support herself and her sons, she becomes a marijuana dealer. Her counterpart in *Breaking Bad* is Walter White, a high school chemistry teacher who, upon learning that he has late-stage lung cancer, begins producing crystal methamphetamine to provide for his family upon his death. Over the course of both series, the main characters become progressively immersed in the criminal drug subculture and engaged in secondary deviance.[9]

Drug User as Harmless and Goofy

The prototype for the movie version of the drug user as goofy and stoned is Jeff Spicoli, the perpetually high surfer played by Sean Penn in 1982's *Fast Times at Ridgemont High*. The creators of this genre, however, are Cheech and Chong, whose movies, based in large part on their stage and record routines, present drug use, especially marijuana, as harmless fun and their users as often confused and comical. In their first movie, 1978's *Up in Smoke*, Chong plays Anthony Stoner,

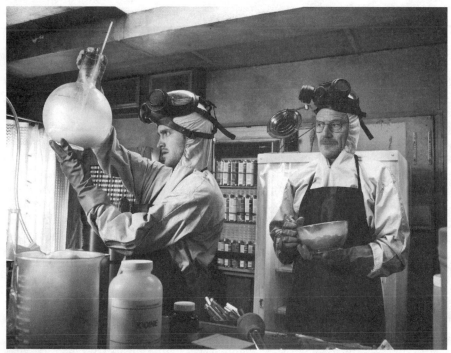

Photo 10.3: A scene from *Breaking Bad* (Season 2).

Photo 12/Alamy Stock Photo

a marijuana-smoking drummer, who is picked up by Pedro de Pacas, a Chicano played by Cheech. The film's plot, which involves loosely connected vignettes, is about their attempt to purchase marijuana in a series of funny misadventures. In one classic scene, they are stoned and sitting in Cheech's smoke-filled 1964 Chevrolet lowrider on a median in traffic when they are approached by a police officer. They get involved with drug dealers and end up driving a van constructed of marijuana, which inevitably ends up on fire. In their second film, 1980's *Cheech and Chong's Next Movie*, they reprise their roles. This time, Cheech also plays his cousin, Red, who grows fields of marijuana and comes to town with a full duffel bag of weed. Cheech sends Chong out to meet his cousin, while he prepares for a date with his girlfriend. The film centers around a stoned Anthony and Red, as they travel around Los Angeles, narrowly escaping arrest, first through an encounter with a hotel clerk, then in a brothel, and later, with the upper-class family of a woman they meet in a music store.

In their third movie, 1984's *Nice Dreams*, playing the same characters, Cheech and Chong sell marijuana out of an ice cream truck. That movie, as in the rest of their filmography,[10] is full of comical characters, many imported from their successful albums, such as Sergeant Stedanko (played by Stacy Keach) and even includes Timothy Leary in a cameo role appearance. Like in their other movies, Cheech and Chong narrowly escape harrowing situations.

Another "stoner" comedy featuring hapless pot-smoking protagonists in the Cheech and Chong genre is the 1998 movie *Half Baked*, starring comedian Dave Chapelle. The plot revolves around Chapelle's character, janitor Thurgood Jenkins, and his two buddies who sell stolen marijuana to raise bail money for a friend. As in the Cheech and Chong movies, the main characters get involved in hair-raising adventures and encounters with the police. To add to the continuity with Cheech and Chong, Tommy Chong appears in a small part in this film.

Pineapple Express, released in 2008, similarly involves a stoner, process server Dale Denton, played by Seth Rogen. Though it has comedic moments, the film is more accurately viewed as an action-comedy. The title refers to a special type of marijuana sold exclusively to Dale's supplier. The plot revolves around Dale's witnessing a murder committed by a corrupt police officer, his attempt to keep one step ahead of the officer's hired killers, and his relationship with his drug dealer.

Chong pops up again in the popular sitcom *That '70s Show*, which aired from 1998 to 2006. This time he has a recurring role as Leo Chingkwake, a middle-aged hippie burnout. *That '70s Show* centers around a group of goofy teenagers and their relationships. At some point in every episode the six friends, Eric Forman, Steven Hyde, Donna Pinciotti, Jackie Burkhart, Michael Kelso, and Fez, are seen sitting around in the Formans' basement (where Hyde also lives), stoned amid dense clouds of marijuana smoke, talking nonsense and generally acting silly. What is unrealistic about all of this is that Eric's parents, Red and Kitty, never seem to notice the pungent smell of marijuana or accidentally come upon the intoxicated youngsters. Similarly, one has to suspend belief in the 1985 film *The Breakfast Club*, about five disaffected teenagers serving a Saturday in school detention. In one scene, the group retrieves a bag of marijuana from a school locker, smokes joints in the school library, and dances wildly to very loud music, yet Mr. Vernon, the assistant principal who monitors the youngsters from his nearby office, never catches them in the act, nor does he seem to notice the very recognizable smell.

Woody Allen's 1977 film *Annie Hall* has a scene in which Allen's character, Alvy Singer, is introduced to cocaine. Instead of snorting the drug, Alvy ineptly blows the powder all over the room.

Drug Subculture

In addition to *Weeds* and *Breaking Bad*, a number of movies and television programs have dealt with the drug subculture, drug dealers, and drug users. One of the earliest films, *The Man With the Golden Arm*, was loosely based on the novel of the same name (Algren 1949) and premiered in 1955. It tells the story of Frankie Machine, a heroin addict, played by Frank Sinatra. Released from prison, where he kicked his habit, Frankie returns to Chicago, moves back with his disabled wife, and rejoins his former criminal associates. He eventually becomes addicted again and later goes through withdrawal with the support of a former girlfriend. Because it depicted addicts as sympathetic, the film was denied certification by the Motion Picture Association of America (Wikipedia 2015b).

The 1969 film *Easy Rider*, which has become a cult classic, is about two motorcycle riders, Captain America (played by Peter Fonda) and Billy (Dennis Hopper), on a drug-financed trip from California to New Orleans. It contains scenes of marijuana smoking and one of an extended LSD trip during Mardi Gras taken by Captain America, Billy, and two prostitutes they meet in a brothel.

Two films, *The Panic in Needle Park*, from 1971, and *Drugstore Cowboy*, from 1989, revolve around drug users and the drug subculture. Set in New York City's Sherman Square, known as "Needle Park" because of its heroin addict habitués, the film tells the story of Bobby, an addict and drug dealer played by Al Pacino, and his relationship with drug suppliers, other addicts, and his girlfriend Helen (Kitty Winn). The film is notable for its grittiness, including realistic scenes depicting addicts shooting up.

Drugstore Cowboy takes place in the Pacific Northwest in 1971. Bob Hughes, an addict (played by Matt Dillon), along with his wife, Dianne (Kelly Lynch), and another couple, support their habits by robbing pharmacies and hospitals. After one of his associates dies from an overdose, Bob is frightened into going into rehabilitation. What is particularly interesting about this film is the casting of William S. Burroughs, himself a former heroin addict and the author of *Junkie*, as Tom the priest.[11]

Blow, from 2001, is the story of real-life cocaine smuggler George Jung, starring Johnny Depp as Jung and Penelope Cruz as his wife, Mirtha. Imprisoned in the 1970s for smuggling marijuana, Jung makes a connection in prison with a cellmate who introduces him to cocaine smugglers. He then becomes the major exporter of that drug into the United States. Also portrayed in the movie is Pablo Escobar, the head of the notorious Medellin cartel in Colombia. The film portrays the various machinations of the cocaine business, including betrayals and murders, and ends with Jung serving a long prison sentence.

Bates Motel, a popular television program also set in the Pacific Northwest, is a prequel to Alfred Hitchcock's 1960 film *Psycho*. Though the series revolves around the character of Norman Bates (Freddie Highmore) and his relationships with others, especially his mother, Norma (Vera Farmiga), underlying the drama is the illegal marijuana industry, which provides the economic base for their town. Many of the town's residents make their living from growing, transporting, or selling marijuana, including some of the wealthiest and most prominent citizens. The sheriff, well aware of that industry, does not interfere with it, and even Norman's half brother Dylan (Max Thieriot) is involved in the marijuana trade.

A more realistic and extensive examination of various drug subcultures, focusing on the economic side of the drug enterprise, is the National Geographic Channel's television series *Drugs, Inc.*, which has covered the production, distribution, and use of a variety of drugs, including heroin, cocaine, methamphetamines, and marijuana. Examples of some of these episodes are "Hawaiian Ice," which documents the use of crystal methamphetamine in Hawaii; "The Real Wolves of Wall Street," which investigates the use of drugs among that population;

"Pittsburgh Smack," which examines the heroin economy in that city; and "Heroin Island, NYC," which looks at the heroin epidemic on Staten Island.

Drug Use and the Police

The French Connection is a 1971 film about New York City narcotics detectives based on a real-life investigation. In the plot, detective Jimmy "Popeye" Doyle, played by Gene Hackman, and his partner, Buddy Russo (Roy Scheider), attempt to intercept a shipment of heroin from France hidden in secret panels in a Lincoln Continental Mark III. The most riveting scene in the movie is a car chase under the elevated train line as Popeye attempts to capture a villain riding in a train above him.

Serpico, from 1973, is based on real-life police officer Frank Serpico, who went undercover to investigate police corruption in the New York City Police Department in the 1960s and early 1970s. Played by Al Pacino, the movie follows Serpico's ill-fated crusade to rid the department of graft-taking officers. He is eventually set up by his colleagues and severely wounded during a drug arrest.

Prince of the City is a 1981 movie based on a book by Robert Daley (1978) about an investigation of corruption in the Special Investigations Unit of the Narcotics Division of the New York City Police Department. Like *Serpico*, the book and film focus on a New York City police officer, Daniel Ciello, played by Treat Williams. Unlike Serpico, however, Ciello was himself involved in corruption and was "turned" by the NYPD internal affairs unit and federal prosecutors to uncover illegal activities of the "princes of the city."[12] Jay Presson Allen, the movie's screenwriter, explains the premise of the film, in a response to the criticism of Murray Kempton, a well-respected journalist, who had criticized the movie as having unrealistic elements:

> The SIU was as corrupt an arm of law enforcement as one is likely to find this side of Hong Kong. It was so corrupt it selfdestructed [sic], which the movie makes abundantly clear to anyone not looking for absolutes. We made a movie about five men, some eagerly corrupt, some not so eager but still corrupt, flawed men trapped in a flawed system. It is not a movie about heroes or villains or societal symbols. And the vast majority of the audience understands this. (Allen 1981)[13]

Relationship Between Licit and Illicit Drug Use and the Media

Although the examples given so far are far from exhaustive, they demonstrate the extent to which illicit drugs have permeated American popular culture. Paralleling this is the widespread presence and acceptance of legal drugs in the media. One cannot watch television for long without being bombarded with advertisements for prescription medications ("Ask your doctor about . . .") or over-the-counter (OTC) pills and remedies. So, for example, there are prescription drug ads for erectile dysfunction, ulcerative colitis, Crohn's disease and irritable bowel syndrome, incontinence, sleep disorders, respiratory problems such as COPD (chronic obstructive pulmonary disease) and asthma, blood thinners, antipsychotics, rheumatoid arthritis, allergies, weight issues, smoking cessation, type 2 diabetes, high cholesterol, bladder problems, pain, Alzheimer's disease, atrial fibrillation and stroke, shingles, toe fungus, and more (Aubuchon 2016). Since the U.S. Food and Drug Administration (FDA) lifted some of its restrictions on prescription drug advertisement in 1997, the use of media to advertise these medications has dramatically increased (Moyer 2015; Thompson 2016). The pharmaceutical industry spent $4.5 billion marketing prescription drugs in 2014, a billion dollars more than it spent the year before (Millman 2015; Moyer 2015). In 2014, television ads made up 61.6% of these expenditures (Millman 2015). The United States and New Zealand are the only countries that permit these advertisements, which are called DTC ads, for direct to consumer (ProCon.org 2014; Thompson 2016; U.S. Food and Drug Administration 2010). Although the FDA requires all advertisements to comply with specific requirements, such as including a narrated list of a drug's potential side effects, the use of DTC ads still remains controversial (Millman 2015; Moyer 2015; ProCon.org 2014; Thompson 2016; U.S. Food and Drug Administration 2010). Supporters of this practice say that the commercials inform patients, encourage them to talk with their physicians, and motivate them to comply with prescribed treatments and remove the stigma from some diseases and medical conditions (ProCon.org 2014; U.S. Food and Drug Administration 2010), whereas medical practitioners and the American Medical Association have concerns about commercials providing misleading information, not presenting enough information about risks, encouraging overuse of prescription medications, causing patients to pressure their medical providers to prescribe unneeded drugs, stigmatizing normal bodily functions, and adding increased health costs (Moyer 2015; ProCon.org 2014; U.S. Food and Drug Administration 2010).

These ads are very creative. For example, one advertisement for a COPD medication shows people lying on a couch with an elephant sitting on their chests and following them around all day. Another freezes people in place to indicate the stress a woman's ulcerative colitis causes her. One ED drug ad features masculine men in their 50s, solving problems in challenging situations. A more recent and controversial ad for the same product features attractive women frankly discussing the problem of achieving and maintaining erections. A competitor's ad is more subtle, showing affectionate middle-aged couples. In addition to television ads, which certainly have the most visceral impact, there are radio advertisements and magazine and newspaper ads, all touting prescription drugs. In contrast to the television ads aimed hit or miss at a general audience, magazine ads are more focused on particular readerships so, for example, men's and women's magazines have some gender-specific ads.

Magazines appealing to older consumers are more likely to have ads for ailments like arthritis and peripheral neuropathy.

Drug ads are nothing new. In the past, they appeared in newspapers and magazines. According to ProCon.org (2014), "Lydia E. Pinkham's Vegetable Compound was mass advertised starting in 1876 and purported to 'cure entirely the worst form of Female Complaints, all ovarian troubles, Inflammation and Ulceration, Falling and Displacements, and the consequent Spinal Weakness, and is particularly adapted to the Change of Life,' in addition to curing headaches, depression, indigestion, insomnia and other ailments." Lydia E. Pinkham's Vegetable Compound was an example of what were called "patent medicines," to distinguish them from "ethical drugs," which appeared in the U.S. Pharmacopeia and were approved by the American Medical Association (ProCon.org 2014). Patent medicines, which often contained cocaine, opiates, and alcohol—such as Coca Beef Tonic, Roger's Specific Cocaine Pile Remedy, and Peruvian Syrup—in various forms (Gomez 1984) made up "nearly half of the total ad revenue for newspapers" in the early 1900s (ProCon.org 2014). Then, as now, the exaggerated advertising claims made for nonprescription drugs were not regulated. In current television ads, OTC potions are often accompanied by a caveat, often in small print at the bottom of the screen, and only momentarily, that "these claims have not been evaluated by the FDA." The FDA categorizes many of these OTC drugs as supplements, rather than medications. Drug companies spend millions of dollars on advertising OTC drugs. Johnson & Johnson's advertising budget for Tylenol, for example, exceeds $100 million a year; in 2008, McNeil Consumer Healthcare, the unit that makes that drug, spent $162 million promoting its product (Gerth and Miller 2013).

The societal acceptance of drug use, especially illicit use, is facilitated by the ubiquity of drugs in the media, including Internet-based social media like Facebook and Twitter. Adolescents appear to be particularly vulnerable to the influence of both Internet-based and traditional media. In an article published in *Pediatrics*, Strasburger (2010) pointed out that positive images of drug use in the media give adolescents mixed messages, so that "the media contribute significantly to the risk that young people will engage in substance use" (p. 791). He further noted that "the power of advertising to influence children and adolescents (and adults, for that matter) is incontrovertible" (p. 792). A study of the followers of a pro-marijuana tweeter found that almost 73% of them were under 19 (Cavazos-Rehg et al. 2014). Some medical professionals are concerned with the influence of "super peers," defined as movies, television, and the Internet, because adolescents spend many times more hours (8.6 versus 1.2) with electronic than nonelectronic media, and 22% of the movies adolescents watch portray illicit drug use (Johns Hopkins Children's Center 2011). One study of 700 middle school students asked them about their current and perceived future use of alcohol and tobacco. They were also asked about their perception of substance use in the media. The researchers found that students who identified with these drug-related messages and saw themselves as similar to the users portrayed in the media were significantly more likely to report substance use (Scull et al. 2010). The *National Survey on American Attitudes on Substance Abuse XVII: Teens*, conducted by the National Center on Addiction and Substance Abuse at Columbia University (CASA) (2012), which surveyed 1,003 12- to 17-year-olds, found that "seventy-five percent of teens say that seeing pictures on social networking sites of kids partying with alcohol or marijuana encourages other teens to want to party like that" (CASA 2012:11). The percentage of teens agreeing with this statement increased with an increase in age cohort. Forty-seven percent of teens who have seen such pictures think that the youngsters in them are having a good time. The researchers found that adolescents who have seen pictures of young people using drugs or alcohol or passing out were 4 times as likely to have used marijuana as those youths who have not seen such images, and they were 3 times as likely to have friends who use marijuana (CASA 2012:12–13). The Center on Media and Child Health (2015) notes that a variety of media present substance use as commonplace, acceptable, and "even cool." It lists a number of ways in which media can influence adolescent attitudes toward the use of alcohol, tobacco, and drugs, including depicting "substance use as hip, sexy and largely consequence-free, not showing the health, social or legal costs" and using celebrity endorsers and attractive actors in commercials, who appear to be independent, adventurous, and rebellious (Center on Media and Child Health 2015). The reference to drugs and alcohol in popular music is also noted. Music "containing references to substance use being normative and without consequences, may lead to adolescents accepting these messages as their beliefs, fueling the potential for them to experiment with substance use" (Center on Media and Child Health 2015).

The relationship between the media and illicit and licit drugs can be understood sociologically on both the macro and micro levels. On the macro level, the media are involved with a number of social institutions, including the economy and legal and political institutions, all of which are intertwined. In this chapter, we have seen the huge sums of money spent by drug companies in advertising their products on television and radio and in print media. In Chapter 2 we noted the large expenditures of the tobacco and alcohol industries on advertising and building a positive image, resulting in increased sales and the powerful influence of the media in creating those images and essentially defining and redefining for us what are "good drugs" and "bad drugs." Alcohol, tobacco, and pharmaceutical companies use their revenue to support and lobby politicians, thus influencing the laws pertaining to their products.

On a microsociological level, the media create the meanings that define drugs and their users. Movies and television often normalize drug use and users and may even make them seem cool and attractive. Pot smoker Jeff Spicoli and the characters created by Cheech and Chong are all "good guys," albeit somewhat unconventional and goofy; their use of marijuana is presented as harmless and even funny. The main characters in *Weeds* and *Breaking Bad* are portrayed sympathetically, and their drug production and dealing are presented as simply a means of survival. The teenagers on *That '70s Show* are normal adolescents, whose pot smoking is seen as a form of social bonding. Drug commercials, whether for prescription drugs or OTC preparations, emphasize the positive qualities of these medications. These ads feature attractive, everyday people who are often introduced as non-actors and the actual users of the medications. They are people with whom the viewer can identify, serving as pseudo reference groups.

Relationship Between Marijuana, Heroin, and Other Harder Drugs: Is Marijuana a Gateway Drug?

One belief in popular culture is that marijuana (and often alcohol and tobacco) is what is termed a gateway drug. That is, smoking marijuana is thought to lead to using other, often harder drugs such as heroin and cocaine. First, from a sociological viewpoint, the concept of a gateway drug is vague and imprecise, with little evidence to show that most people graduate from marijuana to harder drugs (National Institute on Drug Abuse [NIDA] 2015). In fact, though the Substance Abuse and Mental Health Services Administration's (SAMHSA) report for 2014 estimated that 22.2 million Americans aged 12 and over, representing 8.4% of the population of those ages, reported currently using marijuana (SAMHSA 2015a:5), only about 435,000 Americans in that cohort, or about 0.2% of the population aged 12 years and older, reported current heroin use (p. 11). Additionally, the SAMHSA (2015a) report estimated that about 1.5 million Americans currently used cocaine (or about 0.6% of the 12-and-older population), including 354,000 crack users, corresponding to 0.1% of the population (p. 10). The survey also found that there were about 1.6 million current stimulant users, including 569,000 methamphetamine users, corresponding to 0.6% of the population aged 12 and older for all stimulants and 0.2% for just methamphetamine users. Second, precedence in time does not prove causality. Of course, many current heroin, cocaine, and crack addicts have probably also used marijuana prior to becoming involved with these harder drugs, but some of them have not. For some addicts, their first drug experience is with prescription drugs. Third are what are called "intervening variables," factors that may either precede a hypothesized independent or causal variable or cause both the supposed independent and dependent variables. It may be, for example, that some other variable, such as an addictive personality, accounts for the use of both marijuana and heroin, or, following Maslow (1943), the use of drugs may be an attempt to satisfy basic needs like those for esteem, which people may seek within drug subcultures,[14] or the need for self-actualization, for which the use of hallucinogens has often been espoused (Aaronson and Osmond 1970). Fourth, the effects of marijuana are different from the effects of heroin and cocaine, and people differ in the type of effect or high they desire, which will affect their choice of drug. Marijuana is both a stimulant and a depressant (Erowid 2015; Murray 1986); cocaine and methamphetamine are euphoric stimulants, and heroin is a euphoric depressant (Erowid 2015). Fifth, the idea that marijuana is a gateway drug skips over the obvious question: Why should this be so? In other words, what is the mechanism by which marijuana use starts the slippery slope down into hard drug use? Our position is that the notion of a gateway drug is a lay idea, not a scientific concept. The challenge, then, is to account for the small proportion of people who first use marijuana and then go on to use harder drugs. The question is what differentiates those individuals from the much larger group of people for whom marijuana use does not appear to stimulate further drug experimentation. The explanation one uses depends on one's scientific framework. Psychoanalysts, for example, may look within the individual for an explanation, as in the idea of emotional needs or an addictive or experimental personality.[15] Social behaviorists would look outside the individual for patterns of reward and reinforcement. Sociologists such as Cloward and Ohlin (1960) might look for the availability of deviant opportunities that differentiate these drug users from those who have not gone on to harder drugs, and symbolic interactionists might examine the relationships these individuals have with others, focusing on reference groups, significant others, participation in drug subcultures, and their perceptions of the responses of others to them and of themselves as users (Ray 1961).

NOTES

1. Peyote is still being used as part of the ceremonies of the Native American Church.

2. Crumb's art may be seen at https://www.google.com/search?q=psychedelic+comics+by+R.+Crumb&biw=1366&bih=623&tbm=isch&tbo=u&source=univ&sa=X&ved=0ahUKEwiZjNuFkMPKAhULHT4KHeCWCkQQsAQIGw

3. Examples of Robbie's art may be found at http://www.psychedelic-art.com. Examples of works by other contemporary artists can be found on Tumbler: https://www.tumblr.com/tagged/drug-art

4. A Lascar is a sailor from India.

5. In Appendix 2, however, Burroughs (2003) writes, "In this book I have written what I know about junk and the people who use it. The narrative is fiction, but it is based on facts of my experience" (p. 163).

6. In addition to the albums reviewed here, Cheech and Chong's work includes *Cheech & Chong's Wedding Album* (1974), *Sleeping Beauty* (1976), *Up in Smoke* (1978), *Let's Make a New Dope Deal* (1980), *Get Out of My Room* (1985), and *Cheech & Chong's Animated Movie* (2013). The latter is the soundtrack for their movie of the same name, which contains several drug-related tracks such as "Marijuana," "Smoke a Doobie Time," "Paranoid Pot Head," "Medical Marijuana Blues," and "(Another Hit of) Marijuana."

7. http://www.hightimes.com

8. *The Cocaine Fiends* was originally titled *The Pace That Kills*.

9. *Weeds* was produced for 8 seasons, August 7, 2005–September 16, 2012, and *Breaking Bad* for 5 seasons, January 20, 2008–September 29, 2013.

10. Their movies include *Things Are Tough All Over* (1982); *Still Smoking* (1983); *Cheech & Chong's The Corsican Brothers* (1984, which departs from their usual drug-addled characters); *Get Out of My Room*, a short-form video from 1985; and *Cheech & Chong's Animated Movie* (2013).

11. Burroughs wrote *Junkie* under the pseudonym William Lee. In an interview with the CBC in 1989, Burroughs detailed his drug experience and perspective on heroin use. See https://www.youtube.com/watch?v=DnxweVAvE5w

12. The detectives of the Special Investigations Unit of the Narcotics Division of the NYPD were referred to as "princes of the city" because they had free reign to travel and investigate in all parts of the city, in contrast to other officers who were confined to their own precincts.

13. In an interesting development, Ramon (Ray) Viera, an NYPD narcotics detective with whom Bruce Jackson (1970a) rode and whom Jackson quoted as being concerned about the infections of one of his informants (see Chapter 13), was one of the princes of the city who was arrested and convicted for corruption. According to court papers, "The offenses all arose out of appellants' corrupt use of their positions as New York City law enforcement officers to extort and misappropriate money from suspected narcotics dealers" (Open Jurist 1976).

14. See, for example, Philippe Bourgois, *In Search of Respect: Selling Crack in El Barrio* (New York: Cambridge University Press, 2003).

15. The idea of an addictive personality is given some support from the observation that multiple addictions are not uncommon. Anecdotally, all of the present writers know of individuals with multiple addictions, some of which are completely unrelated to drug use. For example, one man of our acquaintance, a recovering alcoholic, also has a gambling addiction and is a transvestite, itself an addiction (see, for example, Vern L. Bullough and Thomas S. Weinberg, "Women Married to Transvestites: Problems and Adjustments," *Journal of Psychology & Human Sexuality* 1(2) (1988): 83–104; and Thomas S. Weinberg and Vern L. Bullough, "Alienation, Self Image and the Importance of Support Groups for the Wives of Transvestites," *Journal of Sex Research* 24 (1988): 262–268). Another individual, who has been a drug user and is a recovering alcoholic, is a shopaholic and food addict.

Becoming a Drug User
Careers, Personalities, and Interaction—Two Perspectives

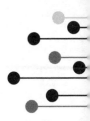

Drug use, abuse, and addiction are complex behaviors that require different perspectives in order to gain a complete understanding of the dynamics involved in their development.[1] An academic sociological framework enables one to understand the place of larger societal structures, culture, and social context in addiction, but an intellectual understanding of the drug phenomenon is not enough. One of the early fathers of American sociology, Charles Horton Cooley, called for sociologists to practice what he called "sympathetic introspection." According to Cooley (1909), the sociologist comes to understand people "largely by what may be called *sympathetic introspection*, putting himself into intimate contact with various sorts of persons and allowing them to awake in himself a life similar to their own, which he afterwards, to the best of his ability, recalls and describes. In this way he is more or less able to understand—always by introspection— children, idiots, criminals, rich and poor, conservative and radical—any phase of human nature not wholly alien to his own" (p. 7; italics in original). In other words, we have to be able to understand the individual's behavior from that person's point of view. This requires an *emotional* comprehension, not just an academic understanding. In the first part of this chapter, Dr. Ursula Adler Falk, a psychotherapist with extensive experience working with drug and alcohol abusers, provides the missing element in our sociological understanding of addiction through an analysis of cases from her practice. Identifying indicators have been removed to protect the anonymity of her patients. Additional case studies of drug users appear in Appendix B.

The second part of this chapter takes a broader approach of more conventional sociological theory, primarily that of symbolic interaction, to discuss the process of becoming a drug user and the factors involved in self-identification as an addict.

A Psychotheraputic Approach

The drugs described here are products that are bought and sold illegitimately and are harmful to the human mind and body. Their purpose is to create addictions in the users and to enrich the criminals who market these chemicals and products. Some are grown and produced in the soil of the United States and elsewhere, others are manufactured to alleviate pain during surgery or from serious injuries, and still others are used by addicts, obtained illegally from pushers who gain materially from their use. Other illegal drugs are imported from other countries. There are many varieties of these products, and variations among their use and their users, which will be described. Their purpose is to enrich the seller, the criminal who trades in this merchandise and in the thoughts, pain, and unhappiness of the purchasers.

There is a long history of the use of mind-altering drugs. The first major morphine addiction occurred during the American Civil War. Soldiers were given morphine to ease the pain of injuries and relieve the symptoms of dysentery. During wars surgeons would use whatever was available to lessen the pain, especially the agony of leg or arm amputations. In this, our 21st century, illegal drugs are used to heighten "enjoyment," to douse unfortunate feelings and emotional problems, to allow the user to practice what he or she could not do were the user in his or her "right mind," to enable the user to act out sexually or in an unacceptable fashion, and much more. It has also been found that some drugs imbibed regularly or heavily create impotence in the male and lack of feeling and/or desire in the female.

Users of all classes of humanity use illegitimate drugs. There are the folks who suffer from severe pain and begin their addiction through a prescription by their physician. They become habituated to these drugs, and when their prescription expires, they find other means of obtaining what they believe they need, that which takes away momentary ill feelings or pain. There are those users who are troubled by their circumstances. They are fighting emotional problems and use drugs to momentarily forget their troubles; they may have lost their jobs and then turn to the "quick fix" by indulging in illegitimate drugs. These folks can become addicted, and their reality is covered by the substance they are imbibing. The drug they are using, be it heroin, marijuana, alcohol, or innumerable other drugs, produces an altered state of consciousness. The person thus addicted is in another place. He or she is not troubled by the painful, the difficult, and the seemingly threatening situation when using the drug. An addiction may begin in many ways. It may originally have occurred accidentally at a party with friends or acquaintances, as the result of an overused or misused prescription drug, because of an erroneous belief that the individual is having a joyful experience, as panacea letting the user become less inhibited, or as a perceived ideation of a magical hallucinatory omnipotence, which would erase the individual's perception of his or her shy or troubled personality traits.

Innumerable situations lead to drug problems. The poor may sell drugs, taste them, and become victims of the temporary "cure," which becomes an addiction. There are those who have inherited an allergy to alcohol and who become very ill early in their usage. A *USA Today* headline read "Binge Drinking Kills 6 a Day—Mostly Men" (Painter 2015). "The report from the Federal Centers for Disease Control and Prevention says that an estimated 2,221 people older than 15 died of alcohol poisoning each year from 2010 to 2012. About 76% were men and nearly

77% were 35–64. Just 5% were ages 15–24" (Painter 2015:1). Robert Brewer, coauthor of the CDC study, noted that "there is a lot of binge drinking going on post-college age" (Painter 2015:1). High blood alcohol concentrations (BACs) impede the areas of the brain that control breathing, heart rate, and temperature, causing death. "The risk rises with binge drinking, which the Center of Disease Control defines as four or more drinks in about two hours for women and five or more drinks in two hours for men" (Painter 2015:1). Ryan Stanton, an emergency room physician in Lexington, Kentucky, told the USA Today reporter that older male drinkers "tend to be the largest category of binge drinkers." Stanton further noted that "most deaths do not happen in hospitals . . . [but] are often found dead on the street or on a porch" (Painter 2015:1).

Those drug users who have inherited allergies and who become very ill in their usage of the drug imbibed, and those who have free access when sampling, are unable to stop. This has been observed in hospitals, pharmacies, and readily accessible places. In addition, the repetitious advertisement of legal drugs can become the beginning of a serious or fatal addiction for the addictive personality convinced of the curative power of a given drug. Any pharmaceutical product can become hazardous when misused, overused, or taken in massive quantities. The promotion of so-called legitimate drugs on television and radio and in other media is known to be enticing to the potentially addictive personality. It appears as a panacea to people who are searching for a cure for their perceived difficulties. When alcohol no longer has the expected effect, the alcoholic will either add another more potent drug or use a stronger means of attempting to erase his or her urges or unhappiness. The addiction becomes more intense, creating severe problems. It affects every part of the human body, including the brain. As the quantity and quality of the intake changes, so does the effect. The drug commonly known as Lortab reduces, or for a time stops, the pain of the user. The person thus affected will feel strong, ready to do whatever is expected. As time passes, the person becomes lethargic, the pain returns, and he or she feels helpless to perform as expected to work and function adequately. As a consequence, he or she may become severely depressed. If fortunate, the person may be able to obtain a counterdrug, possibly Suboxone or another substance, that is less dangerous but also addicting, which enables the self-induced victim to return to a pseudo normal stage. He or she can, if fortunate, return to earning a livelihood and gain strength to work and live a pseudo normal life. Such prescriptions will cost drug abusers a portion of their income that could have been used to enhance their lifestyle and that of their dependents. In addition, the physician who prescribes the counteragent, for example, Suboxone or other antidotes, must attempt to have the user lessen his or her need for the counterdrug. A second professional is required to see the patient at appointed times to determine if any progress has been made in counteracting the original drug and regularly lessen the strength and quantity of the less damaging counterdrug. It is rare that such healing potions achieve their purpose. The prescriber is often not strict in insisting on lessening the pseudo-healing would-be medication. The fear of losing his or her license requires that a third person, a psychotherapist, send a regular notice to the prescriber after examining a given patient in order to report in writing on the so-called progress of the user.

If one drug does not help to curb the emotional or physical pain the drug user experiences, he or she will add or substitute another illegal product. This action usually has dire consequences for the victim. Users' urges may become so strong that they overdose, consuming so much that they cannot speak and their heart stops, ending their life.

Another addict may turn to crime to satisfy his or her addictive needs. He or she will steal whenever possible, associate with drug dealers, possibly sell drugs on the street or elsewhere to other victims, and may find a future in prison, experiencing an indescribable mental and physical state. Addiction also affects the user's family. If married, divorce is one solution for the beleaguered spouse. If there are children, their lives are severely affected by their incarcerated parent. If the addict remains in prison for any length of time, children have a poor role model or none at all. The income of the family is reduced to a point at which necessities to make life comfortable are often not covered. The effects of addiction on the user and his or her significant other and offspring are innumerable. The addict's future, if he or she survives, has many deleterious effects. If he or she is released from prison and in recovery, potential employers will be afraid to give the person an opportunity to function adequately for the job. They will be fearful that the individual will return to his or her addictive behavior and possibly steal from them in order to satisfy cravings. Thus, the prejudice mixed with reality makes normal living difficult for the person released from incarceration. If the released individual cannot find remunerable employment, he or she may repeat the behavior and reenter prison.

There are addicts who want to live and know they must make a difficult decision to change their addiction. Their urges to continue are so strong that their awareness to have themselves incarcerated in an inpatient drug facility gives them an opportunity to abstain because their drug of choice is not readily available and their surroundings are such that their fellow inhabitants suffer from the same or similar addiction as they do. Such surroundings are therapeutic. The healers are individuals who understand the urges, plagues, and problems the people they are attempting to help are suffering from. They also know that if the plagued one does not change, he or she is doomed. Persons thus stricken have innumerable problems other than their urge to continue in their life-threatening addiction. The ordinary poor or middle-class citizen thus affected cannot afford the costs of obtaining the best opportunity to abstain, to heal through inpatient treatment. This form of treatment provides a much better opportunity to stay away from a given drug and its lethal surroundings, because illegal drugs are not readily available. Having other addicts with whom to commiserate and to feel their pain enables individuals to realize as well as experience that they are not alone in their overwhelming urges, feelings, and attitudes. They strengthen each other in reinforcing their desperate need to find a healthy drug-free existence.

There are many reasons why the addicted do not choose or are unable to sign themselves into a healing center where they have the greatest opportunity to save their lives. Aside from having to step out of their ordinary lives, the cost is the greatest barrier toward entering such a facility. A *Buffalo News* article (Michel 2015) detailed the problems an addictive individual may encounter when he or she is ready for rehabilitation. The 21-year-old opiate and alcohol addict featured in the story had convinced himself of the need to be admitted into inpatient therapy to become "clean and sober." However, he was told he was not sick enough. Outpatient therapy was suggested, because insurance companies do not want to pay the enormous costs involved in full-time, inpatient therapy. The man, after a difficult struggle, convinced the insurance company to pay the costs, because he felt this was his only opportunity to get better. Most insurance companies will attempt to only reimburse the costs for outpatient therapy, if at all. This "illustrates a rift in the medical and insurance community about what the most effective treatment is for heroin and opiate addiction—inpatient or outpatient" (Michel 2015:1). The cost is undoubtedly the greatest reason for the ultimate decision made by insurance companies. Indecision, rifts, and nontreatment have added to the deaths of many addicts.

> And this rift is occurring as an epidemic of heroin and opiate addiction sweeps the Buffalo community and the nation. In Erie County [New York] alone, 78 people died from heroin and other opiate overdoses in the first eight months of 2014, according to the County Health Department. . . . Some say the dispute over treatment is about money. Inpatient care, which lasts one to six months, can cost as much as $30,000 per month. Outpatient care costs only $200 per week. (Michel 2015:1)

The following addicts' feelings, experiences, and situations are authentic cases from the files of one of the authors, Dr. Ursula Adler Falk. Some are self-reported and yet others are quoted, but all are authenticated. Their names and incidents are slightly altered to protect their identity. In addition, a reporter who had the opportunity to join the police experience observed and described some of the addicts and incidents that follow (Parlato 2014).

Case #1: Dr. Garner: Habitual Marijuana User

Dr. Garner, a 58-year-old handsome, sturdy-looking professor, spoke of his use of marijuana:

> It takes me away from the difficulties, the difficulties that are in my existence. I am divorced and am expected to give my ex-wife everything I have. She wants my entire salary, my meager income. She already has the house that I struggled to have. My paycheck was enough to cover our necessities, but there was nothing left. She did not work, and has not in the twenty years that we were together. She had a hobby, a donkey she fed

Photo 11.1: Smoking a marijuana joint.

and a few chickens that laid eggs. It was an expensive hobby that was on our land in the country house that she had insisted we live in. Our home was a considerable distance from the university in which I taught. She refused to go to the city with me to meet my colleagues, and she criticized my friends.

One day one of my fellow teachers asked me to sample a marijuana cigarette. He had rolled it himself. It zoned me out. I could forget all my troubles, my unhappiness. After that experience when I felt stressed I would indulge in a marijuana ciggy. They were just what I needed to take me away from that screeching voice that made constant demands of me. I needed peace to enable me to concentrate on my lectures, my writings and all that my position, my profession demanded. She denigrated everything that I accomplished. All the hard work, the years of work, study and time that I sacrificed were minimalized by this person, the female who alleged she cared about me. In order to minimize my psychic pain I sent away for the ingredients that were needed to roll the cigarettes and wrote her name on the return address of the envelope. The purpose was that if the package were investigated I would not be penalized and possibly lose my job, my profession. The wife did not work so it would not matter. She had nothing to lose. It would hardly affect her. When she accidentally found out, she went ballistic. She called me every name in the book and screamed so loud that the neighbors who lived miles away could hear it. This was the beginning of our serious rift, our unhappy union, our unhappy marriage. We had not been sexually intimate for a long time. I had befriended a single middle aged woman who was our nearest neighbor, and the wife accused me of infidelity, which was a figment of her imagination, another accusatory figment of her thinking processes. The marijuana was a relief from the screaming wife. The multitude of accusations and demands she made of me were without cessation, without end. Marijuana relaxed me, it changed my difficult times at least temporarily, and it gave me an escape from the constant criticism that was intolerable. It gave me the strength to begin the divorce procedures. Although it cost me almost half of my meager income, since I was forced to support the ex, it was worth the price I paid. Freedom from this very narcissistic, controlling female gave me the freedom to be myself!

Marijuana is still in my life but to a much smaller amount and less often. My new girlfriend, Rachel, a very intelligent, educated woman, does not want me to indulge in the marijuana weed, and she rationally explained the reason, the possible effects and the addiction that it can become. We agreed that I would not use it in her presence or in her home. She lives in a distant city, far from mine. She has her own practice, has supported herself, is very well educated and made me comfortable when we visited on weekends in her house away from this countrified abode. She seemed to understand my struggles, my concerns. She herself had a difficult existence. She had problems with her mother during her childhood and could not get along with her sister whom she had not contacted for years. The mom was deceased, and only her frail widowed father remained. She had had various male relationships in her life, but at age fifty, she had never found anyone who was satisfactory marriage material, either from her own or former boyfriends' views. She had no "normal" male friend who had asked to marry her. She was happy to have found someone whom she could love and respect. There was one unfortunate situation that occurred after we had dated for twelve months: We went to Europe together. She took leave from her practice in order to accompany me. I was overseas to study the Irish culture and she to take her yearly vacation, which gave us the opportunity to enjoy each other's company at the same time. The problem occurred on a day when we were at a train station awaiting the train that was taking us from one city to another. There was a young woman standing near us who asked me many questions about where we were going and the purpose of our trip. The conversation became very personal and she wondered if we were married. When she learned of our status she became flirtatious with me. Rachel responded jealously and attempted to direct me away from the conversation with the young woman by pulling at my arm. I became so angry that I pushed her away from me and she accidentally fell and hurt her elbow and her hand. She began to weep. She was not only physically injured but also emotionally. My guilt and self-reproach were so strong that I smoked a marijuana cigarette outside of our hotel room. This was an act which would allow me to feel pleasantly numb and enabled me to feel righteous and comfortable. It also reminded me of my very disturbing situations, which occurred so frequently with my divorced wife. Since that incident, regular visits to the local gymnasium and a daily exercise regime have taken away my need to use a mind altering drug to numb myself from the vagaries of everyday life.

Psychotherapist's comments: It has been recognized that the marijuana cigarette is addictive; its use can be minimized and controlled with determination on the part of the user. If folk who began with the use of this drug turn to more dangerous indulgences like heroin and other mind-altering drugs and poisons, these habits will sooner or later bring about damage to the human body and affect life in a multitude of ways. Loss of good health and the inability to think and act in realistic ways cause joblessness, lawlessness, loss of healthy relationships, and if continued for a period of time, the loss of life. Marijuana, like alcohol, is a drug used by the rich, the middle-class, and the poor. In this the 21st century, it has become legal in a number of states, and thus the availability and overuse has become easily accessible to the addictive personality.

Case #2: Julie Kay: Addicted to Heroin

Julie Kay was referred to the therapist's office by her attorney, the court, and her mother. She is an 18-year-old angry, introverted girl, whose eyes look dull and moist. She is of a slim and small stature. She appeared to be tired and not meticulously dressed. She had multicolored hair, which was carelessly groomed. When asked why she came, she was brief with her answer and held her mother, the court, her lawyer, and everyone other than herself responsible. Her tone was an angry accusatory one, and she let it be known that she did not want to be questioned. She painted a picture of pure innocence and the victim of others as well as her surroundings. Her retorts were frequently abbreviations and evasions, as well as contradictive. When reassured, she felt attacked and disbelieved. Every sentence had to be extracted. She spoke with anger about her mother. She had left home to live with friends when she was approximately 17 years of age. She alleged that she had not dealt with her parents for months and only when she was desperate or wanted something. When asked about her current situation and why she needed to visit the office on this occasion, she related the following episode: She was apprehended by the police when she was sitting peacefully on the couch of her friend's house. She had been enjoying an hour "or so" of peace and closeness with her friends. One of the young

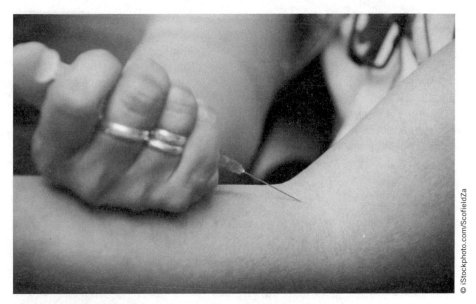

Photo 11.2: Shooting up heroin.

people was allegedly her boyfriend. He supposedly was the renter, the tenant of the apartment in which they were living, but she, Julie, had paid the rent for the premises. The police marched in the day she was arrested, searched her, and found a pair of brass knuckles in her handbag (illegal in New York). She claimed that her boyfriend had thrown them in there in order not to be accused or threatened, because he was on probation. They handcuffed her, brought her before a judge, and from there she was transported to jail. She insisted that she was cheated and wrongly accused.

Julie had a long history of problems. She was the only child of her divorced parents (she contradicted herself as to whether her parents had been married). She hated her mother, who had raised her alone into adulthood. The father remarried and had a number of other offspring. She rarely saw the dad. Only her age mates, her friends, mattered to her. All of these friends were alcohol and drug users. She had begun with marijuana, then alcohol and sometimes both, and ultimately had become addicted to heroin. She alleged that she received it from friends, who were also users and sellers. She insisted that she was a relatively recent user of that drug. When questioned a little more in-depth, she became abusive and insisted that she had abused heroin only once. Her contradictions were frequent and numerous. When the therapist inquired about her graduation from high school, she sullenly responded that she had completed it 6 months before. After graduation she said that she had been employed in a grocery store. She had lost this job because she had stolen money whenever she worked as the cashier there. She was not trusted after being discovered in one of these incidents and was promptly terminated. She was unable to find remunerable work after that, because apparently her reputation had followed her. She described the day she was dismissed. Her employer found her stealing not only from the cash register, but she had also stashed a bottle of wine in her pocket with the intent of taking it with her. She had worked in that store for approximately 2 months. There was a time that she had wanted to be a teacher, but she had no money and no energy to take the courses necessary toward her alleged goal. She was living with several others in an apartment. She refused to live with her mother and insisted that she hates her. She was the only child, a fact she repeated. Julie resented that her mother dated occasionally. She called the mother vile names and held her responsible for the breakup of her family. She also spoke of her father's Asian wife who brought several children into the marriage with her. The father also had a son before he married Julie's mother. She rarely sees or hears about her half brother, who allegedly lives alone and apparently is an adult.

Psychotherapist's comments: Julie minimizes her use of heroin. She insists that it helps her mood. She feels very tired and seems to be very "high" with the heroin in her system. She insists she can quit any time that she desires. She also stated that when she used the drug it induced sleep, and she could barely stay awake at such times. She wants more and more of the drug once she begins her very serious and harmful addiction. She admitted that sometimes she does not know what she is feeling or saying while under the influence. She is lethargic much of the time. When under the influence, she feels satisfied, not angry, not anxious or disinterested in her immediate surroundings. Her ambition to become a teacher left her long ago. She states she has no money nor any great urges to "be someone." She dreads becoming "straight" every day and facing reality. Her theft on the job and her being fired resulted in emotional pain, but it is not sufficient enough to control her addiction. She is not open regarding her use of the drug and minimizes everything about this addiction.

Julie was ordered by the court to live with her father and his wife while she is on probation. Her future is a very questionable one.

Case #3: Timothy Smith: Addicted to Pain Killers

Timothy Smith, a 30-year-old factory worker, revealed the situation that brought him to the therapist's office. He needed a counterdrug to keep him from his addictive product Lortab, which he had been using for nearly 2 years. He worked the midnight shift in the factory where he was employed. He nearly lost his job because he had many absences as his strength failed him. He was overcome by weakness in his entire body; he was nauseous, he could not get up when needed, and after 10 years of steady employment he received a warning that if he had any more unexcused absences, he would be terminated. This sturdy-appearing man had a number of responsibilities, which included a fiancé and their 9-year-old son, whom he supported. His addiction began when he injured his back after falling from a ladder while painting the ceiling of their home's kitchen.

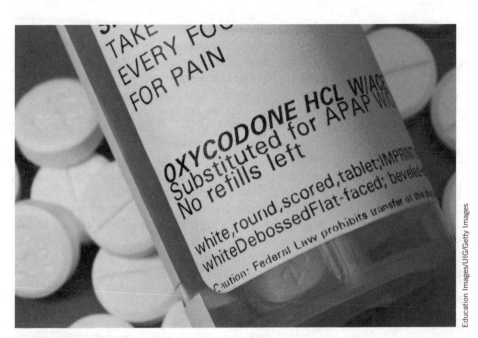

Photo 11.3: Oxycodone pills.

He was prescribed the pain-killing medication that ultimately created the addiction he needed to stop. The physician, Romar Resoy, a general practitioner, was very accommodating and readily prescribed Lortab, assuring the patient that he would feel much better in a relatively short time. It was a miracle for Tim. After a day, Timothy felt like a "new man." The pain was nearly extinguished, and he was able to perform his duties without difficulty. He seemed to be able to enjoy his fiancé, his son, and his colleagues at work, and his job seemed to be "a breeze." Life seemed good. As time passed, he needed to ingest higher dosages of his prescribed drug. In the beginning, his strength appeared to have increased. After a year, he became lethargic and his driving had become problematic. He could barely leave his bed, and his job performance became inadequate. His enthusiasm had disappeared. He desperately needed relief from the misery that beset him. It was in that state that he learned of a physician who would be able to give him the countermedication he believed he needed. He found Dr. Schwind, who wrote a prescription for Suboxone, the miracle drug that would enable him to continue his job and meet his other responsibilities. Dr. Schwind was found through an acquaintance, who used this physician's service. The drug specialist insisted, as the law demanded, that he see a therapist, who would assist him to lessen the new countermedication through counseling sessions, assisting the patient to be emotionally enabled to lessen his urges. The physician needed a written statement for each session that the patient had with the mental health person, lest he lose his practice. This protected him and his remunerative practice. Unfortunately, the dosage did not decrease, although the patient made verbal promises he did not keep. Tim found every excuse that he could not to do as advised, but he would reduce his use at the beginning of his vacation when his responsibilities decreased and the strain of his duties was lessened. A decrease did not occur after 8 months had passed. Tim did once report that he had taken an iota less of the drug. The therapist was unable to dissuade him in his self-destructive behavior and gave him an ultimatum, which ended their relationship.

Psychotherapist's comments: The experience of Timothy is not unusual, and it is extremely difficult to succeed in convincing an addicted person to abandon his very destructive addictions. Dr. Indira, the general practitioner who prescribed Lortab so readily for his addicted patients during many years of practice, was fined, incarcerated for a brief period, and eventually returned to his native India. Dr. Schwind had a reputation of protecting his remunerative practice by shifting his responsibility to the therapist who was working with his patients. The remuneration for visits is excellent because a number of these physicians do not use insurance but receive their considerable fees in cash from the addicts/patients who visit their office.

Dr. Indira was a physician with a large practice of people addicted to illegal drugs who could no longer find what they believed they needed on the street. Their yearning, emotional pain, and desperation sent them on a search through other addicted acquaintances for a doctor who would readily prescribe a "magic pill" that would douse their pain, anguish, and fear. From the proverbial word of mouth they succeeded in locating Dr. Indira, a man in his late 70s who was no longer afraid of being discovered, incarcerated, or excluded from practicing in his field. He was friendly with his contemporaries and the pharmacists in the area and exceptionally fatherly and polite to the frantic addicts who visited his practice. He examined them superficially, questioned them about their life, and asked how long ago their addiction began and how long they had purchased the pain-relieving but killing substances on the street. He comforted them and assured them that they would find satisfaction and relief from their misery and much more. His reassuring voice gave new patients the security they needed to believe they had found their panacea. They were convinced that they would no longer have to pay the high prices demanded by the drug peddlers; they would not be discovered and imprisoned, lose their livelihood, attend expensive court sessions, or steal money. They wanted to avoid the consequences of their deeds and not become outcast from the family that had been so important to them. If an addict had children, he would be a poor role model, his wife would contemplate divorce, and he would have to regress to his infantile childhood by returning to live with his parents for shelter, food, transportation, and support to help him meet his responsibilities. The money-hungry physician was the answer in the mind of the addict. Surely whatever potion the doctor prescribed would be sanctioned. Frequently, the doctor would only take his payment in cash rather than alerting the insurance company to the prescriptions he so readily prescribed.

It is unexpected that a professional, highly skilled, educated man would forget he took the Hippocratic Oath to be there to help humanity, one patient at a time. There are a number of reasons why the well-intentioned physician denounces his profession and honor and "forgets" his promises. They include greed, evasion of taxation, a decrease in everyday patients, a belief that rapid cures can be reached, and possibly a lack of thorough knowledge of the effects of drugs.

A Reporter's Observations

In a midsized city in New York, a reporter (with the assistance of the police) observed five people in an apartment, all white and in their 20s. Kay, the hostess, had been beaten that day and was severely bruised. "She said that her boyfriend had been arrested that day and while he was out of jail she had an order of protection, and since it was his apartment where she lived, she would be forced to move out in a couple of days" (Parlato 2014:1). The other guests in the apartment were all heroin addicts. Billy, age 24, stated that he was trying to quit his drug addiction. His friend had died, so he began using again. Angie, age 23, and Billy both stated that they had used heroin a few hours before and would use it again as soon as they could get it. Billy added that if he could not get it that evening, he would be very ill by morning. Angie stated that she does not take all of her medication all the time. "I don't take my subutex. I don't want to do subs more than two days in a row, because I know then I won't get high the next day" (Parlato 2014). Carl, 26, stated, "I just stopped [heroin] about five days ago. I'm on Suboxone."

Angie: Suboxone blocks it. I was on subs, but I figured out how to go around it.

Carl: Suboxone makes me not sick. It is a way to try to quit. If I take heroin after I take Suboxone, I will get sick.

Reporter: Do you have a craving for heroin?

Carl: All the time. But I know if [I] take Suboxone I can't take heroin. (Parlato 2014)

A Sociological Perspective

Interaction, Sense Making, and Identity

The goal of psychotherapy is different from that of academic sociology. As a clinical approach, its concern is to help drug and alcohol abusers develop insight into their attitudes and behavior and to thus work toward abstinence. Sociologists, on the other hand, are interested in addiction as a process of sense making and the social forces influencing cycles of use, abstention, and relapse. The symbolic interactionist approach taken here focuses on the social context of drug use, that is, on those definitions of the situation brought to it by participants.

Sociologists are interested in how these meanings influence individuals' perceptions and behavior. Examples of this perspective are found in the work of Alfred Lindesmith (1938) and Marsh B. Ray (1961) discussed in Chapters 1 and 8. As noted in Chapter 1, Lindesmith applied George Herbert Mead's emphasis on the important role of significant symbols in an individual's construction of the self to an explanation of the process of becoming an addict. According to Lindesmith (1938), the shared meanings, by which his culture defines a "dope addict," are learned by a person and applied to himself "when the point is reached at which withdrawal symptoms intrude themselves upon the attention of the individual and compel him to go on using the drug" (p. 606). This idea foreshadowed the later work of Ray (1961).

Ray examined the importance of an individual's perception of the responses of others in the cycle of relapse and abstinence. "An episode of cure begins," Ray (1961) writes, "in the private thoughts of the addict rather than in his overt behavior" (p. 134). He or she begins to "call into question" his or her addict identity as the result of interactions with "important others" (p. 134). These interactions cause the individual to examine his or her present identity as addict.

Once the individual is abstinent, he or she enters what Ray terms a "running struggle" period, a time of ambivalence during which addicts attempt to deal with their social identities. The question they must resolve is whether they are more like nonaddicts than addicts, and in this fragile state, they look toward nonaddicts to ratify their new nonuser identities. "The tendency toward relapse," Ray (1961) notes, "develops out of the meanings of the abstainer's experience in social situations when he develops an image of himself as socially different from non-addicts, and relapse occurs when he redefines himself as an addict" (p. 137). Thus, Ray's thesis is that "relapse is a function of the kind of objects ex-addicts make of themselves in the situations they face" (p. 138). The experience of a young woman mentored by the authors illustrates this process. "Juliette" (not her real name) enrolled in our college at age 26. She had left Buffalo 10 years earlier after graduating from high school, seeking a career as a model in New York City. That plan did not work out, and she became involved with a man who was a pimp and a heroin user. She quickly became addicted and engaged in secondary deviance to support their habits by working as a street prostitute. She was introduced to house prostitution by a former police officer, eventually took over managing that business, and became a very successful madam, running an outcall female domination service to the five New York City boroughs and New Jersey.[2] After having some legal problems, she eventually returned to Buffalo, where the authors were introduced to her by a former student, who knew we were doing research on BDSM (bondage, discipline, dominance and submission, sadomasochism).[3] During her first year in college, Juliette frequently sought us out for moral support. She was uncertain that she fit into the college setting, even though she was only a year over the median student age. Her life experience had made her feel older than her student peers. At the end of the summer of her first year, we and Juliette went for coffee at the student union:

Juliette said to me, "Do you know where I've been all summer?"

I replied, "You went back to the city, didn't you?"

"Yes," she said.

"You got back into the life, didn't you? Were you using?"

"Yes," she said. "How did you know that?"

"What happened?" I asked.

"I realized that I didn't belong there anymore," she said. "So at midnight one night, I just threw my clothes in the car and came back to Buffalo."

The recognition that one is, indeed, an addict is often problematic. Sometimes that doesn't happen until the user experiences withdrawal. A former addict writes, "One day I woke up with what felt like a flu, and it wasn't until I got some more dope to 'help my flu' that I realized I was 'junk sick'—the term users have for the early stages of withdrawal. It was after that—*after* I was addicted—that I turned to the needle" (Sargent and Byrne 2014).

Even going through withdrawal may not be enough evidence for the drug user to see himself or herself as being addicted. Sometimes others have to assist in the sense-making process. For example, several years ago, one of us had a student who had been addicted to heroin and was currently on a methadone maintenance program at a local hospital. "Bill" (not his real name) told the following story:

> I went through withdrawal three times before I realized I was hooked. I just thought that I had a bad case of the flu. The third time, a friend stopped by. He said, "You look terrible." "Yeah," I said, "I'm really sick with the flu." "No, you're not," he told me. "You're dope sick. You're going through withdrawal." I didn't believe him, so he cooked up some dope, and I injected it. Immediately, I felt normal again. "See," he said. "You're hooked." (From author's notes)[4]

Bill's experience illustrates the importance of the drug subculture in defining one's experiences. From a symbolic interactionist perspective, the role of other drug users in providing explanations, justifications, neutralizations, and rationalizations for one's substance use and drug-related behavior is at least as critical for the user as facilitating the access to drugs.

Subcultures and the Development of Identity

One of the differences between Dr. Falk's patients and the drug users studied by sociologists, social anthropologists, other ethnographers, and the autobiographical writings of drug users (e.g., Bourgois 1989, 1998a, 1998b, 2003; Bourgois and Schonberg 2009; Hoffer 2006; B. Jackson 1970a, 1970b; W. Lee 1953; C. Pearson and Bourgois 1995; Rettig, Torres, and Garrett 1977) is that, for the most part, they are individual users, some of whom became addicted as a result of medicine prescribed for pain. Most of them do not appear to have been involved in a drug subculture in any way, other than for procuring drugs. The exceptions include "Peter," a low-level drug dealer and not a user, and "Julie Kay," a heroin user who denies she is an addict and is not directly involved in the street addict subculture. Thus, they were usually not involved in the complex world of drug use, in which a user identity is solidified through interactions with others. "Timothy Smith" and the other addicted pill users in Dr. Falk's case studies[5] came to their addictions by being prescribed narcotics for pain control by physicians. Thus, they did not have the support of other pill users to help them, in Matza's (1969) terms, "to conceive a special relationship between doing and being—a unity capable of being indicated" (p. 170). That is, they did not have the reference group support enabling them to interpret their drug use in terms of a special (i.e., addict) identity; they did not convert doing into being.

In contrast, the pill users described by B. Jackson (1970b) were active participants in a drug subculture, complete with a special language, system of stratification, and norms structuring their interactions. Although, like Dr. Falk's patients, "several of the group members were first turned on by physicians, . . . a larger number were turned on by friends" (B. Jackson 1970b:263). Jackson first became aware of what he called "the white-collar drug scene" during a trip to Chicago in 1966. He attended a party at which the main activity was taking pre-scription drugs. Jackson (1970b) observes, "Sometimes the pill-takers meet other pill-takers, and an odd thing happens: instead of taking the drug to cope with the world, they begin to use their time to take drugs. Taking drugs becomes some-thing to do. When this stage is reached, the drug-taking pattern broadens: the user takes a wider variety of drugs with increasing frequency" (pp. 256–257). The upper-middle-class professional or semiprofessional pill users—lawyers, jour-nalists, artists, writers, political aides, housewives, TV executives—described by Jackson pass around pills of various types in a candy dish, much like peanuts or candies would be shared at other parties.

This group has its own terminology. They consult "the Book"—*The Physicians' Desk Reference* or *PDR*—to identify pills and look up their effects and contraindications. Jackson (1970b) calls the *PDR* "the pill-head's *Yellow Pages*: you look up the effect you want ('Sympathomimetics' or 'Cerebral Stimulants') and it tells you the magic columns" (p. 257). These users obtain their pills from "the Source," usually a professional who has access to large quantities. The group's norms are enforced through teasing and storytelling. Jackson, for exam-ple, was chided when it was thought that he was falling asleep during the party, a violation of that subculture's expectation. He was told a story about a young woman who, having used both scotch and marijuana, had fallen asleep during a party, arousing the disgust of the other guests. Using alcohol (but not mari-juana) was viewed negatively, serving to mark the user as really not a member of the in-group. Jackson (1970b) observes: "For the dedicated pillhead there is a slightly narrower definition: the square is someone who has an alcohol dependency: those who use nothing at all aren't even classified. The boozers do bad things, they get drunk and lose control and hurt themselves and other people. They contaminate their tubes, and whenever they get really far out, they don't even remember it the next day" (p. 263).

One's social ranking is an important part of one's self-identity, a point made by both Hoffer (2006) and Bourgois (1989, 1998a, 1998b) in their ethnographies of street dealers and addicts. Like most human enterprises, the world of drugs is stratified, both among dealers and within the ranks of users. Some stratification, as illustrated by Jackson's pill takers' rejection of alcohol, is based on the drug of choice. Bourgois (1998a) notes this ranking within street culture: "I jumped at Mikey's offer to accompany him to a nearby shooting gallery because most of my friends were crack dealers who snubbed anyone who used 'dope' [heroin]" (p. 37).

In this shooting gallery, a room in an abandoned building in New York City's East Harlem where heroin addicts injected their drugs, "Doc," the manager, had the highest status. He controlled the interaction in the room, he provided needles and water, and his authority was deferred to by the addicts. Although he was white and living in a black area, Bourgois's guide, Mikey, was completely integrated into the drug world and accepted by other addicts. As Bourgois (1998a) writes, "Mikey was not needing or paying attention, to any awkward introductions. He no longer needed to prove or justify his identity to anyone as he was instantly recognizable to everyone beyond any shade of doubt, to be what is proudly referred to as a 'dope fiend' among heroin addicts on the street" (p. 45).[6]

In another ethnographic study of homeless heroin addicts in San Francisco shooting encampments, Bourgois (1998b) discussed how the access to heroin defines the social standing of participants in the subculture. The lowest-ranking denizens of the encampments are those addicts who, like "Pete" and "Hogan," are unable to afford their own supply of heroin and therefore depend on the largess of others to give them their used cotton, through which a dissolved heroin solution is filtered, leaving a small amount of residue. Pete and others like him attempt to ingratiate themselves with the more successful addicts by providing them with cups of water, bits of cotton, and the like. "Addicts with more successful income-generating strategies claim they never 'pound cottons,' and they often humiliate those who are regularly reduced to 'begging cottons.' In fact, Hogan, who is the lowest prestige member in the network, is frequently referred to disparagingly as no-hustle-Hogan, the cotton bandit" (Bourgois 1998b:2336–2337). Bourgois (1998b) points out that "the notions of personal respect . . . organize social interaction on the street. Indeed, the search for respect, as well as economic security, is a central organizing dynamic of street culture" (p. 2336).

In his ethnography of junkie/heroin dealers in Denver, Colorado, from 1997 to 2000, Hoffer (2006) also comments that "the issue of respect was important to many of the local junkies; many of them had maintained heroin habits over many years, which was not an easy thing to do" (p. 29). He notes that "heroin dealing is a comprehensive experience that impacts how users think about themselves, how they think about and form relationships with others, and how they survive in the streets while managing their drug addictions" (Hoffer 2006:xix). In the Larimer area of Denver there was a clear hierarchy of drug users. "'Drinkers' or 'winos' constituted a distinct social group and had a separate social identity from other people in the area" (Hoffer 2006:22). Heroin addicts did not associate with them, partly because they drew the attention of the police and partly for their propensity for violence. Another drug-using group was the "huffers," primarily immigrants who used inhalants such as paint because it was inexpensive. "Everyone in the area considered the huffers to be the lowest and most degenerate type of drug user. The locals called them 'golden boys' because the favorite paint to huff was gold metallic spray paint, which inevitably ended up on users' clothing and faces. . . . Golden boys were a popular target of violence" (Hoffer 2006:22).

Much of the drug sales in Larimer were made by transient immigrant dealers. They were not considered by local junkies as part of their community. These dealers "had no particular allegiance to their customers. . . . The immigrant dealers were outsiders to the social conventions and intimate understandings of heroin users. The immigrant dealers were not heroin users, nor were they a part of the users' social groups. As nonmembers, they lacked the intimate knowledge of the normative behaviors and expectations associated with heroin dealing" (Hoffer 2006:29). Thus, the junkie community in Larimer distinguished between their members and outsiders, strengthening a sense of belonging and solidifying identity among addicts, through shared meanings, expectations, and special relationships, which were violated by the immigrant dealers.

Like the drug users studied by Bourgois and Hoffer, the addicts discussed by Finestone (1957) a few generations earlier had a sense of belonging based on their identity as drug users. They saw their drug use as indicative of their membership in an elite society of "cats," knowledgeable in the subtleties of music and fashion. This sort of group identification appears to be lacking in Dr. Falk's patients, who appear to be rather conventional other than in their drug abuse. In fact, for street addicts, drug use is an all-encompassing way of life. Charles Pearson writes,

> Upon completing the first draft of this article, Philippe and I went to visit our homeless heroin addict friends—who no longer had their camp—and we were told through Jim's tears that Scotty had died in his sleep two days earlier on February 15, 1995. This was exactly one week after he had the seizure reported in these pages. Ignoring the busy pedestrians walking past us, Philippe and I reminded each other through our own tears how Scotty enjoyed quoting the righteous dope fiend refrain, "Hope to Die a Dope Fiend." He did. (C. Pearson and Bourgois 1995:593)

NOTES

1. Discussing his 1998 ethnography of heroin addicts in San Francisco, Philippe Bourgois (1998b) writes, "We are documenting through direct observation the complex dynamics of intensive heroin addiction among one of the most socially marginal cohorts with elevated HIV risks in the industrialized world. We are exposed to the subtle interpersonal power hierarchies, hidden income-generating strategies, and repeated mutual personal betrayals and everyday violences that organize the precarious lives of street-based substance misusers in the inner-city United States" (p. 2329).

2. This is highly unusual. Most prostitutes stay at the level at which they first enter sex work. Juliette's intelligence, luck, and persistence helping her to rise in that profession are not the normal case for street prostitutes.

3. Some of Juliette's story can be found in Juliette, "Autobiography of a Dominatrix," in *S & M: Studies in Dominance and Submission*, ed. Thomas S. Weinberg (Amherst, NY: Prometheus Books, 1995), 61–70.

4. Toward the end of the semester, Bill told the author that he was leaving our college and enrolling in another university in the far west.

He planned to get off methadone before he left. His counselors, as well as the author, warned him that it was too soon and reminded him of the consequences for doing so. He also told the author that he was bringing his "works" with him. A few months later he was back. He said that his mother had accompanied him to see his father in a western state, en route to his final destination. During that visit he had become restless and went looking for drugs. He found another junkie in a park and was able to make a drug connection. After arriving at the new university, he discovered that his roommate was also a heroin addict. Bill finally decided that he had to try to end his addiction, so he left the new school and had stopped in Buffalo to see the author on his way back to his home in downstate New York. That was the last he was heard from.

5. The other patients who became addicted to pain pills in the same way as Timothy Smith are found in Appendix B. They are Kenneth Ronfort, Bernard Jones, Lenore Kramer, Trafalger Whittington, and Marlene and Shepard Lyons.

6. The highest accolade in the addict subculture is to be recognized as a "righteous dope fiend."

The Business of Drug Use
Crime and Law Enforcement

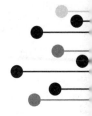

The Mexico–U.S. Drug Connection

There can be little doubt that the importation of illegal drugs into the United States from Mexico has been responsible for a considerable number of murders and other crimes for many years. These drugs include cocaine, heroin, methamphetamines, and marijuana, which are smuggled daily across the southwest border of this country. This drug-smuggling operation is so successful because the border allows a large number of people and goods to legally cross each day. The southern border is barely secured and is 2,000 miles long. This allows drug trafficking organizations considerable opportunities to introduce drugs into the United States by every conceivable method such as small airplanes, speedboats, backpackers, horses and mules, tunnels, trains, and all kinds of vehicles (Perkins and Placido 2010).

For example, the San Diego Tunnel Task Force discovered a tunnel from Tijuana to San Diego at about 35 feet below the surface. It had lights and an electric railway. Several people were arrested in and near the tunnel, and 142 kilos of cocaine and 8 tons of marijuana were seized. These tunnels became more popular as fencing along the U.S.-Mexico border increased (Tuckman 2013).

Drug importation into the United States is mainly controlled by organized crime syndicates such as the recently disbanded La Familia Michoacana, its founders now calling themselves the Knights Templar. Michoacan is a province in Mexico, which was the home base of La Familia. Although this drug cartel is no longer in operation, its successors use the same tactics employed by them, namely murder, assault, and other forms of violence, as well as incentives to cooperate, including bribery of officials and a number of other benefits furnished to the population (Fainaru and Booth 2009).

The cartel bribed Mexican officials and financed their campaigns. This criminal organization claimed to help the poor and defend the people against kidnappers and drug dealers, although they themselves were the most important drug dealers in the state because they succeeded in gaining control of the drug trade in Michoacan from all rival gangs (Kouri 2011).

The Familia Michoacana employed religion as a means of gaining popular support in a community of mostly very poor and superstitious citizens. Relying on murder and the symbolism of religious objects such as Bibles distributed

Photo 12.1: A drug tunnel between Mexico and California. The tunnel included an elevator, wood flooring, and lighting.

by the cartel, the drug dealers became so popular that on the death of their founder, Nazarino Gonzalez, the community marched in his honor and held up signs to the effect that "Nazarino will always live in our hearts" (Associated Press 2010).

Because the Mexican government has evidently lost control of the country, the U.S. State Department has issued a warning in the form of an advisory to all Americans interested in visiting Mexico. That advisory notes that U.S. citizens have been victims of kidnapping, carjacking, highway robbery, and murder. In fact, 81 U.S. citizens were killed in Mexico in 2013 and 100 in 2014 (Llenas 2016). Moreover, gun battles between rival gangs and between the Mexican police and drug dealers in Mexico have trapped U.S. citizens, and gangs have used stolen vehicles to block roads, thereby making the movement of traffic unpredictable. Many of the roadblocks are used to allow drug gangs to kidnap passengers stopped by these gangs; from 2013 to 2015, 241 Americans were kidnapped in Mexico (Llenas 2016). Methods of kidnapping Americans have included bumping moving vehicles or shooting at those attempting to flee. Even buses coming from the United States have been targeted.

U.S. citizens are also victimized by being forced to withdraw money from an ATM or to contact their family, who will then send money to the kidnappers to gain the loved ones' freedom (U.S. Department of State, Bureau of Consular Affairs 2014).

The criminal activities of Mexican drug dealers affect the United States, not only because Americans have traditionally traveled in Mexico, but also because Americans are the principal customers of the Mexican drug merchants. The drugs imported into the United States have devastating consequences for many of their users. This includes prostitutes, who are frequent victims of drug addiction. Because prostitution and drug use are closely associated, the additional crime of drug dealing is a common outcome of prostitution. Moreover, prostitutes also commit other crimes provoked by the need for money used to support the drug habit.

Drugs and Secondary Deviance

It is no secret that those who use expensive drugs, such as heroin and cocaine, are more likely than nonusers to become involved in crimes ranging from confidence games and various property offenses to prostitution. These activities in support of the addict's primary (drug) deviance are called secondary deviance. Prostitution is, of course, a consensual crime in that the "victim" cooperates with the prostitute, whose income is mostly used to buy expensive drugs. One of these expensive drugs is cocaine, which is sold for about $20 a gram when it first comes into the United States. It is then resold to street users at $100 a gram. A gram is a fraction more than 0.035 ounces. The price of a pure gram of cocaine is about $133, or more than 6 times its original price (Cocaine Information and Addiction Resources 2016).

Those who need the drug have to either steal goods of greater value than is needed for the drug habit to be maintained or engage in prostitution or other forms of secondary deviance. No doubt there are some whose wealth or income is great enough to avoid both of these options, although such cocaine users are few.

Drug dealing is the most pervasive crime in the world of addiction. This is true because those who use drugs usually also sell drugs in small or large quantities. This is important to drug users because they must make money every day to feed their habit (Faupel and Klockars 1987). In 2015, 1,488,707 Americans were arrested for involvement with illegal drugs; 83.9% (1,249,025) of these arrests were for possession and 16.1% of arrests were for dealing or manufacturing illegal drugs (Drug War Facts 2017a).

Drug dealing is widespread and far more common than can be recognized by viewing arrest statistics. Inciardi, Potrieger, and Faupel (1982) found that drug dealers completed 1,000 drug deals for every two for which they were arrested. Other studies have come to the same conclusions.

In 2015, an estimated 27.1 million Americans aged 12 or older had used an illegal drug. That means that 10.1% of the U.S. population had done so that year. Marijuana was the most popular illegal drug used in 2015; 22.2 million of the population (8.3%) aged 12 or older were involved. In addition, 1.24 million Americans used hallucinogens in 2015; 3.8 million misused prescription drugs nonmedically, that is, without a prescription; and 1.876 million used cocaine. (Drug War Facts 2017b). Illegal drug use is most common among teenagers and those in their 20s. In 2013, 25.1% of 18- to 25-year-olds reported using an illegal drug that month (SAMHSA 2014).

Women and Drug Dealing

Successful women are also involved in drug dealing. Included are women who operate salons, hotels, and restaurants, which serve as fronts behind which drug-dealing women hide their activities. An example is Sandra Avila Beltran, also known as the "Queen of the Pacific." She is the niece of "godfather of crime" Manuel Gallardo. When he was apprehended in 1989, Beltran seized his assets and became his successor. Her good looks and sex appeal allowed her to become the mistress of Colombia drug boss Diego Espinoza and later Ismael Zampada, boss of Mexican drug dealers. She became the boss of the Mexican-United States drug routes. Her luck ran out in September 2007, when she was arrested for drug possession and extradited to the United States. Released from a U.S. prison, she was deported to Mexico and imprisoned there.

Instead of being viewed as a dangerous criminal, Beltran has numerous followers. Her life was the basis for a novel by Arturo Perez Reverte, leading to a movie starring Eva Mendez and Ben Kingsley.

Another example of a female drug boss is Eledina Arellano Felix. The sister of two notorious drug kingpins, she succeeded them after their arrests and murders. An expert money launderer, she has taken over their organization and is gaining large profits from the drug business every day. Blanca Cazares Salazar, also known as "The Empress," is a major money launderer. She has been designated as key money launderer by the U.S. Office of Foreign Assets Control. Her husband was arrested and her son and brother were murdered. It is remarkable that these women and men are devout Catholics. Evidently, religion and crime can be supported by the same people without difficulty.

There are a number of other well-known female drug dealers in Mexico and the United States. In fact, Miss Hispanic America, Laura Zuniga, was arrested with her boyfriend as they were caught with 9 millimeter pistols, semiautomatic rifles, and over $50,000 in cash. She was briefly imprisoned but released for lack of evidence (Diaz-Duran 2009).

Crack Dealing

Although women are indeed involved in drug dealing, men predominate. Men engaged in that business usually fit into the neighborhood. For example, a man selling drugs at a California beach is most likely a surfer; a man doing the same thing in a downtown office building is most likely a lawyer, accountant, or other professional man. Likewise, dealers are often members of the same ethnic community that includes their friends and relatives (Johnson, Hamid, and Morales 1987). This is particularly true of distributors of crack cocaine. The leaves of the coca plant, the source of cocaine, have long been chewed by the Andean Indians in South America. It was used to decrease hunger and increase work capacity. In the 19th century, cocaine was viewed as a miracle drug. American doctors prescribed it for exhaustion, depression, and other ailments, and it was present in many patent medicines.

After it was discovered that cocaine was addictive, it was no longer prescribed, but crack, a cocaine derivative, became a street drug during the 1970s. At first it was considered harmless. However, crack-infested neighborhoods began to display a great deal of violence as gang warfare led to numerous murders.

The excessive violence attributed to the use of cocaine has been a topic in numerous American newspapers and has become a part of urban legend over the past 20 years. Although such reports may not be viewed as scientific, they are supported by well-grounded studies.

Writing in the *New York Times*, Peter Kerr (1988) reported that "crack has brought a new level of drug violence to New York." This new level of violence has resulted in attacking police officers, killing witnesses to violent incidents, and domestic mayhem. Many of the crack dealers now in the United States are immigrants from South American countries such as Colombia, where violence against police and even innocent bystanders is usual, even as automatic weapons have become common among crack dealers. Crack dealers are usually addicts themselves. According to Kerr, Washington, DC, has become a battleground over the cocaine trade, and Kansas City has become the location of a highly organized drug distribution system. This led to more than 40 drug gang–related homicides in Kansas City.

In Queens, New York, a 25% increase in homicides has been recorded since the advent of crack cocaine. That included the murder of Mildred Green, who had testified before a grand jury about a homicide she had witnessed (Kerr 1988).

This anecdotal evidence concerning the increase in violence through crack cocaine use is more objectively documented by a study conducted by Grogger and Willis (2000). This study confirms the notion that crack cocaine is indeed responsible for increases in violence since its initial development in the 1980s.

Crack cocaine use is largely limited to the inner cities of the United States. There, crack dealers collect large profits from those addicted to the drug. These profits are collected by using violence, including murder, because drug dealers do not have access to the courts to enforce agreements or contracts. If users do not pay as agreed, dealers have to use any means at their disposal to collect their money. That may include violence, although even the threat of violence often has desired consequences (Grogger and Willis 2000).

Profits from selling cocaine are immense. A 15,000% to 20,000% markup from the source to the street customer is usual. The base extract from the coca leaf costs $360 a pound. In the United States, the market price for the same extract

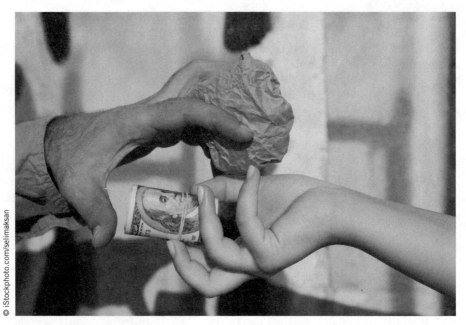

Photo 12.2: A drug transaction.

is about $17,000 a pound, and on the street this rises to $48,000 a pound. As a result, the yearly amount spent by Americans on cocaine is about $4.5 billion. In some localities cocaine sells on the street for $100 a gram or 0.035 ounces. This explains why some will take the risk of imprisonment and even commit murder to sell cocaine (November Coalition 2005).

It has been estimated that murder increases by 4.4% for every 100,000 Americans because of crack cocaine. Increases of 19% have also been recorded for aggravated assault and rape caused by cocaine use. According to Grogger and Willis (2000), "The arrival of cocaine has led crime to rise substantially" with aggravated assault in the lead (p. 528).

Numerous studies over many years have confirmed that a substantial number of people arrested for all kinds of crimes are under the influence of illicit drugs at the time of their arrest. For that reason some states, like California, have avoided incarceration for nonviolent drug offenders and substituted drug treatment facilities instead (Wexler et al. 1999).

Crime costs victims and society a great deal. Some of these costs, such as fear and the memory of the crime and its emotional consequences, cannot be expressed in numbers. However, there are tangible costs such as the victim's medical bills, the cost of crime prevention programs, and the money needed to compensate the crime victim. Four kinds of crime costs have been identified: victim costs; costs of law enforcement; productivity losses by victims; and costs of reaction to crime by the community such as installing special locks or security alarms, procuring weapons, and paying for protection.

Drugs and the Mafia

Although drugs were brought to the United States in the 19th century by Chinese immigrants and others, the Sicilian Mafia, which began its American operations at the start of the 20th century, avoided drug dealing for 30 years. The majority of the crime bosses at that time would not participate in drug dealing, not only because they did not want to alert law enforcement but also because they did not want their own followers to become addicted.

In the early 1930s Charles "Lucky" Luciano became the "Capo di tutti Capi" or boss of bosses of the New York Mafia. He decided that the five crime families he had organized should participate in drug dealing and thereby gain access to a vast amount of money. Indeed, there were some small drug operations active before Luciano made that decision. But it was the "Cosa Nostra," as the American Mafiosi called themselves, who thereafter flooded the country with heroin and other drugs. In 1936, Luciano was convicted of numerous crimes and sentenced to 50 years in prison. However, he was released in 1946 and deported to Italy. Prohibited from entering the United States, he traveled to Cuba to meet his American friends and plan further drug imports to the United States (R. Kelly 1999).

From the mid-1930s on, the American and Sicilian Mafia were making millions from the drug trade. One of the consequences of this commerce was that greedy drug dealers killed one another in order to eliminate the competition. The murders and the huge amount of drugs entering the country finally led to a nationwide raid by law enforcement, when 400 agents arrested 22 major suspects and seized several hundred thousand dollars in cash, as well as shotguns, handguns, rifles, and a huge amount of ammunition. The trial of the suspects was labeled the "Pizza Connection," because a number of pizza parlors were used to distribute the drugs (Amoruso 2010).

The Italian-Sicilian drug dealers and organized criminals have suffered severe setbacks, not only because American law enforcement became more efficient in the mid-20th century but also because Asian and South American drug dealers were competing for the huge market for drugs, which the American public provides. In addition, black drug dealers were avoiding the Sicilians and began to deal on their own. Today, the Mafia or Cosa Nostra deals drugs on the street level. Its former power is gone, as others have seized the lucrative drug trade.

The only Mafia boss to go to Southeast Asia was Frank Lucas, who visited that major source of opium. His exploits were the subject of the 2007 movie *American Gangster*, which depicted Lucas's short reign.

The area of about 370,000 square miles that Lucas visited overlaps Myanmar, Laos, and Thailand and is known as the Golden Triangle. Together with Afghanistan it is the most prolific drug producer worldwide. From the mountains of the Golden

Triangle the opium and heroin base is sent by horse and donkey to refineries in Myanmar and then shipped to Bangkok for distribution on the international market (Bernstein and Kean 1966).

That source is by no means the only supplier of drugs for American consumption, which constitutes one half of the world's recreational consumption of cocaine. About one half of the $80 billion spent on illegal drugs by Americans is spent on coke. This means that in the 21st century the expenditure on coke is 100 times that spent in 1900 (United Nations International Drug Control Program 2008).

After the Spanish-American War in 1898, Cuba became the source of much drug dealing throughout the Americas. By 1950, Cuba was the headquarters for drugs, gambling, prostitution, and bootlegging. American criminals congregated in Havana, which remained "wide open" until the Cuban revolution of 1959, when Fidel Castro and his associates overthrew the dictator Batista and established a communist dictatorship instead. The Castro brothers expelled the dealers and gangsters from Cuba. The United States would not recognize the communist regime in Cuba for 56 years until 2015. That alone made drug trafficking from Cuba to the United States difficult if not impossible, because traffic between the two countries was hardly possible.

The end of the Cuban drug business led to the introduction of the drug trade into Bolivia and Peru, which then hosted the most significant drug trade in the Americas. From these countries the drugs were sent to Chile and then smuggled into the United States by way of Mexico. This led President Nixon to declare a "war on drugs," which was mainly aimed at marijuana. The United States launched "Operation Intercept," which concentrated on the Mexican border and led to the introduction of drug production into Colombia, which is located on the Caribbean Sea and is therefore in a favorable position to send illegal drugs to Florida by means of speedboats and airplanes. These modes of transportation are only one minor aspect of the global network of communication that allows drugs, guns, and humans to be moved across the world for the profit of ruthless entrepreneurs whose greed knows no limits (Hollis 2007).

Drug Cartels and the Market for Drugs

The market for drugs is large and profitable, estimated as yielding over $500 billion a year. It is an international business that has continued to grow since the 1970s. Because the demand for drugs is so great, the industry has several branches, all of which profit from it. Farmers, refiners, traffickers, and dealers all make a profit, although wholesale traffickers earn the most. Because the money is so immense, competition among dealers has led to numerous murders. For example, in 2016 there were nearly 23,000 intentional homicides in Mexico related to the thousands of kilograms of drugs that cross the Mexican-American border every day (Woody and Reuters 2017). These drugs are delivered to dealers and from there end up among consumers (Stares 1996).

Recreational drugs became acceptable in the United States during the 1960s, when the counterculture of so-called hippies and others sought to rebel against American middle-class strictures. One of the means of achieving a sense of rebellion against "the establishment" was to publicly use drugs. The most widely known event promoting the drug culture in that decade was the Woodstock Festival, which took place on a farm several miles from Woodstock, New York. Advertised as "Three Days of Music and Peace," the festival became overrun by 500,000 adolescent women and men who engaged in the use of drugs in public, thereby defying authorities and the prohibition culture (Evans and Kingsbury 2010).

The prohibition of heroin, cocaine, and other drugs leads to the establishment of a black market. That black market is dangerous for producers and distributors, because of the possibility of arrest and imprisonment and because competitors are often violent. Therefore, producers and dealers need to pay for protection, which in turn increases the price of drugs to consumers. The need of consumers allows producers and dealers to increase the price, particularly because dealers usually have a monopoly over illegal drugs, which they enforce with violence, including homicide. About 5,700 Americans were killed in the American drug wars from 2007 to 2010 (Miron 2001). That is more than twice that of those killed in Afghanistan (2,349) during the same period (Haltiwanger 2014).

The illegal drug trade is the second largest profit-making industry in the world after the weapons trade. This is illustrated by the observation that the United States consumes 25 times more illegal drugs than Colombia, although Colombia produces 50% of the world's cocaine. Ninety percent of South American drug production passes into the United States through Mexico. This does not mean that Mexico produces all those drugs, because 104 countries are involved in the drug trade, although usually with far less results than are achieved by Colombia, Peru, and other Latin countries (United Nations International Drug Control Program 2008).

Trafficking is the most important and frequent crime associated with the drug culture. This crime is very difficult to prevent, because each year over 60 million people enter the United States by air, 370 million enter by land in 116 million vehicles, and 6 million enter by sea on 90,000 ships carrying 400 million tons of cargo. This enormous traffic allows drug dealers to move their product into the United States with near impunity (U.S. Drug Enforcement Agency 2004).

In addition to these means of smuggling drugs into the United States are drug tunnels, which have been very effective. Since 1990, over 100 drug tunnels have been discovered at the Mexican-U.S. border, either in Arizona or California. The tunnels have ventilation, cement floors, and pulleys. They begin at a depth of 85 feet and end at 45 feet below the surface. The amount of work and expense to build these tunnels is a reminder of the huge profits that illegal drugs furnish smugglers (Executive Office of the President, Office of National Drug Control Policy n.d.).

Three categories of countries are involved in the illegitimate drug business: the production country, the transshipment country, and the consumer country. The traffickers' job is to get the product from the producer to the consumer without being discovered. Because of the danger associated with trafficking, those who engage in it derive the greatest income from that activity, in that the value added to a drug has increased substantially on delivery. Violence constantly accompanies illegal drug transactions. That violence is caused by the disputes between sellers and buyers, but it is also promoted by the inability of drug dealers to use the courts as enforcers of illegal contracts. Therefore, one of the most effective arguments in favor of legalizing drugs is the reduction of violence. In the 1970s, a number of drug wholesalers combined to gain more profits. These large organizations fought each other as each cartel sought to eliminate threats to its businesses, which are run like all successful American corporations, although they are headed by violent criminals like Pablo Escobar. Escobar kidnapped prominent people and assassinated candidates for political office if he thought the candidate was capable of destroying his business. Bombing public places is also a common means of weakening all governments, making them look incapable of protecting its citizens (Saunders 2009).

In 1966, a guerilla organization calling itself FARC, or Revolutionary Armed Forces of Colombia, was founded as a private army determined to protect drug growers and dealers and make money by "taxing" drug farmers. After the cartels were dismantled, FARC continued where the cartels once existed and has succeeded by using murder and kidnapping for ransom and other forms of criminal activities (Saunders 2009).

FARC is willing to do anything to make money, as are the Mexican drug lords, who have formed their own cartels. This can be recognized by the fact that, as noted, there were nearly 23,000 drug-related murders in Mexico in 2016 (Woody and Reuters 2017). These killings are attributed to drug gangs fighting over the profits. The leaders of these gangs are cruel and ruthless. An example is Miguel Angel Trevino Morales, leader of the Zeta cartel. Morales was an exceptionally brutal leader. He tortured his victims by placing them in a 55-gallon drum and then burning them alive. He used kidnapping to extort money from relatives and was not afraid to attack the police. He was also responsible for beheadings, hanging corpses from bridges, and leaving hundreds of bodies on the roadside. Poor peasants were kidnapped off buses and killed unless they agreed to be a "drug mule" (Weissenstein and Caldwell 2013).

Morales was arrested in July 2013 at the Mexican-U.S. border. In his pickup truck, the police found eight assault weapons, 500 rounds of ammunition, and $2 million in cash. It has been estimated that more than 60,000 Mexican citizens have been killed in 10 years of fighting in the drug wars. Since then, at least eight major organizers of the drug cartels have been killed or imprisoned, only to be replaced by someone else willing to risk all for the sake of profit. The Zeta organization has about 10,000 soldiers in its ranks (Grillo 2011).

The Zeta organization began when some highly trained military men joined one of the Mexican drug cartels and thereafter started their own cartel devoted to extreme brutality so hideous that it can hardly be described. This has terrified its competitors so much that Zeta has gained the majority of the drug trade.

Mexico is not the only country torn by violence related to the drug trade. Across the world, drug-related violence is caused by prohibition. The United Nations has conceded that violence and corruption are fostered by the war on drugs, which makes violence the most important argument against drug control (MacCormack 2009).

It has been 46 years since President Nixon declared a war on drugs in 1971. Yet drug dealing and all the evils associated with it are more widespread than ever in 2017. This increase in drug trafficking began in the 1970s, when a new form of organized crime was created by the global world economy, resulting in open borders, as crime groups changed from domestic organized crime like the Cosa Nostra to criminal organizations that are international and not nearly as hierarchical as the Mafia. These transnational organized crime cartels are usually violent, allowing them to intimidate citizens and law enforcement personnel. Because these traffickers are international, they can exploit differences between countries, which allows them to escape apprehension and conviction. They attain influence in government and politics by bribing and corrupting officials. In their insatiable greed they not only seek to make vast amounts of money from illegal drug deals, but they also enter into legal business and are thereby supported by vast numbers of unsuspecting customers. To ensure that the crime bosses are never held accountable, these cartels develop a structure that insulates each layer of authority from those below them (Picarelli 2011).

The United Nations Office on Drugs and Crime (2005) has estimated that the total international drug trade amounts to $321 billion. This includes cannabis, cocaine, opiates, and amphetamines. Counterfeiting is another source of income for international crime cartels. It is estimated that this yields $250 billion in counterfeit electronics, pharmaceuticals, and cigarettes. Additional money is made by criminal cartels by engaging in human trafficking and selling oil, wildlife, timber, fish, art, gold, human organs, diamonds, and small arms for a total estimated illegal income of $645,717,000,000.

Law Enforcement

The failure of the war on drugs is best understood by looking at arrests made for dealing and possessing illegal drugs. For example, on February 3, 2015, eight people were charged in Arkansas for large-scale drug trafficking of methamphetamine and crack cocaine. These arrests were labeled "Operation Three Amigos." The investigation led to the seizure of two firearms and several rounds of ammunition, four vehicles, and $10,000 in cash. The investigation consisted of agents buying controlled substances, as well as surveillance and monitoring. Some of those arrested had been arrested previously for the same offenses ("Authorities Arrest 8" 2015).

This example is only one instance of concern to drug law enforcement. The best source of understanding the extent of drug crimes in this country is to look at the Bureau of Justice statistics issued by the Department of Justice. This reveals that in 2012, annual drug arrests in the United States were 1,552,432. In 2013, drug arrests came to 1,501,043. Forty years earlier, in 1973, the total number of drug arrests was 328,670. In 1973, the population of the United States was 212 million or 29% less than the 317 million in 2013. Yet drug arrests have increased fivefold since then. Likewise, drug arrests in 1990 were 741,600, a number exceeded by 46% in 2006. The median age of those arrested was 26; 11% of those arrested were juveniles, and 18% were 50 years old or older. The cost of arresting drug users is very high. In New York City alone, 1,096,000 hours of police time is spent on drug possession cases (U.S. Department of Justice 2013).

Police reports and other reports by criminal justice agencies describe the vast amount of time spent by police in dealing with drug arrests. It has been estimated that it takes approximately a million hours of police time to make about 440,000 arrests for drug possession. It has further been noted that 46.8% of violent crimes and 19% of property crimes are drug related. Compared to arrests for all crimes, 46.8% of all violent crimes are cleared by arrest, matching exactly the arrest rates for drug-related crimes. This leads one to believe that violence not associated with drugs is hardly prosecuted, for the alternative explanation, that drug use is associated with all violence, is spurious (Freedman et al. 2011).

A significant number of U.S. citizens with criminal records are associated with drug possession. This high number of criminal activity is undoubtedly related to the war on drugs. It appears that 27.8% of the adult American population has a criminal record because of the war on drugs (Rodriguez and Ensellem 2011). A most disturbing finding concerning drug possession and the enforcement of drug laws is that enforcement increases the homicide rate (Jenson 2000).

Gender, age, and ethnicity make a difference with respect to arrests for possession of illegal drugs. Women account for only 14% of all drug arrests, according to the Drug Enforcement Administration (DEA). Of the 86% of arrests involving men, three out of ten were arrested for possession of cocaine powder and 25% for possession of marijuana. Half of all suspects arrested were 31 years old or younger, Hispanic suspects constituted 46% of all arrests, and black suspects constituted 26%. Hispanic suspects make up more than half of arrests for cocaine possession. Three quarters of crack cocaine arrestees are white (Motivans 2011).

Drug enforcement has been a failure since its inception. However, the number of jobs created by drug enforcement is great, illustrating what structural functionalists would consider to be one of the functions of deviance: creating employment opportunities for those working in the drug enforcement industry. For example, the DEA employs 40,000 individuals, and the Federal Bureau of Prisons employs 17,000 persons. The FBI employs 12,760 people, and the Bureau of Alcohol, Tobacco and Firearms employs 2,540 officers. One may speculate that those employed in drug enforcement have a vested interest in the continued criminalization of the drug industry (Reaves 2012).

A good number of drug addicts obtain large amounts of legal drugs by "doctor shopping," using insurance fraud to pay for their needs. This costs insurance

Photo 12.3: A police TAC team arresting a crack dealer.

companies $72.5 billion annually, and it also affects customers of these companies, who pay higher premiums to cover the insurance companies' expenses (National Drug Intelligence Center 2013).

Medical Professionals and Drugs

Drugs are more available to physicians and other health-related occupations than to the vast majority of Americans, who do not deal with drugs in connection with their daily work. This often makes medical practitioners vulnerable and leads to arrests and convictions of doctors, dentists, nurses, and other health-related professionals.

Goldenbaum and colleagues (2008) looked at 725 doctors who were charged with drug violations between 1998 and 2006. The offenders were accused of prescribing opioid analgesics. Opioid analgesics act like a narcotic and are very effective in helping patients live with otherwise severe pain. It is, of course, the sworn duty of physicians to not only cure disease whenever possible but also to relieve otherwise unbearable pain. The prohibition concerning opioid analgesics has led to some controversy, because this drug is highly addictive, so that patients who were relieved of pain often became dependent on the drug, with disastrous effects.

The other side of the argument holds that lawyers and government bureaucrats interfere in the practice of medicine and condemn thousands of patients to suffer excruciating pain for the sake of imposing drug laws indiscriminately. It is also true that there are undoubtedly some who lie and claim to be in pain solely to get opiates (Rosenberg 2007).

A good example of the manner in which DEA agents interfere in the practice of medicine and ruin well-established doctors appeared in *Time* magazine (Roosevelt 2005). It should be noted that the destruction of a physician's practice not only hurts the doctor so assaulted but also deprives numerous patients who depended on him or her for their health and well-being.

According to Margot Roosevelt (2005), five DEA agents suddenly invaded the offices of Dr. Richard Nelson, a neurologist in Billings, Montana. They confiscated 72 patients' charts, which the 73-year-old doctor, who had been practicing medicine for 40 years, had accumulated. The DEA acted because some anonymous individuals informed them that Dr. Nelson was issuing "suspicious prescriptions," which included even Tylenol. Many of Dr. Nelson's former patients lost their jobs because they could not tolerate the pain they suffered without their prescription. This included people who suffered brain and back injuries from car crashes and other accidents.

The DEA has investigated thousands of doctors on charges of illegally prescribing medications and, in some cases, drug trafficking. As a result, 50 million Americans who suffer severe pain from arthritis, back injuries, and cancer must live without these medications because doctors are afraid of prescribing them. Some doctors are closing their practices for fear that the DEA will prosecute them indiscriminately.

Will Row, executive director of the Pain Foundation, located in Baltimore, Maryland, told Roosevelt that "hundreds of sufferers have contacted them because they cannot get any doctor to prescribe for them." Even patients with prescriptions are refused by pharmacies that also fear the DEA.

Virginia physician Dr. William Hurwitz was sentenced to 25 years in prison for prescribing pain-relieving drugs to numerous patients. Hurwitz made no money by prescribing these medicines, nor had he committed any crime (Tierney 2007). It should be noted that the average sentence for murder in this country is 11 years, less 3 years for "good behavior."

The history of physicians being arrested and prosecuted for prescribing narcotics goes back over 100 years, after the passage of the Harrison Narcotics Tax Act of 1914, when a few thousand doctors were arrested, tried, convicted, and incarcerated for maintaining medically addicted patients on opiates. The law allowed physicians to prescribe narcotics during their "normal medical practice," but this permission pertained only to new cases of patients suffering from the pain of surgery, disease, or accidents. It did not give doctors carte blanche to maintain already addicted patients on these drugs. The more recent prosecution of doctors who prescribe pain killers began in the 1990s, when some celebrities, including Rush Limbaugh and Courtney Love, attained a great deal of publicity for using OxyContin, an opium-related drug. This caused a hysterical reaction among DEA agents, who "rushed in where angels fear to tread" and began to threaten all doctors. In fact, the Cato Institute's report "Treating Doctors as Drug Dealers: The DEA's War on Prescription Painkillers" by Ronald T. Libby denounced the methods of the DEA. The Cato Institute is a libertarian think tank whose publications are viewed as reliable and based on sound research principles (Roosevelt 2005).

The DEA also prosecutes doctors whose patients sell OxyContin to someone else. This makes the patient a drug dealer. Yet the DEA considers the doctor, who knows nothing about the patient's conduct, to also be a drug dealer.

It is evident that the war on drugs has failed. This failure is caused by the public's immense desire for drugs and the huge profits that accrue to illicit drug traffickers. Like the prohibition of alcohol in the 1920s and early 1930s, the prohibition concerning drugs of all kinds cannot succeed.

Prevention and Treatment of Alcohol and Substance Use Disorders

Americans are ambivalent in their feelings about alcohol and drugs. On the one hand, as noted in Chapters 1, 2, 8, and 12, we see drug traffickers, dealers, and users as criminals, deserving of punishment. On the other hand, we see addicts (even some addicts who deal drugs to support their habit) as people deserving of compassion. Even President Nixon (1971b), who spearheaded the war on drugs, called for funds to rehabilitate drug users and set up a new organization within the White House to coordinate efforts of the various rehabilitation agencies. The increasing number of states that have legalized marijuana for medical purposes, and Alaska, California, Colorado, Maine, Massachusetts, Nevada, Oregon, Washington State, and Washington, DC, which have legalized it for recreational purposes, illustrate these inconsistent perspectives on drug use. These conflicting points of view may be understood by couching a question in the language of responsibility: Do we see drug users and addicts as irresponsible, meaning they have the ability to control their substance use but choose not to, or as not responsible, in the sense that they do not have the capacity to make informed decisions? The former is the way we look at criminals; the latter is how we view juveniles, the intellectually disadvantaged, the mentally ill, the criminally insane, and even "the sick."[1] In practical terms, however, there may not be much difference between whether we view drug users as criminal or mentally ill and whether we consequently punish or treat them, for some treatment venues involve involuntary commitment and sometimes rather harsh therapy (see Rettig, Torres, and Garrett 1977 and Yablonsky 1965 on "haircuts" in the Synanon program).

Although federal and state agencies that target the distribution of drugs and the drug cartels that supply them see users and traffickers as criminals, this is not always the case with local police, especially those on narcotics squads, who have day-to-day contact with addicts. They often become what Goffman (1963) calls "the wise." The wise, unlike "the own"—other addicts, fellow alcoholics—do not share the individual's stigma, but nonetheless they understand that person's world and are not necessarily judgmental about it. In the early 1970s, when one of the authors was first teaching a course on the sociology of addiction, one of his students was the captain of the Buffalo, New York, narcotics squad.[2] Toward the end of the course, the captain volunteered to bring in some addicts to talk to the class. The author and he took the addicts to dinner, and the captain slipped them a few dollars. For the next several years, until he retired, the captain would bring addicts to talk to the Sociology of Addiction class. He told the students that addicts would often call him just to talk or stop in to visit, a phenomenon also noted by Bruce Jackson (1970a), who writes, "The narcotics detective must live in the junkie's world, know his language, appreciate his pain; he may be—and often is—antagonistic to all of these, but he is rarely independent of them" (p. 273). The addicts knew that the captain understood their world and did not judge them. He saw addiction as an infectious disease. His solution was to isolate addicts on an island, away from the rest of the population, and then rehabilitate them. That solution is not unlike how therapeutic communities work.

In "Exiles From the American Dream: The Junkie and the Cop," Bruce Jackson (1970a) relates his experiences as a researcher during the summer of 1966, working for an organization charged with gathering information for the President's Commission on Law Enforcement and the Administration of Justice. His job required him to speak with law enforcement and criminal justice personnel and addicts and pushers around the country. In this article Jackson details his experiences in interacting with and accompanying police narcotics squad officers in New York City, Houston, and Austin, Texas. His experience in New York City, riding with two detectives, Ray Viera and Burt Alvins, perfectly illustrates the symbiotic relationship between narcotics police and addicts. The detectives take Jackson to meet "Elmer," one of their addict/informers. Looking decades older than his actual age, Elmer has infected sores oozing on his thighs from where he has injected himself. The detectives suggest to Elmer that he let them put him in a hospital, but he says that he is unable to go at that time. Jackson (1970a) reproduces the following dialogue between the detectives (p. 276):

> They talk about Elmer. "I'm worried about him, Burt. Can't we get him into some hospital?"
>
> "He doesn't want to go. We can't force him."
>
> "Well, how about we get him some antibiotics for those sores? They're just awful."
>
> "You have to have a prescription for that stuff."
>
> "Maybe I can get somebody to let me have some."
>
> "Heroin you can get; for penicillin you need a prescription."

Prevention Efforts

If one wishes to reduce the problem of drug and alcohol abuse, the logical place to start is by preventing its initial use, especially by young people. Therefore, an important question relevant to efforts of prevention is whether there is a significant substance abuse problem among youth. There are a few sources of information about alcohol and drug use within this particular population, including arrest statistics, emergency department visits, and self-reports from a federal survey.

Arrest Data

Data provided by the Uniform Crime Reports on arrests by age for substance-related offenses give a picture (albeit not a complete one) of drug and alcohol use by young people. Table 13.1 shows the number of arrests for various age categories as well as total arrests for selected drug- and alcohol-related offenses for 2015. That year arrests of juveniles under the age of 18 represented less than 7% of all arrests for drug abuse violations, less than 1% of all arrests for driving under the influence, 17% of all arrests for the violation of liquor laws, and slightly more than 1% of all arrests for drunkenness. When these figures are further broken down into specific age categories, it appears that the first large increase in arrests for these offenses comes between the age categories of 10 to 12 and 13 to 14. Traditionally, 13 has been seen as the threshold age for delinquency (at least in terms of official arrest rates; see Caldwell and Black 1971; Empey, Stafford, and Hay 1999; Haskell and Yablonsky 1970; Shafer and Knudten 1970), and this seems to hold for drug and alcohol arrests.

As we can see from Table 13.2, data from the Uniform Crime Reports indicate an overall reduction in substance abuse arrests for those under the age of 18. There are a number of concerns when trying to estimate the scope of substance abuse of juveniles by using arrest data. The first of these is that much, probably most, delinquent behavior is never detected and therefore does not find its way into arrest statistics (Gold 1966, 1970). A second issue is that official data are

Table 13.1 Number of Arrests by Age, 2015

Offense Charged	Total All Ages	Under 18	Under 10	10–12	13–14	15	16	17	18
Drug abuse violation	1,144,021	76,172	79	1,596	10,428	11,997	19,935	32,137	53,900
Driving under the influence	833,833	5,064	20	4	96	223	1,150	3,571	10,593
Liquor laws	204,665	33,155	15	274	3,200	5,033	9,220	15,413	30,639
Drunkenness	314,856	4,243	20	42	476	650	996	2,059	5,606

Note: 12,706 agencies reporting; estimated population 246,947,242 (2015 data).

Source: Modified from Federal Bureau of Investigation 2015, Table 38, "Arrests by Age 2015." Retrieved March 12, 2017 (https://ucr.fbi.gov/crime-in-the-u.s/2015/crime-in-the-u.s.-2015/tables/table-38).

Table 13.2	Ten-Year Arrest Trends, Totals 2006–2015 (Number of Persons Arrested Under 18 Years of Age)		
Offense Charged	**2006**	**2015**	**Percentage Change**
Drug abuse violation	113,132	63,035	−44.3%
Driving under the influence	12,947	4,294	−66.8
Liquor laws	94,729	29,530	−68.8
Drunkenness	11,093	3,528	−68.2

Note: 9,581 agencies reporting; 2015 estimated population 199,921,204; 2006 estimated population 186,371,331.

Source: Modified from Federal Bureau of Investigation 2015, Table 32, "Ten Year Arrest Trends." Retrieved March 12, 2017 (https://ucr.fbi.gov/crime-in-the-u.s/2015/crime-in-the-u.s.-2015/tables/table-32).

rarely complete; not all agencies are included, nor is the total nation's population usually covered. Additionally, juveniles may be picked up, brought home, and not arrested, so that they would not appear in official statistics.

Emergency Department Visits

The Substance Abuse and Mental Health Services Administration (SAMHSA) (2013) provides additional information about substance abuse among young people in its report on emergency department (ED) visits. Table 13.3 presents data on ED visits by type of drug and age category.

In all, there were a total of 1,252,500 visits to EDs for illicit drugs in 2011. Of these, 78,667 were made for youths 12 to 17 years old. The largest number of these adolescents (60,302) went to EDs after having used marijuana. Eighteen to 20-year-olds accounted for 105,274 visits, 59,945 of which involved marijuana (SAMHSA 2013).

The overall rate of ED visits for illicit drugs per 100,000 visits in 2011 was 402.0. For youth 12 to 17 in that year it was 313.3, and for those 18 to 20 it was 779.4. The older cohort, aged 18 to 20, exceeds the overall ED visit rate for heroin (134.6 vs. 83.0), marijuana (443.8 vs. 146.2), amphetamines/methamphetamines (89.8 vs. 51.3), MDMA (Ecstasy) (51.7 vs. 7.2), LSD (14.7 vs. 1.5), and PCP (27.6 vs. 24.2), but the rate for the younger cohort, 12–17, only exceeds the overall rate of ED visits for marijuana (240.2 vs. 146.2) and MDMA (Ecstasy) (12.7 vs. 7.2) (Drug Abuse Warning Network [DAWN] 2013a).

The use of alcohol by youth is a related issue. According to DAWN (2013b), "In 2011, of the nearly 440,000 drug-abuse ED visits made by patients 20 or younger, almost half (188,706 visits, or 43.2%) involved alcohol." Patients aged 12 to 17 accounted for 71,991 of these visits. Of that number, 40,239 trips to the ED were for alcohol alone, and 31,752 were for alcohol combined with other

Table 13.3 Emergency Department Visits Involving Illicit Drugs by Drug and Age Category, 2011

	All Illicit Drugs	Cocaine	Heroin	Marijuana	Amphetamines/ Methamphetamines	MDMA (Ecstasy)	LSD	PCP
Total ED visits	1,252,500	505,224	258,482	455,668	159,840	22,498	4,819	75,538
12–17 years	78,667	5,904	2,141	60,302	5,889	3,184	------	1,965
18–20 years	105,274	15,198	18,179	59,945	12,128	6,986	1,982	3,730

Source: Modified from Substance Abuse and Mental Health Services Administration 2013, Table 6.

drugs (DAWN 2013c). As we saw in Chapter 2, multiple drug use is common. From the SAMHSA report, it appears that both alcohol and marijuana are the most commonly abused. Cocaine accounted for 21,102 ED appearances for youth 12 to 20, heroin for 20,320 visits, amphetamines/methamphetamines for 18,017 visits, MDMA (Ecstasy) for 10,170 visits, and PCP for 5,695 visits. Slightly fewer appearances were reported for LSD problems, and only for the older 17- to 20-year-old group.

Self-Reports: The National Survey on Drug Use and Health

A third source of data on alcohol and drug use among youth is provided by SAMHSA's (2015a) annual report *Results from the National Survey on Drug Use and Health: Summary of National Findings*. This survey uses a scientifically drawn national sample of "the civilian, noninstitutionalized population of the United States aged 12 years or older" (SAMHSA 2015a:iv). In face-to-face interviews, 68,073 respondents were asked about their use of illicit drugs, alcohol, and tobacco.

An interesting finding is that self-reported use of illicit drugs in general, and marijuana use specifically, as well as alcohol and tobacco use, has declined over the past few years among adolescents aged 12 to 17. This is consistent with the decline in arrest rates for that population as shown in Table 13.2. Additionally, these rates are generally low; 8.8% of these youth reported current illicit drug use, 7% said they used marijuana, just 2% admitted current nonmedical use of psychotherapeutic drugs, and only 1.1% said they used nonmedical pain relievers. Percentages of youth reporting the use of tranquilizers, stimulants, sedatives, cocaine, crack, heroin, hallucinogens, and methamphetamines were all under 1%. A greater percentage of youth 12 to 17 used inhalants (0.7%) than those in all other age groups.

In 2015, the rate of alcohol use for this cohort was 9.6%, with binge drinking rates at 5.8% and heavy drinking rates at 0.9%. The rate of past-month tobacco use was 4.2%, about one third of the rate for 12- to 17-year-olds in 2002 (13%). About 20% of these youths were daily smokers, and 1.5% used smokeless tobacco. The 2013 NSDUH[3] report found a strong relationship between tobacco use and the use of illicit drugs for this group. "Among youths aged 12 to 17 who smoked cigarettes in the past month, 53.9 percent also used an illicit drug compared with only 6.1 percent of youths who did not smoke cigarettes" (SAMHSA 2014). A similar relationship was found for youth who were heavy users of alcohol, with 62.3% of them being illicit drug users, compared to 4.9% of those taking illicit drugs who were not using alcohol. Additionally, 57.9% of these heavy-drinking adolescents reported also using marijuana, compared to only 3.3% of youth in this age cohort. Moreover, using both alcohol and cigarettes appears to increase the probability of illicit drug use, with about 16 times the rate of illicit drug use for those who use both substances compared to adolescents who use neither and about 25 times the rate for marijuana use for alcohol and tobacco users versus nonusers. Consistent with the arrest data, which show a marked increase in arrests for illicit drug use from the 10 to 12 age category to the 13 to 14 category, self-reports show a rate increase "from 2.6 percent at ages 12 or 13 to 7.8 percent at ages 14 to 15" (SAMHSA 2013:19).

Programs Directed at Youth

Whether the rate of officially reported drug abuse is a cause for concern is problematic. The numbers do not appear to support the idea that there is a drug abuse epidemic among young people. And, as we have seen, arrests for a variety of illicit substance use–related offenses have dropped over the past several years. Nevertheless, a number of programs are designed to dissuade young people from ever using drugs and alcohol, illustrating early American sociologist William I. Thomas's observation that it is people's perception of situations, rather than the empirical truth of these situations, that guides their behavior. The most publicized of these efforts are the Just Say No campaign pioneered by First Lady Nancy Reagan and the current D.A.R.E. (Drug Abuse Resistance Education) program. Both were developed for children and adolescents with the goal of educating them about the danger of drugs and thereby helping them to avoid their use.

The Just Say No Campaign

Moral crusades usually begin with the identification of a problem by upper-status people who wish to help those less fortunate. These crusaders have been called moral entrepreneurs. The Prohibition movement, discussed in previous chapters and spearheaded by the Anti-Saloon League and the Women's Christian Temperance Union, is a prototypical example. The Just Say No campaign is a more recent illustration of how moral crusades begin and develop.

Nancy Reagan's involvement in the antidrug movement has been variously attributed to a 1980 visit she made to Daytop Village, a therapeutic community in New York City (Wikipedia 2015c), and a trip to a New York City advertising agency in 1983, where she was impressed by a demonstration of an antidrug campaign sponsored by the Ad Council (Stricherz 2014). The slogan itself, Just Say No, was coined by Mrs. Reagan in 1982, when, in response to a schoolgirl's question about how to resist peer pressure to use drugs, she replied, "Just say no" (Ronald Reagan Presidential Foundation and Library 2010; Wikipedia 2015c). With the first lady as a spokesperson, the Just Say No campaign rapidly expanded. Mrs. Reagan appeared on several popular television programs and in a rock music video to popularize her antidrug movement. She got the Girl Scouts, the Kiwanis Club, and the National Federation of Parents for a Drug-Free Youth involved in her cause. Additionally, she convened a First Ladies' Conference on Drug Abuse in 1985, inviting first ladies from many countries to the White House. The campaign subsequently spread to the United Kingdom (Wikipedia 2015c).

"By 1988 more than 21,000 'Just Say No' clubs had been formed across the country and around the world" (Ronald Reagan Presidential Foundation and Library 2010:1). Stricherz (2014) notes, "At its height in the mid '90s, the Just Say No Foundation had more than 1 million members and affiliates in 12 countries. . . . There was a theme song and an annual rally in May" (p. 3). Although drug use among youth dropped during the late 1980s and mid-1990s, there is no way to determine whether the Just Say No campaign was responsible (Ronald Reagan Presidential Foundation and Library 2010; Stricherz 2014; Wikipedia 2015c).

Despite its popularity, the Just Say No movement was not without its detractors. It was said to be too simplistic and too costly, and it ignored related social issues such as poverty and unemployment (Wikipedia 2015c). Currently, the Just Say No movement is essentially defunct (Stricherz 2014).

Drug Abuse Resistance Education (D.A.R.E.)

The D.A.R.E. program is the largest and most popular attempt to dissuade young people from using alcohol, tobacco, and illicit drugs. Founded by former Los Angeles chief of police Daryl Gates and the Los Angeles Unified School District in 1983 as an attempt to prevent crime and substance abuse (Wikipedia 2015d), the program has expanded to 48 countries and taught more than 200 million students, including more than half of them in the United States (ProCon.org 2017). Taught by police officers, who must undergo 80 hours of rigorous training in "classroom management, teaching strategies, communication skills, adolescent development, drug information and curriculum instruction" (Ennett et al. 1994:1395), or in some cases by trained classroom teachers, the D.A.R.E. curriculum was originally developed for later primary school students, specifically fifth and sixth graders, and then later expanded to middle school children and high school students (National Institute of Justice n.d.). The original curriculum consisted of 17 weekly lessons of 45 to 60 minutes each during the regular school day

Photo 13.1: A D.A.R.E. class for fifth graders.

(Ennett et al. 1994; Wysong, Aniskiewicz, and Wright 1994). The presentations included group discussions, question and answer sessions, role-playing, lectures, audio-visual materials, and workbooks (Ennett et al. 1994). They focused on resisting peer pressure, developing social skills, enhancing self-esteem, and drug education. Emphasis was placed on the so-called gateway drugs—alcohol, tobacco, and marijuana (D.A.R.E. officer, detective Robert Goetz, Town of Tonawanda, NYPD, ret., personal communication, May 2015).

The D.A.R.E. program had great popular support from parents, school authorities, and government officials, but it was not without its critics. Studies done in the 1990s concluded that it did not reduce drug use among adolescents. For example, sociologists Earl Wysong, Richard Aniskiewicz, and David Wright (1994) studied D.A.R.E. both quantitatively and qualitatively. They compared a sample of 288 Kokomo, Indiana, high school seniors who had been D.A.R.E. students in the seventh grade with 335 seniors who had not had that experience. They administered a multipart questionnaire that included four scales, a drug use scale, the D.A.R.E. scale, a self-esteem scale, and a locus of control scale, to non-D.A.R.E.-exposed seniors in 1991 and in 1992 to seniors who had been exposed to D.A.R.E. as seventh graders. Additionally, the researchers used what they called "micro-level process evaluation," using a focus group of D.A.R.E. graduates. "The focus group interview," they wrote, "reinforced the quantitative findings and provided insights into students' views on a number of issues related to DARE and drug education. It also revealed a general shared resentment toward adult authorities related to the students' perception that their views about DARE had been ignored" (Wysong et al. 1994:458). Moreover, "DARE was judged by all group members as having no lasting influence on students' drug-related attitudes or behaviors" (p. 459). They concluded that "after tracking DARE for five years, our quantitative and qualitative data both point in the direction of no long-term effects for the program in preventing or reducing adolescent drug use" (p. 467).

In a meta-analysis of the evaluation findings of eight studies that examined the short-term effectiveness of D.A.R.E.'s core curriculum, Ennett et al. (1994) concluded that "the results of this meta-analysis suggest that DARE's core curriculum effect on drug use relative to whatever drug education (if any) was offered in the control schools is slight and, except for tobacco use, is not statistically significant" (p. 1398). They explain D.A.R.E.'s "limited effectiveness" in terms of the instruction staff and curriculum. Noting that in most cases the instructor is a police officer, the authors suggest that law enforcement officers "may not be as well equipped to lead the curriculum as teachers" (p. 1398). Moreover, "the generally more traditional teaching style used by DARE has not been shown to be as effective as an interactive teaching mode. Although some activities encourage pupil interaction, the curriculum relies heavily on the officer as expert and makes frequent use of lectures and question-and-answer sessions between the officer and pupils" (p. 1398).

A number of other studies examined the effectiveness of D.A.R.E. Clayton, Cattarello, and Johnstone (1996), for example, compared elementary school students in Lexington, Kentucky, whose schools used the D.A.R.E. program with students whose schools used another drug education program over a 5-year period, beginning with the first posttest after the programs were completed. They found no significant differences between the two groups in the use of cigarettes, alcohol, or marijuana. Interestingly, in a longitudinal study, Rosenbaum and Hanson (1998) found that D.A.R.E. graduates were more likely than non-D.A.R.E. adolescents to smoke, drink, and use illicit drugs. Given these scientific studies and other criticisms of D.A.R.E., the program adopted a new curriculum in 2009 (Nordrum 2014; Wikipedia 2015d). Developed by Michael L. Hecht and Michelle Miller-Day (2007) at Penn State University (and at Arizona State University), the most recent iteration is called "keepin' it REAL."

Hecht and Miller-Day employed what they termed "translational scholarship" as part of their Drug Resistant Strategies Project. Translational scholarship is "a new approach that addresses everyday problems by utilizing what we learn from knowledge discovery and putting it to the test of application" (Hecht and Miller-Day 2007:343). Simply put, Hecht and Miller-Day trained college students to collect personal stories (which they call "narratives") from adolescents in middle school in Phoenix, Arizona. The interviewers asked these youths about their "substance use and offer-resistance episodes" (p. 345). The researchers felt that "these narratives would reveal the underlying processes through which alcohol and other drug use decisions were made" (p. 345). What strategies, Hecht and Miller-Day wanted to know, do young people use to refuse offers of drug use?

"This gave us a unique way of identifying prevention messages *generated from the experience of teens*," they wrote, "rather than imposing an adult perspective, as was pervasive in many failed interventions such as Drug Abuse Resistance Education" (p. 345; italics added). From an analysis of the collected narratives, Hecht and Miller-Day identified four strategies used by adolescents to reject offers of drugs from their peers: refuse, explain, avoid, and leave (REAL). They then translated their findings into a prevention curriculum, with the help of high school students, developing dramatic role-plays based on these strategies. They used live and video performances of the narratives they had gathered, "modeling competent refusal skills through the representation of adolescent narratives" (p. 347). Later, with the assistance of high school students, who served as script writers and editors, the researchers began developing digital films.

The keepin' it REAL curriculum, in contrast with the original D.A.R.E. program, puts little emphasis on drugs. For example, the lively illustrated workbook for fifth graders directly addresses drugs only in the second lesson of the 10-lesson program, and the discussion is limited to alcohol and tobacco. Instead, the program's focus is on a decision-making model: Define ("Describe the problem, challenge or opportunity"), Assess ("What are your choices?"), Respond ("Make a choice, use the facts and information you have gathered"), and Evaluate ("Review your decision. Did you make a good choice?") (DARE). Other lessons deal with topics such as making choices, resistance strategies, responding to pressure, stress, communication styles, and developing confidence. The workbook includes a journal section for each lesson in which students write "What I have learned today" and various scenarios for discussion, some of which involve drugs, in which students are asked to apply the decision-making model. There is also a lesson on bullying and one on needing help. Students have opportunities to write essays about their own experience in D.A.R.E. and there is also a crossword and word search section.[4]

As a result of research comparing students who went through the keepin' it REAL curriculum with a control group, Hecht and Miller-Day concluded that "as anticipated . . . *keepin' it REAL* influenced the way adolescents think about drugs (their expectations and norms) while teaching them skills that led to less drug use than was reported by the control group" (p. 347). From a sociological perspective, the Hecht and Miller-Day approach makes sense. To understand what people do, it is necessary to understand how they see the world. Taking a phenomenological view enabled Hecht and Miller-Day to develop an effective program based on adolescents' perceptions, rather than on a predetermined view of their situation held by adults.

Diversion: Drug Court

The first drug court, designed to rehabilitate nonviolent offenders, was established in Miami-Dade County in Florida in 1989 (Wikipedia 2015e). There are now more than 3,400 drug courts in the United States, more than half of which are adult drug courts (National Institute of Justice 2015). There are also juvenile drug courts, family drug courts, and tribal healing to wellness courts. According to the U.S. Department of Justice (2016), "Drug courts are specialized court docket programs that target criminal defendants and offenders, juvenile offenders, and parents with pending child welfare cases who have alcohol and other drug dependency problems." The goal of drug court is to enable participants to lead drug-free and productive lives through providing a variety of rehabilitation services. Drug courts use a multidisciplinary approach, including judges, prosecutors and defense attorneys, social workers, and community corrections and treatment professionals (National Institute of Justice 2015; Rempel et al. 2003; U.S. Department of Justice 2016).

Although drug courts vary in terms of eligibility criteria, target population, program design, and so forth, most of them do not accept violent offenders (National Association of Drug Court Professionals n.d.; National Institute of Justice 2015). Eligible offenders enter a revocable plea and are then accepted into the program, which may include self-help groups, support groups, and addiction counseling ("Judge Piotrowski Warns" 2015). The model used by most drug courts involves offender screening and assessment of risks, needs, and responsiveness; frequent interaction with the judge, attorneys, and program staff so that the offender's progress can be reviewed; regular and random drug testing by the courts and/or their treatment program; supervision, sanctions, and rewards for doing well; and intensive treatment and rehabilitation services to get and stay free from drugs ("Judge Piotrowski Warns" 2015; National Association of Drug Court Professionals n.d.; National Institute of Justice 2015; Rempel et al. 2003).

In some courts, after successfully completing a year-long program, the participant can revoke the guilty plea and plead to a nondrug offense. It is not unusual, however, for some offenders to fail during that period ("Judge Piotrowski Warns" 2015; Rempel et al. 2003). When that happens, there are a variety of sanctions the court can use from giving individuals jail time to having them write an essay about their relapse.

Rempel and his colleagues (2003) analyzed the reconviction rates of drug court defendants for six sites across New York State with similar individuals who had not participated in drug court. The courts were located in large- and medium-size cities, a suburban county, and small city/semirural areas. Data were collected for at least 3 years after initial arrests and at least 1 year after completion of the drug court programs. Rempel et al. found that "all six drug courts . . . produced recidivism reductions compared with conventional case processing. . . . The results indicate that positive drug court impacts are durable over time" (p. x). The researchers found a few predictors of success in the drug court program. Older participants were more likely to graduate and stay drug free, whereas those for whom heroin was their primary drug, defendants with prior criminal convictions, and those charged with property crimes rather than drug offenses were most likely to recidivate. Both immediate treatment and graduation from the program were found to predict long-term success. Rempel et al. conclude, "This study provides strong evidence that drug courts produce lasting changes in their participants, persisting even after the period of active judicial supervision" (p. xv). The National Association of Drug Court Professionals (n.d.) puts it more succinctly: "Drug Courts are the most effective justice intervention for treating drug-addicted people."

Psychotherapy

Psychotherapy is used both as a primary treatment for alcohol and drug abuse and as an ancillary program to other treatments such as methadone maintenance, therapeutic communities, acupuncture, and court-ordered rehabilitation. From a sociological perspective, psychotherapy is a resocialization process and the psychoanalyst is an agent of social control. According to Talcott Parsons (1951), "There are such close relations between the processes of socialization and of social control that we may take certain features of the processes of socialization as a point of reference for developing a framework for the analysis of the processes of control" (p. 298). And, "The process of psychotherapy is the case in our own society where these fundamental elements of the processes of social control have been most explicitly brought to light" (p. 301).

For Parsons, the role of the psychotherapist has "special elements" that differentiate it from other social control roles. First, "it is carried out in a professional role of a specialized type." Second, "in its classic form, it is carried out in a one-to-one relationship of two persons, not a group interaction process." Third, "the cultural patterns of scientific knowledge of psychological processes and, hence, the value-standards of scientific objectivity play a prominent role not to be found in many other cases." Fourth, "the therapist extends his conscious manipulation of the situation and of the reward system in the light of his own theory" (p. 301).

The role of the psychotherapist, like the role of physician, has built into it specific societal expectations or institutionalized alternatives from which to choose, which Parsons terms "pattern variables" or "value-orientation patterns." These are affective neutrality (vs. affectivity), collectivity orientation (vs. self-orientation), universalism (vs. particularism), and specificity (vs. diffuseness). In interacting with patients, the psychotherapist, like the physician, is affectively neutral. That is, he or she responds objectively, rather than emotionally. "Whether he likes or dislikes the particular patient as a person is supposed to be irrelevant" (Parsons 1951:435). The therapist is expected to be collectivity oriented, being obligated to "put the 'welfare of the patient' above his personal interests" (p. 435). He or she is expected to treat patients universalistically, without regard to his or her particular relationship to them. Finally, the psychotherapist is not a generalist but rather a specialist with a focused expertise.

Parsons identified "three basic aspects" in the process of resocialization: "support, permissiveness and restriction of reciprocation" (p. 300) as well as the use of rewards, whose expression is structured by the particular value orientations of the psychotherapist's role expectations just noted, as he or she and the patient (client, addict, alcoholic) act and react.

The objective of psychotherapy sessions is to help the patient reduce his or her substance abuse and eventually remain drug or alcohol free. This new information produces anxiety, or what Parsons terms "strain," in the individual. Recognizing this, the therapist gives support. The function of support, according to Parsons (1951), is to reduce "the anxiety component of the reaction to strain, to give a basis or reassurance such that the need to resort to aggressive-destructive and/or defensive reaction is lessened" (p. 299). It is the "collectivity-orientation of the therapist" that is in play, "his readiness to 'help' and his 'understanding' of the patient" (p. 299). However, "support cannot be unconditional" (p. 299) because this would simply reward the patient for continued deviance. Along with giving support, the therapist also shows some permissiveness, recognizing that "people under strain are . . . expected to do and say things which would not be tolerated if the circumstances, or their own states were wholly normal" (p. 300). Yet Parsons notes that this permissiveness must be limited in order to avoid encouraging the undesired behavior. Addicts and alcoholics are notoriously manipulative people, and they may attempt to return to the status quo, trying to get the therapist to allow some backsliding. The therapist, in turn, denies reciprocity, neither responding negatively to the patient's frustrations nor validating his or her regressing. The psychotherapist uses rewards, primarily what Parsons calls "relational rewards," such as social approval, or negative sanctions such as its withdrawal, to control the patient's behavior. The many case histories in the appendices from the files of Dr. Ursula Adler Falk provide insight into both how psychotherapists see their patients and the ways in which patients understand their situations and respond to therapy.[5] Some patients resist labeling themselves as substance abusers, miss appointments without prior notification, and manifest anger and depression. They tend to be manipulative and project blame onto others.

Cognitive-Behavioral Therapy (CBT)

Developed out of the early work of psychotherapist Aaron T. Beck in the early 1960s, CBT is a relatively short-term (10 to 15 sessions) structured, goal-oriented treatment approach that actively engages therapist and patient (Addiction Center 2016; American Addiction Centers 2017; Drug and Alcohol Rehab Asia 2017; New Beginnings 2017). It is a blending of cognitive therapy, which works with patients' thoughts, feelings, and beliefs in order to change their thinking to be more adaptive, and behavioral therapy, which is concerned with changing unhealthy behavior patterns (Addiction Blog 2016). A number of treatment protocols are used under the label of cognitive-behavioral therapy, including motivational interventions, contingency management, functional analysis of cues for substance use, the inclusion of partners and family members, and combination strategies (McHugh, Hearon, and Otto 2010). Regardless of the techniques used, they have in common the application of learning-based interventions and (following reinforcement theory) the recognition that substances serve as reinforcers of behavior.

The basic premise of CBT is that one's thoughts, feelings, and behavior mutually influence one another, that they are learned and can be unlearned and replaced by healthier alternatives (E. Patterson 2017). According to American Addiction Centers (2017), this research-based treatment is "present-oriented, problem-focused and goal-directed." Unlike other forms of therapy, CBT requires both patient and therapist to be actively engaged in therapy. CBT therapists teach patients to identify negative thoughts, which may trigger maladaptive behavior such as substance use, that have become reinforced and help them to develop coping strategies to manage these triggers by engaging in positive alternative behaviors (Addiction Center 2016; American Addiction Centers 2017; New Beginnings 2017; Winerman 2013). Patients are required to keep thought records, participate in various exercises, and use written exercises to help them identify negative thinking (Addiction Center 2016; American Addiction Centers 2017).

An important question is whether CBT works for substance abuse. According to the National Institute on Drug Abuse (2012), the coping skills learned in CBT remain after treatment has been completed. Two meta-analyses examined the research on the efficacy of CBT (Magill and Ray 2009; McHugh et al. 2010). Magill and Ray (2009) analyzed 53 controlled trials of CBT with adult alcohol or illicit drug disorders published between 1982 and 2006. They found that CBT worked particularly well with marijuana users. Additionally, women appeared to benefit more than men from this therapy. CBT also appeared to be effective when it was combined with other psychosocial therapies and when it was short term. Whether it was used as a group or individual therapy did not seem to matter. The authors concluded that their study supported CBT's overall effectiveness as a treatment for substance use disorders.

McHugh et al. (2010) conducted a meta-analysis of 43 randomized, controlled CBT trials, which focused on drug abuse and dependence, and found a moderate effect for this therapy. As in the Magill and Ray (2009) study, they found larger treatment effects for marijuana than for other drugs. They summarized their findings by noting that the CBT trials they studied, although varying in their protocols, demonstrated their efficacy.

Rehabilitation Program Studies

Sociologists have studied the functioning of a variety of programs and efforts to help alcoholics and drug abusers achieve sobriety. Although with few exceptions (e.g., Bullington, Munns, and Geis 1969) these programs have not been conceived by professional sociologists, most of them follow sociological principles as part of their resocialization efforts. As discussed in Chapter 8, these principles include removing the individual from his or her drug-using environment, integrating him or her into another group of former and recovering abusers whose goal is abstinence, providing the individual with opportunities to demonstrate adherence to the new group's norms and to conforming behavior, and rewards for compliance. Sociologists have studied informal self-help programs, such as Alcoholics Anonymous (e.g., Rudy 1986; Trice 1957), and more formal programs like methadone maintenance (Dole and Nyswander 2011) and therapeutic communities (National Institute on Drug Abuse [NIDA] 2011; Yablonsky 1965).

Informal Self-Help Programs: Alcoholics Anonymous and Narcotics Anonymous

David Rudy's (1986) ethnography of Alcoholics Anonymous (A.A.) is the definitive study of how members affiliate themselves with this program. Using a symbolic interactionist framework, Rudy examined this process. He writes, "From an interactionist perspective, 'alcoholism' is what it is taken to be by given people in given situations. The meaning of phenomena from this perspective is a consequence of the definitions and meanings that are attached to them by actors" (p. 95). Looking at how A.A. members construct or reconstruct their alcoholism, he developed a model of affiliation that has six steps: hitting bottom, first stepping, making a commitment, accepting one's problem, telling one's story, and doing twelfth-step work. He summarizes his position early on in his preface: "Becoming alcoholic and the type of alcoholic one becomes has as much to do with the responses of others—treatment agencies, psychiatrists, A.A., and friends—as it does with the drinking activities and life experiences of the person labeled alcoholic" (p. xiv).

Narcotics Anonymous (NA) was formed in July 1953 in Southern California (NA 2008). Although it originated in the A.A. program of the late 1940s and is based on A.A.'s Twelve Steps, there are some differences between the two organizations. According to NA (2008), "We follow the same path with a single exception; our identification as addicts is all-inclusive with respect to any mood-changing, mind-altering substance. Alcoholism is too limited a term for us; our problem is not a specific substance, it is a disease called addiction. We believe that as a fellowship, we have been guided by a Greater Consciousness, and are grateful for the direction that has enabled us to build upon a proven program of recovery" (p. xxv).[6]

NA's early growth was slow, but with the publication of its *Basic Text* in 1983, its membership expanded rapidly. As of May 2014, NA (2015) had over 63,000 meetings in 132 countries worldwide. The worldwide membership of NA is multicultural and multilingual, with literature in 45 languages.

Like A.A., the core of NA's program is the social support provided by its members. According to NA's (2015) website, "One of the keys to NA's success is the therapeutic value of addicts working with other addicts. Members share their successes and challenges in overcoming active addiction and living drug-free productive lives through the application of the principles contained within the Twelve Steps and Twelve Traditions of NA. These principles are the core of the Narcotics Anonymous recovery program." The group meeting, led by individual members of NA, during which members share their experiences, is the primary mechanism through which change is accomplished. NA (2015) has a World Service Conference, which is an international assembly that "provides guidance on issues affecting the entire organization." NA has no affiliation with other groups, takes no financial contributions from nonmembers, and relies solely on voluntary member contributions to cover its expenses.

We do know something about the composition of NA's membership and some of their issues, because since 1966, the organization has distributed a biannual survey to participants at its world conventions and also makes the survey available to members online and through mail and fax. As of this writing, the most recent survey was conducted in 2013 at the convention in Philadelphia, and because of the strong online response, NA (2015) made it available for 5 months. In total, there were 16,750 responses to the survey. Fifty-seven percent of the respondents to the survey were male and 43% were female, 76% were Caucasian, 13% were African American, 5% were Hispanic, 2% were Asian, 1% were indigenous, and 3% were multiracial (NA 2015). NA noted that the ethnic composition of responses was influenced to some extent by the geographic location of the survey. Respondents reported an average of 4.79 meetings a week. The average length of sobriety for NA (2015) participants was 11.07 years. Ninety-two percent of respondents said that their family relationships had improved with participation in the NA program, and 88% reported that their social connections with others had also increased (NA 2015). These are important changes, because drug addicts and alcoholics typically isolate themselves from others, including family members (J. Jackson 1956; Weinberg 1994).

Therapeutic Communities

The National Institute on Drug Abuse (NIDA 2011) has reviewed the literature on residential therapeutic communities (TCs). Unlike A.A.'s alcoholism-as-a-disease perspective, TCs are based on a clinical model that assumes that drug- and alcohol-abusing behavior is a symptom of the individual's underlying problems, and the goal of the TC is to change his or her negative patterns of attitudes and behaviors. To do this, the individual is placed in a group situation separated from the outside world, where a structured environment and group pressure and support are used to promote positive change. The effectiveness of TCs has not been established, but modified versions of them, especially for special populations and multimodality approaches, show some promise (NIDA 2011).

Daytop Village

There are many TCs in the United States. One of the earliest of these was Synanon, founded in 1958, which is discussed in another section. Daytop Village owes its existence in part to Synanon, because its cofounder, Dr. Daniel Casriel, a psychiatrist, visited Synanon in 1962 and lived there in 1963 (Wikipedia 2008). Founded in 1963 by Dr. Casriel and Monsignor William B. O'Brien, Daytop Village

Photo 13.2: Nancy Reagan visiting Daytop Village, New York, on October 23, 1980.

is one of the oldest TCs in the country. First Lady Nancy Reagan visited Daytop Village in 1980, which led to her interest in drug abuse education and prevention for youth, eventually creating the Just Say No campaign discussed earlier in this chapter (Wikipedia 2015c). Originally called Daytop Lodge, the program was founded with a grant and located on Staten Island, having as its first residents 22 male probationers from the Brooklyn corrections system (Daytop Village 2012). According to Daytop Village's (2012) website, "The basics of the treatment program were group therapy sessions, role modeling, job assignments and a hierarchy of peers. As residents progressed, they received more responsible duties, and earned more privileges. Those coming after them could see that others like themselves were gaining respect, and that life without drugs was possible." By 1964, Daytop had become incorporated as Daytop Village and counted among its residents women and voluntary referrals. Within the next few years it had expanded to its first residential facility in Sullivan County, New York, and an outpatient clinic in Westchester County (Daytop Village 2012). Daytop Village is considered "one of the most successful programs of its kind," with an estimated 85% of those whom it has treated staying drug-free (Wikipedia 2014d).

Phoenix House

Phoenix House was founded in 1967 by six heroin addicts who "came together at a detoxification program in a New York hospital. They talked about the struggles of staying clean and decided to help one another through the tough times ahead. Together, they moved into a brownstone on Manhattan's West Side and lived as a community, encouraging and helping each other to stay sober. That is how Phoenix House was born" (Phoenix House 2015). Phoenix House (2015) claims to be "the nation's leading provider of alcohol and drug abuse treatment and prevention services operating more than 120 programs in ten states." The program services over 5,000 patients, including adolescents. Its treatment options include a variety of programs including both residential and outpatient treatments, detoxification, assessment and evaluation, and special programs for women and adolescents. Phoenix House is listed in SAMHSA's National Registry of Evidence-Based Programs and Practices.

Passages Malibu

Passages Malibu is a more recently established TC, founded in 2001 by father and son Chris and Pax Prentice. Pax identifies himself as a former drug and alcohol addict. Passages Malibu is presented as an extremely posh resort. The cost for a month's stay at the for-profit TC was $88,500 for a shared room in 2011 (Wikipedia 2015f). According to its website, "At Passages Malibu we offer more unique treatment methods than any other rehab center in the world. Unlike the cookie-cutter group approach offered by most rehab centers, our program is customized specifically for each client who walks through our doors" (Passages Malibu 2015a). Passages Malibu does not believe that addiction is a disease. Rather, it believes it is the result of one or more of the following causes: a chemical imbalance, unresolved events from the past, beliefs people hold that are inconsistent with what is true, and an inability to cope with current conditions (Passages Malibu 2015b). Although Passages Malibu claims an 84.4% rehabilitation rate (Pringle 2007) and is accredited by the Joint Commission on the Accreditation of Healthcare Organizations, it is not without controversy. It does not believe in group therapy or a multistep approach to rehabilitation, which are used by many other programs.

The Strange Story of Synanon

The story of Synanon, one of the most prominent therapeutic communities from the late 1950s to the late 1970s, is both strange and sad. In 1958, Charles ("Chuck") E. Dederich, a recovering alcoholic, began an informal "free-association" discussion group with some friends from A.A. in Ocean Park, California (Yablonsky 1965). He supported this fledgling "club" with his $33 unemployment check. Within a short time, he had rented a storefront building for meetings. Over time, Synanon added recovering heroin addicts to its members, outgrowing its small quarters and eventually severing its ties with A.A. By 1963, the Synanon Foundation had become a million-dollar enterprise, with chapters in Santa Monica; San Francisco; San Diego; Reno, Nevada; and Westport,

Photo 13.3: Charles E. Dederich at Synanon House.

Connecticut (Yablonsky 1965). In his glowing report on Synanon, *Synanon: The Tunnel Back*, Lewis Yablonsky (1965) hails its "significance as a social movement," which has "steadily moved beyond the limited work of treating drug addiction and crime . . . as a vehicle for constructing personal and social change" (p. v). He notes "the several hundred college and university students currently involved in campus Synanon clubs," predicting that "the magic and usefulness of Synanon thus seems to be growing and spreading to a wider audience" (p. vi). Yablonsky characterized Dederich as "a layman with a genius for understanding and solving human problems" (p. vii) and a "masterful social planner" (p. viii). The central concept of Synanon was called The Game, a group encounter session during which members worked on their own and others' problems, frequently confronting one another about their attitudes and behaviors (Rettig, Torres, and Garrett 1977). The most severe attacks, often directed by Dederich, a master in that technique, were called "haircuts." The object of the encounter sessions and the haircuts was to get individuals to understand their motives and behaviors and change them.

The Synanon program followed the sociological/social psychological principles for successfully working with addicts and alcoholics discussed earlier and in Chapter 8, serving as a new reference group supplanting the individual's previous associations. Manny Torres (Rettig et al. 1977) notes that "I found that the Synanon group sucked me in little by little. In Synanon there is almost total suppression of preexisting statuses, which is achieved by the assimilating function of the group. They won't let you stay outside" (p. 120).

When an addict first came to the Synanon program, he or she was not necessarily automatically admitted. As Yablonsky (1965) notes, "A 'prospect' (the Synanon term for someone seeking entrance) must voluntarily present himself and must prove to an indoctrination committee of older Synanon members that he truly seeks help and wants to change his behavior. He does not enter an organization that is compelled to accept him, as in a government-run jail or hospital. His acceptance comes from a peer group" (p. 161). Some individuals came to Synanon while they were still on drugs. They were required to kick their habit "cold turkey," on a couch in the living room, in full view of others. If the newcomer was admitted, he or she may have been given an informal talk by Dederich. The point of the talk, part of the indoctrination process, was to let the individual know that others have had the same experiences but have begun to overcome their problems through Synanon. He or she was told the rules: turn up at noon seminars, attend synanons three times a week, do your job, no violence, and no substance abuse. The newcomer was on the bottom of the hierarchy. As Torres explains, "New members are totally isolated from the world of their former selves. They are not allowed to venture forth 'outside' again until they have demonstrated stability—until they have been indoctrinated. The new person in Synanon does the shit work. He is assigned low status and soon learns that he has to work for anything he gets. Synanon is the ultimate adjustment center" (Rettig et al. 1977:124).

Over time, as the individual demonstrated adherence to Synanon's norms, he or she was given additional responsibilities and a better job, living in Synanon and working in its growing businesses.[7] In many ways, Synanon became a total institution, keeping members within its boundaries and serving all their needs. Therein lay a fundamental problem with its program. One of the major criticisms of Synanon was that its members were too closely tied to the program and not being prepared for a life outside. So long as they remained in Synanon they were drug-free, but success was not guaranteed if they left. In other words, critics saw members as having substituted addiction to Synanon for addiction to drugs. There was another problem with Synanon, which Yablonsky recognized early on. It resided in the personality of its creator. "In retrospect," Yablonsky (1965) wrote, "it seems that any approach not *completely* developed by Chuck himself was too binding for his roaring ego needs. The development of Synanon confirms this speculation. Chuck appears to need an 'empire' based on his own ideas, and Synanon has fulfilled this prescription" (pp. 48–49; italics in original). Several years later, Manny Torres noted Dederich's autocratic method. He would appear at Synanon Games and violate his own rules. During a confrontation, when according to the rules Manny was allowed to continue talking, Dederich abruptly ended it. When Manny remonstrated with him, Dederich replied, "I say the game is over and I have the final say around here. I'm Chuck Dederich" (Rettig et al. 1977:121). According to Manny, "The Synanon community blots out the outside. . . . The control is a sort of benign dictatorship of the poor proletariat, with Chuck's presence ever felt as the ultimate authority" (Rettig et al. 1977:124). Both Yablonsky and Manny were prescient, as subsequent events would demonstrate.

A 1978 *Buffalo Evening News* article told the story of Chuck Dederich's search for a new wife after his wife, Betty, died of cancer. Using an imperial metaphor, it compared Dederich to a potentate: "Under the bearded Dederich's tight-fisted reign, Synanon has grown into a self-sufficient organization of 1,600 persons, an experimental mini-society" ("Synanon Patriarch" 1978). Dederich said, "'I sent up a flare, like any monarch of old times. I let the word out that I was available.'" Following his marriage to a Synanon member half his age, Dederich decided to see "what would happen if Synanon members . . . ended their marriages and changed partners. 'I'm a statistician,'" he said. "Most of these people were going to be divorced anyway, eventually. I thought, 'Wouldn't it be funny to perform some emotional surgery on people who are getting along pretty well?'" After persuading two couples to divorce and remarry, other couples followed suit. "'They were almost like sacrificial lambs,' Mr. Dederich says, 'After them it was easier. They were on my side'" ("Synanon Patriarch" 1978). At least 230 love matches occurred.

The Synanon story continued to grow more and more bizarre. On Tuesday, October 10, 1978, an attorney who had won a $300,000 default judgment against Synanon on behalf of a couple who claimed that the wife had been kidnapped and physically abused by Synanon put his hand in his mailbox to check his mail. Instead of retrieving mail, he had a 4½ foot rattlesnake with its rattles cut off clamped to his hand. He had been previously warned that he was on a Synanon "hit list." A neighbor who had seen two men put something in the mailbox earlier that day was able to write down their car's license plate number and turn it into the police. The car came back as registered to Synanon ("Police Seek Synanon Car" 1978).

Police arrested two Synanon members in the attack, Joseph Musico and Lance N. Kenton, the latter the 20-year-old son of well-known band leader Stan Kenton. Kenton was "reportedly a leader of the Synanon cult's paramilitary force," a "protective force within the cult known as 'the Imperial Marines,' which trained in commando tactics and martial arts such as karate. Synanon representatives have said in recent years that the group's self-contained communities have arsenals of guns for self-defense" ("Stan Kenton's Son" 1978). An article by the Associated Press, "Violence Shadows Synanon's 'Enemies'," appeared two days later. In it, Synanon was described as "a tax-exempt, $22 million-a-year business and religion" ("Violence Shadows Synanon's 'Enemies'" 1978). The article enumerated several incidents of violence by Synanon members over the previous few years, including misdemeanor assault charges for attacking a rancher and his wife and child who had been harboring Synanon runaways, terrorizing a former member by handcuffing him to a chair and interrogating him while a guard dog stood watch, and beating a former transportation director almost to death with baseball bats ("Violence Shadows Synanon's 'Enemies'" 1978). Dederich pleaded no contest to the charge of putting the rattlesnake in the attorney's mailbox, and in 1982 he was arrested, along with his daughter and son and six other suspects, and charged with illegal stock sales ("Accused of Fraud" 1982). Synanon disbanded permanently in 1989, after its properties were seized by the IRS for back taxes, and was formally dissolved in 1991. Charles Dederich died in 1997 (Wikipedia 2008).

Methadone Maintenance

Methadone maintenance programs (Dole and Nyswander 2011) treat drug addiction as a disease and use methadone, a synthetic narcotic given orally, as a heroin blocker. Ideally, methadone maintenance is accompanied by counseling and other forms of treatment. The idea behind methadone maintenance is to eliminate the addict's need to obtain narcotics on the street and to support his or her habit through secondary (criminal) deviance, while promoting his or her social and psychological adjustment. The Dole and Nyswander program was the first of its kind in the United States and the model for many other programs. They found that criminal activity was reduced while addicts were on their program.

An Innovative Approach

One of the most interesting and unique attempts to rehabilitate narcotics addicts was conceived by Bullington, Munns, and Geis (1969). In this case the authors actually set up the program that they then studied. Based on sociological principles, especially those of exchange theory, their hypothesis was "that a social service job, paying a decent salary to a man who stood small likelihood of commanding such a salary in the open market, would lead the employee to take on values and behavioral patterns (particularly, of course, those involving abstinence from use of opiates) of persons in the middle class" (p. 456). Using federal grant money, the authors opened the Boyle Heights Narcotics Prevention Project in one of the highest drug addiction areas in California. They hired ex-addicts, who had been drug-free for a median time of 2 to 3 years, as paraprofessional street workers to aid current street addicts. In that role they worked with families, counseled addicts, helped addicts to find jobs, testified for addicts in court, and so forth. Some of the ex-addicts also worked in drug use prevention education in two junior high schools. Note that in this project two groups of individuals were the object of study. The first and most obvious was the street addicts. It was anticipated that having ex-addicts work directly with them, modeling nonusing behavior and attitudes, might encourage them to become abstinent. Implicit in this approach is the recognition of the impact of significant others on one's attitudes and behaviors, an important element in reference group theory. The second group of individuals in the study was the ex-addicts. Again, assumptions of reference group theory are operative with this cohort, as well as the idea that money is a powerful agent of exchange in modifying behavior.

Bullington and colleagues collected data on 31 street workers working in the program in February 1968. These data included interviews, psychological write-ups on each individual, and over 500 pages of field notes. The researchers saw a transformation in the behavior of their ex-addict street workers. However, this was not a result of the salary they received. "The tidy relationship which we had anticipated between salary and middle-class conformity did not emerge from the data," they wrote. "There is certainly evidence of adoption of bourgeois styles and affiliation, but salary alone was not the reason. What appear more significant are certain features of the street worker role itself, which allowed intimate observation and colleague (rather than client) interaction with a system heretofore remote and mysterious" (p. 459). Through their participation in the project, these ex-addicts began to develop competencies and social skills that characterize middle-class status. They also developed contacts with individuals in social service and employment agencies. They began, in sum, to begin to see themselves as competent potential professionals. They started to dress like professionals and changed their consumption patterns. Bullington et al. (1969) noted that as these ex-addicts began to see the possibility of a career in social services, their responses to questions indicated "a considerable rise in self-esteem, tied rather directly to enhanced feelings about job marketability" (p. 460). Unfortunately, however, this newly acquired positive self-image came under attack by the very people whose job it was to supervise and support them. Project administrators believed that taking on the trappings of the middle class would undercut the street workers' effectiveness, so they pressured them to maintain a street style. This put the workers in the untenable position of marginal men. They were no longer using drugs or active in the addict subculture, and they had begun to think of themselves as professionals. However, their new status and identity was not being validated by their administrators, who still saw them as addicts. Their dilemma was clearly explained by Ray (1961) in his discussion of the running struggle experienced by abstinent addicts. These cross-pressures ultimately led to the resignation of many of the workers and the premature end of the program.

Unconventional Approaches

Outward Bound Programs

The 1980s featured a number of unconventional attempts to deal with addiction. One of these was developed by Beech Hill Hospital in Dublin, New Hampshire. It combined seminars and counseling sessions with participation in Outward Bound programs (Foster 1983). Outward Bound programs challenge participants to overcome physical obstacles by climbing cliffs, hiking mountains, and so forth. The idea behind the Beech Hill program, and similar programs, was to present alcoholics and other addicts with obstacles that appear to be impossible but that they could overcome, step by step, and then transfer that successful confidence-building experience to confront their addictions. "Outward Bound participants get a chance to succeed at something they never thought they could do; alcoholics at Beech Hill are pushed to do the one thing they've already failed to do—stay sober" (Foster 1983:C-6). A 1980 study of a program at St. Luke's Hospital in Denver begun in 1978 found that 77% to 85% of the more than 200 patients who had gone through their Outward Bound program remained sober, as compared to a 71% success rate for patients who had not gone through that program (Foster 1983). McPeake et al. (1991) reported on a program developed by Beech Hill Hospital specifically for adolescents with chemical dependency issues that combined a Twelve Step drug- and alcohol-oriented program with the Hurricane Island Outward Bound School. They carried out three follow-up studies of two different groups of patients, using structured telephone interviews that asked about "employment/school status, legal difficulties, interpersonal relationships (notably family), perceived self-improvement, participation in Twelve Step Programs, drug or alcohol use and rehospitalization" (McPeake et al. 1991:48). Additionally, as a check on the respondents' veracity, they also interviewed a parent or guardian. They found "a significant decrease in the number of arrests, hospitalizations, work problems and school problems reported by patients . . . and positive changes in all areas (relations within family, attitude about self, etc.)" (p. 48). Also, 75% of the respondents were abstinent at that time, 37% of whom had been drug- and alcohol-free for at least 6 months. A second follow-up study after 2 years showed that the majority of youth were still doing well. A third study of 30 young people who were a year to a year and a half removed from the program found similar improvements. The researchers concluded that "first and foremost the program evaluation studies described above suggest that this model of adolescent treatment is effective. These studies indicate that most of the adolescents contacted . . . had significantly decreased their substance use, were happier with themselves and with others and appeared to be leading productive lives. This information was corroborated by a parent or guardian" (p. 52).

Kennedy and Minami (1993) interviewed 91 youth and a parent by telephone every 3 months for a year after they had left the Beech Hill program. They also administered the Minnesota Multiphasic Personality Disorder Inventory and the Personal Experience Inventory, along with detailed psychosocial assessments to understand what variables affected successful outcomes. Forty-seven percent of their respondents reported being completely free from alcohol and drugs. Outcomes were improved by participation in Alcoholics Anonymous.

Acupuncture

Acupuncture was an innovation begun in the late 1970s to help alcoholics and drug addicts deal with their addictions ("Acupuncture Use Seen" 1986; D'Emilio 1982; Lin, Chan, and Chen 2012; W. King 1981).

The Western application of acupuncture follows the protocol developed in 1985 by Dr. M. Smith, head of the U.S. National Acupuncture Detoxification

Association (NADA). In this procedure, termed *auricular acupuncture*, five needles are inserted at specific points into the outer ear (Lin et al. 2012). This treatment is claimed to relieve withdrawal symptoms, decrease cravings, and retain patients in psychosocial treatments (Lin et al. 2012; Margolin et al. 2002). The mechanism through which acupuncture is thought to work is by activating endorphins, which are pain-suppressing chemicals in the brain (W. King 1981).

Sociologists John A. Newmeyer, Gregory L. Johnson, and Steven Klot (1984) studied 460 heroin addicts in a San Francisco clinic over an 18-month period between October 1979 and April 1981. Subjects were offered an opportunity to participate in one of three conditions: acupuncture only, acupuncture and medication, and medication only. The researchers found that those who chose acupuncture only were significantly more likely to drop out of treatment and that "soft-core" users stayed longer in acupuncture treatment than "hard-core" users (Newmeyer et al. 1984). Johnson explained why this may have been the case to a reporter: "Despite their endorsement of acupuncture's effectiveness, most clients discontinued treatment because of its inconvenience relative to pills and the perceived pain of the needles. . . . We're really fighting people's liking for pills" (D'Emilio 1982:F-6).

Lin et al. (2012) reviewed data from 10 clinical trials involving a total of 1,034 subjects from China, the United States, the United Kingdom, and Iran, published in Chinese and English and going back to 1970, that used acupuncture as a strategy to treat addiction. They found that though "the majority agreed in the efficacy of acupuncture as a strategy for the treatment of opium addicts," 8 of the 10 studies had methodological deficiencies. The researchers concluded that "although many studies have reported positive findings regarding the use of acupuncture to treat drug dependence, the evidence for its effectiveness has been inconclusive and difficult to interpret. There are few randomized controlled clinical trials of acupuncture treatment for opiate addiction, and the methodological methods used in several clinical trials of acupuncture treatment for opiate dependence can be criticized for their poor quality" (Lin et al. 2012).

Bullock et al. (2002) reported on their application of acupuncture on 503 alcohol-dependent subjects. In a single-blind study,[8] subjects were randomly assigned to one of four treatment modalities: specific acupuncture, nonspecific acupuncture,[9] symptom-based acupuncture, or conventional treatment alone. Although 49% of their acupuncture subjects reported reduced desire for alcohol, Bullock and his colleagues concluded that acupuncture did not significantly reduce alcohol use more than conventional treatments alone.

Margolin and his colleagues (2002) studied acupuncture use for cocaine addicts. Their sample consisted of 620 cocaine-dependent subjects recruited from six sites throughout the United States randomly assigned to one of three conditions: auricular acupuncture, a needle-insertion control condition, or a relaxation control condition.[10] The treatment was given five times a week, 40 minutes at a time, for 8 weeks, supplemented with drug counseling. The authors noted that auricular acupuncture, one of the most widely used treatments for cocaine addiction, is being used in more than 400 clinics in the United States and Europe. They observed that it is often a component in numerous drug court programs (Margolin et al. 2002).

Margolin et al. (2002) found that "there were no differences by treatment condition in cocaine use assessed by urine samples or self-report. Throughout the study there were modest reductions in cocaine use by patients in all 3 conditions. Secondary analyses revealed no significant differences among the treatments on any outcome measure. Relative to patients in the 2 control conditions, patients receiving NADA acupuncture were not retained in treatment longer."

In summary, it does not appear that acupuncture treatment for opiate or cocaine addiction or alcoholism is any more effective than other treatment modalities.

As we have seen throughout this book, alcoholism and other drug addictions are complex social situations affected by cultural and social definitions and relationships, political considerations, and economic circumstances. Our society has a long-standing drug culture. We Americans see pills and medications as solutions to all kinds of medical and personal problems. One has only to view television for a couple of hours to realize the cultural impact of drugs and alcohol as demonstrated by the many commercials for beer, wine, and spirits. Both over-the-counter and prescription drug advertisements flood the airwaves, extolling treatments for erectile dysfunction, low testosterone levels, obesity, digestive problems and bowel issues, heartburn, depression, nicotine addiction, congestive obstructive pulmonary disease, asthma, insomnia, high cholesterol, high blood pressure, headaches, and so forth.[11] Combine the cultural belief in drugs as solutions with widespread tolerance of and participation in deviant behavior (e.g., gambling, pornography, pirating) and it is not surprising that we have an illicit drug problem. The question is, what, if anything, can we do about it? In this chapter, we have addressed the wide variety of ways in which drug and alcohol abuse have been addressed, but there are difficulties in assessing the effectiveness of many programs. Definitions of success vary from program to program. Is a reduction in the frequency and amount of a substance consumed a successful outcome, or must success only be measured by the proportion of clients who remain abstinent? And for how long must an individual remain drug- or alcohol-free in order to be considered successful? The baseline for reporting outcomes has sometimes also been manipulated. One therapeutic community, for example, may report the percentage of persons entering its program who graduate from it, whereas other TCs may only count individuals as being part of their program after they have been in residence beyond the time that most people drop out. Few programs have been expressly developed with an intention of making them amenable to evaluation. Methodological problems with outside assessment studies often make definitive conclusions problematic. Some self-help groups, like A.A., do not keep statistics, so we have to rely on anecdotal accounts from current members.

Decriminalization and/or legalization of certain substances has often been proposed as a solution to some drug problems. Decriminalization of marijuana for recreational purposes is so recent that there has not been enough time for assessment. As of this writing, eight states and Washington, DC, have legalized recreational marijuana use.

NOTES

1. Talcott Parsons (1951), in his classic work *The Social System*, makes this distinction between the sick role and other deviant roles. He writes, "If being sick is to be regarded as 'deviant' as certainly in important respects it must, it is as we have noted distinguished from other deviant roles precisely by the fact that the sick person is not regarded as 'responsible' for his condition, 'he can't help it'" (p. 440).

2. In those days, police officers were not required to have a college degree. Many officers, however, took advantage of federal programs to pay for their college educations.

3. The 2014 and 2015 reports do not have data on multidrug use.

4. The authors wish to thank Detective Scott Sprague, D.A.R.E. officer for the Town of Tonawanda, New York, for his assistance and providing us with a copy of the D.A.R.E. workbook.

5. For examples of how written records may be understood, see Rod Watson, *Analysing Practical and Professional Texts: A Naturalistic Approach* (Burlington, VT: Ashgate, 2009).

6. The authors wish to thank Heather R. for providing us with a copy of NA's *Basic Text*, sixth edition.

7. In 1966, during a cross-country trip to California, one of the authors filled up his car at a Synanon-owned service station.

8. In a single-blind study, the individuals analyzing the results do not know which subjects were placed in the various experimental conditions.

9. Specific acupuncture uses the five points identified by NADA—sympathetic nervous system, shenmen, kidney, lung, and liver (Lin et al. 2012), whereas nonspecific acupuncture does not necessarily focus on these areas.

10. The relaxation control condition consisted of videos demonstrating relaxation techniques and showing relaxing images accompanied by soft music.

11. There are also a number of antismoking commercials. Some of these, directed at preteens or early teens, featuring attractive adolescents dancing and singing, present nonsmoking as the cool and popular option. Other commercials graphically illustrate the negative consequences of smoking, showing people with disfigured faces, patients talking about their stomas, colon cancer patients with their colostomy bags, and amputees. There are also numerous lawyers' advertisements soliciting victims of the harmful side effects of prescription drugs.

APPENDIX

A

Case Histories

Alcohol Abusers

These 23 case histories come from the files of Dr. Ursula Adler Falk, a psycho-therapist. The names of her clients have been changed, along with some other details, to protect their anonymity. Although these histories do not represent a scientifically drawn random sample, some conclusions can nonetheless be drawn from them. Dr. Falk's clients represent a diversity of gender, age, ethnicity, socio-economic and educational statuses, and sexual orientation, but they have much in common. Most of them are children of divorce or have parents who were never married. This, of course, is not unusual in contemporary American society and does not differentiate them from most people. Since at least the early 1970s, about half of marriages in the United States have resulted in divorce.

These people illustrate a number of characteristics of the alcoholic person-ality discussed in Chapter 8. They are generally angry; they deny responsibility for their actions, and they blame others for their situation. They are also quite manipulative.

One commonality found within this group of problem drinkers is that their parents were often not only drinkers but heavy users of alcohol. Genetic researchers might therefore attribute their alcoholism to inheritance; a more likely sociological explanation is that drinking is a learned behavior, influenced by the attitudes and behavior of significant others and reference groups, especially within the family. Both positions, of course, are merely speculation. These case histories also pro-vide interesting illustrations of the sociological concept of careers, describing these individuals' progression through the alcoholic career, including abstinence and relapse cycles.

Clifton Brewer

Clifton Brewer is a 27-year-old poorly dressed Caucasian gentleman who came to the office because he had been arrested three times in the past 15 months for driving under the influence of alcohol. He had a court date within 14 days of his last arrest and wanted the counselor to let the public defender know that he was having an evaluation as well as some treatment sessions before the judgment date. He did not want to face another imprisonment (he had already spent some weekends in jail in the last few years because of fights with other drivers and other unacceptable behavior). His history included an alcoholic father, deceased when Clifton was in his teens; a mother who worked as a factory laborer in a salad dressing place; and three brothers who did not get along with each other. Clifton is also the father of four children. He has one 11-year-old daughter who lives with her mother. She was born when he was 16. He also has a 6-year-old son, a 5-year-old daughter, and an 18-month-old son. The last three children were born to his current significant other with whom he had been living for the past 6 years. He saw no reason to marry this 24-year-old woman and did not think he would make the relationship "legal." He thought marriage was unnecessary and was "just a joke" anyway. He spoke about fighting with Jenny because she never saw it "his way." He let it be known that she worked nights in a bar waitressing. He accused her of getting drunk and cheating, although he had no proof of the latter. He did insist that she came home inebriated after work. There were times when Jenny and he had physical battles and locked each other out of the house. Their children were intimidated and frightened and lived in an insecure and hostile environment. The child protection agency had been called on several occasions, but the children had not been removed. Clifton has no job, lives on welfare, and is able to pick up an occasional bit of work repairing things privately for people. When he does have work, he needs to drive to the job, and because he has lost his license, he is unable to get to and from the few jobs available. Clifton has a high school education. He alleges that he cares about his mother, who would always give him some food when he was hungry and desperate. When speaking of his significant other, he often refers to her as a "slut" and a liar.

Clifton did come for counseling/therapy several times. He feels that he has always been disadvantaged and what occurred was not his fault. He had Jenny drive his very old "broken down" truck with his three children in the vehicle while he spoke with the counselor.

When his court date came, it was delayed. He made several other appointments with the therapist. Sometimes he would keep his sessions and other times he did not telephone to cancel but did not appear as agreed. One day he arrived and reported to the counselor that he was to begin a 6-month jail sentence. He insisted that he felt that this should not have occurred. He recited that his acquaintances had been more dangerous on the road than he and that "someone had it in" for him. He recited all of these folk's misdeeds and the fact that they were "drunks" who had some secret connections. He wanted reassurance that his therapist would see him after his sentence ended.

After the 6 months in jail he returned and once again was covered by welfare, as were his children. He did get a job by working privately "off the books" in a car repair garage. He seemed to have the knowledge to solve the problems in vehicles. He found an acquaintance at the workplace who agreed to drive him to and from the place if he paid the gasoline expenses. He did suffer from anxiety lest he would be discovered by the welfare department.

Eventually, his significant other left him. She found a new mate, a man who had two young children of his own. She abandoned her offspring and Clifton was given custody of their children. He was placed on probation but did relapse one evening. He was not apprehended at that time because he had not been driving. His mother, having been laid off from her job, agreed to help with the children. Clifton does attend A.A. meetings as often as he is able. He has found soulmates at these A.A. meetings.

There is no guarantee that he will be able to control his urges, especially when his pressures become great. There have been a number of alcoholics in his family, his late father being one of them. His brothers also have had problems with refraining from using alcohol but have not been incarcerated as a result.

It must be remembered that the surroundings of human beings are essential for creating each person. As infants and children we depend heavily on our caregivers; our parents are our role models. We imitate them and to a great extent follow in their footsteps. As infants our parents are always right. If our parental figure drinks, to the child it seems the acceptable thing to do. Addiction is another variable. Much depends on our bodies and how fast a person becomes addicted to a product if at all, how much control we have, and what is important to each individual. The support a person has and how much influence significant others have are relevant in drinking and abstention. All this and much more are important considerations when we examine the reasons and possible causes of alcoholism.

Richard Burns

Richard Burns is a tall 55-year-old Caucasian male who comes to his sessions by bus because he lost his license after getting a second DUI 2 years ago. His first DUI was in 2005, which was 8 years ago. Neither of these incidents ended in injuries to people. He refused both times to take a Breathalyzer test, because he knew he had many more drinks than he should have had. His actions usually created a situation in which he could not receive his legal privileges back for a minimum of one to one and a half years.

When he entered the office his facial expression was one of a schoolboy awaiting punishment from the principal. It was for the last alcohol infraction that he came to begin his evaluation and treatment that he knew was awaiting him. His history included having two alcoholic paternal grandparents and a father who drank heavily. His mother did not care for alcohol. He revealed what had occurred to bring him to this state: He began drinking in his teens. His father took him along to a bar to show him what "men do," which left a "good" impression on the boy. He learned to enjoy drinking with his buddies as he got a little older and continued using alcohol. He could feel good, tell jokes, and feel free; his "angst" (fear) of being clumsy and dumb left him when he was under the influence. He could relate to others his age.

He became a machinist and did very well in his chosen occupation. He never drank during the day and kept his position for years because he was well qualified and well liked by his contemporaries. He was "one of the guys, a real man." Before he took his first job, he graduated from high school, where he was an average student. His dad owned a bar, and he would sometimes help out with customers and with glasses that had to be washed.

His parents married at a young age, and for the most part, they got along with one another. There was no divorce and he considered his childhood "average." He was third in the family constellation; he has two older brothers and two younger sisters. Only one sister is friendly to him and she lives out of town. The other three siblings do not speak to him. They disagree with his "drunken states" and remind him that he has been apprehended four times, even though only two were on his current record (only two were in the last 10 years; the others were before that time).

At the time of his most recent counseling he had been sober for 30 days, and prior to a one-evening drinking spree, he was sober 146 days and very proud of that accomplishment. He stated that sometimes he can fight his urges by drinking tea accompanied by candy. Sweets do help him somewhat. After the second DUI he was sent to attend drug court for 1 year. He had to be there weekly, and it was much like probation. He had to report and have blood and breath tests taken. During one of his sessions the court staff informed him that his test "came out dirty." He had snorted cocaine. In addition, he had a probationary period of 3 years. Probation and drug court have been of great help and a deterrent. He does attend A.A. sessions fairly regularly, which help his sobriety. He has to walk or find public transportation to get to wherever he has to be.

When he was 19 he left the state in which he was raised and went to California and then Texas. Several times he spent a few days in jail for inebriation. In spite of that, he always worked. He did manage to attend and graduate from a trade school and became a skilled mechanic.

He eventually married a woman whom he met down South and had a son and a daughter with her. When the children were quite young the couple divorced, and he had to pay a considerable part of his paycheck to support them. When he failed, the court handled the situation. Because of the money that he owed over the years, he could not afford a comfortable abode for himself. Eventually he rented a room with a coworker who also drank heavily but currently has been sober for the last 10 years.

Richard has a full-time job now in his home state and has been with the factory for more than 11 years. He visits his octogenarian parents about once a week and enjoys a meal with them when possible. He feels quite close to his mother, who has always been a forgiving person.

He was sober for 3 years at one time but began drinking again when his girlfriend died suddenly. He does have urges to drink and works hard to suppress them. He has difficulty sitting for any length of time in one position. He has a "tick" and rubs his eyes frequently. He is almost unaware that he makes these motions.

He has set goals for himself: 1. He will not drive a car until he is released from drug court and has experienced a full year of sobriety. 2. He will rent an apartment of his own after he has paid all his debts. 3. He will attend A.A. meetings a minimum of two times per week.

He admits his shortcomings, works hard and does not deny his addictions, and holds no one but himself responsible for the situation that brought him here. He is very fond of his adult children and wants to make them proud.

Thomas Cardel

Tom is a 37-year-old man who comes from a dysfunctional family. He dislikes his mother because she smokes and is not his "type." He is very fond of his father, who always "came through" when he needed something. When in desperation he would telephone his dad and the man would come. (I met Mr. Cardel, a very masculine yet nurturing type, who drove to Buffalo from New Jersey repeatedly to calm his son. In fact, he seemed somewhat overprotective.) When all else failed in Tom's manipulations, he threatened suicide.

Tom made a number of appointments with me. Some he kept and others he did not. There were times when he suddenly appeared at odd hours and insisted on being seen no matter who else was scheduled.

Tom had a number of guns in his apartment. This came to the attention of his probation officer and they were removed. His probation was increased. He then decided to violate probation. He was mandated to jail for a period of 6 months. When he was discharged he appeared in my office with an ankle bracelet looking very haggard and distressed. He told me that he had also spent time in the hospital, had a serious physical illness, and had very little to eat, allegedly on a strict diet. He lived mostly on PowerBars. He had diverticulitis and had had several surgeries on his gastrointestinal tract. He had lost considerable weight and had difficulty with the "ankle bracelet leg."

Tom is a man who never became an adult. He is manipulative, uses denial in his dealings with people, vacillates between anger and depression, projects his feelings onto others, and has difficulty assuming responsibilities. He uses alcohol and other drugs to temporarily escape his problems and is suffering severely from the consequences.

Jason Clump

Jason Clump, a 58-year-old laborer, has held his job for 10 years. He is heavyset with a rotund midsection, or "beer belly." His chubby face is graced with a large rosy nose, which appears as if it had been glued together by countless small pieces of flesh. He has sparse white hair and looks closer to 70 than his actual age.

Jason is the second of five children; he has one brother and three sisters. His parents divorced when he was 9. His father was married four times and somehow could not get along with any of the women with whom he attempted to share his existence. His father was an alcoholic, as are two of Jason's sisters. His father stopped drinking a number of years before his death. His mother remarried, and Jason felt more warmly toward the stepfather than toward his dad. The latter was a difficult person with whom to share a good relationship. Jason has one 31-year-old unmarried daughter and three grandchildren. His only child is very needy and he helps her when he is able. Jason works very hard doing manual labor, and his time is too sparse for him to do much else. At the end of the day he would drink to relax and feel a degree of tranquility. The aftermath of his drinking bouts was not the most pleasant, but he adjusted to his feelings. His wife was an alcoholic as well as a user of narcotic/mind-altering drugs. He divorced her 8 years ago.

Jason was in the service on an aircraft carrier for 3 years. Afterward he moved to Florida and also for a stretch to Texas. He returned to Buffalo and its environs because he wanted to be near his daughter and his family.

His drinking history is a long one. He is proud of himself because he has been sober for a few days now. He confessed that he was sober for a few years when he was younger but then reverted back to vodka, mixed drinks, wine, and beer. He would drink mostly beer. He would consume a six-pack followed by a bottle of whiskey or vodka. He insisted that it relaxed him after a heavy day of work or on weekends when he was away from his job. He alleged that at one time he was sober for 9 years. He thought it would make a difference with his family. Unfortunately, it did not, and he has many urges that are extremely difficult to control. During these times he visits with his neighbors and his housemate (an alcoholic male in sobriety). He rented a portion of the house from him because this person shares Jason's dilemma with alcohol. He also deals with his daughter and grandchildren during periods of sobriety. He has warm feelings toward them and does not want them to become addicted. His grandchildren are 10 and 11. The oldest is a girl, and according to Jason, she seems to understand some of his difficulties. She reminds him not to drink.

Jason has been to court twice and has another court session scheduled within a month. He has been given a temporary license so that he is able to drive to and from work. He also has an appointment with a probation officer and will be on probation for the next 5 years. He is quite uneasy about this edict and wonders how he can handle these sessions. He has so little time now and he wonders what his employer will say or do knowing that he will need time to satisfy the many responsibilities that are expected of him. In addition, he will need to meet his sessions with his alcohol/drug counselor over a number of months.

It has been found that, while individuals are on probation, they are much more likely to remain in sobriety than they would be otherwise.

Patrick Condrell

Patrick Condrell is a 59-year-old Caucasian male who came to the office in desperation because he had been sent by his employer, a well-known airline, after reports of lewd behavior while working. He is very frightened that he will lose his lifestyle together with his job as an airline attendant.

Patrick has worked for High Up Airlines (not actual name to protect the company) for more than 35 years as a flight attendant. He is very concerned because he likes his position, the folks with whom he works, and the work atmosphere. He likes seeing different parts of the world, meeting interesting passengers, hearing the sound of foreign languages, and the relative freedom that is part of his profession. It freed him from what he considered the rigid humdrum aspect of everyday home life and the sameness that came with that lifestyle.

We must look at this man's history to understand the situation that threatened his livelihood, his lifestyle, and his identity. Patrick was born in the United States to a strict German mother and an Italian father. The father was an obese, emotionally challenged, well-educated professional man who did not spare the rod, especially when he had too much to drink. His outbursts occurred frequently. He was deeply depressed much of the time. There had been little joy in the father's life since he was raised in an orphanage, both of his parents having died at an early age.

Patrick is the youngest of nine children; he has six brothers and two sisters. He tried a number of jobs after dropping out of high school. He began drinking during his teens; his friends also enjoyed alcohol and life seemed not as complicated to Pat when he could enjoy some "relaxation" with his age mates.

After trying a number of minor jobs, he found his place in the working world. He was able to land a position with High Up Airlines, where he first worked in the "yard," the landing place where airplanes arrived and departed. He enjoyed seeing them soar into the air with relative ease and longed to be included in the rides. He did not object to any of the menial work that had to be done, like cleaning planes, lifting luggage off and on, and much more. He got along with his peers and was fairly comfortable. In time and with effort he applied for a position as an attendant for High Up. He learned rather fast to please the passengers, met whatever needs they had, made their flight as pleasant and as comfortable as possible, and felt good just being in the "clouds" looking at the world in a different fashion, "from up high." He was able to rub elbows with the "best of men" and others who were not so fortunate. Wherever they landed he found new places to see and new situations to encounter. He also learned that he had time to relax and enjoy himself whenever he arrived at a destination. He would join his "crew" (fellow employees), have "both feet on the ground again," have a few drinks, and forget whatever troubled him at home. (He had married when he was 30 years of age and became the father of three children.) His job allowed him to depend on his wife to take care of his offspring, and he rarely had to get involved in their daily upbringing. His wife was able to rely on him to financially support their children. She understood his situation and accepted the fact that his job demanded his absence from home because of the schedule he had to keep.

As time passed, his alcohol consumption appeared to increase. He saw nothing wrong with this until the episode that brought him to the therapist's office and, prior to that, a 30-day stay in an alcohol/drug treatment center. His flight had landed in Antwerp. He and the airline crew were given rooms in a very comfortable hotel. The restaurant and bar in the place was well furnished and elegant. The crew of High Up was treated with deference. Patrick had a drink or two with his dinner and then went to the bar and "drank a few more." He could not recall just how much alcohol he consumed that first night after landing. He apparently became rude to the manager of the restaurant and bar. He was either too inebriated or unable to reach the lavatory, so he relieved himself in the restaurant/bar. He showed no remorse at the time, was crude in his language, and was disruptive to the staff and guests of the establishment. It did not take long before he was reported to his employer and his official problems began. High Up felt strongly that his behavior had diminished the reputation of its business and damaged the good name of the airline.

It became obvious that Patrick had become an alcoholic over the years. Once he began his first alcoholic beverage, he could not control his urges and drank without cessation. He was able to forget his status, his behavior, and his concern for anyone around him. He could not recall specific details of episodes that brought him into the dilemma in which he found himself. His denial was obvious, and he frequently did not hold himself responsible for his actions. It can be readily assumed that there is much in this man's life that contributed to his alcoholism. His father was an alcoholic, a man who was emotionally ill; he had no healthy guidance from a strong healthy father figure; he dealt with others like himself in his youth who also consumed mind-altering substances. Patrick Condrell used alcohol as a medication, a panacea to temporarily forget his problems.

Randolph Crane

Twenty-four-year-old Randolph Crane came to the office for an alcohol/drug evaluation. The first time that he was scheduled he did not appear, and it was 4 weeks later that he insisted on making another appointment and agreed to pay the drug counselor/therapist a portion of the fee in advance.

Although he had been apprehended by the police twice in the last 2 years, he insisted that he is not an alcoholic and is able to control his consumption of beer or other mind-altering drinks anytime he desires. He further stated that he does not need treatment and demanded to know exactly what that "treatment" would be. He stated that he knows everything that any counselor can tell him about inebriation and that his background or current situation has nothing to do with the few "beverages" that he ingested in the past 2 years. He wanted credit because he had given "half of his liver" to his brother, who needed it because of a liver disease he had acquired "that had nothing to do with drinking." He also wanted to be recognized because he had allegedly spent 4 years in the U.S. Air Force.

Randolph revealed the following history. He was the son of a father he did not know. His mother gave him no other information. He has two brothers, both of whom are from different fathers. He liked the last male that his mother had in their home. He adopted the "stepfather's" name at age 13 and ultimately left his mother's home and joined the air force. He alleged that he had one year of college behind him but did not complete school because he needed to go to work to support himself. He rented a house together with a male friend, for his job and his debts did not enable him to pay all the costs of having a home of his own.

Randolph took no responsibility for his actions and insisted that he needs no treatment. He was angry because his friends were also drunk and he drove to "protect them." He uses denial and projection for his actions. He was angry because he had to hire an attorney when he had to appear in court. He also was hostile when he had to pay a relatively small sum to have an alcohol evaluation.

This young man believes he has been "cheated" by life. He has assured himself that he has given too much by being generous to his brother when a partial liver transplant was needed, devoting 4 years to the military, and sparing his mother by not insisting that she tell him about his father. He is unsure whether his mother was really married or how many men she may have married.

Randolph Crane feels cheated and has projected his actions and responsibilities, and lack thereof, on his surroundings. He reminds one of a child who screams out his anger and frustration in the hope of getting what he wants.

Constance Durham

Constance Durham is a 50-year-old well-dressed mother of two adult children who came to the office with an attorney friend who spoke on her behalf, insisting that she is a "good" woman and should be viewed with sympathy. He praised her and underscored all the interesting and good deeds and education (she has a bachelor's degree) she allegedly accomplished in her life. This gentleman himself had problems with drugs and was able to identify with her difficulties.

Constance seemed very frightened by the court hearings she still had to confront and what the outcome might be. In describing her difficulties, she began by stating that she is not an "ordinary" or frequent drinker. She had her last drink 2 weeks before she appeared in the therapist's/evaluator's office. Her first DUI was 6 years before the most recent one. She described what had occurred in the most recent episode: To her recollection she had enjoyed five glasses of wine and was feeling "good." She was a bit tired when on her way home she felt herself "clipping" into a guardrail. At that point she was not able to control her vehicle. It weaved back and forth, hitting the rocks and the rail with unbelievable speed. When the car finally stopped, the police came, and they asked her to take a Breathalyzer test. She was adamant in her refusal. Her reason was that she had been told by her attorney years ago that she was never to agree to be tested because it could incriminate her. It did not take long for the police officer to place her into handcuffs and direct her into his car. From there she was taken to the nearest police station, and her very much damaged vehicle was hauled into a repair station. She was housed in a cell overnight and was released after a friend posted bail for her.

Constance described her feelings as fear, embarrassed/shameful, helpless, and out of the ordinary. She wanted to run and hide but could not. She was faced with paying for court, the attorney's fee, tickets handed out by law enforcement officers, car repairs, and much more. She could not imagine how she would pay for all that. She worried about what her daughter and son would think of her, the poor role model she felt she was, and the unforeseen situations yet to occur. She worried about losing her driver's license and how she would be able to get to work without it.

The following history was given by Constance: She was raised by both parents until she was 15 years of age, when her alcoholic father died. She was married at 23 and was divorced 9 years later. During her marriage she and her husband had two offspring, a son and a daughter. (The son, now age 23, has many emotional problems, has not worked for several years, and is addicted to illicit drugs; the daughter does have a job and is the mother of a 2-year-old girl.) Constance has been able to support herself and has worked at a fairly adequate managerial political job for many years and is apparently well thought of by her employer.

Constance has had a significant other for some years since her divorce. The gentleman was a professional man who was an alcoholic. At this point in her life she is living alone. She works hard to sustain herself and to manage her expenses as well as help her offspring when she can. She has taken up cleaning houses for people in order to stretch her income to meet all of her expenses.

Constance is sincere when she speaks about making every effort to not repeat any of the episodes that brought her to where she is. She hopes that she will never get behind the wheel again with as little as one drink. Unfortunately, she is not convinced that she cannot ever have as little as one alcoholic drink again. She will be undergoing some outpatient treatment to help her with the problems she is facing. The treatment is mandated because she had two DUIs within the last 10 years. There is no absolute cure under the circumstances seen here. The ultimate solution has to come from Constance.

Linda Garner

Linda Garner is a beautiful, slim 39-year-old Caucasian woman who has held an important professional job in a medium-sized business. She came for an assessment and treatment after having been charged with two drinking and driving offenses. She had a high blood alcohol concentration (BAC) and her driver's license was taken after her second court hearing. Linda is suffering from depression. She lives with her mother, never having moved out. Her parents were divorced when she was 8, and her dad took very little interest in his daughter. There was also a son who was seen slightly more by the father. Linda felt worthless. She did not believe in her ability nor that there would be anything happy or exciting in her life. She attempted to drown her unhappiness with alcohol. She also suffered from bulimia and anorexia. She ate very little, and when she did, she would force out the food by vomiting. The only liquid she seemed to retain was alcohol. She came for a number of sessions in order to attempt to receive her driver's license. She drove without a license most of the time and was arrested and had to pay repeatedly for this. She felt deserted; she never had a permanent boyfriend or a marriage proposal in spite of her beautiful face and figure. It was not long before she became very ill and had to have surgery. She had a large growth removed from the side of her throat and her speech became difficult to understand. Her mother took care of her but became more and more discouraged and angry with Linda because somehow she managed to get alcohol into the house, hiding it in her bedroom. She also was on a leave of absence from her job because she was too ill to work. As time passed, Linda became weaker and seemed to drag her body into the office. She denied her excessive drinking and refused to take any responsibility for her actions. I pleaded with her to join an inpatient drug/alcoholism program because of the seriousness of her situation, but she was adamant in her refusal. She insisted she was returning to work because she did not want to lose her job. She began to detest the work assigned to her. She felt cheated, underplaced, and bored. Her employer insisted that she could not return to her job if she did not improve within a given time. Her mother drove her to my office, and Linda staggered up the few stairs; she appeared to be physically and mentally deteriorating. She was suffering from a malignancy, which according to her medical record came from poisoning her body with alcohol. With all of the other growths, her liver was also affected. She was placed on a waiting list to receive a healthy liver. She knew how ill she was, yet she could not control her consumption of alcohol. How she staggered to receive these mind- and body-altering beverages her mother did not know.

The last I saw of Linda she was rail thin; her speech was very weak, garbled and difficult to understand. She found no solace in life, although in her very weak voice she insisted that she wanted to get well. She was unable to give up her addiction at the cost of her life.

Johnson Kashalla

Johnson Kashalla is a 24-year-old sturdily built, tall, blond male who appeared very distressed and angry throughout our interview. He came because he had lost his driver's license after having had a fairly high BAC when tested with a Breathalyzer by the police. (He had six cans of beer and was inebriated while driving.) He alleged that he had been drinking early in the day and "it should not have been so high" (the typical denial). He was returning at night from an amusement park when he was apprehended. He used a very harsh vocabulary when he berated the law enforcement officer as he was relating his situation. He added, as he told his story, that 6 or 7 months ago he used marijuana but preferred the consumption of alcohol. He had been accused of illegal possession of a mind-altering substance when that "happened" to him. It was obvious throughout his drug evaluation session that he took little if any responsibility for his actions. At the time of the marijuana incident, he had been ordered to receive treatment from a drug treatment center where he felt falsely accused of various misdeeds. He did not complete the sessions assigned to him by that organization.

The following history was given by Johnson: His parents were divorced when he was 6 years of age. His father left their home and shortly after the separation he married another woman whom he labeled "stepmonster." He lived with his mother and missed his dad. He was very resentful of his life situation. He felt that he was robbed and cheated of his childhood. Allegedly much was expected of him. This feeling became stronger and more pronounced when his father had another son when Johnson was 9 years old. He insisted that his father and stepmonster spoiled their son, giving him everything he desired and nothing to him. He recited that Embry, that son, was given a cell phone and he was not. That boy had to do no chores like he had to do; he had no privileges and "next to nothing" whereas Embry had everything. His jealousy was so great that he began to despise his half brother. He insisted that the only one who would care for him or do anything for him was himself. He then spoke about having had a girlfriend whom he loved and with whom he hoped to have a permanent relationship. Things were going well when she moved out of town to attend college. They visited each other on weekends for many months. He felt they had a strong affection for one another; he loved her and there appeared to be reciprocity. One day he received a letter from her "out of an orange colored sky" in which she ended their bond. To date he still did not know what happened, and he was too distressed to ask her the reasons for her dismissal of him. This rejection was very difficult. It made him feel less of a person and that he did not deserve to be loved.

Johnson left his mother's house to attend college in Florida. He attended for 4 years and studied engineering, receiving his bachelor's degree at age 22. It was the profession he wanted. Returning home, he could not find a position in that field. He ultimately took a menial job with the help of his father. He did not like the labor he had to perform. His salary was too small to make a dent into the debt he had accrued while attending college. He did not see a way he could rid himself of that enormous obligation. In addition, he had moved in with his father when he returned from his college years. His stepmother disliked him and loved and protected Embry. "He got everything I never had," recited Johnson, naming all the toys, gadgets, and electronic devices Embry had, all denied to him. He became more and more resentful. At one time, after a year of sharing his dad's home, he was given an ultimatum to move out. He managed to make the deadline, which was less than a month from the time he had been asked to leave. It was in the proverbial last minute that he took his departure. Having no funds, he decided reluctantly to move back to his mother. (She had been married twice after leaving Johnson's father.)

Whenever Johnson felt unwanted or deprived, he would use alcohol or another mind-altering substance to make himself feel better. His reactions were infantile. He wanted to be taken care of without making much effort. He denies his part in the situations in which he finds himself. Only superficially does he recognize that he is an adult and must hold himself responsible for his actions.

Brendon McKormick

Brendon McKormick is a 36-year-old man who looks younger than his age. He has fairly long braided hair, which moved back and forth when he spoke to me, emphasizing his situation. He stated that he enjoyed a "beer now and then" and insisted that he no doubt "drank less" than most of his acquaintances. He was quite circumspect when he explained what had occurred the night that he was "picked up" by the police. He had enjoyed drinking since he was 17 and had only been apprehended once in the past 4 years. This time in September 2013, he had attended a football game with a "good friend" (James). The two men had a wonderful time and were able to relax and have a few drinks. They were driving on the New York State Thruway when Brendon had an accident. He did not know how this could have happened, and he attempted to hold the truck driver responsible for the accident. Brendon "ran into the back of a truck probably because the driver of that vehicle was driving too slow." Brendon insisted that he was driving the speed limit. He could not rationally explain how he came to that conclusion. When the sheriff came he found both vehicles severely damaged. The driver in the truck was hurt and had to be transported to the hospital. Brendon and James were injured; James had a leg and back injury and Brendon had severe pain in his neck, which apparently had been "jarred." In addition to all the damage done, the sheriff found marijuana in Brendon's vehicle. Brendon insisted that the drug was not his and must have been his friend's. (This is the usual excuse that the counselor has found to be used by folks who are drug users.)

His greatest worry was that his license would be taken and that he would lose a very responsible job that he had held for the past 4 years. He was also concerned because he is the father of a 10-year-old son, whose custodial parent is the mother and for whom he pays child support.

Looking at the history of this man we found the following: His parents were separated when he was 5 years of age. He lived with his mother and began living with dad part-time, beginning at age 15. The father was a "fairly heavy drinker," and the boy saw nothing wrong when he began using alcohol himself in his teens. He had a car accident at age 17 and his license was revoked. It took 4 years for his license to be reinstated. He was at that time ordered to have counseling.

It was some time after that when he began drinking alcohol again. His friends for the most part were social drinkers, and he found that he was more "relaxed" when he joined them and did not abstain.

Brendon intellectually knows that he cannot stop drinking when he has one drink. It is questionable whether he will be able to permanently refrain from that first glass of alcohol. Experience has taught that it is a very difficult and long road to desist when addiction to drugs or alcohol are to be permanently overcome.

Molly Mentor

Molly Mentor was sent to her therapist by her psychiatrist. She is an attractive, blue-eyed, 58-year-old twice-divorced woman diagnosed with bipolar illness in addition to alcoholism. Her history is that of an only girl in a family of six children of whom she was the youngest. Her parents were always good to her as were her brothers. She was somewhat spoiled by her family and as a young girl felt good about herself.

She attended college and became a representative of a large firm where she excelled at selling products at a wholesale level. She was very much appreciated by her company and won a number of prizes for her excellence in her position. She dealt mostly with men, and she invited them to lunches where drinks were consumed by her customers. Eventually, she joined them, enjoying some alcoholic beverages. She moved away from the town of her birth and represented her company on the West Coast. She worked long hours, traveling to many places, often with her car. It was out West where she met her second husband, a professional man, who worked for himself (although she earned more than he). They had enough income that they were able to purchase a beautiful home and also take vacations together. Jim and she were married for 17 years when problems progressed to the point that the marriage ended. They had no children. Jim could not tolerate Molly's domination and the demands she made of him; she was constantly tired and had very little time for her spouse. She alleged that it was a shock when he presented her with divorce papers.

The pressure she felt became more and more intense, until she drank so much and was so distressed that she had to sell their home, giving more than half of the proceeds to her erstwhile spouse, and resign her very lucrative job. She called her aging parents to inform them of her dilemma. She needed to return home to her mother and father. They sent one of her brothers to help her pack up whatever she wanted to take.

When she returned, she felt like a little girl who could do very little to help herself. She drank more and more in the room where she had grown up. She brought her dog with her, which seemed to be very important to her. She said he would love her and not bite her. Also, he did not care whether she drank. She sneaked alcoholic beverages into her parental home and was able to forget her failures for hours at a time.

Eventually, she found a 63-year-old man, Thomas, who dated her for a time. Thomas had married someone on the "spur of the moment" but annulled the situation after a few days. He made a date with Molly after this episode. He was very judgmental about her attending A.A. meetings and was very critical of her. In between meetings she drank and could not control her urges for too many weeks at a time.

It was Sweetest Day and Thomas made a date with her for that occasion. He did not appear at his summer home where they were to meet. She had the key to the place. After waiting for hours with no sight of Tom, she tore the pictures of his adult children off the wall, cut the pillows on his couch, threw objects all over the place, and in a seriously angry mood found a bottle of wine and drank it to the proverbial last drop. In that inebriated condition she drove 40 miles back to her parental home.

She heard from Thomas two days later. He had discovered what she had done. He threatened to report her to the police, and for a time she was frightened, hiding and walking around in a daze. Ultimately, he did not have her arrested, but his good feelings for her were gone. It took much persuasion and pleading to eventually deal with her again. She sent him text messages, and he was in touch with her by phone occasionally.

Molly had attended an inpatient alcohol recovery center for 30 days. It helped for 3 months, but ultimately she continued her addiction. On and off, she would hide bottles of wine under her bed. She would lock her door to avoid the discovery of bottles in her room by her mother. Her folks treated her well, and they were as supportive as they could be under the circumstances.

Molly does attend A.A. meetings as regularly as she is able. She has some friends in the women's groups she attends. She likes to take an occasional class in subjects that are appealing to her, like drama or play interpretations. She had a sponsor who died, which left her unhappy for a time. With encouragement, she found another alcoholic in sobriety who is somewhat helpful to her. She also visits a psychiatrist for medication. She has occasional anxiety attacks. She also occasionally texts Thomas, who gives her unsolicited advice. Occasionally, she becomes angry with a friend who is more fortunate in her relationships with men than she is. She likes to travel, but at this time she is unable to afford this luxury.

Molly enumerated many fears for this therapist: being abandoned and unloved, losing her parents, being deathly ill, being in severe physical or psychic pain, being without medical insurance, becoming severely depressed, having no money, being seen without clothing, a possible STD (sexually transmitted disease), blindness and/or being incapacitated.

Molly frequently views herself with disdain. She is angry with herself and her circumstances and fluctuates between anger and depression. When angry she sometimes lashes out at her acquaintances. She does not want to be minimized, which is understandable.

She is encouraged by her therapist, her psychiatrist, and the group to which she belongs to attend A.A. meetings on a daily basis, to use her medication as prescribed, and if at all possible to get involved in something worthwhile that will bring her some satisfaction.

Helen Pamisrock

Helen Pamisrock, a 38-year-old woman, needed counseling from the therapist in order to have her license reinstated. Her history was a very complicated one, as was her education. There were multiple contradictions in this woman's life. Her large, expressive eyes conveyed a tragedy; she presented a femininity to which her muscular arms and large bosom were a contradiction, mingling feminine and masculine features in one body. Helen was the daughter of a heavy-drinking Polish American factory laborer and a kind, hardworking mother who had given birth to two daughters. The couple had separated when the two girls were in their late teens. Anna, her sister, became a law enforcement officer and died in a vehicular accident. Anna had been divorced after a brief marriage. She was very serious about her work and enjoyed being a cop. There was a question about the night of her death as to whether she might have had some alcohol in her system when the deadly accident took place. Helen loved her sister and wept when describing her beloved Anna. The two sisters had been such good friends and gave each other strength and understanding. Helen always got along well with her grieving mother, who died a few years after Anna. In the interim, Helen spent time after work comforting her mother, while her own grief was difficult to handle.

Helen graduated with a police science degree from the local college and was excited to be a cop as her sister had been. It was shortly after she graduated that she was apprehended while driving and given a Breathalyzer test. It showed that she had a high alcohol level in her system. This was the end of her dream for a law enforcement career. She knew she had to work to support herself (even when in college she worked nights in a bar as a waitress) and succeeded in obtaining a job in a factory. She was an excellent employee, not afraid of the heavy and often dangerous factory work assigned to her. There were many chemicals in the factory, which created some unhealthy conditions. Heavy precautions had to be taken, with special uniforms needed to protect the body as much as possible. The wages were adequate, and eventually Helen was able to purchase a home of her own in an attractive suburb not too distant from the factory in which she was employed. She frequently worked nights because her job was a 24-hour operation, and shift work was needed. At times, she was happy to take the night assignments because the pay was higher. She dated while in college as much as she could. There was not much opportunity because she was always busy, and with her part-time evening job and the demands of her studies, she had little time for pleasure. She worked mostly with men in the factory. They were engaging, mostly uneducated males, who became her buddies rather than her dates. The majority of them were married or had girlfriends. She would, when possible, have a beer with them after work, but her relationships were limited. She was liked by her coworkers, and they could complain about various work situations to one another. She worked steadily and responsibly for many years in her job. Her drinking increased, and she was apprehended several times for intoxication. Never, however, was she inebriated while at work. After her mother's death she felt totally alone. Her father had predeceased her mother, and her closeness was with her mom. She felt abandoned, worked long tedious hours, and made a few friends, all of whom had some serious problems. These folks frequently used Helen for favors, for a loan of money here and there. One of these friends borrowed a considerable sum, which she never repaid. Therapy did help her to become a bit stronger in not allowing herself to be exploited.

In the beginning of her contact with the drug/alcohol counselor, she hid the fact of her alcoholism. She continued to imbibe. She was able to suppress her loneliness, her failures, the fact that she could not join the police force, the loss of her beloved sister, and her superficial relationship with her late father and the negative influence he had been as a flawed role model. Sometimes she added some antidepressant drugs to her drinking binges in order to sleep better, until she was incarcerated for a few days. This was the signal to attempt to stop. This was when she realized that her job would be in jeopardy if she continued; she would be penniless and helpless. She pictured herself becoming a ward of the welfare system, sitting on stones outside of stores and begging. The change began. She was urged to regularly attend not only her therapy/counseling sessions but also A.A. meetings. Together with these assignments, she slowly suppressed her addiction and depression. For Helen, alcohol had become a poison, which hampered all that she needed to do to make her life more worthwhile. She experienced some happy and some very sad times over the course of her years. She found a man whom she had met years before and he became her significant other. He was divorced with two adult offspring. He had lost his job in another state and returned to the city in which he was born and raised. He eventually moved into Helen's home with her. She was very much in love with him. She supported him and was not only his girlfriend, but she also mothered him. She managed to help him. She read newspaper advertisements, sorted out possible positions on her computer, and did all she could to get him what he needed. The result was that he obtained a position in his field of interest in a southern state. After he left his home town, he regularly visited Helen; they vacationed together, and she found much comfort and solace that she was not alone and had found someone who cared for her. While he was unemployed she paid for his vacation, giving of herself and her material goods. She could not believe her good fortune.

Several years had passed when Helen came into the office of her therapist/counselor, weeping uncontrollably. Her beloved mate had sent her a letter declaring that he wanted to remain friends rather than continuing to be her permanent boyfriend/lover. She was almost inconsolable. She could not understand that he was apparently an exploiter who brutally was able to abandon the person who had hoped and planned to spend her life with him. They had spoken about moving in together permanently after they both retired. Her dream, her future, seemed to have disappeared with his rejection of her. Helen thought about drinking again to wash away the hurt and humiliation caused by the man she loved so deeply. While grieving, she found herself less careful in accomplishing her tasks safely. She took little care of herself. One night, while working in the factory, she found her hand caught in a dangerous machine, and she lost a part of one of her fingers. Psychologically speaking, she had been cut off by the most important person in her life, and she had now cut off a part of her hand. She learned that she had to take care of herself before she could take care of others. Fortunately, she was able to stop herself from using alcohol or drugs to make herself happy. She was convinced that alcohol would destroy her life. Her addiction had to stop. She had to consciously avoid any intake of alcohol and street drugs. She had the ability to heal herself and knew what she had to do when she felt desperate after work. When yearning for relief from the plague that she felt, after a difficult day at work she could heal herself and knew what she needed to do. She could go to bed, turn on a meaningless television program, and manage to sleep. She continued with A.A. meetings, reconnected with one or two long-time acquaintances, and talked about her misery with them or her counselor. She can be a very gregarious human being who is realistic about her work and essential tasks. She does occasionally visit a casino where she spends a few dollars, which gives her some joy. She is bright enough to designate a sum of money that she can afford without depriving herself. She also learned to rid herself of one friend who was a divorced exploiter she had known for years. She began to like herself more and took yearly vacations to places that she had always wanted to see. Instead of distributing her funds for alcohol, she became a better friend to herself and took care of her own healthy needs first. She also had a dog that she enjoyed. She was very caring to him, and he was very responsive to her, sitting by her side whenever she was not working. She took the animal for walks and made friends with her next-door neighbors. These folks helped her, and she reciprocated so that there was no exploitation.

Helen attends A.A. meetings on a regular basis and has been sober for 10 years at the time of this writing. She has become a presenter and leader to many addicted drug/alcohol members. She visits her therapist/counselor on a monthly basis and when she feels needy or depressed or when she needs some positive reinforcement in her sobriety. She is doing well. We cannot predict the future, but at this time we are optimistic that her life will continue to be a satisfactory one.

Robert Peterson

Robert Peterson came to the office for an alcohol evaluation. He is a tall 24-year-old, who was rather belligerent and insisted that the only reason he was "forced" into this was because anyone connected with law enforcement and alcohol merely wants to "make money" from "innocent" people. He stated that most police, lawyers, and others drink also, but they are never apprehended. With much bitterness and anger he told of the following situation: He was allegedly found unconscious in his car. The police officer had great difficulty arousing him. He was unaware that he had created any problem for anyone. After much questioning, he stated that he and his 22-year-old brother had celebrated his move to an independent apartment (he had lived with his mother and brother until that day).

Robert insisted that this was the only DUI he had ever received. "I was not aware that I had been charged." He contradicted himself as he gave me the condition and the situation in which he found himself. Although he had fallen asleep in his vehicle, he talked about being "unconscious" sometimes; at other times he changed his label for the inebriated state in which he was discovered. He insisted that he does not understand why others are not "picked up"; it must be because they know "someone." He also insisted that "everyone" drinks. He was almost paranoid in stating that he was the one chosen to be found and convicted. When he was asked to take a Breathalyzer test at the scene, he refused. (This is frequently the case when the person apprehended has too much to drink and realizes that the alcohol level in his or her body would be high. Those who truly had only one or two drinks were more likely to agree to take the test requested.)

In examining his history, it was found that his mother had him and his brother with the same man. The father and mother of these two sons were never married to one another. In his culture he acknowledged that this was not unique. He rarely saw his dad because the parents were separated from one another. The mother was the breadwinner and his relationship with her was a "casual" one. In the household in which he grew up, the mom was the caregiver. According to Robert, his mother rarely drank, and he insisted that he never saw her have more than a glass of wine on special occasions. His brother, however, enjoyed beer more often than Robert.

Robert had a number of temporary positions; the last was a machinist in a factory. He complained about the long hours and believed that he should have a less strenuous type of work. From the situation in which this gentleman finds himself, it is apparent that he needs to have treatment for his problem. He has to recognize that he has to be responsible for his actions and also have the conviction that no one forced him to drive while intoxicated.

If he continues to hold others responsible for his situation, he will not change his beliefs or behaviors. He will continue to drive without a license until he is discovered in one fashion or another. If he is found to be inebriated at that time, his second conviction will cost him a considerable sum of money, which he does not possess, and in addition, the possibility exists that he will be incarcerated.

Donald Pilczarski

Donald Pilczarski is 28-year-old tall, slender Caucasian male, a father of four. His oldest is a 9-year-old girl he sired with Rosa, one of his first "serious" girlfriends. The other three children, two girls and one 2-year-old boy, are from his most recent significant other, Becky. He lived with this young woman for the past 4 years, but they never got along. They fought daily. He worked repairing, painting, and whatever odd job was necessary in a garage. Becky was a waitress. She served alcoholic beverages five nights a week. Donald exclaimed that he doesn't understand what she was "bitching" about because she had it so good. "We both drank and got angry at the children because they wanted too much and wouldn't leave us alone. I'd give them a swat on the butt and that helped sometimes to shut them up. Becky, that bitch, never stuck up for me, and I got in trouble at work and that pig that worked next to me always thought he knew it all. One day I let him have it and I beat the tar out of him, so he needed to go to the hospital. It was then that the boss fired me. That rat, George, should have gotten canned, not me. He was such a busybody, grumbling all the time. Because of him, I spent 6 months in jail. Becky don't leave me alone; she's always bitching about something; she always wants money, which I ain't got!"

Donald had a very high BAC, as well as four DUI infractions during the last 10 years. He had totaled his last car, which he could not replace because of lack of income. In addition, he had no license. He was willing to do whatever work was available as long as it was in walking distance or a friend or colleague would be willing to drive him. He did find a few small jobs, but he was unable to support his children or himself. Both Becky and he continued to drink, spending whatever time they had "drinking away" their self-induced misfortune.

Donald's hardworking mother was very protective of her derelict son, gave him whatever she could, and helped with food for the three younger children. The 9-year-old girl was raised and supported by her mother, and Donald took next to no responsibility for her existence. When he was under the influence of alcohol, he would sometimes beat Becky and she would retaliate, beating him with objects as best she could. The three children would frequently be the audience for the abuse the couple meted out to one another. They were often frightened and would hide as best as they were able. The 2-year-old son would cry. The fights would most generally occur with the intake of alcohol in various proportions.

Donald was irresponsible as far as attending his treatment/counseling sessions. The welfare department covered the costs so that the bills were not assigned to him. He would come when he pleased, would appear when the spirit moved him, and at other times would be late or absent. He wanted his license back but was unwilling to make the sacrifices necessary. He was angry at his partner Becky, at his children, and at people randomly.

Donald's father was an alcoholic and moved in and out of his wife's household until he recently died. Donald and his brothers saw very little of him, and when they did, he was frequently inebriated, with slurred speech or lying asleep on the couch of the family living room, oblivious to his surroundings.

Donald and his brothers would fight with one another physically with rarely anyone stepping in to stop them because their mom was working in a factory as many hours as she could possibly receive. There was no healthy discipline in that house.

Ultimately, Becky moved out of their shared abode and Donald took temporary positions and private jobs that could not be recognized by the IRS. In addition, he received some governmental funds to help him in supporting the three offspring. Becky moved into the house of a divorced man and his children. She met this man in the bar at which she was a waitress. This gentleman had problems with his separated spouse and was attempting to save some money so that he would be able to file for divorce. He was a hardworking factory worker, was forced to send funds to his separated wife, and spent his spare time in this particular bar after work.

Neither Donald nor Becky held themselves responsible for the poverty, unhappiness, and mayhem they had caused. Both of them are alcoholics, their children are troubled, and the future for Donald is guarded.

Madonna Ringer

Madonna Ringer is a 48-year-old woman who was raised by her mother in a lower-middle-class home. Her parents divorced when she was 5 years of age. Madonna was the fourth of eight children. Her father visited with her on rare occasions but exhibited very little interest in her. Her parents were hardworking people. Her father was a bricklayer who died at age 60. Both of her parents drank alcohol with their meals. Her mother worked as an office clerk when her offspring were all in school. Madonna never felt special or important. At 17 she became pregnant and gave birth to a son. She gave him up for adoption shortly after he was born. She did manage to graduate from high school and then joined the service. She was in the U.S. Army and U.S. Air Force for a total of 28 years. While in the air force, she met her husband. Like her mother, she divorced him. Her marriage lasted only 6 years. He enjoyed drinking when off duty, and although she enjoyed a drink "now and then," she did not consider herself to be an alcoholic. She was self-supporting when she was married and always valued her independence.

As she became older her drinking increased, and she was picked up by law enforcement officers four times, accumulating four drinking and driving charges. She was never incarcerated and did not consider herself to be suffering from alcoholism. When she was 45 years of age she became very ill, but she did not believe that her consumption of alcohol had anything to do with her condition. She had breast cancer and faced a mastectomy, which caused her to suffer from a deep depression. It was not long after her diagnosis that she had the necessary surgery, which left her with one breast. She was convinced that she was no longer the feminine person she used to be. Following this, she attempted to anesthetize herself by drinking more on a daily basis. She had at one time been in inpatient therapy at a veterans hospital and was able to maintain sobriety for a considerable time. She was given chemotherapy to prevent further damage to her body. She was very depressed, feeling that she was at "death's door." She felt weak and helpless and out of control. She stopped drinking for stretches of time, but as the examinations became more frequent and there was a suspicion that her cancer had spread, she drank more and more to suppress the horrors of what she would have to face. The consumption of alcohol suppressed her fright, and she was in alcoholic stupors frequently. She verbalized that nothing mattered anymore and that she does not want to think of her future.

It is difficult to know whether Madonna's disease was brought on because of her excessive alcohol consumption or whether the increase in drinking was caused by the oncoming cancer developing in her body. It is true that the severe pain due to her illness created the situation in which she drank more to anesthetize herself against the agony she suffered.

Johann Ripe

Johann Ripe is a very slim, medium-height Caucasian male who came to the therapist's office with a slip of paper stating that he had been in a substance abuse inpatient therapy treatment program for 28 days at the veterans hospital 2 years ago in 2012. In examining his record, he had two convictions in the past 4 years. In the first, he had a BAC of .20 and the last one indicated a .16. He insisted that he had merely "a couple of drinks" each time. When he was repeatedly informed that he had 10 alcoholic beverages the first time and eight in the most recent situation, he insisted the Breathalyzer was "darn wrong."

He was the illegitimate son of his mother, who left him soon after he was born to be raised by his maternal grandmother. Occasionally, the mom would drop in from another town where she had obtained a menial job and had a boyfriend. She was a high school dropout and at age 16 gave birth to Johann. He was named after an erstwhile boyfriend. When Johann was in his teens he met his putative father, and he learned that this man had two brothers who were alcoholics.

Johann described himself as a feisty little boy who liked fighting with other children while playing with them. When he began school he was restless; he felt different from the other students. He disliked sitting for hours and was sometimes sent to the principal's office in order to not interrupt the teacher. He disliked school and preferred being outdoors whenever possible. He loved his grandmother and explained that he became inebriated when she died, which was 4 years ago. The second time that he was apprehended by law enforcement officers was 2 years ago, when his wife divorced him and he drank himself into unconsciousness.

He signed up for the army when he was barely 18 years of age. His life seemed to change then. He was in the service for 5 years and eventually became a staff sergeant. He stated he was traumatized in Iraq, where he was allegedly exposed to nerve gas. He was terrified of dying. He was 23 when he left the army. He suffered from post-traumatic stress syndrome. After the service he married and had two sons. The older son, almost 9, is autistic; his 6-year-old is within normal limits. He described his life as a very difficult one and hopes to raise his children to have a better life. He is currently the "daddy/mom." His "wife" is pregnant with a third child. Two years ago, his wife divorced him because he was "a different man" than when she married him. The night he learned of the divorce he became inebriated. He could not remember much because he was unconscious after running into a telephone pole and being hospitalized. He already had a leg injury in the service, which became worse after the accident. When he awoke in the hospital, he was informed that he could no longer drive; his license was revoked, and he was eventually an inpatient in the alcoholism division of the veterans hospital. He insisted that he has had no alcohol for the past 2 years. Eventually, his divorced spouse agreed to have him live with her again. She has not officially remarried him as yet. He has recently been awarded full-time compensation from the Veterans Administration and no longer has to work. His significant other (his divorced wife) and he have an excellent income because she works full time and has a very adequate job. He takes care of the household as well as the children.

He came to the therapist in order to receive his driver's license. He feels helpless and somewhat emasculated because his wife has to drive whenever he has to go anywhere. It came to the forefront now that he is accompanying her to take an examination in the state of Washington where she took courses toward her master's degree. She is in her eighth month of pregnancy and has to be the driver.

In summarizing his situation, we see a person who had an insecure childhood. His mother in essence abandoned him, and he was raised by his grandmother. He disliked school and was fidgety without a stable role model. He had two paternal uncles who were alcoholic. Alcohol enabled Johann to forget his problems for a short time. He used denial in talking about his inebriation. For this man, alcohol was an anesthetic for which he paid a heavy price.

Franklin Simsio

Franklin Simsio, a 43-year-old, handsome, masculine-looking, tall male, came to my office for an alcohol/drug evaluation and treatment. He was sent by his employer after he had been accused of "grazing" a tenant's car and cursing the woman when she rightfully accused him of the deed. He maintained the landscaping and janitorial duties for a fairly large housing complex. The woman reported him and claimed he appeared inebriated. When confronted the next day, he denied the allegation. Ultimately, he was placed on probation for 3 years.

Franklin told me that he enjoys "a drink or two." He met his most recent girlfriend in a bar, as he had several others previously. He likes the sociability in bars where he feels happy and surrounded by others like himself. He told me he enjoys watching sports, whether football or baseball, and he finds folks who are also interested in sitting on a bar stool while the games are on.

Franklin never married; he has no children. His parents were divorced when he was 7 years of age. His mother raised him, but he occasionally saw his father, who seemed to be working "all the time." He has a brother who lives on disability payments (he could not tell me his brother's illness or injury, or if he has either). His sister has an important job in Colorado. She is a college graduate with a master's degree and is in a "high position" for the government. His father "enjoyed his drinks," but Franklin did not consider him an alcoholic because he was able to work. The dad was unfaithful to his mother and eventually married one of the women with whom he had a sexual relationship. He seemed to have no regrets.

His mother is a registered nurse and has made an adequate living. He feels close to his mother and visits her at least once or twice a week, and he has a meal with her when possible.

Franklin told me about his most recent girlfriend and how sad he was because she suddenly committed suicide approximately 6 months ago, after she had broken up with him. She too enjoyed "a little drinking," but he did not specify how much. He stated that she wanted to marry him, but he assured her that he is not the "marrying kind." He was the baby of the family and likes his independence. He confided to me that he does not trust women. (That in spite of the fact that his mother was not unfaithful in her marriage. His father was the irresponsible one.) Franklin does not enjoy his job because it is physically straining, manual labor. He would have liked to do better but did not want to attend school past high school. He was interested in becoming a cop, but he had no interest in any other trade or occupation. For reasons unknown he did not pursue taking the necessary courses to enable him to join the police force. He did travel to other states where he worked whatever jobs were available, ultimately returning to Buffalo where his mother lives. Eventually, he accepted whatever job was available, one that did not demand a higher education. He found when he became older that many of his single friends were no longer available because they had either married or were "tied up" with someone or other. He enjoyed the camaraderie of people whom he felt had something in common with him.

Franklin informed me that when he was in his mid-to-older teen years he did smoke marijuana and tried cocaine. He insisted that these so-called adventures lasted only until he was in his early 20s, at which time he "only" enjoyed drinking "sometimes."

To date, Franklin has been able to control his drinking. He is on probation and being tested randomly, as well as receiving therapy regularly. There is no guarantee that Franklin will permanently abstain from mind-altering substances.

Gordon Slender

Gordon Slender is a 40-year-old male who appears much older. He is 5 feet 6 inches tall and weighs over 300 pounds. He was very frank in revealing his situation. He is an alcoholic who consumes at least three or four shots of whiskey per evening. Until 4 months ago he lived with his partner Nancy and their two daughters, ages 2 and 4. He needed an alcohol/drug evaluation demanded by the court in order to have unsupervised visitation rights with his offspring. He had a court order to stay away from his home and family. He has paid full child support and has not deprived his children or Nancy of the home, for which he paid the largest share of the monthly cost. (Nancy has a well-paying job.) He felt abused by Nancy, and when she became physically aggressive toward him, he defended himself by pushing her away. He had taken much verbal abuse from her on a daily basis. She also had an occasional drink but allegedly never drank to excess.

He was the only child of a doting mother and an alcoholic father. His parents were separated when he was quite young. He felt very close to his mother and at this time is living with her (he cannot afford rent and to pay for the house in which his children now live). He stated that Nancy has mood swings and took pride in denigrating his mother whenever she attacked him. This woman took him to court. From there he was referred for the evaluation.

Gordon never had a DUI. In fact, he has a commercial driver's license, which he is able to use in his job where he has worked for the past 16 years. He has never been absent because of inebriation, nor been in jail for anything having to do with alcohol.

Gordon bitterly resents that he can only see his children under supervision of Nancy's mother. He suggested that his mother be permitted to be the supervisor, but this was rejected because she would "defend" him if he were not behaving in an "orderly fashion." He insisted that he never hit or abused his children in any way. According to his explanation, he insisted that they were in bed at night when he drank.

Without a doubt Gordon is an alcoholic. He craves drinking and feels he has no control over his urges. He is able to wait until evening to imbibe in his compulsion and satisfy his urges. When intoxicated, he can for a very brief time put his grievances aside and even sleep. He has been able to control the times that he drinks. He drinks alone. It is not friendship or the bar scene that creates his nightly binges. He is able to work and is sober from early in the morning until the evening. He exhibits all the habits, signals, and personality of an alcoholic: His father was an alcoholic; Gordon had a poor role model; he was introduced to mind-altering substances at an early age; he had little self-confidence; he had parents who did not get along with one another; he "teamed up" with an abusive woman; by his own admission he stated that he was in denial for many years; earlier in life he had a few drinking buddies; he had a difficult time relating to "normal" folk.

Gordon is suffering from a liver problem, which is getting progressively worse. There is little chance he will improve if he continues drinking. He has little money, is in debt, and pays child support. If he were in a financially good position, he could spend 30 to 90 days in an inpatient treatment center with strict follow-up and daily or weekly outpatient treatment sessions including group sessions like A.A. meetings. Such suggestions may be a panacea for someone as accustomed to his mode of life without much possible reward for his recovery.

Nina Solder

Nina Solder is a short, slim, average-appearing young woman with a glittering diamond in the right side of her nose, another small round metal object implanted in her tongue, and a bright smile as she came to the therapist's office for a drug/alcohol evaluation. She was apprehended by the police at three in the morning after coming out of a bar where she had worked the last 8 hours. She was 22 years of age and had been joking and drinking with one of her customers who had bought her "a few drinks." She could not really remember how much wine she had consumed. She was taken to the nearest police station and kept in a cell overnight. It was the second time that she had been apprehended since she was 21 years of age. She never felt "drunk," just more "loose as a goose," as she described it.

Nina was raised by a mother and stepfather. She did not know her natural father until she was 10 years of age when she had supervised visitation with him. She learned that he had been a fairly heavy drinker and that her mother had kept her daughter away from this man because of his behavior, which included too much consumption of alcohol. When she was 11 years of age, the visitations with her father stopped because he moved to Florida. They called and wrote letters back and forth, and Nina believed that she "really" got to know him. Once or twice during the next few years he came to see her in western New York. Unfortunately for Nina, he died last year at a relatively young age. She was unsure whether he died because of an accident, his addiction to alcohol or drugs, or a serious undefined illness. She felt sad because she always believed she could be a "daddy's girl." She missed not having a father-daughter relationship as she pictured it. Although she had a very good stepfather, she insisted she loved her putative father more. She told me that her father became angry with her when she called to inform him that she gave birth to an infant daughter. He hardly dealt with her after that.

With a great deal of effort and assistance from her mother, she managed to somehow, keep her little girl. It had been strongly suggested to her to place the youngster for adoption, but Nina rejected this advice and did all that she could to be with her child. She did get some help from the mother of her former boyfriend, who together with her own mother nurtured the infant as much as they were able. In the interim Nina took any menial job she could obtain until the waitress job, a night position, became available for her. She somehow managed to complete high school and reminded herself how tired she always felt. She described her drinking binges as allowing her to forget her responsibilities, financial problems, and exhaustion from lack of sleep. She is now able to raise her 5-year-old and earn a living for them both.

She feels deeply regretful for the problems she brought on herself. She is proud that she has been able to refrain from alcohol consumption. She has found a young man. Although she is determined to remain in sobriety, she is vulnerable because of past habits and her significant other who also had a drinking and driving violation. The hope is that she has learned from her actions and is still young and wants a healthier, happier childhood for her daughter than what she experienced.

Randolph Spankling

Randolph Spankling had a number of DUI arrests. During the course of his history it was discovered that he had, in addition, experimented with a number of drugs. He had apparently very little self-control and wanted to live the good life, as he perceived it. He denied these occurrences when he visited the therapist to discuss his situation in order to be able to drive legally and safely again. At 23 he had already accumulated three driving infractions, but he claimed that his license had been taken from him when he was 22 years of age for no authentic or verifiable reason. He was sentenced to 3 years of probation and had to report at frequent intervals to a probation officer assigned to him. He stated to the evaluator/consultant that he had one driving arrest and that his BAC, when tested, had been .08 (four alcoholic beverages). He was very anxious to be able to drive to and from his job in order to support himself. He also complained how difficult it was because he needed to meet other essential appointments. He had returned to live with his parents after he had his infraction. His wages were insufficient to pay for an apartment because he needed much more money to cover the cost of his lawyer, the court, the probation department, the necessary laboratory tests, the incidental expenses, and more. His father is a house painter who enjoys a "beer or two, now and then." His mother rarely consumes "a glass of wine" at special occasions. She is employed in a retail establishment. At the time of this writing Randolph had more debts than he could handle.

Randolph urged the counselor to contact his probation officer because he was certain that this man wanted him to have his driver's license restored. Randolph had already been seen by this officer for a year, so he surely must know Randolph. "All he needs is your permission to go ahead and give me my license." (He was very convincing, but the therapist/evaluator was prepared for this pressure having experienced it so frequently by other clients.) When discussing the situation with the probation officer, much was disclosed. Probation Officer Anders revealed the following: Randolph had had three infractions in the last 3 years as reported by the police. One of the numbers on the Breathalyzer was high, indicating nine drinks of alcohol ingested. Another time the client came to court inebriated. He was involved in a number of automobile accidents, fortunately minor. These situations were recorded in the police reports. All the client's mistakes were reasons not to permit him to drive until he learned to take responsibility for his behavior and was seriously convinced that he could not consume as little as one alcoholic beverage and be safe behind the wheel. It was determined that Randolph needed much more counseling. He was transferred to an outpatient group rehabilitation center, where in addition to three group sessions per week he would have individual sessions as indicated.

In summarizing Randolph's case, it was found that his father was a frequent consumer of beer and his mother had no particular aversion to "a little alcohol." His friends were all drinkers whose social life always included alcoholic beverages. He had little interest in education, and his goal was to have the good life. He rarely thought about the consequences of his actions. When he caused his own problems, he used denial. Prevarication was his tool of defense. He held his victims responsible for his actions. He obviously had learned very little after the serious occurrences he caused.

Melissa Steel

Melissa Steel is a 26-year-old very attractive Caucasian woman who came to the office because she had a drinking and driving charge during the summer. She described her situation as flawed, insisting that she could not have had a high alcohol residual in her urine, that the cop was wrong and "full of himself," that she had been very careful to wait one hour after each beer, and that it was the fault of her male companion who was inebriated. She continued by stating that she had stepped out of the car when the boyfriend cursed the law enforcement officer and he connected her with him. Because he was not behind the wheel, he allegedly set her up to be the victim. Her denial was strong and not unusual for the alcoholic or heavy drinker.

Melissa is the second oldest daughter of six children. Her parents were divorced when she was 5 years old. Her mother enjoyed an occasional glass of wine with dinner; her dad frequented his favorite bar where he met his friends on a weekly basis. He felt it was a woman's responsibility to raise the children, because his job as the main breadwinner was more important and he needed freedom to "unwind" on the weekend. His wife was very resentful of his actions. It was no surprise that Mr. Steel married another woman not long after his divorce, and Melissa remained with her mother. Melissa felt that she had raised herself and was also expected to oversee the younger siblings. She is still in contact with several of her sisters and has peripheral dealings with her only brother. She did complete high school and took a course in beauty culture. She received a certificate as a beautician. She likes her job but complained that her salary is inadequate. She works a minimum of 40 hours per week. She is happy that she enjoys her skill in creating some "beautiful hairstyles" and that she is able to give herself some attractive "hairdos." She emphasized that she was never happy sitting in school all day being confined to a chair and desk and having to listen to teachers who spoke about learning that had no interest for her. Working with her hands was her style.

She did readily admit that she enjoys her life and entertains herself by "going dancing" three times a week, where she meets men and women whom she enjoys who have similar interests. She also enjoys "a few drinks," which make her feel "free" and uninhibited. She seems to be very popular when it comes to finding dancing partners/companions who also enjoy their cocktails. She insisted that she never drinks too much and has never had problems driving to and from the places she attends.

Melissa described what occurred on the evening when she, her sister, and a male friend went to a concert at an outdoor stadium. "I only drank one glass of beer per hour. I always waited exactly 60 minutes before I drank another drink. It was a warm night and beer felt good, but I was careful not to have too much. At the end of the evening I had only had six glasses of beer. That should not have been counted as illegal." She obviously is a person who is preoccupied with drinking, enjoys avoiding reality, and does not know or care if alcohol is unhealthy and can damage her mind or body. She feels carefree when inebriated, and to date she has not realistically considered the consequences of her behavior during or following her overconsumption of alcohol. She insists on deluding herself that drinking is not a problem for her. She projects her deeds toward the police; her outspoken, inebriated boyfriend; and anyone else nearby if possible. She does not take responsibility for her actions. She also alleged that the Breathalyzer that measured her alcohol content was defective.

What can be seen in Melissa's case is not unusual in the creation of an evolving alcoholic: a father who drank regularly, a mother not against alcohol, denial of drinking or overdrinking, taking little or no responsibility for inebriation, excuses for actions, projection of actions, and compulsion for imbibing in a mind-altering substance.

Sarginio Trajullio

Sarginio Trajullio is a 40-year-old Puerto Rican native who came to the counselor regarding a drinking and driving incident he had 8 months prior to his appearance in the office. Although he alleged in very poor English that he was 18 years of age when he came to the United States, he also insisted that he graduated from high school locally. He could barely be understood because his English was accented so strongly. Many of his allegations were contradictions intermingled with denials of what occurred and who was responsible for the actions that brought him for help. It was obvious that he attempted to deceive the counselor. He presented blank papers that he wanted to be covered with accounts that proved his innocence. He also was able to obtain letterhead with the Department of Transportation address on it, which he gave to the counselor. He used every distraction to evade what actually did occur.

He also denied that he had been counseled with another organization before engaging the current counselor. When he was questioned, he would hide behind his accented speech to circumvent anything he did not want to reveal and that might indicate he was in serious need of counseling. All he wanted was his license in order to be able to drive without further expense or inconvenience.

After many distractions, he told the following history: Neither of his parents drank. He was divorced and had two offspring, a son age 15 and a daughter age 20. He saw them frequently, and they are "good." He spoke of himself as an admirable father and a hard worker in the construction industry, where he has been a street worker for one and a half years.

He stated that his "wife" raised the children and he did not see them very much or at all for long periods. He also revealed that he saw nothing of his own father and did not really know him. He did not know whether his parents were married, but he thought that they "could have been." He stated that his father "was no good. He cheated on my mother." He did not really know whether his father was an alcoholic or if he did or did not drink alcoholic beverages.

He was very vague in describing the episode in which he was apprehended by law enforcement officers in December 2012. He insisted that no one was hurt, that he had only one drink, and that his score on the Breathalyzer was "minimum." When pressed for the score he talked about ".02." When he was informed that .08 is the minimum, he nodded his head in agreement.

With further investigation, it was discovered that Sarginio had been counseled briefly in an agency, which insisted he remain longer than the few sessions he had with them. The client left the agency with the thought that he could find someone who would evaluate him briefly and assist him in his attempt to regain his license after a brief evaluation.

He insisted that he had only a beer or two, that beer relaxes him and cools him off when he works hard whether it be winter or summer. In addition, he insisted that, if he had been a "big shot," he would not have been apprehended by the police.

David Wenkel

David Wenkel had been apprehended by the police after he and another driver had been in a head-on collision. Both were inebriated, their cars damaged beyond repair.

Eleven months after this incident, he came to the therapist's office for an alcohol evaluation. He insisted that everything he had suffered was the fault of the other driver, who left following the collision. David had been to court; his Breathalyzer test had registered his BAC as .28, which indicated that he had consumed 14 alcoholic beverages. He insisted that he could not believe this because he only had five. For him it was rum. He attempted to deny how many "shots" of rum were in each glass from which he consumed his "drinks." He spoke about the money all this cost. He had briefly attended three group counseling sessions, but because they demanded $85 each time, he could not afford to continue there. He was dismissed from his last two jobs because there was some suspicion of theft. He was a bank teller, and discrepancies in amounts collected could not be proved. In another position he was frequently late because he depended on buses. He did not take any responsibility for any of these occurrences.

His childhood was an unfortunate one. He was the youngest of five, having had two older brothers, one older sister, and one brother very close to him in age. His mother left his dad when David was 4 years of age. His dad left a few years later. David was raised mostly by his older brothers. His sister, the oldest, has a child, and her boyfriend, the father of her child, is serving a prison term for drug smuggling. David related that he is the only one in the family who is gay. He knew this when he was 6 years old when he was teased and tormented by his classmates. He usually played with girls and was considered "one of them." At age 25 he looked back on his tormentors with revulsion and anger. At 17 he moved in with his 18-year-old significant other and the two men have taken care of one another.

David drinks too much and has been reprimanded by his partner. He uses denial and insists that he can control himself. He did admit that his father was a heavy drinker but stopped when he discovered that he is suffering from diabetes. David sees his father fairly often. His mother is not as frequently visited, although she now lives as a married woman with David's paternal uncle (the father's brother) in their hometown about 20 miles from the client's apartment. David realizes that this is not a common situation and is aware that it was difficult for his father to remain on good terms with his brother.

David was very open about his sexual preference and is angry with those who ridiculed and judged him. He feels much better since he is able to let his formerly hidden identity be known. He has had emotional problems and difficulty sleeping. At times hyperactivity overcomes him, depression is not uncommon, and he struggles to overcome the pressures that beset him. He insists he is not an alcoholic but knows that he cannot usually stop with as little as one drink. He knows that he must overcome the need to have that first drink. He does not totally believe that he is as addicted to alcohol as the folk who attend A.A. meetings.

Because of severe problems, disappointments, alcoholism in his family, a poor and emotionally deprived upbringing, a lack of remunerative work, and subsequent poverty, it will be difficult for him to fight his addiction. He agrees that he cannot drive a motorized vehicle with as little as one alcoholic beverage.

Case Histories
Drug Abusers

There are a number of similarities between the dozen individuals whose case histories are presented here and those in Appendix A who have alcohol use disorders. This should not be surprising because many of the individuals discussed here also use alcohol. As Dr. Ursula Adler Falk has pointed out, and as we have discussed in previous chapters, multiple drug use is common. Like the people in Appendix A, some of these people come from broken homes and were abandoned as children. A number of them grew up in homes with neglectful parents who had alcohol or substance use disorders. Some of them appear to be sociopathic. One of the interesting commonalities among the individuals in this appendix is that so many of these men and women became medically addicted to pain killers. This led some of them to abuse prescription drugs or to substitute street drugs. In the majority of cases, drug use was instrumental, used as a means of coping with physical pain, depression, or anxiety.

Harry Haskins

Harry Haskins is the son of a single mother. He did not know much about his dad, except that he was a drug user who was incarcerated because he was also a drug seller. He knew that his father was caught repeatedly and ultimately injured by a prospective buyer, who did not pay for his weekly order of illegal drugs. There was a scuffle and the other man was severely injured and permanently handicapped. Harry was a handsome 12-year-old when he was placed in an institution for delinquent youth. With his blond hair and blue eyes one could barely believe that he was the acting-out youngster who broke dishes, screamed at random, hit other children, and needed constant supervision. His mother had abandoned him when he was a little boy, and he had been sent from one foster home to another because of anger, his serious and difficult behavior, and episodes of running away. His mother did not give him up for adoption, although she had very little interest in him and rarely visited him in his various foster homes. He remained in an institution after his failed foster home placements, in a boys' cottage until he was 18 years of age. At that time he was permitted to join the army, for that was something he appeared interested in doing. Nothing was heard from him until 4 years later when, having been honorably discharged from the army, he visited the social worker in the institution where he had spent so many years. Full of enthusiasm, he told her that he had killed a Vietnamese soldier with a perfectly aimed shot. He described how the blood flowed from this enemy's body and how happy he was with his success. He seemed to experience great joy when he told of his heroism in a sadistic fashion over and over, emphasizing that he "got even." It appeared that he needed some help because he sounded bizarre and overly enthusiastic as he described in detail the joy of annihilating his target. He complained of various aches and pains in his legs. He was offered some assistance from the government and agreed to be examined at the veterans hospital, hoping that he might be helped, especially emotionally, and have some respite there. It would take time to determine the cause of his situation and to recover from the strain that he exhibited, which indicated some mental and emotional abnormality. He accepted the offer to be taken to the VA hospital. He was examined by one of the physicians, who felt that he need not be an inpatient and could remain in the community. The social worker from the former children's institution managed to get Harry a room and board within a Salvation Army housing compound to help him until he found work. He seemed relieved with his temporary domicile. Six weeks had passed when Harry's former social worker received a telephone call from him requesting help. He was in jail awaiting a court date. The social worker responded to Harry's pleading and anxiety and came to the prison to see him. He told her that he had found a friend in the Salvation Army. He had also met an elderly lady who needed to have work done in her house. She needed someone who understood how to repair items and do some cleaning. He was happy to have the income and asked his friend to assist him. He described his temporary employer as a "lovely old lady." "You would have loved her; she was so nice and appreciated what we fixed. The windows looked so clean when we got through washing them. We did that and much more. One day we were very tired and needed money. We knew where she kept her dough. We needed more money so we could buy some weed to feel good. We took a pillow she had on her bed and put it over her face. She was a real nice lady; she was. She struggled, but we held the pillow tight. My buddy held her arms around her back until she stopped breathing. We got money she had in her drawer. We ran out of the house, but someone saw us and somehow we were caught. The woman couldn't breathe and died. She was a nice old lady, she was."

This mentally ill, psychopathic drug user had no conscience and no regrets. He wanted out of the situation. He was rejected from very early childhood and had an uncaring narcissistic mother and a nonexistent father who was a drug addict. There was no stability or healthy role model in Harry Haskin's life, and the outcome was almost predictable.

Bernard Jones

Bernard Jones spoke about his addiction. When he was 21 years of age, he injured his back. His physician, Midda, prescribed the drug that reduced his pain. If he used two Lortabs his discomfort would disappear. The medication at that time was labeled "Blue Watson." He increased his dosage to 3 times daily. He continued using them for approximately 6 years. He became addicted; he could not abstain. He said that each dose cost him $3. After stopping his use of this "miracle drug," he became more and more tired and unable to work. Next, he received Fentanyl patches. When that no longer eased his pain, he had feelings of withdrawal: "You can't move and are achy; you can't do anything," he told the therapist. "You can't even sleep or walk. I laid in my bed for two days. I sweated and got hot and cold flashes and then I got real cold." He was depressed. He bought the patches from people on the street. Some peddler on the street introduced him to Suboxin. He insisted that this drug made him feel normal. He continued to further explain his problems and how "tough" one has to be to accept and attempt to change his problems through the injection of "pain killers." He described Suboxin as little pieces of film. Suboxin allowed him to sleep. He spoke of his childhood as having been an ordinary one, although there were some sad and difficult times. One of his brothers died a few months ago. He was hit by a truck. Five of his brothers and two half sisters were still alive. None of the siblings received much positive attention from their parents. Two of his brothers use crack. His parents fought daily. He has the conviction, the "strong feeling," that marriage is not for him because "it costs too much and is too much trouble."

Lenore Kramer

Lenore, a frail, well-groomed 37-year-old unmarried woman, was guarded in her disclosure of the reason she had entered the therapist's office. She revealed her history of growing up with parents who did not get along. She was a beautiful girl who had a number of boyfriends and ultimately found one whom she dated for a year and anticipated marrying and loving for the rest of her life. He had been admitted to a very prestigious university a considerable distance from home. They saw each other rarely after he left his hometown but kept in touch by telephone and correspondence. They had planned for a future together. As time passed she found that their contact with one another became more infrequent. His telephone calls came less often, and one day he wrote her that marriage was not in his future. Like her father, this male had abandoned her and crushed her hopes, her dreams, and her future. She began to recognize the reality of her situation. She felt unwanted, unloved, and unlovable. The abandonment, the unthinkable rejection, was a terrible, unreal disappointment to her. She could not expect anything in her life to allow her to have satisfaction, normalcy, and happiness. She would have to force herself to drudgingly slave every day without any satisfaction.

She was an only daughter of her divorced parents, and she clung to her mother. Her brother was married and the father of an infant son. The only close relationship that Lenore had was with her mother. (The mother was a white-haired, overweight woman who seemed to be disgusted with her clinging, dependent daughter.)

Lenore was a college graduate. She worked in a position that was demanding and frequently overwhelming. She felt driven and bored all at the same time. She frequently felt inadequate and suffered from headaches and blurred vision. No physical reason was found for her occasional visual complaints. To feel better, she would have a cocktail before retiring. At least it would allow her to sleep at night. She had been on her job for many years and was lauded and rewarded for her exactness and ability to handle the very detailed assignments. As time elapsed she added prescribed drugs that she would use nightly. She had received these from a specialist in pain management. She was frequently unstable and had too many sick days, which ultimately caused dismissal from her assignments. It did not take long before she was placed on sick leave. She had also been apprehended for inability to drive safely, and her license was revoked so that she could no longer drive legally. She was confused in her description of the exact cause of her problem. For a time she drove without a license, with the constant fear of being discovered, reprimanded, and ultimately serving a prison sentence. This did not occur. Her mother drove her where she needed to be. As time passed the mother chauffeured her more and more grudgingly. This 65-year-old woman resented spending her retirement frequently having to take her infant grandson, waiting with him in the car while her emotionally ill adult daughter visited her numerous physicians and attended other necessary appointments.

Lenore was frantic and sometimes irrational; she could not sleep, and the rare moments that she slept, she had indescribable terrifying nightmares. Nothing seemed to help her. The father who had abandoned her in her early teens was brought into the situation at the request of her mother, but when seeing her several times in her frightful condition, he wanted no more contact with her. She was thus emotionally abandoned. The last time her therapist saw her she was very frail; her face was distorted; and her broken, confused, garbled speech was barely understandable. Tears rolled from her eyes. She wanted to explain herself and her condition, but her sounds were strained and tortured. She wanted desperately to be understood and express her agony. She was the picture of a severely tormented human being, an unloved adult infant who was disliked and doomed.

Marlene and Shepherd Lyons

Marlene and Shepherd were married for 25 years. He had a well-paying job until his company closed and he was out of work. His wife enjoyed her position in the company in which she was employed. She had been rewarded for her competency and her ability to get along with her employers and fellow employees, many of whom she taught to function effectively. She had the ability to explain the operation of the computers and new machinery and equipment that were bought and sold. Her position included traveling to other cities to teach employees and others about the functional aspects of the machines and other products. She enjoyed her position, her tasks, her contacts with new people, her trips, and being admired for her knowledge, ability, skills, and expertise. She cheerfully informed her husband about all she was teaching, learning, and examining. She missed Shep when she had to leave him, but he was occupied taking care of their house, repairing what he could, and giving attention to the health and needs of their German shepherd. He loved their animal and frequently joked that he was named after his dog's breed. When Marlene was on her work assignments, his dog would follow him around the house and would sit by his master's easy chair. Shep was always happy when his wife returned after one of her assignments. He would have a meal ready or they would eat in a nearby restaurant to celebrate her return. He often searched for jobs in the newspaper and called employment agencies and offices in an attempt to find employment. Because of his age and a lack of suitable jobs, his opportunities were exceptionally sparse. The longer he was at home, the more depressed he became. He felt that he should be the provider or at least contribute to his wife's income. He was college educated in a subject that was already overcrowded, and openings either did not exist or those that were available were offered to new, young graduates who were satisfied with a beginner's wage. The longer he was rejected by potential employers, the more depressed he became. He felt more and more useless and a burden to his beloved wife. He did, on occasion, mention his feelings of impotence to his spouse. She attempted to distract him by praising him for taking such good care of the household, the dog, and more. He felt overwhelmed by the reversal of roles, of being placed into what he considered the female role after their 25 years of a once happy marriage. He did not want to play the part of the servant, a house husband, or feel the eternal pain of the proverbial castrated male. The more his wife left for work, especially for her out-of-town demonstrations, the more dejected and useless he felt. As time wore on and jobs became fewer for a man of his age, and as he was rejected more often by prospective employers when applying for work, the more morbid became his outlook. Frequently, when his wife returned from out-of-state monthly assignments, she found him asleep in his easy chair, their dog by his side. His appearance changed, and his former carefree nature was gone. He had little interest in household chores, and at times his wife found their home in disarray, unwashed dishes left on a chair or table. The fresh smell of soap had disappeared and she noted a stale atmosphere. She did not say much nor chastise him regarding the situation but worried silently about him. At other times she became angry and reproachful. The love that had been theirs, so intense and satisfying over their 25 years of togetherness, seemed to have disappeared at times, which made Marlene very sad and distressed. She wanted to help him, but she did not know quite what steps to take. She suggested he see a physician to give him some tranquilizers or antidepressants to make his situation more bearable. He assured her he would attempt to follow her suggestions and surprise her when she returned from one of her longer trips. She in turn assured him of her love and, with a positive attitude and demeanor, left with hopefulness in her heart. She optimistically believed that their life would improve. She had 14 days to cover three towns that were near one another. Her students did well in learning techniques she taught them to operate the computers. After three days away from home, she received a telephone call that she was to return home immediately. It sounded like her husband's voice, but she was uncertain. She packed her few belongings, placed them in her car, and sped the 10-hour distance home. Upon arrival, she unlocked the door, walked into her living room, and found her husband slumped in his favorite chair, with his dog sitting next to him. There was a strange odor in the room and some empty nondescriptive cans were on the floor. She called his name, lifted his arms, and realized he was not moving. He was dead! A scream escaped her lips as she raced out the door. When an autopsy was performed, it was found that he had been on some poisonous drugs, which took his life. She was informed that her husband must have been taking the poisonous drugs for a considerable length of time. The postmortem report revealed that his body was damaged bit by bit by all the so-called prescription drugs that had been taken to relieve his depression. He had wittingly or otherwise committed suicide.

Peter Mason

Peter, a young man when he had nearly completed high school, found a job that was physically very straining; he felt he was not sufficiently reimbursed for the energy he put forth and muscle pain he was experiencing. His compatriots seemed to have an easier existence than his. At age 19 he was invited by a close friend to try the trade he had found satisfying and remunerative. Peter was excited when he met a person who could lead him into receiving some "real money" without exerting himself. For authenticity, he saw the new car this young man had and how the opposite sex was interested in his fortunate friend. Girls flirted with him, and he seemed to have no difficulty finding dates. This person wore stylish clothing, and his income allowed him to purchase what he particularly desired. With little coaxing Peter was introduced to the drug supplier who would make him a wealthy man. This person explained the process used to sell the product. The commission was much more than he could ever earn working hard from 40 to 50 hours per week climbing roofs, carrying heavy loads, and having discolored swollen hands. He gleefully accepted the job. He met dealer M. once every 2 weeks at various designated areas as prearranged to accept a container with drugs. After the first amount was sold, he met M. and gave him the money as agreed. He was able to keep a certain sum of the profit for himself. After the first time, he had to pay immediately when he received the product. A number of public places like hotels, bus stations, and certain housing projects were designated by the dealer for this business exchange. Peter was delighted to have the opportunity to be a part of this money-making business. He would take the product to his apartment, bundle a certain number of the particular drug in a small bag, and sell the contents to the users. In the beginning of his employment he was given names of general and particular users. Eventually his business grew because the addicts would inform others where he could be found. Peter was successful. It did not take long before he was able to purchase a large dog that would bark when someone came to his door. At last he felt like the proverbial he man. For 3 years he was very successful and purchased a number of luxuries that he had always desired.

He had agreed to meet M. in the Loyola Hotel on a Tuesday at two o'clock in the afternoon to purchase a quantity of drugs. He had $37,000 in cash. The dealer sat in a designated prearranged room. He asked for the money agreed upon as he handed Peter the package. Suddenly, there was a knock on the door, and after a few moments of no response the door was forcefully opened, just as Peter handed the dealer the money. Three large men entered. They were out-of-uniform police officers who then arrested Peter. M. was released because he had confessed to law enforcement and had "squealed." He had exposed Peter as a drug seller to get his own freedom. This was only the beginning. Peter was incarcerated and eventually transferred to a federal prison where he spent 10 years. Because of the distance from his erstwhile home, only his mother visited him on rare occasions. He lost all his earthly possessions, including his dog. His girlfriend instantly severed their relationship. When he was released from prison his appearance had changed. He seemed much older than his chronological age. He temporarily found a domicile with his mother and stepfather. His plan was to be a barber and possibly to join an uncle who owned a barbershop. Although he was one of the more fortunate drug traffickers, his youthful hopes and dreams were shattered.

Mark Nagel

Mark Nagel, a handsome, tall, educated, well-dressed man entered the therapist's office 3 years after his first wife had divorced him. He feared that his current wife would also leave him if he did not succeed in discontinuing his habit. She is nearly 4 years older than he, and there is something "motherly" about her personality and her "warmth." With a great deal of hesitancy and evasion, he described his sexual addiction. He would have urges at frequent and sudden times to have sex with women. He would find these partners wherever and whenever he could and had no problem being intimate with them, even at the spur of the moment. If nothing else, he would pay prostitutes to satisfy his pressing urges. He shared his feelings with his wife, which left her suspicious and feeling unloved, abandoned, and frightened. He had been married to this wife for a number of years and kept insisting that he loved her very much in spite of his actions and very frequent sexual encounters with other females. His sexual addiction began when he was approximately 27 years old. At various times he attempted to use marijuana to counteract his sexual feelings, but with no success.

In examining the history of this very troubled, physically attractive man, we find a person who is lacking his identity. He was born somewhere in the United States to a young woman who was possibly in her late teens. She abandoned him when he was born because she could not raise her child at her young age. How she felt is unknown. He was temporarily placed in a foster home, and from there, after a few weeks, he was adopted by his "parents." The new mother, following the suggestions that she had learned in preplacement meetings, informed him as soon as he could speak that he was not her birth child, but she emphasized that she loved him very much, and she and her husband were happy to have a child because her siblings also had children.

The adoptive father was a good man, sparse of words, who left Mark's upbringing to his wife. He came from an old-fashioned Germanic belief, "Kinder, Küche, Kirche" (children, kitchen, church), meaning that women should take care of children, do the kitchen and household tasks, and attend church. The new father was a hard worker and faithful husband but only on rare occasions verbalized that he loved his adopted son. The mother always informed the dad each day when he came home what the child had achieved, tasks done, behavior exhibited, what personality traits he might have exhibited, and minute changes she observed. Sometimes the child overheard his parents in their discussions, but that was rare. He recalled that he felt left out of those discussions. He did not recall any unusual punishments, especially not physical attacks. He, like most children, was raised to be obedient and polite and to behave within the normal stages of his age. From his description, he seemed to have had responsible, caring parents who wanted the best for their child. He recalled that he did not physically resemble either his mother or his dad. Although his parents are still living, he has a strong yearning to know his birth parents—who they are, how the mother might have felt toward him, and much more. He is searching for his identity and why his birth mother did not love him enough to keep him. His anger was often unjustifiably directed toward his parents, especially his adoptive mother.

On the surface he led the "good life." He was an excellent student, always on the honor roll, and he went to a well-known university out of town. He was educated in the sciences and continued to be a superior student. He had a girlfriend from his high school years who was the proverbial love of his life. They dated for 4 years. She was very distressed when he left for college. Although he came home to see her as often as he could, she felt rejected and eventually left him for another man. He was very upset over the situation and felt deserted. It was after that situation that his sexual addiction began. After each sexual episode, he felt only temporarily satisfied until he was plagued again with indescribable urges, which caused him to find another willing female to gratify his physical/sexual needs. He completed his schooling and married "on the rebound." It was not long after that they had a son. The marriage lasted a few years, and he had been given almost no contact with his boy, by edict of his divorced wife.

Although his current wife was emphatically described as warm and loving, his praise of her frequently sounded as if he were speaking of a very motherly figure. He painstakingly revealed that he could barely have sex with this woman because she had physical difficulties. She had had a hysterectomy and intercourse was very painful and problematic for her. He felt guilty pushing her to engage in the sex act. One night he left the bedroom at three in the morning and went to have a cup of coffee to distract himself from the pressure of his addiction. It hardly changed his pressure, and his wife was furious when he returned. She quizzed him and in not very veiled language alluded to possible separation, although she emphasized that she still loved him. He strongly wanted to believe that she did and that he loved her as well.

As we examine this situation, we find a man who felt he had no identity; a man who had been rejected from birth; a person with needs for love, kindness, and fulfillment. He keenly felt the rejection of his birth mother, his first love, and his divorce and was unable to bond with his son and current wife, who could not freely meet his physical/sexual needs. For this man, marijuana was unable to douse the addiction with which he was plagued. At the time of this writing, he has joined a group of folks who are suffering from the same addiction as his. He found a sponsor who is of some help to this very distressed, intelligent, plagued human being.

Dragoner Piranan

Dragoner Piranan, a very tall, muscular-appearing man, was in the office for an alcohol/drug evaluation as requested by the court. He was angry from the beginning, having been ordered to be exposed for such an evaluation. He threatened that he would annihilate anyone who attempted to incarcerate him. He was sparse of words and guarded any information needed to authenticate the reason for his contact with the police. He alleged that he had been stopped on the road because he drove through a stop sign, missing another vehicle by a fraction. He further stated that he was apprehended merely because of the color of his skin, because the police hated him, and because of owning a bright red car. His thought processes and allegations were frequently irrational, and his verbalizations were crude. He threatened to use the law to counteract the accusations hurled at him. He insisted that the police who had stopped him had it "in" for him, even though the specific law enforcement people had never met him previously. He pounded his fist on the desk, shouting loudly that he would get revenge for the injustice meted out to him. He produced his license, which had apparently not been taken from him. After a difficult interview and an examination of his "bill of particulars," also known as a rap sheet, some facts were clarified. He had many traffic violations, some small and others more serious; he had been in jail for relatively brief periods. He had been treated with the synthetic opiate methadone to counteract his dependency on heroin. Although methadone stops the pain and dependence on heroin, it can cause death if overused or given to a very frail or vulnerable individual. In a menacing, frequently irrational, and sometimes exceptionally loud tone, he held the police, the Caucasians, the "race haters," and most human beings responsible for all the hardships and evil of the universe. It was difficult to terminate the 90-minute interview with this man, for his free associations were countless. He threw his feet on the desk and left the therapist's office shouting that the thieves of the world are determined to make life impossible for him. "I won't take it and they'll find out who they're dealing with." In piecing together his history, this 31-year-old was an abandoned child from infancy. His parents were not married. His mother had a number of children who were left to take care of themselves at various stages in their life. Their father was a brutal person. When inebriated he would beat whoever was in his path. No one could determine whether he ever held a job. He was allegedly taken to jail and released. Dragoner's mother had mood swings, dealt sexually with various men, and collected welfare payments and any remuneration for her "services" from various males. Neglect of Dragoner and his siblings was regular in the disorderly place that he grew up. On rare occasions he was briefly placed into temporary foster homes before being returned to his unstable mother. He was afraid of his violent, angry father, who came in and out of his life. His multiple siblings let their frustrations out on Dragoner, who was the youngest of this brood of brothers and sisters. Dragoner was unsure of the whereabouts of most of his siblings, but he did know that his mother was frequently incarcerated. "Dragon," as he was nicknamed by those who knew him, had a violent, plagued, abnormal childhood. Normal love and caring were not in his life. He stated often and emphatically that "I hate people!" He declared in a menacing tone that he would never permit either the police or anyone else to take away his right to use methadone or any other "medication" that would help him to be free of pain. His future seems bleak because he has never been in a peaceful or normal environment. At the time of this writing he is awaiting yet another court appearance.

Bonnie Puerta

Bonnie Puerta is a beautiful 37-year-old woman who was directed by her attorney to have a drug/alcohol evaluation. She had been apprehended by the police in the early morning hours while driving home from her managerial job in an upscale restaurant. When a Breathalyzer recorded that she had consumed 11 glasses of alcohol, she was taken to the local police station and incarcerated for several hours. This was not the first time that she had been discovered in an inebriated state. She had the opportunity to drink with the consumers of the upscale establishment in which she was employed. She was very proud that she could advise her clientele what wine to drink—the taste and age of each product, the place of its origins, and the type of grapes or fruits used to create the wine.

Bonnie revealed the following history of the most recent drinking episode and her situation. She is the only daughter of an Italian American couple. She has two brothers, one who was addicted to drugs and the other who was a normal, hardworking man. Neither of her parents was an alcoholic. They enjoyed an occasional glass of beer with their dinner meal on weekends, but they had never been inebriated. Their three children had a happy childhood; their parents were described as very normal loving people. Except for one adult son, there were no unusual problems. At age 18, Bonnie graduated from high school and from there entered the local state college, where she did well. After a 2-year attendance, she was lured away by a well-paying, full-time job where she had worked part-time while attending school. She could not resist this opportunity and was promoted from cook and waitress to the managerial position, which she still had. She was respected, liked, and trusted by her employers, and she felt very comfortable with them. She worked long hours, often the night shift when the place was the busiest. She felt comfortable in the situation and had no complaints. She met her significant other there. He also was the manager of a dining establishment. He was the son of an alcoholic father, but he was against drinking and abstained from any and all alcoholic beverages. It had spoiled his childhood, for his father and mother did not get along and divorced when he was in his teens. He was opposed to official legal marriage because he felt that love is more than an official legal directive. Bonnie had a very similar belief, and the two young people were satisfied with their union. He was a good father to her child and the love of her life. He was helpful to her, especially with the problems she was facing. She is an independent person; she contributes to the household and handles her problems as she is able.

Bonnie was close to her parents and lived in a suburb near her family, with her teenage son and significant other. She had been with her "spouse" for 14 years. Although they were not officially married, their union was strong, and they were very much in love. Their son, as she described him, was a normal child, a good student, and had no unusual or negative traits or behaviors.

Bonnie was very open and honest when she came to the therapist for her first visit and an evaluation of the situation in which she found herself. She needed a written report of the history of her illegal, dangerous inebriated condition the night she was apprehended. Her visit was two days before her appearance in front of the judge, and the report was essential to determine the outcome of the sentence that was to be administered. When she was asked to have a urine test for alcohol before the court date, she became very frightened. When questioned, she admitted using marijuana for headaches. She did not want this drug to be found in her body. She seemed to be aware that marijuana can remain in the bodily system for as long as 3 months. She was also concerned because this was the second conviction for alcohol/drug abuse that she had in the last 7 years.

The outcome of Bonnie's case is not fully determined at the time of this writing. It is again observed that addictions to one drug are often combined with more and other drugs. The person thus plagued by indulging in one physically and/or emotionally damaging product will attempt to lessen his or her pain by indulging in or adding other harmful products to feel better, to find the very best panacea for the alleged physical or psychic pain. Once addicted, drug yearnings are indescribable. There is physical and psychological pain involved. The friendships addicts have are usually superficial. Addiction may begin with shyness and feelings of inability to be loved. It may occur after a very unhappy childhood. Perhaps one of the parents was an addict or there was desertion by one or both parents; perhaps the growing child had access to a readily available potent product. Friends may have introduced the victim; there may have been strong feelings of being unloved, alone, or burdensome. Maybe it was a lack of identity and feelings of worthlessness, abandonment, inferiority, and helplessness.

Kenneth Ronfort

Kenneth Ronfort, a pleasant, tall, somewhat overweight gentleman, came to the therapist's office because he needed a legal reason to use the drug Suboxin. It was prescribed to counteract the painkiller Lortab. The latter medication was prescribed by his physician during his recovery from spinal surgery. The healing process was successful. His gait was normal; his appearance was that of an attractive 32-year-old male. His addiction to Lortab continued. He could not stop. His addiction was complete. Dr. Lorencio, his medical doctor, was very accommodating, and his prescription had no end. After using this drug for a year, Kenneth felt weak, helpless, and extremely tired. He had to force himself to go to work in a managerial position that in itself was stressful but one he had attained because of his education, ambition, and hard work. He could barely lift 5 pounds and felt helpless and extremely tired until even his walking became a chore. He knew that he needed help to cope with daily living. Every muscle in his body seemed to fail him. Fortunately, he learned from an acquaintance about a counterdrug, Suboxin, that would help him into normalcy again. He was given the name of a physician who would assist him. Dr. Gesundheit, a specialist in addictions, agreed to assist him, but he was urged to lessen the dosage regularly as directed. Kenneth agreed to follow the directives of his new medical doctor. The daily intake of Suboxin was a panacea for Ken. It was not long before he recovered his strength; there was no pain, and he felt like a "new man." He was directed to see a psychotherapist on a regular basis to assist him to adjust and to help him to slowly have his prescription titrated, lowered to a lesser dosage, eventually allowing him to be free of any unnecessary, ultimately dangerous fix. He agreed to follow the edict of Dr. Gesundheit, including reporting to the physician a minimum of twice per month in order to be drug tested and to verify his visits to the therapist. He had to bring written proof that he visited her once a month to report his progress.

Kenneth had a very difficult childhood. His father was an alcoholic who beat him and his two sisters at random. The mother of these three children was a very kind, submissive person who also received her share of physical attacks when her husband came home inebriated. Weekends were always difficult. There was no cessation in this man's outbursts. When Ken was 16 years old, the mother, Bess Ronfort, divorced her spouse. Fortunately, by then she had a job with which she could somehow, together with what the court had allotted, support her three offspring. Ken had an afterschool job and contributed what he could to the mom he loved, who had changed his life for the better. He adored his mom and "made her proud" by being a good student. He graduated from high school and managed to accumulate 2 years of additional education while working. He remained good friends with his two younger siblings and became a pseudo substitute father for them. His sadistic father never left his son's psyche. He appeared in his dreams, and Ken would wake up screaming. This situation lasted a considerable length of time.

Kenneth was ambitious. He used to enjoy observing his mother cook, and at times he would help her try a special recipe. He also was a good manager of money. Financial situations were of interest to him. In his early 20s he found a job in a restaurant. He was very well liked by his employers (they owned several upscale eating establishments in a number of cities), and it did not take long before he became a manager in the city in which he grew up.

Despite his success, his drug problem persisted. He attempted repeatedly to lessen the use of the counterdrug, but he struggled. He promised himself, his therapist, and his physician to reduce his intake. He sometimes deluded himself. Dr. Gesundheit gave him an ultimatum that either he titrate the use of the drug or he will have to terminate him as his patient. Ken found another physician, an older gentleman, who was eager to have Ken's twice-monthly visits and the income that would add to his practice. This man was not as insistent that patients reduce their amount of Suboxin. He merely suggested that the therapist send him a monthly report that Ken is doing well. This would cover the physician's responsibility, and it would protect him from allegations that his greed and resistance to give up his lucrative business was the motivation for not persisting toward the ultimate goal of persuading an addict to become a drug-free, healthy human being. Lessening the addiction has been extremely difficult for Ken, and he is still struggling at the time of this writing. He has lessened his monthly visits to his therapist to avoid having to account for his failure to lessen the quantity of his Suboxin prescription. Avoidance of the pressure the therapist has attempted to instill has become the patient's tool for continually failing to face his problem realistically. It can be compared to a young diabetic child who hides candy and eats it when his mother is not present.

Addictions are extremely difficult to change, and it takes unusual control, effort, and more to abandon this state of compulsion.

Lorrie Speed

Lorrie Speed is a personable 22-year-old woman who was apprehended by the police after partying in a local bar with friends to celebrate one of the group's birthdays. She was raised in a medium-sized town in New York State until she was 6 years of age. Her mother died of breast cancer when Lorrie was 5 years old. She then remained with her father who did not stay in the same house where he had lived with his late wife and little daughter. He took her to new surroundings, so that she not only missed her mother but her neighborhood playmates and familiar surroundings. The dad was a music teacher who was not only busy during the day in the classroom but also at night giving piano lessons. Being in charge of his child and her care was difficult for both father and daughter. He loved her very much, but with his busy schedule he could not give her as much attention as she desperately needed. She compared herself to the other children who had mothers who were alive, and she felt lonely, abandoned, and deprived. She felt different from her classmates. Mr. Speed's ways were strict; he was overworked and felt he had to be both mother and father to his only child.

Lorrie was distressed as a teenager and spent a year away when her father sent her to an aunt. The child had periods of depression for which she was hospitalized for one week on two separate occasions. She did not attend school for a time when she was 14 and 15 years old, but she did return. After those occasions, she found little joy in life, and her dad, upon the suggestions of her teachers, sent her to a few counseling sessions at a neighboring outpatient agency. She somehow learned that her mother had two children, who were considerably older than she, by a first husband. Her father had also been married and divorced before he met and married Lorrie's mother.

At 16 years of age Lorrie left high school because she could not concentrate. She did eventually receive a general education diploma (GED). She managed to get a job in a restaurant where she became a kitchen employee and did some cooking. She learned that others at work could relax and abandon their worries with a few drinks. That also seemed to be true when they felt pressured and overworked. She also wanted to feel good and forget her frequent bouts of depression. The alcohol she consumed made her feel happy for brief periods. When that was not enough to satisfy her, she learned about drugs. This occurred when she met a gentleman in a bar who eventually became her boyfriend. He introduced her to marijuana, which she added to her occasional drinking episodes. According to Lorrie, no one in her family is an alcoholic. She has never seen her father inebriated, and he insisted that to his knowledge there was no one in his late wife's family who was a heavy drinker or drug abuser. In summarizing this young woman's situation, it is understandable that she felt abandoned because of the death of her mother when she was so very young. Her father was grief-stricken and overworked and could not successfully be mother and father to his needy little girl. Because of her youth and determination, as well as a therapeutic environment and meaningful job, there is the possibility for Lorrie to be enabled through strict self-control, effort, determination, and motivation to remain in sobriety.

Addictions are extremely difficult to fight. If ignored they will not only be hazardous and costly but ultimately lethal. Alcohol and other addictive drugs must be handled by the persons thus affected. They must consciously abandon whatever drugs they were imbibing, never to use them again, for any reason whatsoever. There is no room for exceptions. It is the addicted personality that must have the monumental strength to desist in causing its own demise. The longer the individual is a user of illegal, dangerous drugs, the more hazardous are the consequences both physically and emotionally. As is known, people who are addicted have an extremely difficult struggle to consciously fight and ultimately abandon their cravings. The folks most vulnerable are people whose parents were addicts, those who turned to drugs to artificially bury their problems, or those who had friends or other persons introduce them to ultimately poisonous substances as an artificial panacea. A number of organizations attempt to help addicts achieve a healthier state of body and mind, but ultimately it is the addict who must convince himself or herself to abstain.

Tracey Thompson

Tracey had been sent to the therapist's office by her physician, a general practitioner. She had contusions in her face; the skin around her right eye could be described in common terms as a black eye; and her shoulder was painful. She could not recall what occurred the night before she came to the office. She vaguely remembered that she had attended "some party." She also remembered some cigarettes that had been rolled differently than those that are bought in stores. She recalled vaguely that she might also have consumed some wine. She explained that she never drank more than one or two glasses of wine. She proceeded to explain that all she fully recalled was that she found herself at the bottom of her basement stairs, where she hurt from "top to bottom." She also could not remember how she came home and why she was so painfully injured. Her greatest concern was that she might have been raped by one of the men where the celebration took place and that she could have been infected with a venereal disease or possibly been impregnated. Her blackout was so severe that she felt helpless. When discussing her factory job, which she had held for the past 6 years since leaving high school, she said that it was sometimes tedious.

Her social life was sparse; although she had dated in the past, no serious commitment had been made. After much prodding and exploring her activities and feelings, it appeared that the alcohol and marijuana combined created a situation where she lost consciousness and recall. She did believe that she fell down her basement stairs and awoke in severe pain. She returned to the therapist's office 4 weeks after the episode described. Her physical wounds had healed, she joyfully disclosed that her menstrual period had returned, and she very fortunately was not pregnant. She did insist that she would never again smoke as much as one marijuana cigarette. A year after her traumatic episode, Tracy has not used marijuana.

As is well known, there is no guarantee that drugs are ever permanently out of the lives of addicted users. It takes much self-control and a good support system, as well as separation from former friends or acquaintances who are still active in the consumption of the forbidden products described. Recurrence can take place for many reasons: severe pain, mental or physical disappointments, lack of joy in daily living, reintroduction of a forbidden product, the degree of compulsiveness of a given individual, and the motivation needed to give up damaging drugs.

Trafalger Whittington

Trafalger, a 32-year-old, tall, slim Caucasian male with a very red countenance and a scarred face, was sent to the therapist by his attorney. He was awaiting a court hearing regarding an accident in which he had been involved. He had been injured 6 months earlier as he was scaffolding for a company. He had a dangerous, unsafe job, and the street repair outfit for which he had worked for the past 3 months did not have the proper precautionary equipment essential for safety. As a consequence, Trafalger fell on his head from a height of 15 feet; he was unconscious, his left shoulder was injured, and his face was severely scarred. He wore a knitted hat, which emphasized his somewhat grotesque appearance. Traf, as he was called, remembered the following history: He was the younger of two sons born to a mother who was a severe alcoholic and a factory laborer father who worked very hard to support his wife and two sons. The mother's addiction became greater as the years passed. Although her first child was not as affected as Traf, he too had his problems, but he was able to marry and was the dad of two offspring. Trafalger frequently prepared his own breakfast as a young boy while his mother slept, recovering from her drinking bouts the night before. Little Traf became self-sufficient out of necessity. When his father was home from work he was a good dad who did not drink and attempted to help his offspring in the brief time he had away from the strenuous factory labor and the long hours he had to work to meet the expenses that faced him. He encouraged his sons to become educated. They both were bright and attended some college. The loneliness and example that Traf followed led him to sample liquor combined with some potent drugs, which he found soothing. He had a number of jobs after school; he was a delivery boy for a pizza place, a night worker in a grocery store where he stocked shelves, and a newspaper delivery boy. He was always ready to earn some money to buy himself a used vehicle. He looked up to his father regarding the need to work. He loved his dad but did not have the physical or emotional strength of this very responsible man. As a young adult, he had many problems, including driving dangerously, which ultimately led to his incarceration. He was imprisoned for 11 months for the multiple vehicle infractions he accumulated with his risky driving. Seven years before the time of this writing he lost his license. He could not drive, nor did he have the necessary means to purchase another vehicle. He was in numerous institutions following his incarcerations. He attended A.A. and Narcotics Anonymous meetings, he was placed in a special place for rehabilitation, and he associated with alcoholics and drug users. He could not find an available job or was rejected when an opening existed. He was rejected by numerous young women when he attempted to find someone whom he could date. Eventually, he met someone his age who had drug problems in one of the A.A. meetings. This young woman had been divorced and had two very young children who were under the custody of their father; she was not permitted to visit them by court order. She minimized her problems when she spoke of the reason for not being able to visit her children. Trafalger was very happy to have found her, and after many years of loneliness he felt worthy of a relationship. He lives near the housing project where his girlfriend has found shelter.

Trafalger had much difficulty finding a place to live. He had to abandon an apartment in a house where there was criminal activity, an apartment he had occupied for 8 months. He found another inexpensive small apartment where he could sleep and heat his food in a microwave oven. He discovered some space in the basement of the house where he could store his tools. At this time, he is very eager to heal. He was ordered to attend counseling sessions to be allowed to drive. He has another job now where he works on street projects. It is hard physical labor, but he is very pleased to earn money. He works fairly long hours but feels proud that he is able to function. He still suffers from severe pain at times, especially in his injured shoulder. He is medicated for the pain and visits a rehabilitation physician at regular intervals. To date, he has been very responsible in keeping his appointments and has the incentive to permanently conquer his addictions. His elderly retired father has been of great assistance to him. This man drives him wherever his son has to be. He is very supportive and does not reproach his son for past misdeeds. He shows him affection and understanding. Traf's brother lives with their father and was reported to have a very amiable relationship with him. Despite both sons having suffered from the alcoholism of their mother, they speak with love about their deceased parent, who died when Trafalger was 17 years of age.

References

Aaronson, Bernard and Humphry Osmond. 1970. *Psychedelics: The Uses and Implications of Hallucinogenic Drugs*. Garden City, NY: Anchor Books.

Abbey, Antonia. 2002. "Alcohol-Related Sexual Assault: A Common Problem Among College Students." *Journal of Studies on Alcohol and Drugs*, Supplement No. 14:118–128.

Abbey, Antonia, Tina Zawacki, Philip O. Buck, A. Monique Clinton, and Pam McAuslan. 1994. "Alcohol's Role in Sexual Assault." Pp. 97–123 in *Drug and Alcohol Abuse Reviews*. Vol. 5, *Addictive Behavior in Women*, edited by R. R. Watson. Totowa, NJ: Humana Press.

Abbey, Antonia, Lisa Thomson Ross, Donna McDuffie, and Pam McAuslan. 1996. "Alcohol and Dating Risk Factors for Sexual Assault Among College Women." *Psychology of Women Quarterly* 20:147–169.

Abel, Ernest L. 1998. "Prevention of Alcohol Abuse Related Birth Effects: Public Education Efforts." *Alcohol & Alcoholism* 33(4):411–416.

Abrahamian, Atossa Araxia. 2013. "Baking Bad: A Potted History of 'High Times.'" *The Nation*. Retrieved January 25, 2016 (http://www.thenation.com/article/baking-bad-potted-history-high-times/).

"Accused of Fraud." 1982. *Buffalo Evening News*, December 15, p. A-19.

"Acupuncture Use Seen as Cure for Alcoholism." 1986. *Buffalo Evening News*, May 7.

Adams, Jad. 2005. "The Drink that Fuelled a Nation's Art." *Tate Etc.* 5(1). Retrieved December 6, 2013 (http://www.tate.uk/context-comment/articles/drink-fuelled-nations-art).

Addiction Blog. 2016. "The Efficacy of Cognitive Behavioral Therapy (CBT) for Addiction Treatment." Retrieved March 7, 2017 (http://addictionblog.org/treatment/the-efficacy-of-cognitive-behavioral-therapy-cbt-for-addiction-treatment).

Addiction Center. 2016. "Cognitive Behavioral Therapy." Retrieved March 7, 2017 (https://www.addictioncenter.com/treatment/cognitive-behavioral-therapy/).

"Administration About-Face." 1969. *Science News* 96(17):37.

Agius, Paul, Angela Taft, Sheryl Hemphill, John Toumbourou, and Barbara McMorris. 2013. "Excessive Alcohol Use and Its Association With Risky Sexual Behaviour: A Cross-Sectional Analysis of Data From Victorian Secondary School Students." *Australian and New Zealand Journal of Public Health* 37(1):76–82.

Akers, Ronald L., M. D. Krohn, L. Lanza Kaduce, and M. J. Radusevich. 1979. "Social Learning and Deviant Behavior: A Specific Test of General Theory." *The American Sociological Review* 44:635–655.

Alberty, Erin. 2012. "Football Dad Accused of Assaulting 13 Year Old Player." *Salt Lake Tribune*, October 11, Athletic Business 1.

"Alcohol Kills Baby." 1930. *New York Times*, June 23, p. 16.

"Alcohol-related Deaths: How Does Your State Rank?" 2014. CBS This Morning. Retrieved August 4, 2017 (http://www.cbsnews.com/news/alcohol-related-deaths-how-does-your-state-rank/).

Alcoholics Anonymous. 1981. *Twelve Steps and Twelve Traditions*. New York: Author.

"Alcoholism Is a Disease." 1956. *Journal of the American Medical Association* 268(8):1012–1014.

Aldaronda, Etiony and Glenda Kaufman Kantor. 1997. "Social Predictors of Wife Assault Cessation." Pp. 183–193 in *Out of the Darkness: Contemporary Perspectives on Family Violence*, edited by Glenda Kaufman Kantor. Thousand Oaks, CA: Sage.

Algren, Nelson. 1949. *The Man With the Golden Arm*. Garden City, NY: Doubleday.

Allen, Jay Presson. 1981. "Prince of the City." *New York Review of Books*. Retrieved January 18, 2016 (http://www.nybooks.com/articles/1981/12/17/prince-of-the-city/).

American Academy of Pediatrics, Committee on Substance Abuse and Committee on Children with Disabilities. 2000. "Fetal Alcohol Syndrome and Alcohol Related Neurodevelopmental Disorders." *Pediatrics* 106:358–361.

American Addiction Centers. 2017. "Cognitive Behavioral Therapy and Addiction Treatment." Retrieved March 7, 2017 (http://americanaddictioncenters.org/cognitive-behavioral-therapy/).

American Beer Institute. 2013. "Tax Facts-No Drink Tax." Retrieved August 17, 2017 (www.beerinstitute.org).

American Cancer Society. n.d. "Smokeless Tobacco." Retrieved August 6, 2014 (http://www.cancer.org/cancer/cancercauses/tobaccocancer/smokeless-tobacco).

American Medical Association. n.d. *Code of Medical Ethics* (Section E815 "Substance Abuse").

American Society of Addictive Medicine. 1990. "The Definition of Alcoholism." Chevy Chase, MD: Author.

Amerman, Kevin. 2014. "Three More Platinum Plus Strippers Get ARD on Prostitution Charge." *The Morning Call.* Retrieved April 26, 2014 (http://articles.mcall.com/2014-01-24/news/mc-allentown-platinum-plus-strippers-hearing-20140124_1_jennifer-beth-jenna-shonk-jamayra-jesse-andrews).

Amoruso, David. 2010. "How the Sicilian Mafia Flooded the US with Heroin." Gangsters Inc. Retrieved May 30, 2016 (http://gangstersinc.ning.com/profiles/blogs/how-the-sicilian-mafia-flooded).

Amory, Deborah P. 1997. "'Homosexuality' in Africa: Issues and Debates." *Issue: A Journal of Opinion* 25(1):5–10. Retrieved March 19, 2017 (http://www.jstor.org/stable/1166238).

Ancient-Wisdom. n.d. "The Role of Drugs in Prehistory." Retrieved July 7, 2015 (http://www.ancient-wisdom.com/prehistoricdrugs.htm).

Andel, Robert. 2005. "Strategies to Reduce the Risk of Cognitive Decline and Dementia." *Aging Health* 1(1):107–117.

Anderson, Nels. 1923. *The Hobo: The Sociology of the Homeless Man.* Chicago: University of Chicago Press.

"Anheuser-Busch Profit Up as Beer Volume Recovers." 2015. Market Watch. Retrieved August 8, 2017 (http://www.marketwatch.com/story/anheuser-busch-profit-up-as-us-economy-recovers-2015-02-26).

Anna, George J. 1997. "Reefer Madness—The Federal Response to California's Medical-Marijuana Law." *New England Journal of Medicine* 337 (August 7):435–439.

Anonymous. 1888. "The Opium Habit." *Catholic World* 33 (September).

Anslinger, Harry J. and Will Ourslee. 1961. *The Murderers: The Story of the Narcotics Gangs.* New York: Farrar, Straus and Cudahy.

Aronson, Elliot, Timothy D. Wilson, and Robin M. Akert. 2013. *Social Psychology* (8th ed.). New York: Pearson.

Artalejo, Fernando Rodriguez. 2001. "Any Alcohol in Moderation May Boost Health." *Journal of Epidemiology and Community Health* 551:648–652.

Asch, Solomon E. 1940. "Studies in the Principles of Judgments and Attitudes: II. Determination of Judgments by Group and by Ego-standards." *Journal of Social Psychology* 12:433–465.

Asch, Solomon E. 1956. "Studies of Independence and Conformity. A Minority of One Against a Unanimous Majority." *Psychological Monographs* 70(9):1–70.

Associated Press. 2010. "Mexicans March in Support of Craziest Kingpin." Huffington Post (December 12).

Associated Press. 2014. "Growing Pot Use as Pain Reliever Puts NFL in Tight Spot." *Buffalo News,* August 15, p. B5.

Aubuchon, Vaughn. 2016. "Vaughn's Summaries: Medicine Summaries: Prescription Drugs, Prescription Drug TV Ads." Retrieved January 27, 2016 (http://www.vaughns-1-pagers.com/medicine/prescription-drug-tv-ads.htm).

"Authorities Arrest 8 in Drug Trafficking Sting, Operation Three Amigos." 2015. Local News KHBS (Fayetteville and Fort Smith, Arkansas). Retrieved May 29, 2016 (http://www.4029tv.com/news/8-arrested-in-drug-trafficking-sting-operation-3-amigos/31073390).

Axelbank, Evan. 2016. "Polk County Deputies Arrest 3 in Undercover Moonshine Investigation." FOX 13 News Retrieved August 4, 2017 (http://www.fox13news.com/news/local-news/77902685-story).

Babor, Thomas. 2003. "Alcohol: No Ordinary Commodity." *Addiction* 98(1):1343–1350.

Bacon, Selden. 1962. "Alcohol and Complex Society." Pp. 78–93 in *Society, Culture and Drinking Patterns,* edited by David J. Pittman and Charles R. Snyder. New York: John Wiley and Sons.

Baer, Paul E., Robert J. McLaughlin, Mary A. Burnside, and Alex D. Pokorny. 1988. "Alcohol Use and Psychosocial Outcome of Two Preventive Classroom Programs With Seventh and Tenth Graders." *Journal of Drug Education* 18(3):171–184.

Bahr, Howard M. 1973. *Skid Row: An Introduction to Disaffiliation.* New York: Oxford University Press.

Banner, Lois W. 1980. *Elisabeth Cady Stanton: A Radical for Women's Rights.* Boston: Addison-Wesley.

Barkley, Roy. 1990. *The Catholic Alcoholic.* Huntington, IN: Our Sunday Visitor.

Barnes, Andrew J. and E. Richard Brown. 2013. "Occupation as an Independent Risk Factor for Binge Drinking." *American Journal of Drug and Alcohol Abuse* 39(2):108–114.

Barnes, Grace M., M. F. Farrell, and M. Dwindle. 1994. "Longitudinal Effect of Parenting on Alcohol Misuse Among Adolescents." *Alcoholism: Clinical and Experimental Research* 18:916.

Barrows, Susanna and Robin Room. 1991. *Drinking Behavior and Belief in Modern History.* Berkeley: University of California Press.

Baum, Stephen. 2000. "Drunk Driving as a Social Problem: Comparing the Attitude and Knowledge of Drunk Driving Offenders and the General Community." *Accident Analysis and Prevention* 32:689–694.

Becker, Howard. 1951. "The Professional Dance Musician and His Audience." *American Journal of Sociology* 57(2): 136–144.

Becker, Howard S. 1953. "Becoming a Marihuana User." *American Journal of Sociology* 59(3):235–242.

Becker, Howard S. 1963. *Outsiders: Studies in the Sociology of Deviance.* New York: Macmillan.

Beeghley, Leonard E., Wilbur Bock, and John K. Cochran. 1990. "Religious Change and Alcohol Use: An Application of Reference Group and Socialization Theory." *Sociological Forum* 5(2):261–278.

"Behind Americans' 162 Billion Alcohol Tab." 2013. Huffington Post. Retrieved August 11, 2013 (http://www.huffingtonpost.com/2012/12/31/americans-alcohol_n_2389375.html).

Bell, Daniel. 1953. "Crime as an American Way of Life." *Antioch Review* 13(2):131–154.

Benton, Glenn H. 2003. "Prohibition Party." P. 502 in *Dictionary of American History* (Vol. 6, 3rd ed.), edited by Stanley I. Kutler. New York: Charles Scribner's Sons.

Berger, Lawrence M. 2005. "Income, Family Characteristics and Physical Violence Toward Children." *Child Abuse and Neglect* 28(2):107–133.

Bernstein, Dennis and Leslie Kean. 1966. "People of the Opiate: Myanmar's Dictatorship of Drugs." *The Nation* 263(20):11–15.

Bersamin, Melina M., Mallie J. Paschall, Robert F. Saltz, and Byron L. Zamboanga. 2012. "Young Adults and Casual Sex: The Relevance of College Drinking Settings." *Journal of Sex Research* 49(2–3):274–281.

Bertelli, Alberto and L. I. Richardson. 2008. "The Behavioral Impact of Drinking and Driving Laws." *Police Studies Journal* 36:545–569.

Beulens, Joline W. J., Ronald P. Stolk, Yvonne T. van der Schouw, Diederick E. Grobbee, Henk F. J. Hendriks, and Michiel L. Bots. 2005. "Alcohol Consumption and Risk of Type 2 Diabetes Among Older Women." *Diabetes Care* 28(12):2933–2938.

Billings, Andrew G. 1979. "Marital Conflict Resolution of Alcoholic and Non-Alcoholic Couples." *Journal of Studies on Alcohol* 40(3):183–195.

Birkmeier, Johanna D. and David Hemenway. 1990. "Minimum Age Drinking Laws and Youths Suicide, 1970–1990." *American Journal of Public Health* 89(9):1365–1368.

Bittner, Egon. 1967. "The Police on Skid Row: A Study of Peace Keeping." *American Sociological Review* 32(5):699–715.

Bland, Joan Hibernian. 1951. *Crusade.* Washington, DC: Catholic University of America Press.

Bock, E. Wilbur, John K. Cochran, and Leonard Beeghley. 1987. "Moral Messages: The Relative Influence of Denominations on the Religiosity-Alcohol Relationship." *Sociological Quarterly* 28(1):86–105.

Borstein, Tim. 1984. "Drug and Alcohol Issues in the Work Place: An Arbitrator's Perspective." *The Arbitration Journal* 39(3):19–24.

Botvin, Gilbert J., Eli Baker, Anne D. Filazzola, and Elizabeth M. Botvin. 1990. "A Cognitive Behavioral Approach to Substance Abuse Prevention: One-Year Follow-up." *Addictive Behavior* 15(1):47–63.

Bouchery, Ellen E., Henrick J. Harwood, Jeffrey J. Sacks, Carol J. Simon, and Robert D. Brewer. 2011. "Economic Costs of Excessive Alcohol Consumption, 2006." *American Journal of Preventive Medicine* 41(5):516–524.

Bourgois, Philippe. 1989. "In Search of Horatio Alger: Culture and Ideology in the Crack Economy." *Contemporary Drug Problems* 16:4:619–649.

Bourgois, Philippe. 1998a. "Just Another Night in a Shooting Gallery." *Theory, Culture & Society* 15(2):37–66.

Bourgois, Philippe. 1998b. "The Moral Economies of Homeless Heroin Addicts: Confronting Ethnography, HIV Risk, and Everyday Violence in San Francisco Shooting Encampments." *Substance Use and Misuse* 33(11):2323–2351.

Bourgois, Philippe. 2003. *In Search of Respect: Selling Crack in El Barrio*. New York: Cambridge University Press.

Bourgois, Philippe and Schonberg, Jeff. 2009. *Righteous Dopefiend*. Berkeley: University of California Press.

Breslow, Jason M. 2015. "The Staggering Death Toll of Mexico's Drug War." *Frontline*. Retrieved May 18, 2017 (http://www.pbs.org/wgbh/frontline/article/the-staggering-death-toll-of-mexicos-drug-war/).

Brown, Emma, Steve Hendrix, and Susan Svriuga. 2015. "Drinking Is Central to College Culture—and to Sexual Assault." *Washington Post*. Retrieved March 5, 2017 (https://www.washingtonpost.com/local/education/beer-pong-body-shots-keg-stands-alcohol-central-to-college-and-assault/2015/06/14/7430e13c-04bb-11e5-a428-c984eb077d4e_story.html? utm_term=.230ecd58bb38).

Bruce, Lenny. 1963. *How to Talk Dirty and Influence People*. Chicago: Playboy Press.

Buddy, T. 2012. "The Michigan Alcohol Screening Test Measures Lifetime Drinking Problems." About.com. Retrieved August 15, 2013 (http://alcoholism.about.com/od/tests/a/mast.htm).

Bukowski, Charles. 1977. "Beer" in *Love Is a Dog From Hell*. New York: HarperCollins.

Bullington, Bruce, John G. Munns, and Gilbert Geis. 1969. "Purchase of Conformity: Ex-Narcotic Addicts Among the Bourgeoisie." *Social Problems* 16(4):456–463.

Bullock, M. L., J. T. Kiresuk, R. E. Sherman, S. K. Lenz, P. D. Culliton, T. A. Boucher, and C. J. Nolan. 2002. "A Large Randomized Placebo Controlled Study of Auricular Acupuncture for Alcohol Dependence." *Journal of Substance Abuse Treatment* 22(2):71–77.

Bullough, Vern L. and Thomas S. Weinberg. 1988. "Women Married to Transvestites: Problems and Adjustments." *Journal of Psychology & Human Sexuality* 1(2):83–104.

buppractice. 2017. "DSM 5 Criteria for Substance Use Disorder." Retrieved March 12, 2017 (http://www.buppractice.com/node/12351).

Burk, Kathleen and Michael Bywater. 2008. *Is This Bottle Corked? The Secret Life of Wine*. New York: Harmony Books.

Burroughs, William S. 2003. *Junky*. Edited and with an introduction by Oliver Harris. New York: Grove Press.

Burton, Vanessa. 2014. "Why Do Men Love Strip Clubs?" *AskMen*. Retrieved January 14, 2014 (http://www.askmen.com/).

Byse, Clark. 1940. "Alcoholic Beverage Control before Repeal." *Law and Contemporary Problems* 7:544–569.

Caba, Justin. 2015. "America's Heroin Epidemic Explained: The Number of People Under the Age of 25 Using Heroin Has Doubled in the Past Decade." *Medical Daily* (July 8). Retrieved February 26, 2017 (http://www.medicaldaily.com/americas-heroin-epidemic-explained-number-people-under-age-25-using-heroin-has-341910).

Cacioppo, John T. 2008. *Loneliness: Human Nature and the Need for Social Connection*. Chicago: W. W. Norton.

Caldwell, Robert G. and James A. Black. 1971. *Juvenile Delinquency*. New York: Ronald Press.

Camargo, Carlos A. 1997. "Prospective Study of Moderate Alcohol Consumption and Mortality in US Male Physicians." *Archives of Internal Medicine* 157:79–85.

"Cannabis Cup." 2015. *High Times*. Retrieved January 25, 2016 (http://www.cannabiscup.com/).

Carpenter, Christopher. 2004. "How Do Zero Tolerance Drunk Driving Laws Work?" *Journal of Health Economics* 23:61–83.

Carson, Ann E. 2014. *Prisoners in 2013*. Washington, DC: U.S. Department of Justice, Bureau of Justice Statistics (September):15–16.

Cavan, Sherri. 1966. *Liquor License: An Ethnography of Bar Behavior*. Chicago: Aldine.

Cavazos-Rehg, Patricia, Melissa Krauss, Richard Grucza, and Laura Bierut. 2014. "Characterizing the Followers and Tweets of a Marijuana-Focused Twitter Handle." *Journal of Medical Internet Research* 16(6):e157. Retrieved February 1, 2016 (http://www.jmir.org/2014/6/e157/).

Census Scope. 2000. "Age Distribution 2000." Retrieved August 18, 2017 (http://www.censusscope.org/us/s27/chart_age.html).

Center on Alcohol Marketing and Youth. 2003. *Summary Brochure: Alcohol Marketing and Youth*. Washington, DC: Author.

Center on Media and Child Health. 2015. "Alcohol, Tobacco and Drugs." Retrieved February 1, 2016 (http://cmch.tv/parents/alcohol-tobacco-and-drugs/).

Centers for Disease Control and Prevention. 2008. "Alcohol Use Among Women of Childbearing Age." *Data and Statistics*, pp. 1–6. Atlanta, GA: Author.

Centers for Disease Control and Prevention. 2011. "Drinking and Driving: A Threat to Everyone." Retrieved August 18, 2017 (https://www.cdc.gov/vitalsigns/drinkinganddriving/index.html).

Centers for Disease Control and Prevention. 2014. "Smoking and Tobacco Use: Tobacco-Related Mortality." Retrieved August 6, 2014 (http://www.cdc.gov/tobacco/data_statistics/fact_sheets/health_effects/tobacco_related_mortality/).

Centers for Disease Control and Prevention. 2016a. "Smoking & Tobacco Use: Trends in Current Cigarette Smoking Among High School Students and Adults, United States, 1965–2011." Retrieved May 30, 2016 (http://www.cdc.gov/tobacco/data_statistics/tables/trends/cig_smoking/).

Centers for Disease Control and Prevention. 2016b. "Fact Sheet—Alcohol Use and Your Health." Atlanta, GA: Author. Retrieved May 30, 2016 (http://www.cdc.gov/alcohol/fact-sheets/alcohol-use.htm).

Centers for Disease Control and Prevention. 2016c. "Drug Overdose Death Data." Retrieved February 23, 2017 (https://www.cdc.gov/drugoverdose/data/statedeaths.html).

Centers for Disease Control and Prevention. 2017a. "Heroin Overdose Data." Retrieved February 23, 2017 (https://www.cdc.gov/drugoverdose/data/heroin.html).

Centers for Disease Control and Prevention. 2017b. "Motor Vehicle Safety: Impaired Driving; Get the Facts." Retrieved August 4, 2017 (https://www.cdc.gov/motorvehiclesafety/impaired_driving/impaired-drv_factsheet.html).

Centers for Disease Control and Prevention. n.d.-a. "Alcohol and Public Health: Data, Trends and Maps." Retrieved October 6, 2014 (http://www.cdc.gov/alcohol/data-stats.htm).

Centers for Disease Control and Prevention. n.d.-b. "Trends in the Prevalence of Alcohol Use National YRBS: 1991–2011." Retrieved October 6, 2014 (http://www.cdc.gov/healthyyouth/yrbs/pdf/us_alcohol_trend_yrbs.pdf).

Chaloupka, Frank J., Michael Grossman, and Henry Saffer. 1996. "Drinking in College: The Impact of Price, Availability and Alcohol Control Policies." *Contemporary Economic Policy* 14:112–124.

Chalupka, Frank J., Henry Saffer, and Michael Grossman. 1993. "Alcohol Control Policies and Motor Vehicle Fatalities." *Journal of Legal Studies* 22(1):161–186.

Chambliss, William J. 1969. *Crime and the Legal Process*. New York: McGraw Hill.

Chapman, Kenneth L. 1963. "Narcotics Addiction and Its Treatment." *Federal Probation* (June):23.

Charrington, Ernest H. 1920. *The Evolution of Prohibition in the United States*. Westerville, OH: American Issue Press.

Chatters, Linda M. 2000. "Religion and Health: Public Health Research and Practice." *Annual Review of Public Health* 21:335–367.

Childs, Randolph W. 1947. *Making Repeal Work*. Philadelphia: Pennsylvania Alcoholic Beverages Study:260–261.

Chinese Exclusion Act. 1882. Ses. I, Chap. 126; 22 Stat. 58. 47th Congress (May 6).

Chiu, Brian C., J. R. Cerhan, S. M. Gapstur, T. A. Sellers, W. Zheng, C. T. Lutz, R. B. Wallace, and J. D. Potter. 1999. "Alcohol Consumption and Non-Hodgkin Lymphoma in a Cohort of Older Women." *British Journal of Cancer* 76(11):1476–1482.

Chong, Tommy. 2008. *Cheech & Chong: The Unauthorized Autobiography*. New York: Simon Spotlight Entertainment.

Clayton, Richard R., Anne M. Cattarello, and Bryan M. Johnstone. 1996. "The Effectiveness of Drug Abuse Resistance Education (Project DARE): 5-year Follow-up Results." *Preventive Medicine* 25:307–318.

Cloward, Richard A. 1977. *Poor People's Movements*. New York: Vintage.

Cloward, Richard A. and Lloyd E. Ohlin. 1960. *Delinquency and Opportunity: A Theory of Delinquent Gangs*. Glencoe, IL: Free Press.

Clyde, Paul H. 1940. *United States Policy Toward China*. Durham, NC: Duke University Press.

Cocaine Information and Addiction Resources. 2016. "About Cocaine." Retrieved May 28, 2016 (http://www.aboutcocaine.com).

Cohen, Albert K. 1955. *Delinquent Boys: The Culture of the Gang*. Glencoe, IL: Free Press.

Cohen, Albert K. 1966. *Deviance and Control*. Englewood Cliffs, NJ: Prentice-Hall.

Cohen, Sheldon. 1993. "Smoking, Alcohol Consumption and Susceptibility to the Common Cold." *American Journal of Public Health* 83(9):1277–1283.

Commonwealth Foundation. 2011. "The Failure of Government Run Liquor Stores." Retrieved May 31, 2016 (http://www.commonwealthfoundation.org/research/detail/the-failure-of-government-run-liquor-stores).

Comprehensive Drug Abuse Prevention and Control Act of 1970, Pub. L. No. 91-513, 84 Stat. 1236.

Congressional Budget Office. 2016. "Increase All Taxes on Alcoholic Beverages to $16 Per Proof Gallon." Retrieved May 17, 2017 (https://www.cbo.gov/budget-options/2016/52284).

Congressional Research Service. 2015. *Alcohol Excise Taxes: Current Law and Economic Analysis*. CRS Analysis of Department of the Treasury Alcohol and Tobacco Tax and Trade Bureau, Various Years. (http://www.ttb.gov/tax_audit/tax_collections.shtml). Figure 4. Alcohol Excise Tax Collections as a Share of Excises Collected by the Alcohol and Tobacco Trade Bureau (TTB), FY1990–FY2015.

Conroy, Bill. 2012. "Drug War Related Homicides in the United States." The Narcosphere. Retrieved May 31, 2016 (http://narcosphere.narconews.com/notebook/bill-conroy/2012/03/drug-war-related-homicides-us-average-least-1100-year).

Coohey, Carol. 2003. "Defining and Classifying Supervisory Neglect." *Child Maltreatment* 8:154–156.

Cook, Philip and Michael Moore. 1993. "Violence Reduction Through Restrictions on Alcohol Availability." *Alcohol, Health and Research World* 17:148–153.

Cooley, Charles Horton. 1909. *Human Nature and the Social Order*. New York: Scribner.

Cooper, Arnie. 2013. "An Anxious History of Valium." *Wall Street Journal*. Retrieved January 24, 2016 (http://www.wsj.com/articles/SB10001424052702303289904579195872550052950).

Cooper, M. Lynne. 2002. "Alcohol Use and Risky Sexual Behavior Among College Students and Youths." *Journal of Studies on Alcohol* 14:101–117.

Courtwright, David. 1982. *Dark Paradise: Opium Addiction in America Before 1940*. Cambridge, MA: Harvard University Press.

Cowboy Lyrics.com. "Roger Miller Chug-a-Lug Lyrics." Retrieved February 23, 2014 (http://www.cowboylyrics.com/lyrics/miller-roger/chug-a-lug-1167.html).

Coyle, Marcia. 1988. "Prosecutors Admit: No Victory in Sight." *National Law Journal* 10(48):S2–S3.

Cressey, Paul Goalby. 1932. *The Taxi-Dance Hall: A Sociological Study in Commercialized Recreation & City Life*. Chicago: University of Chicago Press.

Crow, James W. and William J. Bailey. 1995. "Self-Interest and Attitudes About Legislation Controlling Alcohol." *Psychological Reports* 76:995–1003.

Cunradi, Carol B., R. Caetano, C. L. Clark, and J. Schafer. 1999. "Alcohol Related Problems and Intimate Partner Violence Among White, Black and Hispanic Couples in the U.S." *Alcoholism: Clinical and Experimental Research* 23(9):1492–1501.

Dabney, Joseph E. 1974. *Mountain Spirits*. Asheville, NC: Blue Mountain Books.

Daileda, Colin. 2016. "The Drug Next Door: Why Every American Should be Worried About Heroin." Mashable. Retrieved February 25, 2017 (http://mashable.com/2016/02/25/americas-heroin-epidemic).

Dairdron, D. M. 1989. "Cardiovascular Effect of Alcohol." *Western Journal of Medicine* 151(4):430–439.

Daley, Robert. 1978. *Prince of the City: The True Story of a Cop Who Knew Too Much*. Boston: Houghton Mifflin.

Dannenbaum, Jed. 1981. "Immigrants and Temperance: Ethnocultural Conflict in Cincinnati." *Ohio History* 87 (Spring):125–139.

Davenport, Courtney L. 2012. "Organizers of Teen Party Liable for Drunk Driving." *Trial* (July):54–55.

Davis, Henry L. 2016. "Wave of Opioid-Related Deaths Hits Erie County." *Buffalo News*, December 29. Retrieved February 25, 2017 (https://buffalonews.com/2016/12/29/wave-opioid-related-deaths-hits-erie-county).

Davis, Jeanie Lerche. 2004. "Researchers Identify Alcoholism Gene: Alcohol Addiction, High Anxiety Linked to Same Gene." WebMD Health News. Retrieved August 8, 2013 (http://www.webmd.com/mental-health/news/20040526/researchers-identify-alcoholism-gene).

Davis, Marli. 2012. *Jews and Booze*. New York: New York University Press.

Dawson, Deborah and B. F. Grant. 1997. "Age of Onset of Alcohol Use and Its Association With Alcohol Abuse and Dependence." *Journal of Substance Abuse* 9:103–110.

Day, Nancy L. and Gale A. Richardson. 2004. "An Analysis of the Effects of Prenatal Alcohol Exposure on Growth: A Teratologic Model." *American Journal of Medical Genetics* 127:28–34.

Daytop Village. 2012. "The History of Daytop New York in Substance Abuse Treatment." Retrieved July 1, 2015 (http://www.daytop.org/history.html).

Deep Underground Poetry. 2017. "Drug Poems." Retrieved August 8, 2017 (https://deepundergroundpoetry.com/drugs-poems/).

DeKaseredy, Walter and Katherine Kelly. 2003. "Women Abuse in University and College Dating Relationships: The Contributions of the Ideology of Familial Patriarchy." *Journal of Human Justice* 4:25–52.

D'Emilio, Frances. 1982. "Drug Addiction Treated With Acupuncture." *Buffalo Courier-Express*, February 7, p. F-6.

Denzin, Norman K. 1991. *Hollywood Shot by Shot: Alcoholism in American Cinema*. New York: Aldine de Gruyter.

"Details Emerge From Fracas at Youth Wrestling Tournament in Belveder." 2010. *Express-Times*. Lehigh Valley Live, February 2.

Devos-Comby, Loraine, Jason Daniel, and James E. Lange. 2013. "Alcohol Consumption, Dating Relationships, and Preliminary Sexual Outcomes in Collegiate Natural Drinking Groups." *Journal of Applied Social Psychology* 43:2391–2400.

Di Castelnuovo, Augusto 2006. "Alcohol Dosing and Total Mortality in Men and Women: An Updated Meta-Analysis of 34 Prospective studies." *Archives of International Medicine* 166:2437–2445.

Diaz-Duran, Constantino. 2009. "Queenpins of the Drug Cartels." The Daily Beast. Retrieved May 31, 2016 (http://www.thedailybeast.com/articles/2009/04/16/queenpins-of-the-drug-cartels.html).

Dickens, Charles. 1980/1870. *The Mystery of Edwin Drood*. Concluded by Leon Garfield; introduced by Edward Blishen. New York: Pantheon Books.

Dietler, Michael. 1990. "Driven by Drink: The Role of Drinking in the Political Economy and the Case of Early Iron Age France." *Journal of Anthropological Archeology* 9:352.

DiFilippo, Dana and Phillip Lucas. 2012. "Dirty Dancing: Strippers Bring Prostitution, Violence, Cops Say." Philly.com. Retrieved April 26, 2014 (http://articles.philly.com/2012-03-28/news/31250072_1_penthouse-club-undercover-prostitution-sting-strip-clubs).

Digital Poet. n.d. "Drug Poems, Slam Poetry About Drugs & Addiction." Retrieved August 8, 2017 (http://www.digitalpoet.net/drug-poems.html).

DiJulio, John J. 1996. "Help Wanted: Economists, Crime and Public Policy." *Journal of Economic Perspectives* 10:3–24.

Distilled Spirits Council of the United States. 2017. "Economic Contributions of the Distilled Spirits Industry." Retrieved August 4, 2017 (http://www.discus.org/economics/).

Dobosz, Robert P. and Lee A. Beaty. 1999. "The Relationship Between Athletic Participation and High School Leadership Ability." *Adolescence* 34:215–220.

Dole, Vincent P. and Marie Nyswander. 2011. "Methadone Maintenance: A Theoretical Perspective." Pp. 445–450 in *The American Drug Scene: An Anthology* (6th ed.), edited by James Inciardi and Karen McElgrath. New York: Oxford University Press.

Doyle, Sir Arthur Conan. 2009a. "The Man With the Twisted Lip." Pp. 211–226 in *The Complete Works of Sherlock Holmes*. Introduction by Christopher and Barbara Roden. New York: Barnes and Noble.

Doyle, Sir Arthur Conan. 2009b. "The Sign of the Four." Pp. 75–141 in *The Complete Works of Sherlock Holmes*. Introduction by Christopher and Barbara Roden. New York: Barnes and Noble.

Doyle, Sir Arthur Conan. 2009c. "The Missing Three-Quarter." Pp. 588–602 in *The Complete Works of Sherlock Holmes*. Introduction by Christopher and Barbara Roden. New York: Barnes and Noble.

Drug Abuse Warning Network. 2013a. "National Estimates of Drug-Related Emergency Department Visits, 2011." Table 7. Washington, DC: U.S. Department of Health and Human Services.

Drug Abuse Warning Network. 2013b. "National Estimates of Drug-Related Emergency Department Visits, 2011." Washington, DC: U.S. Department of Health and Human Services.

Drug Abuse Warning Network. 2013c. "National Estimates of Drug-Related Emergency Department Visits, 2011." Table 16. Washington, DC: U.S. Department of Health and Human Services.

Drug and Alcohol Rehab Asia. 2017. "Cognitive Behavior Therapy in Rehab." Retrieved March 7, 2017 (http://alcoholrehab.com/drug-addiction-treatment/cognitive-behavior-therapy/).

Drug Enforcement Agency. n.d. "Drug Scheduling." Washington, DC: U.S. Department of Justice. Retrieved August 18, 2013 (http://www.justice.gov/dea/druginfo/ds.shtml).

"Drug Overdose Deaths Rise Across the United States." 2015. Lifescript. Retrieved February 25, 2017 (http://www.lifescript.com/health/centers/health_care/news/2015/06/17/drug_overdose_deaths_rise_across_the_United_States).

Drug War Facts. 2017a. "Crime, Arrests and US Law Enforcement." Retrieved August 10, 2017 (http://www.drugwarfacts.org/chapter/crime_arrests).

Drug War Facts. 2017b. "Drug Use Prevalence." Retrieved August 10, 2017 (http://www.drugwarfacts.org/chapter/prevalence).

Ducci, F. and D. Goldman. 2008. "Genetic Approaches to Addiction: Genes and Alcohol." *Addiction* 103 (September):1414–1428.

Durant, Will. 1950. *The Age of Faith*. New York: Simon and Schuster.

Durkheim, Emile. 1966. *Suicide, a Study in Sociology*. Translated by John A. Spaulding and George Simpson, edited with an introduction by George Simpson. New York: Free Press.

Dutchman-Smith, Victoria. 2004. "Is Alcohol Really a Feminist Issue?" The F Word: Contemporary UK Feminism. Retrieved February 27, 2017 (https://www.thefworkd.org.uk/2004/09/is_alcohol_really_a_feminist_issue/).

Dutton, Donald G. and Catherine E. Stachan. 1987. "Motivational Needs for Power and Spouse Specific Assertiveness in Assaultive and Non-Assaultive Men." *Violence and Victims* 2:145–156.

Eaton, Virgil G. 1888. "How the Opium Habit Is Acquired." *Popular Science Monthly* 33:663–667.

Elyrics.org. n.d. "Memphis Jug Band Lyrics." Retrieved January 21, 2016 (http://www.elyrics.net/read/m/memphis-jug-band-lyrics/cocaine-habit-blues-lyrics.html).

Emmerich, Alexander. 2010. *Die Geschichte der Deutschen in Amerika*. Köln: Fackenträger Verlag.

Empey, Lamar T., Mark C. Stafford, and Carter H. Hay. 1999. *American Delinquency: Its Meaning and Construction* (4th ed.). New York: Wadsworth.

Ennett, Susan T., Nancy S. Tobler, Christopher L. Ringwalt, and Robert L. Flewelling. 1994. "How Effective Is Drug Abuse Resistance Education? A Meta-Analysis of Project DARE Outcome Evaluations." *American Journal of Public Health* 84(9):1394–1399.

Epstein, Joan F. and Joseph C. Gfroerer. n.d. "2. Heroin Abuse in the United States." SAMHSA. Retrieved September 29, 2014 (http://www.samhsa.gov/data/treatan/treana11.htm).

Erenberg, Debra F. and George A. Hacker. 1997. *High Risk Bar Promotions That Target College Students*. Washington, DC: Center for Science in the Public Interest.

Erowid. 2015. "Erowid Psychoactive Vaults: Drug Humor, Jokes Related to Psychoactives and the Drug War."

Retrieved February 1, 2016 (https://www.erowid.org/psychoactives/humor/humor.shtml).

Eskew Law. 2016. "America's Heroin Epidemic Explained in 6 Charts." Retrieved February 26, 2017 (http://eskewlaw.com/need-know-heroin/).

Espeland, Mark A., L. H. Coker, R. Wallace, S. R. Rapp, S. M. Resnick, M. Limacher, L. H. Powell, and C. R. Messina. 2006. "Association Between Alcohol Intake and Domain Specific Cognitive Function in Older Women." *Neuroepidemiology* 1(27):1–12.

Esslinger, Dean R. 1967. "American German and Irish Attitudes Toward Neutrality, 1914–1917." *Catholic Historical Review* 53 (July).

Evans, Michael and Paul Kingsbury. 2010. *Woodstock: Three Days That Rocked the World.* New York: Sterling Press.

Executive Office of the President, Office of National Drug Control Policy. n.d. Retrieved August 17, 2017 (http://www.whitehouse.gov-ondcp).

Fagan, Ronald, Ola Barnett, and John Patton. 1998. "Reasons for Alcohol Use in Maritally Violent Men." *American Journal of Drug and Alcohol Abuse* 14(3):371–392.

Fainaru, Steve and William Booth. 2009. "A Mexican Cartel's Swift and Grisly Climb." *Washington Post,* June 13, p. 3.

Falk, Gèrhard. 2005. *Football and American Identity.* New York: Hayworth Press.

Faupel, Charles E., and Carl B. Klockars. 1987. "Drug-Crime Connections: Elaborations from the Life Histories of Hard Core Heroin Addicts." *Social Problems* 34:54–86.

Federal Aviation Association. n.d. Regulation 91.17.

Federal Bureau of Investigation. 2013. Uniform Crime Reports. *Crime in the United States, 2013.* U.S. Department of Justice, Federal Bureau of Investigation, Criminal Justice Information Services Division. Retrieved August 18, 2017 (https://ucr.fbi.gov/crime-in-the-u.s/2013/crime-in-the-u.s.-2013/cius-home).

Federal Bureau of Investigation. 2015. Uniform Crime Reports. *Crime in the United States, 2015.* U.S. Department of Justice, Federal Bureau of Investigation, Criminal Justice Information Services Division. Retrieved March 12, 2017 (https://ucr.fbi.gov/crime-in-the-u.s/2015/crime-in-the-u.s.-2015/tables).

Federal Trade Commission Cigarette Report for 2011. 2013. Retrieved August 13, 2014 (http://www.ftc.gov/sites/default/files/documents/reports/federal-trade-commission-cigarette-report-2011/130521cigarettereport.pdf).

Felt, Joseph B. 1827. *The Annals of Salem.* London: W. & S. B. Ives.

Finestone, Harold. 1957. "Cats, Kicks, and Color." *Social Problems* 5(1):3–13.

Fitzgerald, F. Scott. 1992. *The Great Gatsby.* New York: Collier Books.

Floyd v. Floyd. 1963. 218 Ga. 606, 129 S.W. 2nd, 786.

Ford, Gene. 1988. *The Benefits of Moderate Drinking: Alcohol, Health and Society.* San Francisco: California Wine Appreciation Guild.

Fosdick, Raymond B. and A. L. Scott. 1933. *Toward Liquor Control.* New York: Harper.

Foster, David. 1983. "Survival Course Helps Alcoholics." *Buffalo News,* September 9, p. C-6.

Freedman, Samuel P., E. R. Pouget, S. Chatterjee, C. M. Cleland, B. Tempalski, J. E. Brady, and H. L. Cooper. 2011. "Drug Arrests and Injection." *American Journal of Public Health* 101(2):344–349.

Freiberg, Malcolm, ed. 1929. *The Winthrop Papers, vol. III.* Boston: Massachusetts Historical Society.

Freisthler, Bridget. 2011. "Alcohol Use, Drinking Venue Utilization, and Child Physical Abuse." *Journal of Family Violence* 26(3):185–193.

Friedan, Betty. 1963. *The Feminine Mystique.* New York: W. W. Norton.

Friedman, Steven. 2005. "Photographers Witness Highs and Lows at Weddings." *Jewish News Weekly,* June 17, p. 2b.

Frone, Michael R. 2006. "Prevalence and Distribution of Alcohol Use and Impairment in the Workplace: A U.S. National Survey." *Journal of Studies on Alcohol* 67(1):147–156.

Fuchs, Marek. 2004. "Gay Bars, Lifeline to Some, to Close." *New York Times,* January 11, p. WE5.

Furnas, Joseph C. 1965. *The Life and Times of the Late Demon Rum*. New York: W. H. Allen.

Galliher, John F. and Allynn Walker. 1977. "The Puzzle of the Social Origins of the Marihuana Tax Act of 1937." *Social Problems* 24(3):367–376.

Garfinkel, Harold. 1956. "Conditions of Successful Degradation Ceremonies." *American Journal of Sociology* 61:240–244.

Gasnier, Louis. (Director). 1965. *Reefer Madness*. New York: Goodtimes Home Video Corp. (first produced in 1936.)

Gellman, Irving. 1964. *The Sober Alcoholic*. New Haven, CT: College and University Press.

"The Genetics of Alcoholism: Alcohol Alert from NIAAA." 2013. Retrieved August 8, 2013 (http://alcoholism.about.com/cs/alerts/1/blnaa18.htm).

Gerth, Jeff and T. Christian Miller. 2013. "Use Only as Directed." ProPublica. Retrieved February 1, 2016 (https://www.propublica.org/).

Gieringer, Dale. 2006. "The Opium Exclusion Act of 1909." Counterpunch. Retrieved June 1, 2006 (http://www.counterpunch.org/2009/02/06/the-opium-exclusion-act-of-1909/).

Gilmore, Amanda K., Hollie F. Granato, and Melissa A. Lewis. 2013. "The Use of Drinking and Condom-Related Protective Strategies in Association With Condom Use and Sex-Related Alcohol Use." *Journal of Sex Research* 50(5):470–479.

Glad, David D. 1947. "Attitudes and Experiences of American-Jewish and American-Irish Male Youths." *Quarterly Journal of Studies on Alcohol* 8:406.

Glatter, Robert. 2016. "Heroin Is Now the Leading Cause of Overdose Deaths in the U.S." *Forbes*. Retrieved February 23, 2017 (http://forbes.com/sites/robertglatter/2016/12/22/heroin-is-now-the-leading-cause-of-overdose-deaths-in-the-u-s).

Glazer, Nathan. 1952. "Why Jews Stay Sober." *Commentary* 13:181–186.

Goffman, Erving. 1959. "The Moral Career of the Mental Patient." *Psychiatry, Interpersonal and Biological Processes* 22(2):123–142.

Goffman, Erving. 1961. *Asylums: Essays on the Social Situation of Mental Patients and Other Inmates*. New York: Anchor Books.

Goffman, Erving. 1963. *Stigma: Notes on the Management of Spoiled Identity*. Englewood Cliffs, NJ: Prentice-Hall.

Gold, Martin. 1966. "Undetected Delinquent Behavior." *Journal of Research in Crime and Delinquency* 3(1):27–46.

Gold, Martin. 1970. *Delinquent Behavior in an American City*. Belmont, CA: Brooks/Cole.

Goldberg, Leonard. 1977. "Epidemiology and Alcoholism." *Nutrition and Metabolism* 21(1–3):144–152.

Goldenbaum, D. M., M. Christopher, R. M. Gallagher, S. Fishman, R. Payne, D. Joranson, D. Edmondson, J. McKee, and A. Thexton. 2008. "Physicians Charged With Opioid Analgesic-Prescribing Offenses." *Pain Med* 9(6):737–747.

Goldstein, David. 2001. "Drugs in the Comics." Retrieved August 8, 2017 (https://www.erowid.org/psychoactives/humor/humor_drugs_in_the_comics.pdf).

Golgowski, Nina. 2013. "Dark Side of the Hippie Lifestyle: Stunning Photographs Capture the 1969 War on Dealers Who Supplied America's Counter-Culture Revolution With Its Drugs." Daily Mail.com. Retrieved August 4, 2014 (http://www.dailymail.co.uk/news/article-2267979/Operation-Intercept-Americas-1969-war-drug-dealers-supplied-counter-culture-revolution.html#ixzz39SEcS81l).

Gomberg, Edith S. Lisansky and Ted D. Nirenberg, eds. 1993. *Women and Substance Abuse*. Norwood, NJ: Ablex.

Gomez, Linda. 1984. "Cocaine: America's 100 Years of Euphoria and Despair." *Life* 7(5):57–68.

Gonzalez, Turmo I. 2001. "Drinking and Almost Silent Language." Pp. 130–143 in *Drinking: Anthropological Approaches*, edited by V. deGarine. New York: Berghan.

Goode, Erich. 2008. *Drugs in American Society* (8th ed.). New York: McGraw Hill.

Goode, Erich. 2014. *Drugs in American Society* (9th ed.). New York: McGraw-Hill.

Goodfellow, Marianne and Katherine Kilgore. 2014. "DUI Offenders' Beliefs About DUI Statutes and DUI Law Enforcement: Implications for Deterrence." *Journal of Drug Issues* 44(3):269–280.

Goodman, Tim. 2013. "Drunk History: TV Review." *The Hollywood Reporter* (July 7). Retrieved January 28, 2014 (http://www.hollywoodreporter.com/review/drunk-history-tv-review-581507).

Gordon, Anna A. 1898. *The Beautiful Life of Frances Willard.* Chicago: The Women's Christian Temperance Association.

Goyder, John. 2005. "The Dynamics of Occupational Prestige: 1975–2000." *Canadian Journal of Sociology and Anthropology* 42(1):1–23.

Grant, Bridget F. and Deborah A. Dawson. 1997. "Age at Onset of Alcohol Use and Its Association With Alcohol Abuse and Dependency." *Journal of Substance Abuse* 9:103–110.

Greenfield, Joshua T. and J. D. Rogers. 1999. "Beer Drinking Accounts for Most of the Hazardous Alcohol Consumption Reported in the United States." *Journal of Studies on Alcohol* 60(6):732–739.

Greenfield, Lawrence A. 1998. *Alcohol and Crime: An Analysis of National Data on the Prevalence of Alcohol in Crime.* Washington, DC: United States Department of Justice, Office of Justice Programs, Bureau of Justice Statistics.

Griffin, Larry and Ashley B. Thompson. 2002. "Appalachia and the South—Collective Memory, Identity, and Representation." *Appalachian Journal* 29(3):296–327.

Grillo, Joan. 2011. *El Narco.* New York: Bloombury Press.

Grogger, Jeff and Michael Willis. 2000. "The Emergence of Crack Cocaine and the Rise in Urban Crime Rates." *Review of Economics and Statistics* 82(4):519–529.

Gruenewald, Paul J., W. R. Ponicki, and H. D. Holder. 1992. "The Relationship of Outlet Densities to Alcohol Consumption: A Time Series Cross-Sectional Analysis." *Alcoholism: Clinical and Experimental Research* 17(1): 38–47.

Hall v. Hall. 1964. 178, Neb.91132 N.W. 2ns 21 7.

Halsey, L. G., J. W. Huber, R. D. J. Bufton, and A. C. Little. 2010. "An Explanation for Enhanced Perceptions of Attractiveness After Alcohol Consumption." *Alcohol* 44(4):307–313.

Haltiwanger, John. 2014. "The Mexican Drug War Has Killed More Americans Than ISIS or Ebola Ever Could." Elite Daily. Retrieved August 10, 2017 (http://elitedaily.com/news/world/mexican-drug-war-kills-more-americans-than-isis-and-ebola/806049/).

Ham, Lindsay S., Byron L. Zamboanga, Ana J. Bridges, Hilary G. Casner, and Amy K. Bacon. 2013. "Alcohol Expectancies and Alcohol Use Frequency: Does Drinking Context Matter?" *Cognitive Therapy and Research* 37:620–632.

Harckham, Peter B. 2000. "Parental Modeling Key to Teenage Drinking." *New York Times*, January 30, p. 14.

Harner, Michael J. 1965. "Common Themes in South American Indian Yahe Experiences." Paper presented at the American Anthropological Association Meetings, Denver, Colorado. Retrieved January 9, 2016 (http://www.lycaeum.org/diseyes/fresh/yagecomm.htm).

Harris v. Harris. 1960. 186 Cal. App.2nd 788 9 Cal. Rptr.300 Dist. Crt App.

Harrison, Leonard V. and Elizabeth Laine. 1936. *After Repeal: A Study of Liquor Control Administration.* New York: Harper.

Harrison Narcotics Act. 1914. Public Law No.223, 63rd Congress.

Haskell, Martin R. and Lewis Yablonsky. 1970. *Crime and Delinquency.* Chicago: Rand McNally.

Head, Jenny, J. Siegrist, and S. A. Stansfeld. 2004. "The Psychosocial Work Environment and Alcohol Dependence: A Prospective Study." *Journal of Occupational and Environmental Medicine* 61(3):219–224.

Hecht, Michael L. and Michelle Miller-Day. 2007. "The Drug Resistance Strategies Project as Translational Research." *Journal of Applied Communication Research* 35(4): 343–349.

Hein, Kenneth. 2006. "The Bar Scene: Signs of the Times." *Brandweek* 47(16).

Hemingway, Ernest. 1929. *A Farewell to Arms.* New York: Grosset & Dunlap.

Hijek, Barbara. 2012. "16 Strippers, Ages 18 to 61, Busted on Prostitution Charges in Tampa Before Upcoming RNC." *SunSentinal*, August 19. Retrieved April 26, 2014 (http://articles.sun-sentinel.com/2012-08-19/news/sfl-16-strippers-20120819_1_prostitution-charges-rnc-tampa-cops).

Hingson, Ralph W., T. Heeren, M. Winter, and H. Wechsler. 2009. "Magnitude of Alcohol Related Mortality and Morbidity Among U.S. College Students Ages

18–24: Changes from 1998 to 2001." *Annual Review of Public Health* 57:587–595.

Hirschi, Travis and Michael R. Gottfredson, eds. 1994. *The Generality of Deviance*. New Brunswick, NJ: Transaction.

History.com. n.d. "This Day in History: April 1, 1970: Nixon Signs Legislation Banning Cigarette Ads on TV and Radio." Retrieved August 5, 2014 (http://www.history.com/this-day-in-history/nixon-signs-legislation-banning-cigarette-ads-on-tv-and-radio).

Hoffer, Lee D. 2006. *Junkie Business: The Evolution and Operation of a Heroin Dealing Network*. Belmont, CA: Thompson Wadsworth.

Hollis, Andre D. 2007. "Narcoterrorism." Pp. 23–35 in *Transnational Threats: Smuggling and Trafficking in Arms, Drugs and Human Life*, edited by Kimberly Thachuck. Westport, CT: Praeger.

Holloway, Frank A. 1995. "Low Dose Alcohol Effects on Human Behavior and Performance." *Alcohol, Drugs & Driving* 11(1):39–56.

Holt, James B., Jacqueline W. Miller, Timothy S. Naimi, and Daniel Z. Sui. 2006. "Religious Affiliation and Alcohol Consumption in the United States." *The Geographical Review* 96(4):523–542.

Horowitz, Evan. 2017. "The Heroin Epidemic Is Spreading." *Boston Globe*, December 22. Retrieved February 25, 2017 (https://www.bostonglobe.com/metro/2016/12/22/the-heroin-epidemic-spreading/xA6vxWHhGMncXW6xfDCzFI/story.html).

Horvath, A. Tom, Kaushik Misra, Amy K. Epner, and Galen Morgan Cooper. 2016. "The Diagnostic Criteria for Substance Use Disorders (Addiction)." Retrieved March 12, 2017 (https://www.mentalhelp.net/articles/the-diagnostic-criteria-for-subsance-use-disorders-addiction).

Hotaling, Gerald and David Sugerman. 1986. "An Analysis of Risk Markers in Husband to Wife Violence: The Current State of Knowledge." *Violence and Victims* 1:101–124.

Howe, Hubert S. 1955. "A Physician's Blueprint for the Management and Prevention of Narcotic Addiction." *New York State Journal of Medicine* 55 (February 1):341–348.

Hu, Tun-yuan 1950. *The Liquor Tax in the United States, 1791–1947*. New York: Columbia University Press.

Huang, Wenyong, Chengxuan Qiu, Bengt Winblad, and Laura Fratiglioni. 2002. "Alcohol Consumption and Incidence of Dementia in a Community Sample Aged 75 Years and Older." *Journal of Clinical Epidemiology* 55(10): 959–964.

Hull, J. G. and C. F. Bond. 1986. "Social and Behavioral Consequences of Alcohol Consumption and Expectancy." *Psychological Bulletin* 99:347.

Hutchinson, George M. et. al. 1959. *Alcohol in the Work Place: Cost and Responses*. Research Monograph. University of Strathclyde, Glasgow, Scotland.

Hylton, Jeremy. n.d. *The Complete Works of William Shakespeare*. Retrieved February 18, 2014 (http://shakespeare.mit.edu/).

"Imprisoned by U.S. in Narcotics Ring: Stromberg Leader Gets 5 Years and Fine." 1958. *New York Times*, April 24, p. 27.

Inciardi, James A., Anne E. Potrieger, and Charles E. Faupel. 1982. "Black Women, Heroin and Crime: Some Empirical Notes." *Journal of Drug Issues* 12(3):241–250.

Inciardi, James A., Hilary L. Surratt, and Steven P. Kurtz. 2011. "African Americans, Crack, and the Federal Sentencing Guidelines." Pp. 252–263 in *The American Drug Scene: An Anthology* (6th ed.), edited by James A. Inciardi and Karen McElrath. New York: Oxford University Press.

"Increase in Smokers Prompts Ad Campaign." 2014. *Buffalo News*, September 16, p. A7.

Ingalls, Z. 1984. "Campus Programs Called Ineffective in Ending Student Alcohol Abuse." *Chronicle of Higher Education* (May 21):17.

Inglis-Arkell, Esther. 2015. "This Is the Drug in the Rolling Stones' Song, 'Mother's Little Helper.'" Retrieved January 24, 2016 (http://io9.gizmodo.com/this-is-the-drug-in-the-rolling-stones-song-mothers-li-1693032181).

Ingraham, Christopher. 2017. "How an 'Abuse-deterrent' Drug Created the Heroin Epidemic." *Washington Post*, January 10. Retrieved January 24, 2017 (https://www.washingtonpost.com/news/wonk/wp/2017/01/10/how-an-abuse-deterrent-drug-created-the-heroin-epidemic).

Internet Sacred Text Archive. 2011. "The Canterbury Tales and Other Works of Chaucer (Middle English), by

Geoffery Chaucer [14th cent.]." Retrieved August 4, 2017 (http://www.sacred-texts.com/neu/eng/mect/index.htm).

Jackson, Bruce. 1970a. "Exiles From the American Dream: The Junkie and the Cop." Pp. 272–287 in *Observations of Deviance*, edited by Jack D. Douglas. New York: Random House.

Jackson, Bruce.1970b. "White-Collar Pill Party." Pp. 255–265 in *Observations of Deviance*, edited by Jack D. Douglas. New York: Random House.

Jackson, Joan K. 1956. "The Adjustment of the Family to Alcoholism." *Marriage and Family Living* 18(4):361–369.

Jackson, Joan K. 1962. "Alcoholism and the Family." Pp. 472–492 in *Society, Culture, and Drinking Patterns*, edited by David J. Pittman and Charles R. Snyder. Carbondale: Southern Illinois University Press.

Jacobs, Julius J. and Albert C. Goebel. 1962. *Cases on Domestic Relations*. Eagan, MN: Foundation Press.

Jacobs, Shayna. 2010. "Midtown Strippers Caught on Video in Prostitution Den, Say Prosecutors." DNAinfo. Retrieved April 26, 2014. (http://articles.mcall.com/2014-01-24/news/mc-allentown-platinum-plus-strippers-hearing-20140124_1_jennifer-beth-jenna-shonk-jamayra-jesse-andrews).

Janson, H. W. 1971. *History of Art: A Survey of the Major Visual Arts From the Dawn of History to the Present Day*. Englewood Cliffs, NJ: Prentice-Hall.

Jellinek, E. M. 1943. "Sociology and the Problems of Alcohol: An Introductory Note." *Quarterly Journal of Studies on Alcohol* 4:399–401.

Jellinek, E. M. 1962. "Phases of Alcohol Addiction." Pp. 356–368 in *Society Culture and Drinking Patterns*, edited by David J. Pittman and Charles R. Snyder. Carbondale: Southern Illinois University Press.

Jennings, Justin, Kathleen L. Antrobus, Sam J. Atencio, Erin Glavich, Rebecca Johnson, German Loffler, and Christine Luu. 2005. "Drinking Beer in a Blissful Mood: Alcohol Production, Operational Chains, and Feasting in the Ancient World." *Current Anthropology* 46(2):275–303.

Jenson, Gary F. 2000. "Prohibition, Alcohol, and Murder: Unchaining Countervailing Mechanisms." *Homicide Studies* 4(1):18–36.

Jernigan, David. 2008. "Intoxicating Brands: Alcohol Advertising and Youth." *Multinational Monitor* 30(1) (July/August). Retrieved August 20, 2014 (http://www.multinationalmonitor.org/mm2008/072008/jernigan.html).

Jewish Publication Society of America. 1917. *The Holy Scriptures According to the Masoretic Text, A New Translation*. Philadelphia, PA: Author.

Johns Hopkins Children's Center. 2011. "Media and Adolescent Substance Abuse." Retrieved February 1, 2016 (http://www.hopkinschildrens.org/media-and-adolescent-substance-abuse.aspx).

Johnson, Bruce D., Ansley Hamid, and Edmundo Morales. 1987. "Critical Dimensions of Crack Distribution." Paper presented at Annual Conference of the American Society of Criminology, Montreal, Canada.

Johnston, L. D., P. M. O'Malley, and J. G. Bachman. 1996. National Survey Results on Drug Use From the Monitoring the Future Study, 1975–1995. Volume I: Secondary School Students (NIH Publication No. 96-4139). Rockville, MD: National Institute on Drug Abuse.

Johnston, L. D., P. M. O'Malley, and J. G. Bachman. 2000. *Monitoring the Future: National Results on Adolescent Drug Use: Overview of Key Findings, 1999* (NIH Publication No. 00-4690). Bethesda, MD: National Institute on Drug Abuse.

Johnston, L. D., P. M. O'Malley, and J. G. Bachman. 2003. *Monitoring the Future: National Study Results on Drug Use*. Bethesda, MD. National Institute on Drug Abuse.

Johnston, L. D., P. M. O'Malley, and J. G. Bachman. 2005. *Monitoring the Future: National Results on Adolescent Drug Use* (NIH Publication No. 02105). Bethesda, MD: National Institute on Drug Abuse.

Jones, Barry T., Ben C. Jones, Andy P. Thomas, and Jessica Piper. 2003. "Alcohol Consumption Increases Attractiveness Ratings of Opposite-Sex Faces: A Possible Third Route to Risky Sex." *Addiction* 98:1069–1075.

Jones, Jonathan. 2012. "Death by Drinking: William Hogarth's Gin Lane." Retrieved December 6, 2013 (http://www.theguardian.com/artanddesign/picture/2012/sep/12/william-hogarth-gin-lane).

Joy, Janet E., Stanley J. Watson Jr., and John A. Benson Jr., eds. 1999. *Marijuana and Medicine: Assessing the Science*

Base. (Prepublication copy. Uncorrected Proofs.) Institute of Medicine. Washington, DC: National Academy Press.

"Judge Piotrowski Warns of Heroin Dangers." 2015. *Am-Pol Eagle.* Retrieved April 1, 2015 (http://ampoeagle.com/judge-piotrowski-warns-of-heroin-dangers-p7279-1.htm).

Justice Policy Institute. 2010. *How to Safely Reduce Prison Populations and Support People Returning to Their Communities.* Washington, DC: Author.

Kalant, O. J. 1971. "Ludlow on Cannabis." *International Journal of the Addictions* 6(2):309–322.

Kallberg, Henrik, S. Jacobsen, C. Bengtsson, M. Pedersen, L. Padyukov, P. Garred, M. Frisch, E. W. Karlson, L. Klareskog, and L. Alfredsson. 2009. "Alcohol Consumption Is Associated With Decreased Risk of Rheumatoid Arthritis." *Annals of the Rheumatoid Diseases* 68(2):222–228.

Kanazawa, Mark. 2005. "Immigration, Exclusion and Taxation: Anti-Chinese Legislation in Gold Rush California." *Journal of Economic History* 65(3):779–805.

Kandall, Stephen R. 1997. "Women and Addiction in the United States—1850 to 1920." *Journal of American History* 84(2):687–688.

Kann, Laura, Tim McManus, William A. Harris, Shari L. Shanklin, Katherine H. Flint, Joseph Hawkins, Barbara Queen, Richard Lowry, Emily O'Malley Olsen, David Chyen, Lisa Whittle, Jemekia Thornton, Connie Lim, Yoshimi Yamakawa, Nancy Brener, and Stephanie Zaza. 2016. "Youth Risk Behavior Surveillance—United States, 2015" *Surveillance Summaries* 65(6):1–174.

Kantor, G. Kaufman and M. A. Straus. 1989. "Substance Abuse as a Precipitant of Wife Abuse Victimization." *American Journal of Drug and Alcohol Abuse* 15(2):173–189.

Keen, Judy. 2012. "Chicago's Corner Taverns Fade Away." *USA Today,* February 13, p. 3A.

Kelly, Liz. 1996. "Tensions and Possibilities: Enhancing Informal Responses to Domestic Violence." Pp. 67–86 in *Future Interventions With Battered Women and Their Families,* edited by John Edleson and Ziv Eisikovitz. Thousand Oaks, CA: Sage.

Kelly, Robert J. 1999. *The Upperworld and the Underworld.* New York: Kluwer Academic.

Kennedy, Bruce P. and Masahiko Minami. 1993. "The Beech Hill Hospital/Outward Bound Adolescent Chemical Dependency Treatment Program." *Journal of Substance Abuse Treatment* 10(4):395–406.

Kerr, Peter. 1988. "Submachine Guns and Unpredictability Are Hallmarks of Crack's Violence." *New York Times,* March 8, p. 1.

Khayyam, Omar. 1889. *The Rubaiyat,* 1120, as it appears in Edward FitzGerald, *Rubaiyat of Omar Khayyam* (5th ed.). New York: Cosimo.

Kiechal, William. 1982. "Looking Out for the Executive Alcoholic." *Fortune* (January 11):36–39.

Kilbourne, Jean. 1999. *Deadly Persuasion.* New York: Free Press.

Kilmer, Beau, Susan S. Everingham, Jonathan P. Caulkins, Gregory Midgette, Rosalie Liccardo Pacula, Peter H. Reuter, Rachel M. Burns, Bing Han, and Russell Lundberg. 2014. "What America's Users Spend on Illegal Drugs: 2000–2010." Santa Monica, CA: RAND Corporation. Retrieved June 5, 2016 (http://www.rand.org/pubs/research_reports/RR534.html).

King, Rufus. 1972. *The Drug Hang-Up: America's Fifty Year Folly.* Springfield, IL: Charles C. Thomas.

King, Wayne. 1981. "Acupuncture Used to Treat Drug Abuse." *New York Times,* June 14. Retrieved June 28, 2015 (http://nytimes.com/1981/06/14/us/acupuncture-used-to-treat-drug-abuse.html).

Kinkel, Donald S. 2005. "Are Alcohol Tax Hikes Fully Passed Through to Prices?" *American Economic Review* 95(2):273–277.

Kirby, David. 1999. "AIDS Fears Rise as Gay Bars Offer Fewer Condoms." *New York Times,* April 25, p. 625.

Kitsuse, J. I. 1962. "Societal Reaction to Deviant Behavior: Problems of Theory and Method." *Social Problems* 9(Winter):247–256.

Kleck, Gary. 1981. "Racial Discrimination in Criminal Sentencing." *American Sociological Review* 46:783–804.

Kokemuller, Neil. 2016. "The Role of a Bartender." *Houston Chronicle.* Retrieved June 5, 2016 (http://work.chron.com/role-bartender-8352.html).

Komro, Kelli A., C. L. Perry, and S. Veblen-Morrison. 2008. "Outcome From a Randomized Controlled Trial of a Multi-Component Alcohol Preventive for Urban Youth." *Addiction* 103:606–618.

Kopper, Lawrence E. 2005. "Moderate Alcohol Consumption Lowers the Risk of Type 2 Diabetes." *Diabetes Care* 28:719–725.

Koss, Mary P. and Thomas E. Dinero. 1988. "Predictors of Male Aggression Among a National Sample of Male College Students." *Annals of the New York Academy of Sciences* 528(1):133–147.

Kosterman, Rebecca and J. D. Hawkins. 2000. "The Dynamics of Alcohol and Marijuana Initiation." *American Journal of Public Health* 90:360–366.

Kouri, Jim. 2011. "La Familia Michoacana Cartel Battered by U.S. Agents." *Examiner* (July 28).

Krebs, Christopher P., Christine H. Lindquist, Tara D. Warner, Bonnie S. Fisher, and Sandra L. Martin. 2007. *The Campus Sexual Assault (CSA) Study, Final Report.* Washington, DC: National Institute of Justice.

Kutter, C. J. and D. S. McDermott. 1997. "The Role of the Church in Adolescent Drug Education." *Journal of Drug Education* 27(3):293–305.

La Barre, Weston. 1989. *The Peyote Cult* (5th ed). Norman: University of Oklahoma Press.

Landesco, John. 1943. "Prohibition and Crime." *Annals of the American Academy of Political and Social Science* 163:120–129.

Lantis, Nancy T. 1997. "California, Arizona Law Permit Medical Use of Marijuana." *American Journal of Health System Pharmacy* 54 (January 15):126.

LaPiere, R. T. 1934. "Attitudes vs. Actions." *Social Forces* 13:230–237.

Lee, Harper. 2006/1960. *To Kill a Mockingbird.* New York: Harper Perennial.

Lee, Jung Eon, David J. Hunter, Donna Spiegelman, Hans-Olov Adami, Demetrius Albanes, Leslie Bernstein, et al. 2007. "Alcohol Intake and Renal Cell Cancer in a Pooled Analysis of 12 Prospective Studies." *Journal of the National Cancer Institute* 99(10):801–810.

Lee, William. 1953. *Junkie: Confessions of an Unredeemed Drug Addict.* New York: Ace Books.

Lemert, Edwin M. 1967. *Human Deviance, Social Problems, & Social Control.* Englewood Cliffs, NJ: Prentice-Hall.

Lemle, Russell and Mark Mishkind. 1989. "Alcohol and Masculinity." *Journal of Substance Abuse Treatment* 6:213–222.

Lengermann, Patricia Madoo and Gillian Niebrugge. 2010. "Contemporary Feminist Theories." Pp. 193–228 in *Contemporary Social Theory & its Classical Roots: The Basics* (3rd ed.), edited by George Ritzer. New York: McGraw-Hill.

Levine, Harry G. 1978. "The Discovery of Addiction: Changing Conceptions of Habitual Drunkenness in America." *Journal of Studies on Alcohol* 39(1):143–174.

Levine, Harry G. 1985. "The Birth of American Alcohol Control: Prohibition, the Power Elite and the Problem of Lawlessness." *Contemporary Drug Problems* 12:63–115.

Li, Guohura, Susan P. Baker, Yandong Qiang, George W. Rebok, and Melissa L. McCarthy. 2007. "Alcohol Violations and Aviation Accidents: Findings from the U.S. Mandatory Alcohol Testing Program." *Aviation, Space and Environmental Medicine* 78(5):510–513.

Liang, L. and J. Huang. 2008. "Go Out or Stay In: The Effects of Zero Tolerance Laws on Alcohol Use and Drinking and Driving Patterns Among College Students." *Health Economics* 17(1):1261–1275.

Lichtenberg v. Lichtenberg. 1942. 15 Wash. 2d. 226130 P. 371. 2nd.

Lichtenstein, Perry M. 1926. "Thirteen Years Observation on Drug Addiction." Proceedings of the First World Conference on Narcotics Education, Philadelphia.

Lightner, Candice. 1985. "Man of the Year." *Time*, January 7, p. 77.

Lin, Jaung-Geng, Yuan-Yu Chan, and Yi-Hung Chen. 2012. "Acupuncture for the Treatment of Opiate Addiction." *Evidence-Based Complementary and Alternative Medicine.* Retrieved June 28, 2015 (http://www.ncbi.nlm.nih.gov/pmc/articles/PM3296192/).

Lindesmith, Alfred R. 1938. "A Sociological Theory of Drug Addiction." *American Journal of Sociology* 43:593–613.

Lindesmith, Alfred R. 1940. "Dope Fiend Mythology." *Journal of Criminal Law and Criminology* 31:198–208.

Lippmann, Walter. 1931. "The Underworld: Our Secret Servant." *Forum* (January):1.

Llenas, Bryan. 2016. "U.S. Renews Travel Warning to Mexico as Killings of Americans Climb." Fox News

Retrieved August 10, 2017 (http://www.foxnews.com/world/2016/01/20/us-renews-travel-warning-to-mexico-as-killings-americans-climb.html).

London, Jack. 1913. *John Barleycorn*. Retrieved February 19, 2014 (http://www.gutenberg.org/ebooks/318?msg=welcome_stranger).

Lopez, German. 2016. "The Opioid Painkiller and Heroin Epidemic, Explained in Fewer Than 600 Words." Vox. Retrieved February 26, 2017 (http://www.vox.com/2016/9/13/12901708/opioid-painkiller-heroin-epidemic-overdose).

Ludlow, Fitz Hugh. 2013/1857. *The Hasheesh Eater: Being Passages from the Life of a Pythagorean*. New York: Harper & Bros.

Lyons, Mike. 2012. "Man Arrested for Selling Moonshine." *First Coast News*, January 4. Retrieved August 4, 2017 (http://downtownjax.firstcoastnews.com/news/news/68489-man-arrested-selling-moonshine).

Lyricsfreak. 2016. "Kenny Rogers—Just Dropped In Lyrics." Retrieved January 21, 2016 (http://www.lyricsfreak.com/k/kenny+rogers/just+dropped+in_20077868.html).

Lyvers, Michael, Emma Cholakians, Megan Puorro, and Shanti Sundram. 2011a. "Alcohol Intoxication and Self-Reported Risky Sexual Behaviour Intentions With Highly Attractive Strangers in Naturalistic Settings." *Journal of Substance Use* 16(2):99–108.

Lyvers, Michael, Emma Cholakians, Megan Puorro, and Shanti Sundram. 2011b. "Beer Goggles: Blood Alcohol Concentration in Relation to Attractiveness Ratings for Unfamiliar Opposite Sex Faces in Naturalistic Settings." *Journal of Social Psychology* 151(1):105–112.

MacAndrew, Craig and R. Edgerton. 1969. *Drunken Comportment: A Social Explanation*. Chicago: Aldine.

MacAndrew, Craig and Harold Garfinkel. 1962. "A Consideration of Changes Attributed to Intoxication as Common-Sense Reasons for Getting Drunk." *Quarterly Journal of Studies on Alcohol* 23:252–266.

MacCormack, John. 2009. "Drug War Under Fire at Policy Summit." *San Antonio Evening News*, September 23, p. 1A.

Mackinem, M. and P. Higgins. 2008. *Drug Court: Constructing the Moral Identity of Drug Offenders*. Springfield, IL: Charles Thomas.

Madonia, Joseph F. 1981. "Managerial Responses to Alcohol and Drug Abuse Among Employees." *Personnel* 29(6):134–139.

Madsen, William and Claudia Madsen. 1979. "The Cultural Structure of Mexican Drinking Behavior." Pp. 38–53 in *Beliefs, Behaviors & Alcoholic Beverages: A Cross-Cultural Survey*, edited by Mac Marshall. Ann Arbor: University of Michigan.

Magill, Molly and Lara A. Ray. 2009. "Cognitive-Behavioral Treatment With Adult Alcohol and Illicit Drug Users: A Meta-Analysis of Randomized Controlled Trials." *Journal of Studies on Alcohol and Drugs* 70(40):516–527.

Maher, Lisa and Kathleen Daly. 1996. "Women in the Street-Level Drug Economy: Continuity or Change?" *Criminology* 34:465–491.

Maloff, Deborah H., H. S. Becker, A. Fonaroff, and J. Rodin. 1979. "Informal Social Controls and Their Influence on Substance Abuse." *Journal of Drug Issues* 9(2):161–184.

Margolin, Arthur, Herbert D. Kleber, S. Kelly Avants, Janet Konefal, Frank Gawin, Elena Stark, et al. 2002. "Acupuncture for the Treatment of Cocaine Addiction: A Randomized Controlled Trial." *Journal of the American Medical Association* 287(1). Retrieved June 29, 2015 (http://jama.jamanetwork.com/article.aspx?articleid=194524).

Marjorie Jacobs Community Learning Center. 1997. "From the First to the Last Ash: The History, Economics & Hazards of Tobacco." Health Literacy World. Retrieved August 24, 2014 (http://healthliteracy.worlded.org/docs/tobacco/Unit1/2history_of.html).

Markowitz, Sara. 2000. "Anheuser-Busch Profit Up as Beer Volume Recovers." *Southern Economic Journal* 67(2):279–303.

Marmor, Jane B. 1998. "Medical Marijuana." *Western Journal of Medicine* 168(6):540–543.

Marshall, Jane E. and Robin M. Murray. 1991. "The Familial Transmission of Alcoholism: Imitation and Inheritance." *British Medical Journal* 303(6794):72–73.

Martens, Matthew, K. Dams O'Connor, and N. C. Beck. 2006. "A Systematic Review of College Student-Athlete Drinking." *Journal of Substance Abuse Treatment* 31(3):305–316.

Martin, Barbara A., T. P. McCoy, H. Champion, M. T. Parries, R. H. Durant, A. Mitra, and S. D. Rhodes. 2009. "The Role of Monthly Spending Money in College Student Drinking Behavior and the Consequences." *Journal of American College Health* 57(6):587–596.

Marty, Martin E. 1972. "Ethnicity: The Skeleton of Religion in America." *Church History* (March):4–21.

Maruschak, Laura M. and Thomas P. Bonczar. 2013. "Probation and Parole in the United States." Washington, DC: U.S. Department of Justice, Bureau of Justice Statistics (December):19–21.

Maryland Collaborative to Reduce College Drinking and Related Problems. 2016. *Sexual Assault and Alcohol: What the Research Evidence Tells Us*. College Park, MD: Center on Young Adult Health and Development.

Maslow, Abraham H. 1943. "A Theory of Human Motivation." *Psychological Review* 50:370–396.

Massey, Carissa. 2007. "Appalachian Stereotypes: Cultural History, Gender and Sexual Rhetoric." *Journal of Appalachian Studies* 13(1–2):124–136.

Mass Observation. 2009/1943. *The Pub and the People: A Worktown Study*. London: Author. Republished by Faber & Faber, 2009.

Matthee, Rudi. 1995. "Erotic Substances: The Introduction and Global Spread of Tobacco, Coffee, Cocoa, Tea and Distilled Liquor, Sixteenth to Eighteenth Centuries." Pp. 24–51 in *Drugs and Narcotics in History*, edited by R. Porter and M. Teich. Cambridge: Cambridge University Press.

Matza, David. 1969. *Becoming Deviant*. Englewood Cliffs, NJ: Prentice-Hall.

Maxwell, James R., I. R. Gowers, D. J. Moore, and A. G. Wilson. 2010. "Alcohol Consumption Is Inversely Associated With Risk and Severity of Rheumatoid Arthritis." *Rheumatology* 49(11):2140–2146.

Maxwell, Jane Carlisle. 2006. "Trends in the Abuse of Prescription Drugs." Austin: University of Texas. The Center for Excellence in Drug Epidemiology. The Gulf Coast Addiction Technology Transfer Center. Retrieved October 3, 2014 (http://www.utexas.edu/research/cswr/gcattc/documents/PrescriptionTrends_Web.pdf).

Mayhew, Mary. 2010. "Economic Cost and Substance Abuse, 2010." Washington, DC: U.S. Department of Health and Human Services.

McCallum, J. C., L. A. Simons, and J. Simons. 2003. "The Dubbo Study of the Health of the Elderly 1988–2002. An Epidemiological Study of Hospital and Residential Care." Australian Health Policy Institute at the University of Sydney.

McClalland, David C. 1971. "The Power of Positive Drinking." *Psychology Today* 4:40–41.

McCoy, Alfred W. 1972. *The Politics of Heroin in Southeast Asia*. New York: Harper and Row.

McDonald, Mac. 1994. Introduction: A Socio-anthropological View of Gender, Drink and Drugs. Oxford, UK: Oxford University Press.

McDougall, Graham. 2004. "Older Women's Cognitive and Affective Responses to Moderate Drinking." Annual Meeting of the National Congress on the State of Science in Nursing Research, Bethesda, MD.

McFly, Marty. 2013. "A Naked and Burning Richard Pryor Running Down Parthenia Street." *San Fernando Valley Blog*, June 9. Retrieved January 19, 2016 (http://sanfernandovalleyblog.blogspot.com/2013/06/a-naked-and-burning-richard-pryor.html).

McHugh, Kathryn R., Bridget A. Hearon, and Michael W. Otto. 2010. "Cognitive-Behavioral Therapy for Substance Use Disorders." *Psychiatric Clinics of North America* 33(3):511–525.

McKenzie v. McKenzie. 1957. 306 S.W. 2nd. 588 Mo. App.

McKinder, Evan. 2011. "Politics on Tap." *Open Secrets Blog*, March 23, pp. 1–4.

McPeake, John D., Bruce Kennedy, Jim Grossman, and Leonard Beaulieu. 1991. "Innovative Adolescent Chemical Dependency Treatment and Its Outcome: A Model Based on Outward Bound Programming." *Journal of Adolescent Chemical Dependency* 21(1):29–57.

Melville, Herman. 1851. *Moby Dick*. New York: Harper & Brothers.

Melville, Herman. 1930. *Moby Dick*. New York: Random House.

Merrill, Ray M., Jeffrey M. Folsom, and Susan S. Christopherson. 2005. "The Influence of Family Religiosity on Adolescent Substance Use According to Religious Preferences." *Social Behavior and Personality* 8(33):821–836.

Merton, Robert K. 1957. *Social Theory and Social Structure* (revised and enlarged ed.). Toronto, ON: Free Press.

Messinger, Sheldon. 1955. "Organizational Transformation: A Case Study of a Declining Social Movement." *American Sociological Review* 20 (February):3–10.

MetroLyrics. 2016a. "Minnie the Moocher Lyrics." Retrieved July 7, 2015 (http://www.metrolyrics.com/minnie-the-moocher-lyrics-cab-calloway.html).

MetroLyrics. 2016b. "Cocaine Blues Lyrics." Retrieved January 21, 2016 (http://www.metrolyrics.com/cocaine-blues-lyrics-johnny-cash.html).

Michel, Lou. 2014. "Ten Videos to Air in Movie Theaters as Part of Combat Heroin Effort." *Buffalo News*, December 20, p. D5.

Michel, Lou. 2015. "Struggling to Escape Addiction Amid the Epidemic of Opiate and Heroin Abuse Locally, Patients Confront Conflicting Choices in Battle to Recover." *Buffalo News*, January 13, p. 1.

Miller, Julie. 1993. "Alcohol Abuse Among the Elderly: A Growing, Often Hidden Problem." *New York Times*, November 28, pp. 1–2.

Millman, Jason. 2015. "It's True: Drug Companies Are Bombarding Your TV With More Ads Than Ever." *Washington Post*, March 23. Retrieved January 27, 2016 (https://www.washingtonpost.com/news/wonk/wp/2015/03/23/yes-drug-companies-are-bombarding-your-tv-with-more-ads-than-ever/).

Mills, C. Wright. 1940. "Situated Actions and Vocabularies and Motives." *American Sociological Review* 6:904–913.

Mills, C. Wright. 1959. *The Power Elite*. New York: Oxford University Press.

Miron, Jeffrey A. 2001. "The Economics of Drug Prohibition and Drug Legislation." *Social Research* 68:835–838.

Mishane, Larry. 2013. "Booze, Drugs and Bride Boat Crash." *Daily News*, November 8, p. 12.

Mizruchi, Ephraim H. and Robert Perrucci. 1962. "Norm Qualities and Differential Effects of Deviant Behavior: An Exploratory Analysis." *American Sociological Review* 27:395–396.

Mokdad, Ali H., J. S. Marks, D. F. Stroup, and J. L. Gerberding. 2004. "Actual Causes of Death in the United States." *Journal of the American Medical Association* 291(11):1238–1245.

Monroe, Keith. 1955. "They Made the Cigar Respectable." *Harper's*, February, pp. 37–41.

Moore, Mark H. 1979. "Limiting the Supply of Drugs to Illicit Markets in the United States." *Journal of Drug Issues* 9:291–308.

Morgan, Edmund. 1966. *The Puritan Family Religion and Domestic Relations in Seventeenth Century New England*. New York: Harper and Row.

Morison, Samuel Eliot. 1930. *Builders of the Bay Colony*. New York: Houghton Mifflin.

Morley, Miranda. 2011. "Revenue That Comes With Selling Alcohol." *Houston Chronicle*, September 13, p. 3.

Morton, Lindsay M., T. Zheng, T. R. Holford, E. A. Holly, B. C. Chiu, A. S. Costantini, et al. 2005. "Alcohol Consumption and Risk of Non-Hodgkin Lymphoma: A Pooled Analysis." *Lancet Oncology* 6(7):469–476.

Mosher, James F. 1996. "Alcopops Create Sales and Controversy in U.S. Market." *Impact* 26(14–15):7–8.

Motivans, Mark. 2011. "Federal Justice Statistics 2009." Washington, DC: U.S. Department of Justice, Bureau of Justice Statistics.

Moyer, Justin Wm. 2015. "American Medical Association Urges Ban on TV Drug Ads." *Washington Post*, November 19. Retrieved January 27, 2016 (https://www.washingtonpost.com/news/morning-mix/wp/2015/11/19/american-medical-association-urges-ban-on-tv-drug-ads/).

Mulkamal, Kenneth J. 2003. "Prospective Study of Alcohol Consumption and Risk of Dementia in Older Adults." *Journal of the American Medical Association* 289:1405–1413.

Muller, Heidi. 2014. "Why Do Women Go to Nightclubs?" *AskMen*. Retrieved January 14, 2014 (http://www.askmen.com/).

Mumola, Christopher and Jennifer Karberg. 2005. "Drug Use and Dependence." Washington, DC: Department of Justice, Bureau of Justice Statistics.

Murray, J. B. 1986. "Marijuana's Effects on Human Cognitive Functions, Psychomotor Functions and Personality." *Journal of General Psychology* 113(1):23–55.

Musto, David F. 1999. *The American Disease: Origin of Narcotic Control*. New York: Oxford University Press.

Naff, Kevin and Gregg Marzullo. 2007. "Two Views of the Bar Scene." *Washington Blade* 38(1).

Nakate, Shashank. n.d. "Drunk Driving Statistics." *Buzzle*:2.

Namibia, Sister. 2012. "What to Know About Date Rape." *Gender Watch* 24(3):13.

Narcotics Anonymous. 2008. *The Basic Text of Narcotics Anonymous* (6th ed.). Chatsworth, CA: Author.

Narcotics Anonymous. 2015. Website. Retrieved June 25, 2015 (http://na.org/? ID=PR-index).

Nash, Ogden. 1931. *Hard Lines*. New York: Simon and Schuster.

National Association of Drug Court Professionals. n.d. "What Are Drug Courts? The Most Effective Justice Strategy Addressing the Drug-Addicted and Mentally Ill." Retrieved June 21, 2015 (http://www.nadcp.org/learn/what-are-drug-courts).

National Center for Victims of Crime. 2012. "Statistics of Perpetrators of Child Sexual Abuse." Retrieved May 17, 2017 (https://victimsofcrime.org/media/reporting-on-child-sexual-abuse/statistics-on-perpetrators-of-csa).

National Center on Addiction and Substance Abuse at Columbia University (CASA). 2012. "The National Survey on American Attitudes on Substance Abuse XVII: Teens." Retrieved August 14, 2017 (https://www.centeronaddiction.org/download/file/fid/515).

National Council on Alcohol and Drug Dependence. 2015. "Alcohol, Drugs and Crime." Retrieved August 4, 2017 (https://www.ncadd.org/about-addiction/alcohol-drugs-and-crime).

National Drug Intelligence Center, Drug Enforcement Administration. 2013. "National Prescription Drug Threat Assessment." Washington, DC: Author.

National Highway Traffic Safety Administration. 2003. "Traffic Safety Facts: Alcohol" (Pub No. DOTHS 809-606). Washington, DC: U.S. Department of Transportation.

National Highway Traffic Safety Administration. 2013. *Alcohol-Impaired Driving: Traffic Safety Facts, 2012 Data.* Retrieved August 18, 2017 (https://crashstats.nhtsa.dot.gov/Api/Public/ViewPublication/811870).

National Institute of Justice. 2015. "Drug Courts." Retrieved June 21, 2015 (http://www.nij.gov/topics/courts/drug-courts/pages/welcome.aspx).

National Institute of Justice. n.d. "Program Profile Drug Abuse Resistance Education (DARE)." Retrieved June 9, 2015 (https://www.crimesolutions.gov/ProgramDetails.aspx?ID=99).

National Institute on Alcohol Abuse and Alcoholism. 2009. "Apparent Per Capita Ethanol Consumption for the United States, 1970–2007." Bethesda, MD: Author.

National Institute on Alcohol Abuse and Alcoholism. 2015. "Beyond Hangovers: Understanding Alcohol's Impact on Your Health." Retrieved August 4, 2017 (https://pubs.niaaa.nih.gov/publications/Hangovers/beyondHangovers.pdf).

National Institute on Drug Abuse. 2011. "Advances in Therapeutic Communities." Pp. 430–445 in *The American Drug Scene: An Anthology*, edited by James A. Inciardi and Karen McElrath. New York: Oxford University Press.

National Institute on Drug Abuse. 2012. "Principles of Drug Addiction Treatment: A Research-Based Guide" (3rd ed.). Retrieved March 7, 2017 (https://www.ncbi.nlm.nih.gov/pmc/articles/PMC2897895/).

National Institute on Drug Abuse. 2014. "Drug Facts: Nationwide Trends." Retrieved October 6, 2014 (http://www.drugabuse.gov/publications/drugfacts/nationwide-trends).

National Institute on Drug Abuse. 2015. "Is Marijuana a Gateway Drug?" Retrieved December 1, 2015 (http://www.drugabuse.gov/publications/marijuana/marijuana-gateway-drug).

National Institute on Drug Abuse. 2016. "National Survey Results on Drug Use From the Monitoring the Future Study." Retrieved July 31, 2017 (https://www.drugabuse.gov/related-topics/trends-statistics/infographics/monitoring-future-2016-survey-results).

National Institute on Drug Abuse. 2017. "Overdose Death Rates." Retrieved February 23, 2017 (https://www.drugabuse.gov/related-topics/trends-statistics/overdose-death-rates).

National Research Council. 1999. "Alcohol, Other Psychoactive Drugs and Violence. Understanding and Preventing Violence." Washington, DC: National Academy Press.

Neave, Nick, Carmen Tsang, and Nick Heather. 2008. "Effects of Alcohol and Alcohol Expectancy on Perceptions of Opposite-Sex Facial Attractiveness in University Students." *Addiction Research and Theory* 16(4):359–368.

Neff, James A. and Bagar Husaini. 1982. "Life Events, Drinking Patterns and Depressive Symptomatology: The Stress Buffering Role of Alcohol Consumption." *Journal of Studies on Alcohol* 43:301–318.

Nelms, Linda W., Edwin Hutchins, Dorothy Hutchins, and Robert J. Pursley. 2007. "Spirituality and the Health of College Students." *Journal of Religion and Health* 46(2):249–265.

Nelson, Bryce. 1983. "The Addictive Personality: Common Traits Are Found." *New York Times*, January 18. Retrieved August 25, 2013 (http://www.nytimes.com/1983/01/18/science/the-addictive-personality-common-traits-are-found.html).

Nelson, Margaret. 1968. "Prohibition: A Case Study of Societal Misguidance." *American Behavioural Scientist* 12(2):37–43.

New, Catherine. 2012. "Income Gap Closing." The Huffington Post. Retrieved August 14, 2017 (http://www.huffingtonpost.com/2012/03/21/income-gap-women-make-more-men_n_1368328.html).

New Beginnings Drug & Alcohol Rehabilitation. 2017. "Cognitive Behavioral Therapy and Drug Addiction." Retrieved March 7, 2017 (http://www.newbeginningsdrugrehab.org/cognitive-behavioral-drug-therapy/).

New York State. 2014. "Governor Cuomo Signs Legislation to Combat Heroin, Opioid and Prescription Drug Abuse Epidemic." Retrieved September 20, 2014 (https://www.governor.ny.gov/press/06242012-drug-abuse-legislation).

New York State Department of Health Emergency Medical Services. n.d. Code 800.16.

Newmeyer, John A., Gregory Johnson, and Steven Klot. 1984. "Acupuncture as a Detoxification Modality." *Journal of Psychoactive Drugs* 16(3):241–261.

Nieters, Alexandra. 2005. "Tobacco and Alcohol Consumption and Risk of Lymphoma: Results of a Population-Based Case-Control Study in Germany." *International Study of Cancer* 118(2):422–430.

Nixon, Richard. 1971a. "Special Message to the Congress on Drug Abuse Prevention and Control." Retrieved August 4, 2014 (http://www.presidency.ucsb.edu/ws/?pid=3048).

Nixon, Richard. 1971b. "Remarks About an Intensified Program for Drug Abuse Prevention and Control." Retrieved August 4, 2014 (http://www.presidency.ucsb.edu/ws/? pid=3047).

Nordrum, Amy. 2014. "The New D.A.R.E. Program—This One Works." *Scientific American*, September 10. Retrieved June 9, 2015 (http://www.scientificamerican.com/article/the-new-d-a-r-e-program-this-one-works/).

November Coalition. 2005. "Profits From Selling Cocaine Make It a Lucrative Business Venture." *Winona Daily News*, May 31, p. 1.

Nurco, David N. 1985. "The Criminality of Narcotics Addicts." *Journal of Nervous and Mental Disease* 173(2):94–102.

O'Brien, John. 1929. "The St. Valentine's Day Massacre." *Chicago Tribune*, February 14, p. 1.

O'Brien, John. 2016. "Lethal Heroin Batch Has Killed 23 in Buffalo Over Past Two Weeks." Syracuse.com (February 10). Retrieved February 25, 2017 (http://www.syracuse.com/crime/index.ssf/2016/02/lethal_heroin_batch_has_killed_23_in_buffalo_over_past_two_weeks).

Ogle, Maureen. 2006. *Ambitious Brew*. Orlando, FL: Harcourt Books.

Okrent, Daniel. 2010. *Last Call: The Rise and Fall of Prohibition*. New York: Scribner.

Olien, Jessica. 2013. "Loneliness Is Deadly." *Medical Examiner* (August 23):1.

O'Malley, Patrick M. and L. D. Johnson. 2003. "Epidemiology of Alcohol and Other Drug Use Among American College Students." *Journal of Studies on Alcohol* 14:23–39.

Open Jurist. 1976. "528 F.2d 1250 *United States v. McClean*." Retrieved January 18, 2016 (http://openjurist.org/528/f2d/1250/united-states-v-mcclean).

Open Secrets.org, Center for Responsible Politics. 2014. "Tobacco." Retrieved August 20, 2014 (http://www.open secrets.org/industries/indus.php?ind=N02).

Open Secrets.org, Center for Responsible Politics. 2016. "Beer, Wine & Liquor." Retrieved June 5, 2016 (http://www.opensecrets.org/industries/indus.php?ind=N02).

"Opium in China." 2015. "Facts and Details." Retrieved August 6, 2017 (http://factsanddetails.com/china/cat11/sub74/item139.html).

Opium Poppy Control Act of 1942. Public Law No.400 78th Congress.

Ostrander, Gilman M. 1957. *The Prohibition Movement in California.* Berkeley: University of California.

Owens, Robbie. 2017. "CDC Report: Heroin Epidemic Back With a Vengeance." CBS Dallas/Fort Worth. Retrieved February 25, 2017 (http://dfw.cbslocal.com/2017/02/24/cdc-report-heroin-epidemic-back-with-a-vengeance).

Page, Ann L. and Donald A. Clelland. 1978. "The Kanahaw County Textbook Controversy." *Social Forces* 57:265–281.

Painter, Kim. 2015. "Report: Binge Drinking Kills 6 a Day, Mostly Men; Age of Victims Stuns CDC Researchers." *USA Today,* January 7, p. 1.

Pandey, Subhash C., Adip Roy, Huaibo Zhang, and Tiejun Xu. 2004. "Partial Deletion of the cAMP Response Element-Binding Protein Gene Promotes Alcohol-Drinking Behaviors." *Journal of Neuroscience* 24(21):5022–5030.

Papa, Anthony. 2013. "40th Anniversary of the Rockefeller Drug Laws: A Window of Opportunity for a Better Path." Huffpost New York. Retrieved June 5, 2016 (http://www.huffingtonpost.com/anthony-papa/rockefeller-drug-laws_b_3230594.html).

Parker, Robert N., Kirk R. Williams, Kevin J. McCaffree, Emily K. Acensio, Angela Browne, Kevin J. Strom, and Kelle Barrick. 2011. "Alcohol Availability and Youth Homicide in the 91 Largest US Cities, 1984–2006." *Drug and Alcohol Review* 30:505–514.

Parlato, Frank. 2014. "Young, White, Addicted to Heroin. Drug Addicts—On the Record." *Niagara Falls Reporter,* December 3, p. 1. Retrieved March 21, 2016 (http://www.niagarafallsreporter.com/Stories/2014/DEC03/drug.html).

Parsons, Talcott. 1951. *The Social System.* New York: Free Press.

Pascarelli, Emil. 1972. "Alcoholism and Drug Addiction in the Elderly: Old Drug Addicts Do Not Die, Nor Do They Just Fade Away." *Geriatric Focus* 11(5):1, 4–5.

Passages Malibu. 2015a. "Substance Abuse Treatment Center: Alcohol and Drug Addiction Treatment." Retrieved July 1, 2015 (http://www.passagesmalibu.com/addiction-treatment/).

Passages Malibu. 2015b. "Passages Holistic Addiction Treatment Philosophy—Addiction Ends Here." Retrieved July 1, 2015 (http://www.passagesmalibu.com/addiction-treatment-philosophy).

Patterson, Eric. 2017. "Cognitive Behavioral Therapy (CBT) Techniques for Addiction." DrugAbuse.com. Retrieved March 7, 2017 (http://drugabuse.com/library/cognitive-behavioral-therapy/).

Patterson, Gerald R. and Magda Stouthamer-Loeber. 1984. "The Correlation of Family Management Practices and Delinquency." *Child Development* 55(4):1299–1307.

Patton, W. E. and Michael Questell. 1986. "Alcohol Abuse in the Sales Force." *Journal of Personal Selling and Sales Management* 6(3):39–52.

Payscale. 2017. "Bartender Salaries." Retrieved May 13, 2017 (http://www.payscale.com/research/US/Job=Bartender/Hourly_Rate).

PDMP Center of Excellence, Brandeis University, The Heller School for Social Policy and Management. n.d. "The Prescription Drug Abuse Epidemic." Retrieved October 6, 2014 (http://www.pdmpexcellence.org/drug-abuse-epidemic).

Pearson, Charles and Philippe Bourgois. 1995. "Hope to Die a Dope Fiend." *Cultural Anthropology* 10(4):587–593.

Pearson, Thomas A. 1996. "Alcohol and Heart Disease." *Circulation* 94:3022–3025.

Pentz, Michael A. 1985. "Social Competence and Self Efficacy." Pp. 117–142 in *Coping and Substance Use,* edited by S. Schiffman and T. A. Wills. New York: Academic Press.

Peralta, Robert L. and Daniela Jauk. 2011. "A Brief Feminist Review and Critique of the Sociology of Alcohol-Use and Substance-Abuse Treatment Approaches." *Sociology Compass* 5(1):882–897.

Perkins, Kevin L. and Anthony P. Placido. 2010. "Testimony." Washington, DC: U.S. Senate Caucus on International Narcotics Control.

Perry, Cheryl L., C. L. Williams, K. A. Komro, S. Veblen-Mortenson, M. H. Stigler, K. A. Munson, K. Farbakhsh, R. M. Jones, and J. L. Forster. 2002. "Project Northland: Long-Term Outcomes of Community Action to Reduce Adolescent Alcohol Use." *Health Education Research* 16(5):101–116.

Peters, Jeremy W. 2009. "Rockefeller Drug Laws in New York to Be Repealed." *New York Times*, April 26. Retrieved May 27, 2016 (http://www.huffingtonpost.com/2009/03/26/rockefeller-drug-laws-in-_n_179818.html).

Petrunik, Michael. 1972. "Seeing the Light: A Study of Conversion to Alcoholics Anonymous." *Journal of Voluntary Action Research* 1:30–38.

Pew Center on the States. 2009. "One in 31: The Long Reach of American Corrections." Washington, DC: The Pew Center Charitable Trust.

Pew Forum on Religion and Public Life. 2010. "Religion Losing Influence in America." Washington, DC: Author.

Pew Forum on Religion and Public Life. 2013. "Statistics on Religion in America." Washington, DC: Author.

Peyser, Herbert S. 1982. "Stress and Alcohol." Pp. 584–598 in *Handbook of Stress: Theoretical and Clinical Aspects* (2nd ed.), edited by Leo Goldberger and Shlomo Breznitz. New York: Free Press.

Philbrick, H. R. 1939. "Legislative Investigative Report." California Legislature, Senate Journal. Sacramento: State Printing Office.

Phoenix House. 2015. "Our History." Retrieved July 1, 2015 (http://phoenixhouse.org/our-history/).

Picarelli, John T. 2011. "Responding to Transnational Organized Crime." *National Institute of Justice Journal* 268. Retrieved June 5, 2016 (http://www.nij.gov/journals/268/pages/transnational.aspx).

Pierce, Todd G. 1999. "Gen-X Junkie Ethnographic Research with Young White Heroin Users in Washington, D.C." *Substance Use and Misuse* 34:2095–2114.

Pittman, David J. and Charles R. Snyder, eds. 1962. *Society, Culture, and Drinking Patterns*. Carbondale: Southern Illinois University Press.

Podolsky, Edward. 1960. "The Obsessive-Compulsive Chronic Alcoholic." *American Journal of Psychiatry* 117(3):236–238.

Podolsky, Edward. 1964. "The Passive-Aggressive Alcoholic." *Samiska: Journal of the Indian Psychoanalytic Society* 17(4):198–206.

"Police Continue Investigation Into Underage Dancers at Cheaters." 2013. *Providence Journal*, August 8. Retrieved April 26, 2014 (http://www.providencejournal.com/breaking-news/content/20130808-police-continue-investigation-into-underage-dancers-prostitution-at-cheaters.ece).

"Police Seek Synanon Car in Rattlesnake Ambush." 1978. *Buffalo Evening News*, October 12.

Pollin, William. 1980. "Health Consequences of Marijuana Use." *Drug Enforcement* 7 (March):4–7.

Presley, Cheryl, Philip W. Meilman, and Rob Lyerla. 1996. *Alcohol and Drugs on American College Campuses: Use, Consequences, and Perceptions of the Campus Environment.* Volume I: 1989–91. Carbondale: Southern Illinois University Press.

Price, L. H. 2004. "Light Drinking Lowers Bad Proteins." *Washington Times*, February 11.

Pringle, Paul. 2007. "The Trouble With Rehab, Malibu-Style." *Los Angeles Times*. Retrieved July 1, 2015 (http://articles.latimes.com/2007/oct/09/local/me-rehab9/3).

"Prison for Three Northwest Pilots Who Flew Jet While Drunk." 1990. *New York Times*, October 27, p. 1.

ProCon.org. 2014. "Prescription Drug Ads: Should Prescription Drugs Be Advertised Directly to Consumers?" Retrieved January 27, 2016 (http://prescriptiondrugs.procon.org/).

ProCon.org. 2017. "D.A.R.E. Pros and Cons. Is the D.A.R.E. Program Good for America's Kids (K–12)?" Retrieved August 12, 2017 (http://dare.procon.org).

Prus, R. 1983. "Drinking as Activity: An Interactionist Analysis." *Journal of Studies on Alcohol* 44:460–475.

Pryor, Richard. 2013a. "Cocaine." Retrieved January 19, 2016 (https://www.youtube.com/watch?v=Ad6fJy8aOuw&list=RD5Kr0TnhToek&index=30).

Pryor, Richard. 2013b. "Freebase." Retrieved January 19, 2016 (https://www.youtube.com/watch?v=5Kr0TnhToek&list=RD5Kr0TnhToek#t=0).

Pryor, Richard. 2013c. "Burn Up." Retrieved January 19, 2016 (https://www.youtube.com/watch?v=GQRXtvIO_e4&index=6&list=RD5Kr0TnhToek).

"Public Health Issue: Methadone Maintenance Therapy." 2000. *American Family Physician* 62(2):428–432.

Pulliam, Tim. 2014. "Tax Fraud, Bootlegging Charges Against Man Dropped." News4Jax. Retrieved August 4, 2017 (https://www.news4jax.com/news/local/-tax-fraud-bootlegging-charges-against-man-dropped-).

Quora. n.d. "Art Criticism: How Can the Spot Paintings of Damien Hirst Be Interpreted?" Retrieved January 24, 2016 (https://www.quora.com/Art-Criticism/How-can-the-spot-paintings-of-Damien-Hirst-be-interpreted?).

Rabow, Jerome and Marilyn Duncan-Schill. 1995. "Drinking Among College Students." *Journal of Alcohol and Drug Education* 40(3):52–64.

Rawlings, Nate. 2013. "Baby Shroomers and the Heroin Spike: 6 Surprising Trends in Americans' Drug Use." *Time*, September 6. Retrieved October 1, 2014 (http://nation.time.com/2013/09/06/baby-shroomers-and-the-heroin-spike-6-surprising-trends-in-americans-drug-use/).

Ray, Marsh B. 1961. "The Cycle of Abstinence and Relapse Among Heroin Addicts." *Social Problems* 9(2):132–140.

"Readers Respond: What Were Your Toughest Alcohol Withdrawal Symptoms and How Did You Cope?" 2012. About.com. Retrieved August 7, 2013 (http://alcoholism.about.com/u/ua/withdraw/withdrawals.htm).

Reaves, Brian. 2012. "Federal Law Enforcement Officers." Washington, DC: Bureau of Justice Statistics.

Rechy, John. 1963. *City of Night*. New York: Grove Press.

Rehm, Jürgen, Kevin D. Shield, Narges Joharchi, and Paul A. Shuper. 2011. "Alcohol Consumption and the Intention to Engage in Unprotected Sex: Systematic Review and Meta-Analysis of Experimental Studies." *Addiction* 107:51–59.

Rempel, Michael, Dana Fox-Kralstein, Amanda Cissner, Robyn Cohen, Melikssa Labriola, Donald Farole, Ann Bader, and Michael Magnani. 2003. "The New York State Adult Drug Court Evaluation: Policies, Participants and Impacts." New York: Center for Court Innovation.

Research Institute on Addictions. 2014. "RIA Reaching Others: Alcohol and Sexual Assault." Retrieved March 3, 2017 (http://www.buffalo.edu/ria/news_events/es/es11.html).

Resig, Martin I. 1998. "Rediscovering Rehabilitation: Drug Courts, Community Corrections and Restorative Justice." *Michigan Bar Journal* 77:172–176.

Rettig, Richard P., Manual J. Torres, and Gerald R. Garrett. 1977. *Manny: A Criminal Addict's Story*. Boston: Houghton Mifflin.

Rettner, Rachel. 2016. "Deaths From Fentanyl Overdoses Double in a Single Year." The Huffington Post. Retrieved February 24, 2017 (http://www.huffingtonpost.com/entry/deaths-from-fentanyl-overdoses-double-in-a-single-year).

Reuter, Peter and Mark A. R. Kleiman. 1986. "Risks and Prices: An Economic Analysis of Drug Enforcement." Pp. 289–340 in *Crime and Justice: An Annual Review of Research*, edited by Michael Tonry and Norval Morris. Chicago: University of Chicago Press.

Rice, Prudence M. 1996. "The Archeology of Wine: The Wine and Brandy Haciendas of Moquegua, Peru." *Journal of Field Archeology* 23:187–204.

Richman, Judith A., S. A. Shinsako, K. M. Rospenda, and J. A. Flaherty. 2002. "Workplace Harassment, Abuse and Alcohol Related Outcomes." *Journal of Studies in Alcohol* 63(4):412–419.

R. J. Reynolds Tobacco Company. n.d. "Public Health Information." Retrieved August 6, 2014 (https://www.rjrt.com/pubhealth.aspx).

Rodriguez, Michelle and Maurice Ensellem. 2011. "65 Million Need Not Apply: The Case of Reforming Criminal Background Checks." New York: The Law Project.

Roebuck, Julian and S. Lee Spray. 1967. "The Cocktail Lounge: A Study in Heterosexual Relations in a Public Organization." *American Journal of Sociology* 72(4):388–395.

Ronald Reagan Presidential Foundation and Library. 2010. "Just Say No." Retrieved April 2, 2015 (http://www.reaganfoundation.org/details_f.aspx?p=rr1008nrhc&tx=6).

Roosevelt, Margot. 2005. "Why Is the DEA Hounding This Doctor?" *Time*, July 18. Retrieved June 5, 2016 (http://

content.time.com/time/magazine/article/0,9171,1083911,00
.html).

Root, Grace N. 1934. *Women and Repeal: The Story of the Women's Organization for National Prohibition Reform.* New York: Harper.

Rorabaugh, William J. 1976. "Estimated U.S. Alcohol Beverage Consumption." *Journal of Studies on Alcohol* 37 (March):360–361.

Rosenbaum, Dennis P. and Gordon S. Hanson. 1998. "Assessing the Effects of School-Based Drug Education: A Six-Year Multilevel Analysis of Project D.A.R.E." *Journal of Research in Crime and Delinquency* 35(4):381–412.

Rosenberg, Tina. 2007. "When Is a Pain Doctor a Drug Pusher?" *New York Times Magazine*, June 17. Retrieved June 6, 2016 (http://www.nytimes.com/2007/06/17/magazine/17pain-t.html?_r=0).

Rosenthal, M. P. 1977. "The Legislative Response to Marihuana: When the Shoe Pinches Enough." *Journal of Drug Issues* 7(1):61–77.

Ross, H. Lawrence. 1992. *Confronting Drunk Driving.* New Haven, CT: Yale University Press.

Rossing, Mary Anne. 2000. "Risk of Primary Thyroid Cancer in Women in Relation to Smoking and Alcohol Consumption." *Epidemiology* 11:49–54.

Rossner, Judith. 1975. *Looking for Mr. Goodbar.* New York: Simon and Schuster.

Rudy, David R. 1986. *Becoming Alcoholic: Alcoholics Anonymous and the Reality of Alcoholism.* Carbondale: Southern Illinois University Press.

Russell, Theodore G. 2003. "Medicine in Egypt at the Time of Napoleon Bonaparte." *British Medical Journal* 321(7429):1461–1464.

Sacco, Ralph L. 2001. "High Density Lipoprotein Cholesterol and Ischemic Stroke in the Elderly." *Journal of the American Medical Association* 285:2729–2735.

Samorini, Giorgio. 1992. "Prehistoric Psychoactive Artifacts." *Integration* (2/3):69–78.

Sandbrook, Dominic. 2012. "How Prohibition Backfired and Gave America an Era of Gangsters and Speakeasies." *The Guardian*, August 25. Retrieved August 4, 2017 (https://www.theguardian.com/film/2012/aug/26/lawless-prohibition-gangsters-speakeasies).

Sanders, Jolene M. 2009. *Women in Alcoholics Anonymous: Recovery and Empowerment.* Boulder, CO: First Forum Press.

Sargent, J. F. and Ed Byrne. 2014. "5 Unexpected Things I Learned From Being a Heroin Addict." Cracked. Retrieved March 4, 2016 (http://www.cracked.com/personal-experiences-1306-5-unexpected-things-i-learned-from-being-heroin-addict.html).

Saunders, Debra J. 2009. "A Failed Drug War's Rising Body Count." *San Francisco Chronicle*, March 15, p. A6.

Schaffer Library of Drug Policy. n.d. "The Report of the National Commission on Marihuana and Drug Abuse." Retrieved May 18, 2017 (http://www.druglibrary.org/schaffer/library/studies/nc/nc2_7.htm).

Schelling, Thomas C. 1971. "What Is the Business of Organized Crime?" *Journal of Public Law* 20:71–84.

Schmidt, Wolfgang and Robert E. Popham. 1976. "Impressions of Jewish Alcoholics." *Journal of Studies on Alcohol* 37:931–939.

Schneckebier, Lawrence F. 1929. *The Bureau of Prohibition: Its History, Activities and Organization.* Washington, DC: The Brookings Institution.

Schneidman, Edward S. 1984. "Personality and 'Success' Among a Selected Group of Lawyers." *Journal of Personality Assessment* 48(6):609–616.

Schuckit, Marc A. 1986. "Genetic Aspects of Alcoholism." *Annals of Emergency Medicine* 15(9):991–996.

Schuckit, Marc A. 1992. "Alcoholism, A Familial Disorder: Genetic Aspects." Pp. 3–12 in *Alcoholism and the Family*, edited by Satoru Saitoh, Peter Steinglass, and Marc Alan Schuckit. Philadelphia: Brunner/Maezel.

Schumaker, Erin. 2016. "Heroin Deaths Topped Gun Homicides Last Year, Depressing CDC Data Shows." The Huffington Post. Retrieved February 25, 2017 (http://www.huffingtonpost.com/entry/heroin-deaths-gun-homicides-last-year-opioids_us_584ada87e4b0e05aded38bec?utm_hp_ref=heroin-epidemic).

Scott, Marvin B. and Stanford M. Lyman. 1968. "Accounts." *American Sociological Review* 33:46–62.

Scull, Tracy M., Janis B. Kupersmidt, Alison E. Parker, Kristen C. Elmore, and Jessica W. Benson. 2010. "Adolescents' Media-Related Cognitions and Substance Use in the Context of Parental and Peer Influences." *Journal of Youth and Adolescence* 39(9):981–998.

Sesso, Howard, Meir J. Stampfer, Bernard Rosner, Charles H. Hennekens, JoAnn E. Manson, and J. Michael Gaziano. 2000. "Seven Year Changes in Alcohol Consumption and Subsequent Risk of Cardiovascular Disease in Men." *Archives of Internal Medicine* 160(17):2605–2612.

Shafer, Stephen and Richard D. Knudten. 1970. *Juvenile Delinquency: An Introduction*. New York: Random House.

Shanfield, Stephen B., G. Andrew, and H. Benjamin. 1985. "Psychiatric Disorders in Law Students." *Journal of Legal Education* 65:68–69.

Siegel, Michael, Jody Grundman, William DeJong, Timothy S. Naimi, Charles King III, Alison B. Albers, Rebecca S. Williams, and David H. Jernigan. 2013. "State Specific Liquor Excise Taxes and Retail Prices in 8 U.S. States, 2012." *Substance Abuse* 34(4):415–421.

Sinclair, Upton. 1906. *The Jungle*. New York: Doubleday, Page & Co.

Skolnick, Jerome H. 1958. "Religious Affiliation and Drinking Behavior." *Quarterly Journal of Studies on Alcohol* 19:452–470.

Smith, Roger C. 1966. "Status Politics and the Image of the Addict." *Issues in Criminology* 2:157–175.

Snyder, Charles R. 1958. *Alcohol and the Jews*. Glencoe, IL: Free Press.

Snyder, Charles R. 1978. *Alcohol and the Jews*. Carbondale: Southern Illinois University Press.

Social Issues Research Centre. 1998. "Social and Cultural Aspects of Drinking: A Report to the European Commission." Oxford, UK: Author.

Sommers, Ira, Deborah R. Baskin, and Jeffrey Fagan. 1994. "'Getting Out of the Life': Crime Desistance by Female Street Offenders." *Deviant Behavior* 15(2):125–149.

Songfacts. 2016a. "White Rabbit by Jefferson Airplane." Retrieved January 21, 2016 (http://www.songfacts.com/detail.php?id=1250).

Songfacts. 2016b. "One Toke Over the Line by Brewer and Shipley." Retrieved January 21, 2016 (http://www.songfacts.com/detail.php?id=2506).

Songfacts. n.d. "Songs About Alcohol." Retrieved January 21, 2016 (http://www.songfacts.com/category-songs_about_alcohol.php).

Sorensen, Andrew A. 1973. "Need for Power Among Alcoholic and Nonalcoholic Clergy." *Journal for the Scientific Study of Religion* 12(1):101–108.

Spergel, Irving. 1964. *Racketville, Slumtown, Haulburg: An Exploratory Study of Delinquent Subcultures*. Chicago: University of Chicago Press.

Spradley, James P. 1988. *You Owe Yourself a Drunk: An Ethnography of Urban Nomads*. New York: University Press of America.

Squeglia, Lindsay, J. Jacobus, and S. F. Tapert. 2009. "The Influence of Substance Abuse on Adolescent Brain Development." *Clinical EEG and Neuroscience* 40(1):31–38.

Stampler, Laura. 2014. "The New Dating Game." *Time*, February 17, pp. 42–45.

"Stan Kenton's Son Held in Snake Attack." 1978. *Buffalo Evening News*, October 13, p. 2, sec. I.

Stares, Paul. 1996. *Global Habit: The Drug Culture in a Borderless World*. Washington, DC: Brookings Institute Press.

Steele, C. M. and R. A. Josephs. 1990. "Alcohol Myopia: Its Prized and Dangerous Effects." *American Psychologist* 45:921–933.

Steinbeck, John. 1935. *Tortilla Flat*. New York: Grosset & Dunlap.

Steinglass, Peter and Janet P. Moyer. 1977. "Assessing Alcohol Use in Family Life." *The Family Coordinator* 26(1):53–60.

Stempse, William M. 1998. "The Battle for Medical Marijuana in the War on Drugs." *America* 178(12):14–16.

Stephens, Toni. 1995. *Women and Substance Abuse: A Feminist Perspective*. Ph.D. Dissertation. Macquarie University.

Stewart, Bruce E. 2004. "Attacking 'Red Legged Grasshopper': Moonshiners, Violence and the Politics of Federal Liquor Taxation." *Appalachian Journal* 32:36–48.

Stolberg, Sheryl Gay. 1999. "For a Very Few Patients the U.S. Provides Free Marijuana." *New York Times*, March 19, p. A-10.

Strasburger, Victor C. 2010. "Policy Statement—Children, Adolescents, Substance Abuse, and the Media." *Pediatrics* 126(4):791–799. Retrieved February 1, 2016 (http://

pediatrics.aappublications.org/content/pediatrics/126/4/791.full.pdf).

Straus, Robert and Selden D. Bacon. 1954. *Drinking in College*. New Haven, CT: Yale University Press.

Stricherz, Mark. 2014. "What Ever Happened to 'Just Say No'?" *The Atlantic*, April 29. Retrieved April 2, 2015 (http://www.theatlantic.com/politics/archive/2014/04/ghost-of-just-say-no/361322/).

Strunin, Lee. 2011. "Assessing Alcohol Consumption: Developments From Qualitative Research Methods." *Social Science and Medicine Journal* 53(2):215–226.

Stryker, Susan. 2008. "Transgender History, Homonormativity and Disciplinarity." *Radical History Review* (Winter):145–157.

Substance Abuse and Mental Health Services Administration. 2011a. *Drug Abuse Warning Network, 2009: National Estimates of Drug-Related Emergency Department Visits*. Table 19: "Trends in ED Visits Involving Nonmedical Use of Pharmaceuticals, by Selected Drugs, 2004–2009." HHS Publication No. (SMA) 11-4659, DAWN Series D-35. Rockville, MD: Author. Retrieved October 3, 2014 (http://www.samhsa.gov/data/2k11/dawn/2k9dawned/html/dawn2k9ed.htm#Sect4.1).

Substance Abuse and Mental Health Services Administration. 2011b. *Drug Abuse Warning Network, 2009: National Estimates of Drug-Related Emergency Department Visits*. Table 4: "ED Visits Involving Illicit Drugs, 2009." HHS Publication No. (SMA) 11-4659, DAWN Series D-35. Rockville, MD: Author. Retrieved October 3, 2014 (http://www.samhsa.gov/data/2k11/dawn/2k9dawned/html/dawn2k9ed.htm#Tab4).

Substance Abuse and Mental Health Services Administration. 2011c. *Drug Abuse Warning Network, 2009: National Estimates of Drug-Related Emergency Department Visits*. Table 11: "ED Visits Involving Drugs and Alcohol Taken Together: Most Frequent Combinations, 2009." HHS Publication No. (SMA) 11-4659, DAWN Series D-35. Rockville, MD: Author. Retrieved October 3, 2014 (http://www.samhsa.gov/data/2k11/dawn/2k9dawned/html/dawn2k9ed.htm#Tab11).

Substance Abuse and Mental Health Services Administration. 2011d. "Results from the 2010 National Survey on Drug Use and Health." NSDUH Series H-41. Rockville, MD: Author.

Substance Abuse and Mental Health Services Administration. 2013. *Drug Abuse Warning Network, 2011: National Estimates of Drug-Related Emergency Department Visits*. Table 6. HHS Publication No. (SMA) 13-4760, DAWN Series D-39. Rockville, MD: Author.

Substance Abuse and Mental Health Services Administration. 2014. "Results from the 2013 National Survey on Drug Use and Health: Summary of National Findings." NSDUH Series H-48, HHS Publication No. (SMA) 14-4863. Rockville, MD: Author.

Substance Abuse and Mental Health Services Administration. 2015a. "Behavioral Health Trends in the United States: Results from the 2014 National Survey on Drug Use and Health." Retrieved November 30, 2015 (http://www.samhsa.gov/data/sites/default/files/NSDUH-FRR1-2014/NSDUH-FRR1-2014.pdf).

Substance Abuse and Mental Health Services Administration. 2015b. "Mental and Substance Use Disorders." Retrieved March 12, 2017 (https://samhsa.gov/disorders/substance-use).

Substance Abuse and Mental Health Services Administration. n.d. *National Registry of Evidence-Based Programs and Practices*. "Glossary." Retrieved March 24, 2017 (http://www.nrepp.samhsa.gov/glossary.aspx).

Suleiman, Daniel. 1997. "Dying for a Drink." *The Harvard Crimson*, October 6. Retrieved June 6, 2016 (http://www.thecrimson.com/article/1997/10/6/dying-for-a-drink-pbsbcott-krueger/).

Susann, Jacqueline. 1966. *Valley of the Dolls*. New York: Grove Press.

Susman, Ralph M. 1975. "Drug Abuse: Congress and the Fact Finding Process." *Drugs and Social Policy* 417:16–26.

Sweeting, Adam. 2013. "J. J. Cale Obituary." *The Guardian*, July 28. Retrieved January 21, 2016 (http://www.theguardian.com/music/2013/jul/28/jj-cale).

Sykes, Gresham M. and David Matza. 1957. "Techniques of Neutralization: A Theory of Delinquency." *American Sociological Review* 22:664–670.

"Synanon Patriarch Now Urges Members to Try New Mate." 1978. *Buffalo Evening News*, January 1, p. A8.

Tan, Sandra. 2016. "Overdose Deaths Wiping Out Erie County Population Gains." *Buffalo News*, April 28. Retrieved

February 25, 2017 (http://buffalonews.com/2016/04/28/overdose-deaths-wiping-out-erie-county-population-gains).

Tapert, Susan F., E. H. Cheung, G. G. Brown, L. R. Frank, M. P. Paulus, A. D. Schweinsburg, M. J. Meloy, and S. A. Brown. 2003. "Neural Response to Alcohol Stimuli in Adolescents With Alcohol Use Disorder." *Archive of General Psychiatry* 60(7):727–735.

Taubman, Stephen. 1986. "Beyond the Bravado: Sex Roles and the Exploitative Male." *Social Work* 31:12–18.

Tax Foundation. 2009–2010. "State Sales: Gasoline, Cigarette, Alcohol Tax Rates by State." Washington, DC: Author.

Tax Law Firm. 2011. *JD Supra Business Advisor.* "Excise Tax Fraud." Retrieved June 5, 2016 (http://www.jdsupra.com/legalnews/excise-tax-fraud-69831/).

Tennyson, Alfred Lord. 2015/1832. "The Lotus-Eaters." Poetry Foundation. Retrieved January 24, 2016 (http://www.poetryfoundation.org/poem/174631).

Terry, Charles E. and Mildred Pellens. 1928. *The Opium Problem.* New York: Committee on Drug Addictions, Bureau of Social Hygiene.

Tersine, Richard and James Hazeldine. 1982. "Alcoholism: A Productivity Turnover." *Business Horizons* 25(6):68–72.

Testa, Maria and Michael J. Cleveland. 2017. "Does Alcohol Contribute to College Men's Sexual Assault Perpetration? Between- and Within-Person Effects Over Five Semesters." *Journal of Studies on Alcohol and Drugs* 78(1):5–13.

Thio, Alex. 2010. *Deviant Behavior* (10th ed.). Boston: Allyn & Bacon.

Thomas, Jeffrey L., Joshua E. Wilk, Lyndon A. Riviere, Dennis McGurk, Carl Andrew Castro, and Charles W. Hoge. 2010. "Prevalence of Mental Health Problems and Functional Impairment Among Active Component and National Guard Soldiers." *Archives of General Psychiatry* 67(6):614–623.

Thompson, Dennis. 2016. "As TV Drug Ads Increase, So Do Concerns." MedicineNet.com. Retrieved January 27, 2016 (http://www.medicinenet.com/script/main/art.asp?articlekey=106198).

"Thousands Present at MacSwiney's Mass." 1920. *New York Times*, November 26, p. 2.

Tierney, John. 2007. "Juggling Figures, and Justice, in a Doctor's Trial Findings." *New York Times*, July 3. Retrieved May 19, 2017 (http://www.nytimes.com/2007/07/03/science/03tier.html).

Toby, Jackson. 1971. *Contemporary Society, An Introduction to Sociology* (2nd ed.). New York: John Wiley & Sons.

Tocasz, Jay. 2013. "Dispatcher Pleads to Vehicular Assault." *Buffalo News*, July 31, p. 1.

Tomlinson, Stuart. 2012. "Cottage Grove Man Pleads Guilty to $879,000 Tax Fraud." *The Oregonian*, October 31.

Townes, Charles B. 1912. "The Peril of the Drug Habit." *Century Magazine* 84:580–587.

Trice, Harrison M. 1957. "A Study of the Process of Affiliation with A.A." *Quarterly Journal of Studies on Alcohol* 18:38–54.

Trice, Harrison M. and Paul Michael Roman. 1970. "Delabeling, Relabeling, and Alcoholics Anonymous." *Social Problems* 17(4):538–546.

Tuckman, Jo. 2013. "U.S. Shuts Mexican Drug Smugglers' Cross-Border 'Super Tunnel.'" *The Guardian*, November 1. Retrieved June 6, 2016 (http://www.theguardian.com/world/2013/nov/01/us-discovers-mexican-drug-smuggling-tunnel).

Twain, Mark. 1885. *Adventures of Huckleberry Finn.* New York: Charles L. Webster.

Ullman, Albert D. 1962. "First Drinking Experience as Related to Age and Sex." Pp. 259–266 in *Society, Culture and Drinking Patterns*, edited by David J. Pittman and Charles R. Snyder. Carbondale: Southern Illinois University Press.

Ullman, Sarah E. and Cynthia J. Najdowski. 2010. "Understanding Alcohol-Related Sexual Assaults: Characteristics and Consequences." *Violence and Victims* 25(1):29–44.

United Nations International Drug Control Program. 2008. *World Drug Report.* Oxford, UK: Oxford University Press.

United Nations Office on Drugs and Crime. 2005. *World Drug Report.* Vienna, Austria.

Urban Dictionary. 2009. "Kick the Gong Around." Retrieved January 21, 2016 (http://www.urbandictionary.com/define.php?term=Kick+the+Gong).

U.S. Congress. 1924. House Committee on Foreign Affairs. Hearings on H.J. Res. 21, The Traffic in Habit Forming Drugs, 68th Congress, 1st Session. Washington, DC: U.S. Government Printing Office No. 2924.

U.S. Department of Commerce, Bureau of the Census. 1910. *Thirteenth Census of the United States, Taken in the Year 1910.* Volume I: "Population." Retrieved August 18, 2017 (https://www.census.gov/library/publications/1913/dec/vol-1-population.html).

U.S. Department of Commerce, Bureau of the Census. 2009. "Marital Status." Table A1. Washington, DC: Author.

U.S. Department of Health and Human Services. 1996. "Drug Use Among U.S. Workers." Rockville, MD: Author.

U.S. Department of Health and Human Services, Administration on Children, Youth and Families. 2010. "Child Maltreatment, 2009." Washington, DC: Author.

U.S. Department of Justice. 1985. "A Guide to Interpol: The International Criminal Police Organization in the United States." Washington, DC: Author.

U.S. Department of Justice. 1998. "The Coach's Playbook Against Drugs." Washington, DC: Author.

U.S. Department of Justice. 2002. "Drinking in America: Myths, Realities and Prevention Policy." Washington, DC: Author.

U.S. Department of Justice. 2004. "Screening and Assessing Mental Health and Substance Use Disorders Among Youth in the Juvenile Justice System." Washington, DC: Author.

U.S. Department of Justice. 2008. "Alcohol Use Increases the Risk of Sexual Assault." Washington, DC: Author. Retrieved March 3, 2017 (https://www.nij.gov/topics/crime/rape-sexual-violence/campus/pages/slcohol.aspx).

U.S. Department of Justice, Office of Justice Programs, Bureau of Justice Statistics. 2013. *Preliminary Semi-Annual Uniform Crime Report, January–June 2013.* "Crime in the United States." Washington, DC: Author.

U.S. Department of Justice. 2016. "Drug Courts." Retrieved June 6, 2016 (https://www.ncjrs.gov/pdffiles1/nij/238527.pdf).

U.S. Department of Labor, Bureau of Labor Statistics. 2012. "Drinking Places." Washington, DC: Author.

U.S. Department of Labor, Bureau of Labor Statistics. 2017a. *Occupational Outlook Handbook* (2016–17 ed.). "Wholesale and Manufacturing Sales Representatives." Retrieved August 4, 2017 (https://www.bls.gov/ooh/sales/wholesale-and-manufacturing-sales-representatives.htm).

U.S. Department of Labor, Bureau of Labor Statistics. 2017b. *Occupational Outlook Handbook* (2016–17 ed.). "Flight Attendants." Retrieved August 4, 2017 (https://www.bls.gov/ooh/transportation-and-material-moving/flight-attendants.htm).

U.S. Department of Labor, Bureau of Labor Statistics. 2017c. *Occupational Outlook Handbook* (2016–17 ed.). "Occupational Employment Statistics: Occupational Employment and Wages, 53-2012 Commercial Pilots." Retrieved August 4, 2017 (https://www.bls.gov/oes/current/oes532012.htm#nat).

U.S. Department of Labor, Bureau of Labor Statistics. n.d. "Occupational Employment Statistics." Washington, DC: Author.

U.S. Department of State, Bureau of Consular Affairs. 2014. "Mexico Travel Warning." Washington, DC: Author.

U.S. Department of Transportation. 2012. *Code of Federal Regulations. Title 49. Transportation.* Washington, DC: Author. Retrieved July 30, 2017 (https://www.gpo.gov/fdsys/pkg/CFR-2012-title49-vol2/pdf/CFR-2012-title49-vol2.pdf).

U.S. Drug Enforcement Agency. 2004. "Drug Trafficking in the United States." Almanac of Policy Issues. Retrieved May 28, 2016 (http://www.Policyalmnanc.org/crime/archive/drug.trafficking/shtml).

U.S. Food and Drug Administration. 2010. "Keeping Watch Over Direct-to-Consumer Ads." Retrieved January 27, 2016 (http://www.fda.gov/ForConsumers/ConsumerUpdates/ucm107170.htm).

Usery v. Usery. 1961. 229 Ore. 196, 357 P.2d 449.

Vander Ven, Thomas and Jeffrey Beck. 2009. "Getting Drunk and Hooking Up: An Exploratory Study of the Relationship Between Alcohol Intoxication and Casual Coupling in a University Sample." *Sociological Spectrum* 29:626–648.

Vasser, R. M. 1998. "Association Between Work Stress, Alcohol and Sickness Absence." *Addiction* 93:231–241.

Vejnoska, Jill. 1982. "Citizen Activist Group Affecting Policy on Drinking and Driving." *Alcohol, Health and Research World* 7(1):16.

Verhoeven, Jef C. 1993. "An Interview with Erving Goffman, 1980." *Research on Language and Social Interaction* 26(3):317–348.

Vicary, Judith and Jaqueline Lerner 1986. "Parental Attitudes and Adolescent Drug Use." *Journal of Adolescence* 9(2):115–122.

Victorian Web. n.d. "Opium Smoking—The Lascar's Room in 'Edwin Drood.'" Retrieved August 1, 2017 (http://www.victorianweb.org/art/illustration/dore/23.html).

Villafuerte, S., M. M. Heitzeg, S. Foley, W.-Y. Wendy Yau, K. Majczenko, J.-K. Zubieta, R. A. Zucker, and M. Burmeister. 2012. "Impulsiveness and Insula Activation During Reward Anticipation Are Associated With Genetic Variants in GABRA2 in a Family Sample Enriched for Alcoholism." *Molecular Psychiatry* 17:511–519.

"Vince Gilligan Talks 'Breaking Bad' Beginnings, 'Weeds.'" 2012. Huffington Post. Retrieved November 21, 2015 (http://www.huffingtonpost.com/2012/07/17/vince-gilligan-breaking-bad_n_1679038.html).

"Violence Shadows Synanon's 'Enemies.'" 1978. *Buffalo Evening News*, October 15, p. A-6.

Volkow, Nora D. 2014. "Heroin: Letter From the Director." National Institute on Drug Abuse, the Science of Drug Abuse and Addiction. Retrieved September 29, 2014 (http://www.drugabuse.gov/publications/research-reports/heroin/letter-director).

Von Dras, Dean, R. A. Schmitt, and D. Marx. 2007. "Association Between Aspects of Spiritual Well Being, Alcohol Use and Related Social Cognitions in Female College Students." *Journal of Females and Health* 40: 500–515.

Wagenaar, Alexander C. 1993. "Research Affects Public Policy: The Case of the Legal Drinking Age in the United States." *Addiction* (January) 88:Suppl.75S–81S.

Wagennar, Alexander C., Eileen M. Harwood, Traci L. Toomey, Charles E. Denk, and Kay M. Zander. 2000. "Public Opinion on Alcohol Policies in the United States: Results From a National Survey." *Journal of Public Health Policy* 21(3):303–327.

Walsh, Brendan M. and Dermot Walsh. 1973. "Validity of Indices of Alcoholism." *British Journal of Preventive and Social Medicine* 27(1):18–26.

Walsh, Jennifer L., Robyn L. Fielder, Kate B. Carey, and Michael P. Carey. 2014. "Do Alcohol and Marijuana Use Decrease the Probability of Condom Use for College Women?" *Journal of Sex Research* 51(2):145–158.

Walsh, Paul. 2010. "Burnsville Basketball Commissioner Attacked." *Star Tribune*, February 15.

Wang, Lin. 2002. "Predictors of Functional Change: A Longitudinal Study of Non-demented People Aged 65 and Over." *Journal of the American Geriatric Society* 50(9):1525–1534.

Watson, Rod. 2009. *Analysing Practical and Professional Texts: A Naturalistic Approach*. Burlington, VT: Ashgate.

Weeden, William B. 2011/1890. *Economic and Social History of New England*. Berkeley: University of California Press.

The Week Staff. 2016. "America's Painkiller Epidemic, Explained." Retrieved February 26, 2017 (http://theweek.com/articles/605224/americas-painkiller-epidemic-explained).

Weinberg, Thomas S. 1994. *Gay Men, Drinking, and Alcoholism*. Carbondale: Southern Illinois University Press.

Weinberg, Thomas S. 2012. "The Sociology of Addiction." In *Encyclopedia of Life Support Systems*, edited by UNESCO-EOLSS. Oxford, UK: Eolss.

Weinberg, Thomas S. 2015. "Introduction." Pp. xiii–xxi in *Selves, Symbols and Sexualities: An Interactionist Anthology*, edited by Thomas S. Weinberg and Staci Newmahr. Los Angeles: Sage.

Weinberg, Thomas S. and Conrad C. Vogler. 1990. "Wives of Alcoholics: Stigma Management and Adjustments to Husband-Wife Interaction." *Deviant Behavior* 11:331–343.

Wengert v. Wengert. 1950. 208 Ore. 290, 301 P.2d 190.

Weiss, R. M. 1978. "Determining the Effects of Alcohol Abuse on Employee Productivity." *American Psychologist* 40:378–580.

Weissenstein, Michael and Alicia A. Caldwell. 2013. "Miguel Angel Trevino Morales Captured." Huffington

Post. Retrieved August 14, 2017 (http://www.huffing-tonpost.com/2013/07/18/miguel-angel-trevino-morales-protection-from-torture_n_3614739.html).

Wexler, H. K., G. Melnick, L. Lowe, and J. Peters. 1999. "Three-Year Incarceration Outcomes for Amity In-Prison Therapeutic Community and Aftercare in California." *The Prison Journal* 79:321–336.

White, Standley. 2017. "Nevada Liquor Laws. What You Should Know About Drinking Alcoholic Beverages in Nevada." Retrieved August 4, 2017 (https://www.tripsavvy.com/nevada-liquor-laws-2885655).

Wickersham, George W. 1931. "Report on the Enforcement of the Prohibition Laws of the United States." Washington, DC: U.S. Department of Justice.

Wihbey, John. 2014. "Heroin Use in the United States: Data and Recent Trends." Journalist's Resource. Retrieved September 29, 2014 (http://journalistsresource.org/studies/society/public-health/heroin-use-in-the-united-states-data-and-recent-trends).

Wikipedia. 2008. "Synanon." Retrieved March 27, 2015 (http://en.wikipedia.org/wiki/Synanon).

Wikipedia. 2014a. "The History of Tobacco." Retrieved August 24, 2014 (http://en.wikipedia.org/wiki/History_of_tobacco).

Wikipedia. 2014b. "Tobacco and Art." Retrieved August 24, 2014 (http://en.wikipedia.org/wiki/Tobacco_and_Art).

Wikipedia. 2014c. "Summer of Monuments: Legality of Cannabis by U.S. State." Retrieved September 4, 2014 (http://en.wikipedia.org/wiki/Legality_of_cannabis_by_U.S._state).

Wikipedia. 2014d. "Daytop." Retrieved July 1, 2015 (http://en.wikipedia.org/wiki/Daytop).

Wikipedia. 2015a. "Minnie the Moocher." Retrieved July 7, 2015 (https://en.wikipedia.org/wiki/Minnie_the_Moocher).

Wikipedia. 2015b. "The Man With the Golden Arm." Retrieved November 4, 2015 (https://www.wikipedia.org/wiki/The_Man_with_the_Golden_Arm).

Wikipedia. 2015c. "Just Say No." Retrieved April 2, 2015 (http://www.wikipedia.org/wiki/Just_Say_No).

Wikipedia. 2015d. "Drug Abuse Resistance Education." Retrieved April 2, 2015 (http://www.wikipedia.org/wiki/Drug_Abuse_Resistance_Education).

Wikipedia. 2015e. "Drug Courts in the United States." Retrieved June 21, 2015 (https://en.wikipedia.org/w/index.php?title=Drug_courts_in_the_United_States&oldid=661764383).

Wikipedia. 2015f. "Passages Malibu." Retrieved July 1, 2015 (http://en.wikipedia.org/wiki/Passages_Malibu).

Wikipedia. 2016a. "Archie Bunker." Retrieved April 20, 2016 (http://en.wikipedia.org/wiki/Archie_Bunker).

Wikipedia. 2016b. "List of Fictional Bars and Pubs." Retrieved April 20, 2016 (http://en.wikipedia.org/wiki/List_of_fictional_bars_and_pubs).

Wikipedia. 2016c. "Show Me the Way to Go Home Lyrics." Retrieved April 20, 2016 (http://en.wikipedia.org/wiki/Show_Me_the_Way_to_Go_Home).

Wikipedia. 2016d. "Beer Barrel Polka." Retrieved April 20, 2016 (http://en.wikipedia.org/wiki/Beer_Barrel_Polka).

Wikipedia. 2016e. "Robert Crumb." Retrieved April 20, 2016 (https://en.wikipedia.org/wiki/Robert_Crumb).

Wikipedia. 2017a. "Guest House." Retrieved July 30, 2017 (https://en.wikipedia.org/wiki/Guest_House).

Wikipedia. 2017b. "Alcoholic Beverage Control State." Retrieved August 4, 2017 (https://en.wikipedia.org/wiki/Alcoholic_beverage_control_state).

Wilford, John Noble. 2013. "Ancient Ruins Yield Large Wine Cellar." *Buffalo News*, November 23, p. A5.

Wilkerson, Isabel. 1988. "Crack House Fire: Justice or Vigilantism?" *New York Times*, October 22, p. 6.

Wilkie, Scott. 1997. "Global Overview of Drinking Recommendation and Guidelines." *AIM Digest*, June, p. 4.

Williams, David E. 1966. "The Drive for Prohibition: A Transition From Social Reform to Legislative Reform." *Southern Communications Journal* 3 (Spring):185.

Williams, Timothy. 2012. "Indian Beer Bill Stalled: Industry Money Flows." *New York Times*, April 11. Retrieved July 28, 2017 (http://www.nytimes.com/2012/04/12/us/nebraska-bill-on-beer-sales-near-reservation-is-stalled.html).

Wilson, Edward O. 1975. *Sociobiology*. Cambridge, MA: Harvard University Press.

Wilson, George F. 1945. *Saints and Strangers*. New York: Reynal and Hitchcock.

Wilson, Thomas M. 2005. *Drinking Cultures*. New York: Berg.

Winerman, Lea. 2013. "Breaking Free From Addiction." *Monitor* 44(6). Retrieved March 7, 2017 (http://www.apa.org/monitor/2013/06/addiction.aspx).

Wiseman, Jacqueline P. 1970. *Stations of the Lost: The Treatment of Skid Row Alcoholics*. Englewood Cliffs, NJ: Prentice Hall.

Woody, Christopher and Reuters. 2017. "Mexico's Drug-War Death Toll in 2016 Reportedly Exceeded Murder Levels in Many Countries Mired in War." *Business Insider*, May 9. Retrieved August 10, 2017 (http://www.businessinsider.com/r-mexicos-2016-murder-tally-exceeds-those-of-many-countries-at-war-study-2017-5).

World Health Organization. 2015. "WHO Report on the Global Tobacco Epidemic 2015." Retrieved July 18, 2017 (http://who.int/tobacco/surveillance/policy/country_profile/usa.pdf?ua=1).

World Lung Foundation. 2012. "New Tobacco Atlas Estimates U.S. $35 Billion Tobacco Industry Profits and Almost 6 Million Annual Deaths." Retrieved August 13, 2014 (http://www.worldlungfoundation.org/ht/display/ReleaseDetails/i/20439/pid/6858).

Wren, Christopher. 1997. "Maturity Diminishes Drug Use, a Study Finds." *New York Times*, February 2, Sec. 1:28.

Wysong, Earl, Richard Aniskiewicz, and David Wright. 1994. "Truth and DARE: Tracking Drug Education to Graduation and as Symbolic Politics." *Social Problems* 41(3):448–472.

Yablonsky, Lewis. 1965. *Synanon: The Tunnel Back*. New York: MacMillan.

Yeats, William Butler. 1916. "A Drinking Song." Poetry Foundation. Retrieved August 4, 2017 (https://www.poetryfoundation.org/poems/50337/a-drinking-song).

Young, Donald and Agnieska Bielinska. 2006. "Alcohol Prices, Consumption and Traffic Fatalities." *Southern Economic Journal* 72(3):690–703.

YouTube. 2009. "Cocaine Habit Blues." Retrieved January 21, 2016 (https://www.youtube.com/watch?v=SKxZBvE8bjM).

YouTube. 2011. "Dope Head Blues." Retrieved January 21, 2016 (https://www.youtube.com/watch?v=wSX-oidnLQE&feature=youtu.be).

YouTube. 2013. "Cocaine Blues Ray Hensley." Retrieved January 21, 2016 (https://www.youtube.com/watch?v=X8qyQ0pJWAk).

Yu, Jiang. 2006. "Punishment and Alcohol Problems: Recidivism Among Drinking-Driving Offenders." *Journal of Criminal Justice* 28:261–270.

Yuan, J. M. 1997. "Follow-Up Study of Moderate Alcohol Intake and Mortality Among Middle Aged Men in Shanghai, China." *British Medical Journal* 314:18–23.

Zuccala, Giuseppe. 2001. "Dose Related Impact of Alcohol Consumption on Cognitive Function in Advanced Age: Results of a Multicenter Study." *Alcoholism Clinical and Experimental Research* 25:1745–1748.

Zullo, Roland, Xi (Belinda) Bi, Yu (Sean) Xiaohan, and Zehra Siddiqui. 2013. *The Fiscal and Social Effects of State Alcohol Control Systems*. National Alcohol Beverage Control Association. Retrieved August 18, 2017 (http://www.nabca.org/Resources/Files/20141114_092905_Zullo_Study_Final.pdf).

Index

for substance use violations, 6–7
for vagrancy, 159
Arrow War, 178
Art
    drinking and alcohol depicted in, 119–122,
        121 (photo)
    drug use depicted in, 195–196
    smoking depicted in, 31
Arthritis, moderate alcohol intake and, 96
ASAM. *See* American Society of Addictive Medicine
Ask Men, 99
Aspirin, 181
Assassin, derivation of term, 177
Assault, alcohol abuse and, 107, 108–112
Association Against the Prohibition Amendment, 62
ATF. *See* Bureau of Alcohol, Tobacco, Firearms, and
    Explosives
Athletes, masculinity, alcohol consumption, and, 80
Ativan, as Schedule IV drug, 27
Attractiveness of potential sexual partners, beer
    goggles phenomenon and, 143–145
Auricular acupuncture, 277, 278
Automatic weapons, crack dealers and, 241
Ayahuasca, 195
Aztecs and Aztec empire
    teonanacatyl use and, 195
    widespread drunkenness and, 165

BAC. *See* Blood alcohol concentration
Bacchanal of the Andrians, The (Rubens), 120
"Backstreet" methods, prostitution and,
    152, 156n10
Back to the Barrooms (Haggard), 127
Bacon, Selden D., 6, 164
"Bad, Bad Whiskey," 128
"Bad drugs," media, labeling, and changing image of
    marijuana, 33
Bahamas, drug distribution from, 183
Bahr, Howard M., 169
Barbarini Faun, 119
Barkley, Roy, 78
Barmaids, 148
Bar Rescue, 124
Bars
    alcohol profits and, 92
    description of, 98
    economic strain on families and, 49
    marketplace, 148–149, 149 (photo)
    material alcohol culture and, 51

sitcoms set in, 123–124
    social function of drinking and, 55
Bars and Bartending website, 135
Bar scene
    bartender in, 103–104
    dealing with loneliness and, 98–100
    social stratification and, 100–103
Bartenders
    in bar scene, 103–104
    drinking and, 67
    in movies, 123
    wages for, 92
Basic Text (NA), 267
Baskin, Deborah R., 20
Bates Motel (movie), 209
Baum, Stephen, 114
BDSM research, 230
Beck, Aaron T., 265
Beck, Jeffrey, 138, 140, 142
Becker, Howard S., 4, 10, 14, 35, 165, 166, 168
Becoming a drug user, 217–234
    interaction, sense making, and identity in, 229–231
    psychotherapeutic approach to, 217–229
    reporter's observations, 229
    sociological perspective on, 229–234
    subcultures and development of identity in, 231–234
Becoming alcoholic, 166–170
    being caught and exposed as a deviant, 166,
        167–168
    commission of a nonconforming act, 166
    development of deviant motives and interests,
        166, 167
    joining subcultural group of like-minded people,
        166, 168–170
"Becoming a Marijuana User" (Becker), 10
Bed, The (Emin), 196
Beech Hill Hospital (New Hampshire), Outward
    Bound program at, 275–276
Beeghley, Leonard E., 43
Beer
    American consumers and, 39
    in colonial America, 57, 104
    cost of, 51
    dispensing of, 50
    federal excise taxes on, 85
    German immigrants to U.S. and, 58
    magazines, 128
    mass production of, 52
    polkas written/sung about, 126

Spergel's typology and use of, 16
trends in use of, 35–36
Heroin addiction
  inpatient *vs.* outpatient treatment for, 221
  secondary deviance and, 230
Heroin addiction case study
  feelings, experiences, and situations in, 224–226
  psychotherapist's comments, 226
Heroin addicts
  acupuncture in treatment of, 277
  relapse and abstinence cycles and, 170
  reporter's observations of, 229
  subculture, identity, and, 233–234
  withdrawal symptoms and, 161
Heroin dealers
  exchange theory on, 9
  Hoffer's ethnography of, 9
Heroin economy, Hoffer's study of, 22
Heroin epidemic, nationwide growth of, 1–4
Heroin overdoses
  in Erie County, New York, 221
  in United States, 2
  See also Drug overdoses
Heroin subculture, 15–16
Heterosexual bars, pickups in, 149
Highball glass, 51
Highmore, Freddie, 209
High school athletes, masculinity-alcohol connection and, 80, 81
High school students
  alcohol consumption by, 80
  binge drinking by, 44
  drinking and disinhibition and, 138
  seeing results of drinking and driving, 80 (photo)
High Times magazine, 203
Highway 101, 127
Hip Hip Hurrah (Kroyer), 121
Hirst, Damien, 196
Hispanics, drug arrests and, 248
Hispanic youths, alcohol industry advertising and, 45
Hitchcock, Alfred, 209
Hobo, The (Anderson), 22, 168
Hobos, characteristics of, 168
Hoffer, Lee D., 9, 21, 22, 189, 233, 234
Hogarth, William, 120, 121 (photo)
Hogsed, Roy, Rainbow Riders and, 200
Home drinking, social integration and, 55
Homeless, alcoholic men, 170

Homeless heroin addicts (San Francisco), Bourgois' ethnographic study of, 233, 234, 235n1
Homer, 200
Home territory bars, subcultural group of like-minded people and, 168
Homicide
  alcohol-related, 47, 80, 107
  drug-related, 189
  gang-related, in Kansas City, 241
Homosexuality, 5
Homosexuals, bar pickups and, 150
Hookup culture, alcohol-related sexual assault and, 147
Hoover, Herbert, 183
Hopper, Dennis, 209
How to Talk Dirty and Influence People (Bruce), 18, 33
Huffers, in Denver, Colorado, 234
Human trafficking, 244, 247
Hurricane Island Outward Bound School, 276
Hurricanes, dispensing of, 51
Hurst, Paul, 32 (photo)
Hurwitz, William, 250
Husbands, alcoholism in the family and, 171, 172
Hustle, use of term, 23n6
Hustlers
  male bar prostitution scene and, 153
  use of term, 156n11
Hydromorphone (Dilaudid), as Schedule II drug, 27

Ian and Sylvia, 127
Idaho, state-owned liquor stores in, 63, 85
Identity
  alcohol use and construction of, 69
  drug use and, 229–230
  drug users, subcultures, and development of, 231–234
Ideological alcohol culture, 39–44
  drinking and religious beliefs, 41–44
  drinking and stress relief, 39–41
Illegal/illicit drugs
  age and use of, 240
  arrests for involvement with, 239
  black market for, 245
  emergency department visits related to, 256–257, 257 (table)
  Mexico-U.S. drug connection and, 237–239
  self-reports on, 257–258
  wide use of, 218
Illinois, medical marijuana legalized in, 34, 192

Multiple addictions, 25, 37
   addictive personality and, 216n15
   relapse and abstinence cycles and, 170
Munns, John G., 10, 274
Murder
   average sentence for, in U.S., 250
   crack cocaine and, 241, 242
   drug-related, in Mexico, 191, 246
   drug wars and, 189
   market for drugs and, 244
   of U.S. citizens in Mexico, 238
Murray, Robin M., 160
Music, drug use referenced in, 200–201
Music and alcohol, 125–128
   alcohol anthropomorphized, 127
   alcohol as a means of coping with difficulties, 127
   negative effect of alcohol on lives, 127–128
   songs about drinking, 126–127
   songs sung while drinking, 125–126
Musico, Joseph, 273
Muslims
   alcohol prohibition and, 41, 55, 75
   Ismaeli, 177
Myanmar, in Golden Triangle, 243
Mydivebar.com, 128
Myers, William, 116
Mystery of Edwin Drood, The (Dickens), 195, 196–197

NADA. *See* National Acupuncture Detoxification
   Association
"Nancy Whiskey," 127
Napoleon, hashish and Egyptian campaign of, 177
Narcotics, physicians arrested for prescribing, 250
Narcotics Addict Rehabilitation Act of 1966, 186
Narcotics Anonymous, 267–268
   composition of membership, 268
   core of program for, 267–268
   formation of, 267
   World Service Conference, 268
Narcotics Control Act of 1956, 184–185
Narcotics Drug Import and Export Act of 1951
   (Boggs Act), 183–184
Narcotics squads, drug addicts and, 253–254
Nash, Ogden, 137
National Academy of Science, 83, 160
National Acupuncture Detoxification Association,
   276–277
National Association of Drug Court
   Professionals, 264

National Beer Wholesalers Association, 30
National Commission on Law Observance and En-
   forcement, 62
National Council on Alcohol Abuse, 64
National Council on Alcoholism, 64, 65
National Council on Alcoholism and Drug Depen-
   dence, 106
National Football League, marijuana use and, 34–35
National Highway Traffic Safety Administration,
   drunken driving statistics, 65
National Institute of Justice, Drug Use Forecasting
   System, 189
National Institute on Alcohol Abuse and Alcoholism,
   33, 93, 94
National Institute on Drug Abuse, 2, 5, 36, 266, 268
National Minimum Drinking Age Act of 1984, 44
National Prohibition Act of 1919, 182
National Registry of Evidence-Based Programs and
   Practices, 5
National Stroke Association, Stroke Prevention
   Guidelines, 95
*National Survey on American Attitudes on Substance
   Abuse XVII: Teens,* 213
National Survey on Drug Use and Health (SAMHSA), 36,
   257–258
Native Americans, alcohol, fur trade, and, 57
Natural drinking groups (NDGs), 139
Neave, Nick, 143
Nelson, Richard, 250
Neolithic culture, alcohol use in, 55
Neutralization techniques. *See* Techniques of
   neutralization
Nevada
   alcohol profits in, 92
   legalization of marijuana in, 18, 34, 194
   medical marijuana legalized in, 34, 192, 253
New Belgium Brewery (Colorado), 54
Newbury, Mickey, 200
New Hampshire
   medical marijuana legalized in, 34, 192
   state-owned liquor stores in, 63, 85
New Jersey
   alcohol-attributable deaths in, 86
   Jewish population in, 76
   medical marijuana legalized in, 34, 192
New Mexico
   alcohol-attributable deaths in, 86
   medical marijuana legalized in, 34, 192